DOCTORS' DELUSIONS
CRUDE CRIMINOLOGY
SHAM EDUCATION

LONDON

PUBLISHED BY

Constable and Company Ltd.

10–12 ORANGE STREET W.C.2

•

INDIA AND PAKISTAN

Orient Longmans Ltd.

BOMBAY   CALCUTTA   MADRAS

•

CANADA

Longmans, Green and Company

TORONTO

•

SOUTH AND EAST AFRICA

Longmans, Green and Company Ltd.

CAPE TOWN   NAIROBI

DOCTORS' DELUSIONS
CRUDE CRIMINOLOGY
AND SHAM EDUCATION
BY BERNARD SHAW

LONDON
CONSTABLE AND COMPANY
LIMITED

First published in the Limited Collected Edition 1931
Revised and reprinted for this Standard Edition 1932
Reprinted 1950

PRINTED IN GREAT BRITAIN
BY R. & R. CLARK, LIMITED, EDINBURGH

CONTENTS

v

class of 1904

47950

CONTENTS

CONTENTS

vii

CONTENTS

viii

CONTENTS

A WORD FIRST

PLEASE do not class me as one who "doesnt believe in doctors." One of our most pressing social needs is a national staff of doctors whom we can believe in, and whose prosperity shall depend not on the nation's sickness but on its health. There should be no such thing as a poor doctor and no such thing as an ignorant one. The great majority of our doctors today are both poor and ignorant with the conceited ignorance of obsolete or spurious knowledge. Our surgeons obtain the highest official qualifications without having had a single hour of specific manual training: they have to pick up the art of carving us as paterfamilias picks up the art of carving a goose. The general education of our citizens (the patients) leaves them so credulous and gullible, that the doctor, to whom they attribute magical powers over life and death, is forced to treat them according to their folly lest he starve. Those to whom these menacing facts are known, and who are capable of understanding their gravity (including all our really able doctors), will not mistake my aim nor wish me anything but a sympathetic hearing. As for the simpletons (bless their anything-but-sacred simplicity!), if they dont like it, why, they must lump it.

Our mechanist-surgeons and chemist-physicians must, however, forgive me for differing fundamentally and flatly from the scientific basis (if it can be called scientific) of their crude practices. In my view surgeons and physicians should be primarily biologists. To tackle a damaged living organism with the outlook of a repairing plumber and joiner, or to treat an acid stomach by pouring an alkali into it, is to behave like a highly unintelligent artisan, and should entail instant and ignominious disqualification by the Privy Council. There are many unlearned amateur pathologists and hygienists, from Mary Baker Eddy to George Hackenschmidt, who are safer guides than the Harley Street celebrities who laugh at them, their secret being simply that they have had the gumption to guess that it is the mind that makes the body and not the body the mind.

I also expect a doctor to be an evolutionist, and, as such, to regard all habits as acquired habits, a man being nothing but an amœba with acquirements. Any doctor found parroting the obsolete nineteenth century cackle about non-acquired heritable habits and non-heritable acquired habits should be removed to the nearest museum of quaint antiquities.

I hope this is clear. If not, please read the preface to my Back to Methuselah until it *is* clear.   G. B. S.

1931.

DOCTORS' DELUSIONS

Invited to contribute to a series of articles in a
Manchester paper in reply to the question "Have
We Lost Faith?" Mr George Bernard Shaw gives
his answer in this single sentence:
"Certainly not; but we have transferred it from
God to the General Medical Council."

DOCTORS' DELUSIONS

WHAT IS TO BE DONE WITH THE DOCTORS?

From The English Review, December 1917 *to March* 1918

In the English Review for October 1916, a protest was made against the denial to wounded soldiers of any treatment except that of legally qualified operators. This would at first sight appear a very necessary measure of protection for the soldier against unskilled treatment. And if the legally qualified doctor was a completely qualified healer, nobody would question its entire propriety. Unfortunately he is not so qualified, as might be expected from the fact that we have only his own word for the completeness of his equipment and his proficiency in his art. There are now several techniques which he has not acquired and cannot afford to acquire. He is, therefore, bound to denounce them as delusive quackeries or confess his insufficiency. This would not matter if the public could always choose freely between the legally qualified doctor and the unregistered practitioner whom the legally qualified doctor calls a quack. But the public has no such freedom. We call in the unregistered practitioner at the risk of being prosecuted for criminal neglect if the patient dies, like the Peculiar People. The unregistered practitioner cannot sign a death certificate. His prescriptions are not current at the pharmacist's shop, and will not be made up there if they include scheduled drugs. He cannot call in a legally qualified consultant; at least, if he does, the legally qualified consultant will refuse to consult with a quack. He must operate without anæsthetics or administer them himself (a very limited possibility); for the qualified anæsthetists are struck off the register for "infamous professional conduct" if they chloroform the patients of unregistered practitioners. Also the panel doctor, the army doctor, the navy doctor, the medical officer of health, the infirmary doctor: in short, the officially or collectively appointed and paid doctor must always be a legally qualified doctor.

Under such circumstances not only is the unregistered practitioner heavily handicapped in his competition with the registered, but the patient, representing the British public, is equally handicapped in his choice of a doctor. When he is a soldier, a sailor, a hospital patient, or a pauper, there is no question even of a handicap; he is flatly and forcibly cut off from all medical aid except that of the registered doctor. The publicly insured panel patient is virtually, if not legally, in the same position. The assumption is that the registered doctor or surgeon knows everything that is to be known and can do everything that is to be done. This means that the dogmas of omniscience, omnipotence, and infallibility, and something very like the theory of the apostolic succession and kingship by anointment, have recovered in medicine the grip they have lost in theology and politics.

It must not be rashly concluded that the unregistered practitioner is necessarily a despised and impoverished outcast, picking up a precarious living among the dregs of the population. On the contrary, his fees may be from eight to twenty times as high as those of most registered doctors, his practice a West End practice, and the rent of his consulting rooms in excess of the entire income of many an L.R.C.P., M.R.C.S., because the supply of technically qualified but unregistered practitioners is very much smaller relatively to the demand than that of registered ones. Besides, the unregistered man must deliver the goods; he cannot live by the faith of his patients in a string of letters after his name. Nobody will dream of calling him in unless he is believed to have some special technical accomplishment or some knowledge of drugs that the registered doctor does not possess. People send for the registered doctor because they do not consider it decent to be ill without one, and indeed because they may get into trouble if they neglect to secure his aid for children and others in their charge; and they regard his arrival as a solemnity akin to that of death, to which it is so often a prelude. But they go to an unregistered practitioner solely in the hope of being cured; and unless they get well in his hands they drop him, and his practice collapses. The President of the Royal College of Surgeons may "attend" cripples, but Sir Herbert Barker must enable them to take up their beds and walk.

The number of practitioners who can comply with these conditions is not large; and their services are consequently not cheap. It may be said roughly that only people who are rich enough to do what they like, and their servants and *protégés*, can obtain the benefit of any serious technique that is outside the routine of legal qualification. Thus the wounded soldier may stumble through his whole life on crutches just because the legally qualified surgeon does not know how to reduce certain dislocations, or any of us may succumb slowly to the living death of creeping paralysis because the most eminent spine specialists on the register have not acquired the knack of straightening a ricked spine as some bonesetters do without knowing more of anatomy or physiology than a farm laborer can learn through the tips of his fingers.

Orthodox Origin of all the Heresies

The modern unregistered bonesetter, who makes the lame man leap as a hart, may be a learned anatomist far removed from the rough and ready village empiric who puts in a slipped shoulder for you in the hunting-field. He has captivated the public imagination because it delights in miracles and miracle-workers; and the feats of a born bonesetter like Sir Herbert Barker look very like the traditional miracles of the saints. But most of the new techniques, including those which the General Medical Council most fanatically excommunicates, have been discovered within the legalized profession itself. Hahnemann, the founder of homeopathy, was a duly hall-marked M.D.; Ling, the founder of the modern Swedish system of physical therapeutics, had not only all the medical and surgical degrees, but a divinity degree as well, and he was a member of the Swedish Medical Council. Sir Almroth Wright, who discovered the functions of opsonins in phagocytosis, and whose invention of the technique of inoculation rescued vaccine therapy, in theory if not in practice, from the farmyard crudities of Jesty and Jenner, and the disastrous empiricism of Koch, is, as all the world knows, as overladen with diplomas, degrees, gold medals, and prizes as his opponent, Colonel Sir William Watson Cheyne, or Dr Hadwen, the leader of the Anti-Vaccinationists. If academic professional qualifications could secure infallibility, these three gentlemen would need nothing but unanimity to rank them with the Trinity. Unfortunately they have expressed their opinion of one another in print in terms which I dare not apply to the humblest herbalist. Andrew Taylor Still, the founder of osteopathy, is a qualified physician. Crichton Miller, the fashionable psycho-therapist of today, is within the pale. In short, all the so-called quackeries which have established any serious claim to consideration, with one notable exception, have precisely the same credentials as the canon of the British Medical Council. That exception is the Church of Christ Scientist, which may claim that anyone questioning its divine authority can be prosecuted for blasphemy, though anyone acting on it may be prosecuted for manslaughter.

I will therefore ask the reader to clear his mind of the notion that the State-established systems of therapeutics have any greater or other scientific or academic authority than the Nonconformist ones. But he must not rush to the conclusion that every man who calls himself a homeopath, or a bonesetter, or a serum therapist, or a medical gymnast, or a masseur, or an osteopath, or a psycho-analyst, or an electronic specialist, is necessarily as highly qualified as any M.D., L.R.C.P., M.R.C.S., or even L.S.A. These letters, it is true, do not give the public any guarantee that the person to whose name they are affixed is an efficient healer, or even that he is not the victim of sedulously inculcated errors of the most dangerous sort, besides having anti-hygienic commercial interests which make him, economically speaking, an enemy of mankind. What they do guarantee is that he has had a minimum of liberal education; that he has had some clinical practice; that he has been coached in the main facts of anatomy and physiology; and that the awkwardness with which a novice performs minor operations and obstetric deliveries has been worn off, under skilled supervision, on the bodies of the poor. And such guarantees have obviously a very high value to us when our lives or those of our children may depend on whether they are in the hands of an ignoramus or an instructed person. It is true that the village doctor may be beaten by a dislocation that the village bonesetter can correct literally in a brace of shakes. He may fail even to diagnose a lesion which the bonesetter will spot at once. But the village bonesetter may have the strangest notions as to his patient's inside, and, when the case is outside his experience, may allege imaginary bones and organs and do fantastic mischief. The qualified practitioner often enough makes ghastly or ridiculous mistakes; and his very knowledge may lead him to argue himself into errors from which unqualified men are protected by their ignorance, antiseptic surgery being a crying instance. But when all is said that can be said against the registered practitioner, we risk the imperfection of his knowledge rather than the darkness of an uncertified rival's ignorance. In the same way, the penn'orth of Greek which enables the curate to obtain ordination on the report of the bishop's chaplain may not constitute him a Plato; but as far as it goes, it raises presumptions in his favor as against total illiteracy.

It follows that when a discovery is made in therapeutics the discoverer will always begin by trying to induce the medical profession to adopt it. He has everything to gain and nothing to lose by succeeding. Sometimes, as in the case of Jenner, he succeeds with startling suddenness and completeness, and even gets £20,000 from Parliament into the bargain. Sometimes, as in the case of Hahnemann, the profession turns on him with fury, and drives him out of the town, compelling him finally to set up a new therapeutic sect. Sometimes, as in the case of Sir Almroth Wright, the profession is overawed by his authority and dares not openly denounce him or attempt to banish him, but is enabled to evade the consequences of his discovery by popular ignorance of its nature, all the doctors giving it loud mouth honor, and leaving the public to infer that they have adopted it, whilst really continuing their old procedure or no-procedure unchanged.

And we have the converse of this when a practice repudiated by the profession is nevertheless adopted slyly by those of its members who are converted to it but dare not say so. Side by side with the inoculator who sticks to the barbarous procedure of Jenner and Koch whilst professing the technique of Almroth Wright, we have the drug prescriber who fills his patients with the pillules and millionfold dilutions of Hahnemann as the latest form of the drenches and doses of Galen, not to mention the doctor who takes his crippled wife to the famous bonesetter to be cured, and, when the cure is effected, dares not testify to it even as a simple fact when the professional character of the bonesetter is controversially assailed.

SCIENCE AT THE PROW AND COMMERCE AT THE HELM

The contrast between the fortunes of Hahnemann and Jenner invites inquiry, because at first sight it would seem that Hahnemann's apparently harmless observation that though a dose of cinchona would produce headache and fever in a healthy man it would cure one already suffering from those symptoms, and the elaboration of this observation by persistent experiment into a rule that different doses of the same drug produce opposite effects, thus making poison its own antidote, was nothing that the doctors need have quarrelled about. As to some six or seven drugs in the authorized Materia Medica, there is no dispute about the facts: they do admittedly act in this way. On the other hand, Jenner's innovation, a revolting practice picked up from a farmer named Jesty, seems one which would naturally be repudiated with disgust, both from its unpleasantness and its illiterate lay origin. Yet, as we have seen, Hahnemann was hounded into exile (in which, however, he was very prosperous); whilst the profession jumped eagerly at Jenner, whose fame is still so cherished by medical tradition that Sir Almroth Wright, in the very act of reducing Jenner scientifically to the rank of the crassest of empirics, called his new preparations vaccines, though the only cow they are concerned with is the cow that jumped over the moon.

We have not to go very far for the explanation. Hahnemann's discovery threatened a professional trade interest: Jenner's created one. It was the apothecaries who ostracized Hahnemann. When we remember that, long after Hahnemann's time, the Iron Duke of Wellington, when he felt the hand of death descending on him at last, said, not "Send for Sir William So-and-so," but "Send for the apothecary," it will be understood that the doctors whom Hahnemann confronted *were* apothecaries. They lived by selling drugs at stupendous prices (bills of £10 a week for drugs in an illness are on record); and the drugs were paid for and believed in according to their bulk and the offensiveness of their flavor. When Hahnemann proposed to substitute drops for table-spoonfuls and pillules for pills, both almost tasteless, the apothecaries saw ruin staring them in the face. They were wrong, as was proved towards the end of last century by Count Mattei, who put up tiny tubes of colorless fluid (possibly genuine homeopathic infinitesimals) labelled as "electricities," and sold them at higher prices than the largest jorums of chalk and opium could command; but in Hahnemann's day Mattei was still in the womb of time. Hahnemann was hounded out of his first practice not as the discoverer of homeopathy, but as the destroyer of apothecaries' profits.

Jenner, on the other hand, succeeded, not as the plagiarist of Jesty's rough-and-ready way with his farm-servants and his family, but as the popularizer of a means by which doctors could make money out of people who were quite well, and who, before his time, might have passed their whole lives without paying a farthing to a doctor. Such a discovery was irresistible. If its effects had been ten times worse than they were, it would have carried everything before it in the profession. It did no great apparent harm; for even when the population had increased beyond thirty millions, and the operation was ruthlessly enforced, it only killed one baby a week so undeniably and undisguisably that even the doctors could find no other name for the cause of death; and if the great epidemic of 1871 had not shattered its main pretension, or if it had not gone so horribly wrong when it did go wrong, it might have been as little challenged as baptism. When the manufacture and supply of lymph began to take root as a commercial interest outside the profession (except in so far as doctors took shares), capital began to work the oracle, and it was suddenly discovered that the established method of using second-hand lymph by vaccinating from arm to arm was a dangerous and deadly practice. Since then every vaccination involves a fresh expenditure for lymph. What is called scientific progressive medicine is thus seen to be largely dictated by the hygiene of the pocket. It may be none the worse for that; but Sir Isaac Newton would have insisted on a certain distinction.

Diagnosis, Sham and Real

Sir Almroth Wright's hushed-up failure to convert the profession to his technique of the opsonic index has the same economic root. That technique is essentially a very delicate form of diagnosis; and the art of diagnosis has now gone far beyond the private means and public resources of the general practitioners whose incomes are at stake, and who, to feed their families, must perforce stake our lives on their incomes. The ordinary process of diagnosis consists of a mildly obscene conversation between doctor and patient, in the course of which the doctor feels and counts the patient's pulse; looks at his tongue; sounds him with a stethoscope; takes his temperature with a clinical thermometer; and even, if he is a young and ardent modernist, tests his reflexes. He then makes a guess; writes a prescription; administers a little agreeable conversation, in the course of which, having ascertained whether the patient regards fresh air as the elixir of life or as a poison to be warded off by every practical method of exclusion, he advises him to sleep in the garden or in a heated and sealed apartment, as the case may be, and leaves him to his fate until the next visit. If matters become serious, he may go so far as to have a sample of the patient's secretions, and perhaps of his domestic water supply, sent to a laboratory with a few shillings; and the laboratory, after doubtless making as much of an analysis as the shillings will run to, makes a report. The report, by dwelling on "organic matter," may make a job for the plumber, or by mentioning albumen may convince the doctor that it is his duty to warn the patient quite unnecessarily that his days are numbered. All this is better than nothing; but it is far too loose and vague to be scientific; and as to the final diagnosis: that is, the word which is to define the pathological condition of the patient, it is often a word which has never itself been defined with anything like scientific exactitude. Sometimes it is simply a Greekish cloak for British ignorance. In Ireland the question "What did he die of?" is sometimes answered by the formula "Shortness of breath." This mockery has more than once produced a fight. But when the doctor says "Dyspnœa," which means exactly the same thing, we are profoundly impressed by his knowledge of the secrets of life and death.

Battle Creek and Sir Horace Plunkett

Now if this were the best that can be done, we might accept it with gratitude. But it falls far short of the possibilities of modern diagnosis. An eminent public man in Ireland some years ago had reason to be dissatisfied with his digestion. On taking first-rate medical advice in London he was informed that he was suffering from a deficiency of hydrochloric acid, and naïvely advised to put matters right by drinking hydrochloric lemonade at his meals. This he did, and found that the hydrochloric lemonade (a beverage which really exists, fabulous as it sounds) was very nasty, and that his digestion got worse. He then went to America, where he discovered Battle Creek. Battle Creek is the site of a sanatorium with a very elaborate anthropolytical laboratory in which the patients' ills are diagnosed. They eat test meals and have their secretions and excretions analysed; they swallow masses of bismuth and are X-rayed; their opsonic indices are ascertained; and they are not delivered to the doctor until their condition has been ascertained by physical and chemical tests to the utmost modern limit of investigation.

11

On the Irish publicist being put through all these processes it was discovered that he was suffering from a marked excess of hydrochloric acid. His London advisers would no doubt have said, "Oh, indeed; then take bicarbonate of soda instead of hydrochloric lemonade, thus correcting the acid by the alkali." I do not know what they said at Battle Creek; but the case called Sir Horace Plunkett's attention to the inadequacy of the primitive methods of diagnosis prevalent in English general practice; and he, calling the attention of the public to it in turn, had his criticism described as "an attack on the medical profession"; for the British medicine man is primitive in other things besides diagnosis, and takes any utterance that implies the smallest doubt of his omniscience, infallibility, and finality as a personal insult, like a minor poet reading his first review. Sir Horace Plunkett pointed out that the ordinary private surgery or consulting room could no more produce a complete modern diagnosis than a tinker's budget can produce a ten-inch gun, and that laboratories and sanatoria of the Battle Creek sort should be accessible everywhere. As far as I know, the result has been the establishment of one such institution in Great Britain; and that is in Aberdeenshire, a spot chosen as the most remote from Harley Street practically available for the purpose.

"My Poverty, but not my Will—"

Now it is evident that however true Sir Horace's contention may be, the medical profession, as at present syndicalized, cannot admit it, nor even refrain from angrily and contemptuously denouncing it, without confessing that the solemn consultations and visits of private practice are, scientifically speaking, gropings in the dark, and that, skilful as some doctors may become by clinical practice and natural aptitude, they are only artists, diviners, and practitioners like Paracelsus, and not men of science. They cannot be expected to say, "Go to Battle Creek or Aberdeen, leaving us to starve." When the patient hints uneasily that he has been reading a paper by Sir Horace Plunkett, it is mere self-preservation to assure him that Sir Horace, being a layman, cannot possibly know anything about it, and that only last week a patient who went to Battle Creek died, leaving the terrified patient to infer that patients treated in Harley Street are immortal. Better one patient die deluded than a whole profession perish. Besides, the deluded patient does not always die. The doctor who always kills is as unsubstantial a figment of the popular imagination as the doctor who always cures. In most cases Nature does the trick: the doctor only takes round the hat.

The Eternal Struggle between the Old Ways and the New

But even when a new technique needs no publicly instituted laboratories, and can be practised by private practitioners in their own surgeries and consulting rooms and on domestic visits, the young men who have learnt the technique are opposed and denounced by the old ones who have learnt only that which it has superseded, and who cannot return to school to requalify themselves. This sort of schism is chronic in the profession, but occasionally it reaches a crisis; and here again Sir Almroth Wright's analytic power, literary dexterity, and ingenuity in devising technical methods have brought him into conflict with his own generation by unintentionally confirming the guesses and instinctive protests of the unqualified sentimental amateurs who have all through opposed Lister and Listerism, Pasteur and Pasteurism, as godless and cruel; by explaining the success of certain famous operators who steadily and contemptuously refused to use anything but common pipe-water for cleansing; and by making it clear that the improvements claimed for Lister's antiseptic methods were really due to the incidental reform in the personal habits of the old doctors who operated in filthy old coats, and provided themselves with a third hand at a pinch by holding their instruments in their mouths as a dressmaker holds pins.

After half a century of assertions as to the marvellous efficacy of antiseptic surgery, Sir Almroth has now explained to us that

13

antiseptic surgery is not only impossible, but that the procedure based on it is an active source of auto-infection and a powerful hindrance to healing. We now know why sinuses, which healed in a fortnight in the hands of the dirty old doctors, suppurated for months, and were, in fact, incurable when they were plugged daily with iodoform guaranteed to slay every microbe within reach of it. This war has carried Sir Almroth to his greatest clinical triumph: the invention of the salt and water treatment which has swept away the antiseptic treatment by its irresistible success. And he delights in explaining that it is neither Pasteurian nor Listerian, but a scientific rationalization of the procedure of the old Irish peasant women who treat wounds successfully with a mixture of sugar and soap. It is true that Listerian antisepsis for the surgical operations of civil life had broken down almost at the outset and been largely supplanted by asepsis in the hands of the pipe-water operators. But battle wounds are all infected wounds, virulently septic as a matter of course; and it was to these that Wright's revolution applied.

I ask the reader whose memory, like mine, embraces the fifty years' vogue of the antiseptic system, to pause for a moment and contemplate with awe the mountain of plain, earnest, high-minded, indignant lying that has kept the Listerian romance in credit during that deluded period. I can recall no more stupendous instance, even in politics, of the part that sheer mendacity plays in the formation of public opinion in our times.

How these Doctors love one another!

I warmly recommend to those who love a good polemic the controversy lately concluded on the subject between Colonel Sir William Watson Cheyne and Colonel Sir Almroth Wright. Sir William stands at bay in the third-line trench of Antisepticism, and tries to defend that last ditch against his victorious and contemptuous antagonist. He admits that the sterilization of wounds by antiseptics is impossible if you let the wound get a day ahead of you, but still maintains that you can sterilize it by first intention, as it were, if you can shove in the germicide soon enough after the bayonet. But Sir Almroth will not have antiseptic surgery at any price. His intellectual scorn for his opponent gives a stimulating vituperativeness to his part of the debate which makes it highly entertaining, if somewhat cruel, reading. It was Lessing who, according to Heine, not only cut off his adversary's head, but held it up to shew that there were no brains in it. Sir Almroth, knowing that this is an anatomical impossibility, puts Sir William Watson Cheyne's brains on his operating table, and shews that Sir William has never learnt how to use them—never squarely faced even such vital questions as, "What is the exact weight of a little piece of cheese?" He shews that Sir William has no conception of scientific method, and that though he has no standards of quantity or of anything else, he yet makes statements that have no ascertainable meaning except with reference to fixed standards, falling short even of the clergyman who, when reading the lessons, informs the congregation that an omer is the tenth part of an ephah. Indeed, Sir Almroth often loses sight of the controversy in hand in his preoccupation with the defects of Sir Watson's ratiocination; for Sir Almroth has such a devouring interest in and curiosity about the pathology of controversial cerebration, and takes such a delight in playing with it, that if Sir William challenges him to a duel (and the controversy at one moment reached a crisis at which no other reply seemed possible) he will write a most interesting pamphlet on the *rationale* of duelling, ending with an ingenious new technique of fencing, before he takes the field. I have in my own manner, timidly as becomes a layman, hinted more than once that the notion that a medical or surgical degree implies qualification in modern science could not exist if the nation understood either science or conventional surgery and medicine; but never would I dare to handle a medical baronet, a Hunterian professor, a medalled, in-despatches-mentioned consultant to the Forces, a M.B., C.M., C.B., F.R.C.S., F.R.S., LL.D., and D.Sc. (Oxon), as Sir Almroth handles him. I shall not be believed unless I give a sample. Here is a typical one:

"CHEYNE. Another point, which I confess had not occurred to me until I came across it in the course of my experiments, is also of importance: viz., that the antiseptic is used up in killing bacteria.

"WRIGHT. We have here a generalization which ranks in the order of obviousness with the adage that you cannot both eat your cake and have it, and with the scientific platitude that you cannot carry out a chemical operation without expending chemicals.

"CHEYNE. The difficulty of obtaining a proper depth of agar has been overcome in a very ingenious manner by taking a metal ring, placing it on a sheet of glass, and superimposing on it another similar sheet; and though when two men work together it is not usual to refer to any one man's share in particular, still I think I ought to say that it was devised by Mr Edmunds; and I shall speak of it as Mr Edmunds's cell.

"WRIGHT. Some day we shall be told that the difficulty of carrying sugar into one's tea has been overcome in a very ingenious manner by the device of sugar-tongs; and that, in connection with it, this or that re-inventor's name ought to go down to posterity.

"CHEYNE. Lister observed the very curious phenomenon that if blood were drawn aseptically into a glass flask sterilized by heating, the clot which formed did not contract and squeeze out serum, as is the case when blood is received into an ordinary non-sterilized glass vessel. I fancy bacteriologists are not familiar with this fact.

"WRIGHT. Everyone who has drawn blood into a sterile syringe, and, of course, every laboratory worker, knows that this is fiction. Let us tell Sir Watson Cheyne that the method of serum therapy, and indeed the whole serum industry, depends upon the fact that blood, when drawn into a vessel sterilized by heating, *does* contract and squeeze out serum. [*Here Sir William may be conceived as dropping senseless. His colleague proceeds.*] So far, my task of criticism has been simple as child's play. For we have up to this remained entirely in the domain of the particular

16

and the concrete, referring our author's utterances to the touch-
stone of fact. Let us now, rising to a more abstract and general
point of view, deal with those three intellectual requisites of a
scientific worker in which Sir Watson Cheyne comes, as it
appears to me, hopelessly short. [*Sir Almroth proceeds to demonstrate that Sir William exhibits all the characteristic symptoms of
scientific imbecility, including the substitution of adjectives and
adverbs for numerals, and describes his apparently learned remarks
on hypochlorites as patter.*]"

Sir William Watson Cheyne's opinion of Sir Almroth Wright's
scientific competence will never be known to us in its fulness,
because he withdrew from the controversy on the ground that it
had entered the region of the unprintable. Only lack of space
prevents me from adding Dr Hadwen's opinion of both of them,
Dr Hadwen representing as a thinker the chronic indignation of
humanitarian common sense at the attempt of his profession to
exempt the pursuit of cures from the restraint of the moral law,
and as a practitioner that clinical common sense which keeps the
nose of the theorist hard down on the grindstone of practice.
Cheyne merely challenges Wright's practice as to wounds;
Wright retorts that Cheyne cannot use his mind; but Hadwen
execrates most of his colleagues as liars and inhuman scoundrels
as well as bedside bunglers. Here we have no vulgar attack by
our Dulcamaras, our Sequahs, our Mother Seigels, our Count
Matteis, on a dignified and learned profession. We have the most
highly qualified members of that profession throwing their gold
medals at one another's heads; clubbing one another with their
professorial chairs; strangling one another in their pigtails of
capital letters; and denying one another's clinical efficiency,
mental competence, and moral rectitude.

Fortunately, nothing is more false than the proverb that when
doctors differ patients die. On the contrary, when doctors differ
wounded soldiers get well, and even general practitioners are
forced to think instead of to dogmatize and pontificate. When
doctors agree we are face to face with a conspiracy of pretentious

17   C

ignorance with that sordid side of trade unionism which is forced by common need to struggle for its livelihood even to the point of saying, "Thou shalt die ere I starve." As long as we are fools enough to make healing and hygiene a matter of commerce, and give joint-stock companies powerful vested interests in blood poisoning (note the passage about "the whole serum industry" in my last quotation above from Sir Almroth Wright), we shall get the worst of that alternative; and serve us right! When it comes to American States having to pass laws making it illegal for general practitioners to take commissions from the operating surgeons called in on their own suggestion, it is time to inquire whether Colorado produces a special type of human nature, and, if not, whether the same abuse, in less crude forms, may not help to boil our own pots in Harley Street.

The Case of Sir Herbert Barker

I now come to the case of Sir Herbert Atkinson Barker as set forth in The English Review. Sir Herbert is what doctors call a bonesetter, though without any intention of emphasizing the fact that he can apparently set displaced bones better than they can. The war has produced a number of cases which have beaten the primitive manipulative surgery of the R.A.M.C. and the General Medical Council. Benevolent rich persons have taken crippled soldiers to Barker, who has set them on their legs again. Officers who can afford it have taken themselves to Barker with the same result. Barker, though in opulent practice, has finally offered his services, both as operator and instructor, to the Army gratuitously as a patriotic duty. The Army refuses both his operations and his instructions on the ground that Barker is not qualified. Barker and his multitude of converts argue that if he can make the lame walk he *is* qualified. The R.A.M.C. replies that if it admits Barker it must admit Mrs Eddy and Count Mattei and Mother Seigel and the elders of the Peculiar People and Tom, Dick, and Harry. The sensible way out of the difficulty would be to give Barker an honorary degree, just as Oxford makes Mr

Lloyd George a D.C.L., or as the War Office gives a commission to a ranker of obvious qualifications for command. The General Medical Council is less liberal, because it is, first, last, and all the time, a trade union. Therefore you have this silly scandal of a surgical manipulator of genius forbidden to treat our disabled soldiers, not because it is denied that he has mastered a valuable technique omitted from the regulation equipment, but simply because the profession is too preoccupied with its own privileges to provide, as all the other professions have provided, a means by which overwhelming evidence of ability can be accepted and acted on as well as the very doubtful evidence afforded by the examination system, which annually lets loose the most disastrous duffers in the sick-rooms of the nation. Had our universities been governed by doctors, Brahms and Joachim would have been refused their honorary degrees as Doctors of Music unless they had stopped composing and playing for five years to pass an Arts examination; do exercises in counterpoint to the satisfaction of professors incapable of writing three bearable bars of original music; and qualify themselves to name, on demand, the age at which Bach's fourth son was confirmed.

The case of Sir Herbert Barker is thus quite a simple one, as cases of exceptionally gifted individuals always are. I dismiss it by appealing to one of the universities to give him an honorary medical degree and have done with it. Such a degree would not place him automatically on the register; but a refusal to recognize it would bring the General Medical Council into conflict with its constituents, who have, as we shall see presently, the power to transform it into a predominantly lay body.

If the universities are too superstitious to take this step, it can be taken by the Archbishop of Canterbury, who can make anybody a legally qualified doctor.[1]

But the general point at issue has become far more complicated than any individual case. The technique of the bonesetter,

---

[1] As none of my suggestions were acted upon, the King stepped in and conferred a knighthood on Sir Herbert and a slap in the face on the G.M.C.

handed down from Hutton to Atkinson, from Atkinson to Barker, and by him greatly developed, is not an alternative to recognized surgical practice, but an extension of it. Every surgeon should be a bonesetter, especially in the country, where accidents are common and there are no specialists at hand. In fact, many a country surgeon is a bit of a bonesetter, by force of circumstances and natural aptitude. And every bonesetter should have a minimum of liberal education and the technical knowledge of an ordinary surgeon. If Sir Herbert Barker were an ignoramus, or knew less about the anatomy of the knee-joint than the President of the Royal College of Surgeons, it would be quite right to stand between him and the bedside of the maimed soldier and cry, "Hands off." The importance of a test of general surgical knowledge is so obvious that it seems reasonable and salutary to say to a bonesetter, or any other professor of a special technique, "Qualify yourself to practise as a physician or surgeon, and you may employ your technique to your heart's content; for the General Medical Council is actually forbidden by Act of Parliament to impose any test of orthodoxy on you." Let us see how this plausible position would work out in practice.

Swedish Therapeutics

Take the case of the Swedish practitioners so much resorted to of late. First there are the Medical Gymnasts trained by the Central Institute in Stockholm. They go through a three years' course of training, and receive a degree which entitles them to undertake the manipulative treatment of a long range of diseases, with full recognition in consultation, though they may not prescribe nor give death certificates. Much better known in fashionable London are the followers of Kellgren, who evolved from Ling's system a technique of massage which is almost unlimited in its pretension to cure every evil under the sun. Kellgren, who charged enormous fees and had a princely practice, handed down his method by the old system of private apprenticeship, two years' training being considered the minimum. The Kellgrenites are not recognized by the Medical Gymnasts, whose status is official; but both have an elaborate technique taking about the same time to acquire; for it may be taken roughly that two years' apprenticeship to a practising masseur is equivalent to the keeping of terms at the Institute for three years. An already qualified doctor can, however, obtain the Central Institute certificate in one year.

Some time ago a Kellgrenite masseur, now in prosperous practice in the West End, qualified himself for the British register in order to secure professional status, to be authorized to give death certificates, to be eligible for consultation, and generally to enjoy the privileges conferred by the recognized diploma. His opinion of general medical practice is not more flattering than Sir Almroth Wright's opinion of antiseptic surgery. Probably no Swedish doctor thinks highly of British practice, because in Sweden you pay your doctor so much a year to keep you well, whereas in the British Empire you pay him nothing until he makes you ill (or chance or your own bad habits does it for him), the Swedish doctor thus having a vested interest in your health and the British doctor a vested interest in your disease, with the results that might be expected. The Swedish doctor in question believes in the Kellgren manipulative system, and practises it quite as successfully, to say the least, as his British colleagues who pursue the orthodox routine. When he was going through his courses of study at a famous medical school attached to a London hospital, he succeeded in persuading the authorities that every student should qualify himself as a masseur. They actually went so far as to commission him to purchase the necessary apparatus, doubtless remembering that massage is as old as Hippocrates, and has been practised from time to time ever since, sometimes quite systematically, as a part of hospital treatment and instruction. But before the commission was executed, the medical school informed the Swedish expert that the students must qualify as masseurs in a month. Now this, to a trained Kellgren masseur, was horrifying. The shortest period in which a Kellgren masseur can qualify is two years; and of all quacks, the most abhorrent and dangerous in the eyes of the Swedish school is the quack,

21

disastrously common now in England, and usually, I regret to say, on the register as a qualified physician or surgeon, who professes to teach massage in a month for ten guineas to women driven by economic desperation to seek employment as nurses, or worse. He regarded himself as the recipient of an infamous proposal, and indignantly dropped the whole affair.

ECONOMIC LIMIT TO THE PERIOD OF TRAINING

But let us look at this not very reassuring transaction from the point of view of the medical school. Its course of study and training now extends to five years. This is two years less than the traditional apprenticeship of a mason or carpenter; but the mason's apprentice has not to be supported by his parents. He pays his way, and is, in fact, avowedly kept in the bonds of apprenticeship to make money for his master as well long after he has mastered his trade. But the medical student earns nothing, not even his board and lodging, and must keep up a presentable middle-class standard of life, and find time for study, and money for books, fees, etc., during the five years. It is not in all cases absolutely impossible to do this and earn a living as well; but the possibility is too limited to count as a factor in the general problem. The consequence is that much first-rate professional material is driven into the city office because professional training is beyond the family means. Every year added to the course of training cuts off a portion of the supply and recruits the city at the expense of the professions. Had the medical school in question added two years to the five years' period in order that its students should all be fully qualified masseurs, it might just as well have put up the shutters at once; for it would have lost all its students, and none of the other schools would have followed its example.

THE ADVENT OF THE OSTEOPATH

Since that time a far more terrible rival to the registered doctor has come into the field under one of those barbarous names in which doctors delight. The Homeopath and the Allopath alike found themselves confronted with the Osteopath. He, like the masseur, had a new and elaborate manipulative technique; but his training demanded a four years' course in addition to certificates of a minimum of liberal education. The extension of the four years to five, as in the case of our registered practitioners, is probably only a matter of time. Had the General Medical Council admitted the technique of the masseurs and osteopaths to its canon without sacrificing any part of its present curriculum, the period of training for an ordinary general practitioner would have been 5 years + 2 years + 4 years = 11 years, at which rate the calling in of a registered doctor would become a plutocrat's hobby, and the actual practice of medicine and surgery be driven into the hands of unregistered practitioners, leaving the General Medical Council high and dry. Harley Street would become a sort of Faubourg St Germain, and the employment of a registered doctor would become an eccentricity like Jacobitism.

Consequently at this moment the registered doctors in England are engaged in a struggle for life against the osteopaths, who have won all along the line in America, and are flourishing exceedingly already in London. The methods of resistance are petty and futile. For example, Harley Street and the medical region about it belong in great part to one of our monster London ground landlords, a peer to whose liberal tastes and munificence our theatrical and musical art owes a good deal. On his estate is a certain street once occupied by private residences, and still let on old leases containing clauses forbidding the use of the houses for purposes of trade, though by this time almost every house in the street is a shop. An osteopath who was not very well acquainted with London (they all come from America) took rooms in this street and began to practise there. No sooner did the managers of the estate discover his brass plate, with the hated D.O. on it, than they offered his landlady the alternative of ejecting him or having her lease broken under the clause forbidding the use of the premises for trade purposes. That unhappy osteopath was homeless for many weeks, all the eligible houses which he tried

23

being either on the same estate or already partly let to authorized doctors who threatened notice to quit if an osteopath were admitted to any floor. Of course, the final result was that the estate lost a good tenant, and that the osteopath's guineas and his distinguished *clientèle* soon secured him a much less dowdy set of rooms than those to which he had clung in his American innocence. But he was none the less amazed that it was possible for a D.O. to be turned out of doors in the West End of London as a Methodist laborer can be (and sometimes is) in the country on the estate of a bigoted Anglican lord of the manor. Another osteopath who has effected a lodgment in Harley Street itself is forbidden to put his name on his door, even without letters indicating his profession; but as the vogue of osteopathy makes him independent of brass plates, there is no prospect of his moving until the address becomes a bar to public confidence, as it seems likely enough to do presently.

The Electronic Rayman

The most startling of all the new biological discoveries is that made during the present century by a Jewish doctor in San Francisco. The scientific world had become excited about the phenomenon of radio-activity. A metal which was dangerously active in this way was named radium; and for some time the grossest credulity prevailed as to its therapeutic possibilities. Many varieties of rays were discovered and classified; and it was soon found that some of them could pervert the operation of the vital forces so horribly that a process which began by a slight inflammation of our skin would finally and inexorably destroy us after we had sacrificed our limbs joint by joint in the vain endeavour to cut off the attack.

Dr Abrams, the Jewish physician aforesaid, was rich enough to risk the loss of his practice and try experiments. He presently announced not only that he had found that our blood is radioactive, which was credible enough, but that if you had a patient, A, whose complaint you wished to diagnose, you could do so by taking a healthy person, B (called the Subject), and passing through him an electric current influenced by the rays from a drop of A's blood, whereupon you could read off on the body of B any disease from which A was suffering very much as you can read on the spectrum of a light thrown by an incandescent substance the salts and metals which are burning in it. This statement was tested by the simple and obvious experiment of taking samples of blood from hospital patients suffering from known diseases, and from healthy persons, and challenging Dr Abrams to diagnose and sort them out by his method. He passed the test. In London an investigating committee of qualified physicians had finally to report that the British disciples of Dr Abrams had made out their case as far as diagnosis is concerned, though it refused to admit that the method of treatment founded on it had any value. Nevertheless the disciples, pointing to satisfactory results following the treatment, persisted in practising it; and some of them were too eminent to be infamonized (Shakespear's word) and deregistered. As the matter stands, any registered practitioner may both diagnose and treat by the Abrams method; but as it is a new method and therefore unknown to the examiners, and as, moreover, the necessary plant costs much more than a stethoscope, and the examination of the Subject (who has to be paid) takes much longer than the old routine of auscultation and pulse feeling, not to mention cubicles to be provided and nurses to be paid, the process is quite beyond the means of the average private patient and the ordinary private practitioner, who is therefore directly interested in ridiculing it as a notorious quackery if he ever happens to learn of its existence from facetious allusions in the Press to "the Abrams box."

Certainly the procedure is ridiculous even among medical procedures, which are almost all fatal to human dignity. You enter a consulting room and are greeted with professional courtesy by the physician, who then suddenly assaults you by seizing the lobe of your ear and squeezing it hard enough to produce local anæsthesia. When he lets go, he has in his hand a piece of blotting paper stained with a drop of your blood; and this he shuts up in a little box on a special form of rheostat (a rheostat is an instrument for varying and calibrating electrical resistances). Then the Subject enters and is introduced. In the practice of Dr Abrams the subject was a negro, possibly because nobody else could then be induced to adopt so strange a profession. In first-rate London practice she is a young lady, all the more attractive as her necessary qualification is that there is nothing the matter with her. Her dress is so contrived that she can denude herself for auscultation in the regions mapped out by Abrams as diagnostic. She stands facing the north; for the charm will not work unless she heads for the magnetic pole. She is connected with the circuit passing through the rheostat. The doctor then sounds her all over the diagnostic region by placing two fingers of one hand on her and tapping them smartly with two fingers of the other. No stethoscope is needed: not only the doctor's trained ear, but the patient's untrained one, can hear quite distinctly the change in resonance from hollow to stuffy when the fingers reach the tell-tale spot which indicates the patient's disease, according to the localizations determined by the experiments of Abrams. This is the technique of Abrams himself; but some practitioners, using later forms of his instrument, roll a glass rod over the region and discover the tell-tale place by the rod sticking at it instead of rolling freely on.

The treatment follows logically. The rheostat gives the vibration rate of the blood rays at the disease point. The patient is accordingly made comfortable in a cubicle for an hour, during which an electrical current, adjusted by another rheostat to produce a rate of vibration which neutralizes the disease rate, is brought to bear on him. If he gets well, so much the better for the doctor. If not, so much the worse for the patient. There is no doubt that he does get well sometimes; and that is all that can be said, so far, for any medical treatment.

It is evident that here the diagnosis and the treatment do not stand and fall together. The investigating committee in London was convinced of the soundness of the one, but shook its head over the other. I am not concerned here with the effectiveness of the treatment. I cannot repeat too often that treatments can justify themselves only by cures; and as there is no treatment, from the crudest cathartic pill to the subtlest Abrams rheostat, that cannot shew an imposing list of cures, which its rivals usually counter by a bloodcurdling list of kills, I must not pin my present contention to the efficacy of any treatment or theory of treatment. But it is clear that Abrams opened up a medical path which must be explored to the end, and that no doctor who has not been instructed concerning it is, whether he accept or reject the treatment, a fully qualified doctor. The current mockeries about "the Abrams box," and the fantastic speculations attributed to Abrams as to whether Shakespear might not have conveyed enough of the radio-activity of his blood to his ink to establish a diagnosis of his health by putting an authentic signature of his into the rheostat, are beside the point. Nobody would dream of excluding radium therapy from the medical curriculum merely because more nonsense has been written about radium than about the philosopher's stone. Enough has been demonstrated to suggest very strongly that a doctor who poohpoohs "electronic vibrations" nowadays is as hopelessly out of date as a chemist who poohpoohs spectrum analysis.

The important feature of the Abrams rheostat is that it is the beginning of diagnosis by machinery. And machinery may come to mean a great extension of the use of comparatively unskilled labor in the handling of patients. The Abrams machine is not the only one in the market. A gentleman calling himself a spinal specialist, who would be classed ordinarily as an unregistered osteopath, surprised me by diagnosing spinal lesions, not with his fingers, but by applying to each of my vertebræ in succession a fork attached to a galvanometer, which instantly registered any displacement. And there are in existence medical rheostats, notably one invented by a Scottish homeopath, of which I can give no account. But they all point one way. When I was young big business offices employed hosts of book-keepers, skilled in writing and arithmetic, who, when the books came to be balanced, passed many distracted hours discovering and correcting their own errors. Clerks in those days had to make calculations of all sorts, deducting rates from rents, income tax from dividends, ordinary discounts from ordinary accounts, or translating foreign into home currencies for money changing. Nowadays these operations are performed by persons who need know neither how to write nor to add two and two correctly, by the use of calculating-cum-printing machines which are becoming as common as inkstands, though not quite so cheap. In the clinics and hospitals of the near future we may quite reasonably expect that the doctors will delegate all the preliminary work of diagnosis to machine operators as they now leave the taking of a temperature to a nurse, and with much more confidence in the accuracy of the report than they could place in the guesses of a member of the Royal College of Physicians. Such machine work may be only a registration of symptoms; but I can conceive machines which would sort out combinations of symptoms and deliver a card stating the diagnosis and treatment according to rule. It would not do the work done by the clinical instinct of the born healer; but the proportion of practising doctors possessing this instinct can hardly be more than ten per cent. With the rest the diagnosis follows from the symptoms; and the treatment is prescribed by the text-book. And the observation of the symptoms is extremely fallible, depending not only on the personal condition of the doctor (who has possibly been dragged to the case by his nightbell after an exhausting day), but upon the replies of the patient to questions which are not always properly understood, and for lack of the necessary verbal skill could not be properly answered if they were understood. From such sources of error machinery is free. But of modern machinery the General Medical Council seems to know just as much as Newman Noggs knew of typewriters. The sort of doctor it turns out is, as far as his registration guarantees, a medical Newman Noggs. He knows that he can call in a specialist when a case is too difficult for him; but he does not know that he may be wearing himself out by trying to do in a very difficult and uncertain way things that he could get done with ease and certainty by a machine which his typist-secretary could operate.

To many readers this suggestion of Robot doctors operating diagnosing and prescribing machines may read like a reduction to absurdity of the routine of medical practice. Perhaps it is. I have not forgotten an occasion on which my mother, finding her heart palpitating, called in a young doctor, who soon disposed of the case in the most business-like fashion. It was quite simple. My mother herself provided the diagnosis: heart trouble. He looked it up and found that digitalis is the drug for hearts. Accordingly, he "shoved in" a stiff dose which all but killed the patient, who, however, being of a hardy constitution, survived to forswear doctors for ever, and physicked herself thenceforth with the homeopathic specifics of Count Mattei, which had the advantage over "allopathic" digitalis of leaving her none the worse for them. Still, as she did survive, many of my readers will conclude that the digitalis doctor cured her; and as what he did could obviously have been done just as well or better by machinery, it is in their interests that a knowledge of such machinery should be made part of the qualification for registration as general practitioner.

The Infinitesimal Dose

I used to be a collector of uncanonical therapeutics. Whenever I heard of a new method of treating illness I presented myself for treatment when next I had a spare hour. Though my celebrity made me an interesting patient I was medically a very disappointing one, as there was nothing more serious the matter with me than the occasional headaches which, like common colds, reduce Harley Street to impotence. The cure of a man who is obviously not ill cannot be claimed as a triumph by any physician, orthodox or unorthodox. Still, if I could not credit the practitioner with success, at least I could not reproach him with failure. And I gathered a good deal of first-hand information which I could not have obtained by any other means.

But at last I had really something unpleasant the matter with me. I developed a very inconvenient sort of localized dropsy called by doctors a hydrocele. It did not hurt; but it was an unseemly nuisance. My medical friends assured me that it could be dealt with by a very simple operation, and that it was positively indecent of me to go about with such a disfigurement when its removal was so easy.

But on reading up the subject I found that the operation was one of the mechanical kind practised by Mrs Squeers. It consisted of just boring a hole in me over the dropsical region. Its ease and simplicity for the surgeon was beyond question; and it was perhaps natural for him to conclude that it was equally easy and simple for me. But it seemed to me that the same might be said of a bayonet thrust. According to the books there was much more diversity of opinion as to the operation than my medical friends had been taught in the course of their training. It was suggested that as the operation did not cure, and had to be repeated over and over again as the dropsical condition recurred, a speculative antiseptic injection of iodine might follow the tapping. Also that the only radical operation was excision of the sac of the gland. As it happened, I had an opportunity of observing the case of a sufferer who obeyed his doctor and underwent the recommended simpler operation. It was much more distressing and disabling than the doctors thought; and the condition recurred.

On this evidence it did not seem to me that I could, as a sane man, allow myself to be coopered in the proposed manner, especially as I was aware that Nature has a therapy of her own for which there is at least more to be said than for Mrs Squeers. However, I exhibited my misfortune to an osteopath. He noted that the gland most nearly concerned was not quite normal, and warned me, with a somewhat grave expression, that if it became painful I should have to do something about it. And indeed it presently began to blacken rather ominously, and to protest uncomfortably against being disturbed in any way.

Here was a rare opportunity for one of my therapeutic experiments. I knew that Mr Raphael Roche claimed that chronic malignant conditions are amenable to treatment by drugs in infinitesimal doses. I challenged him to try his hand on my hydrocele. He accepted the challenge without hesitation; and for some weeks or perhaps less I every day solemnly put on the tip of my tongue a grain or two of some powdered sugar which he gave me.

Mr Roche won the game: whether by luck or cunning I know not. All I can say is that the appearance of the gland became less threatening, and that the hydrocele suddenly discharged itself without notice. Fortunately I was in bed at the time. Twice afterwards it discharged a blob of transparent lymph. And that was the last of it. My return to healthy normality was complete; and though many years have elapsed there has never been the slightest recurrence.

Now Harley Street would certainly have claimed this as a cure if it had treated a case with a similar result. As Mr Roche, who denounces Harleian practice as lethal, treated it, the Street will no doubt contend that the relation of his treatment to my cure was one of pure coincidence, and that I should have done just as well without his sugar as with it. That is the *coup de Jarnac* for all medical treatments, registrable or unregistrable. I can only state the facts as they occurred, and confess that I prefer Mr Roche's pleasant coincidences to distressing operations that admittedly do not cure. I did not ask Mr Roche what drug he used, as he strenuously denies that he has any specific drugs for specific diseases. I cannot prove that he used any drug at all, as he defied me to discover it by any known process of analysing the sugar. I had, he held, cured myself by the operation of my own vital forces, roused from their previous neglect by the attack made on them by an infinitesimal quantity of a drug which in a larger quantity would have aggravated or even produced not merely the symptoms and sensations attendant on the hydrocele, but those of the entire Shavian diathesis, physical and mental, representing the vulnerable idiosyncrasies of my vital force—what he calls the directions in which I have a tendency to be wounded. This is much more than the serum therapists claim for their inoculations. And who would not prefer the taste of Mr Roche's sugar to the *malaise* and risks of inoculation with preparations which disgust healthy-minded people and involve ill-usage of animals?

It also, by the way, is much subtler than ordinary homeopathy, which, though it prescribes infinitesimal doses, is still obsessed by lists of specific diseases curable by specific drugs, and to that extent can be practised by anyone with intelligence enough to look up a number in a telephone directory.

It is plain that the ordinary counteractive use of drugs, as when croton oil is prescribed for constipation or chalk and opium for diarrhœa, is only the crudity of Mrs Squeers transferred from surgery to medicine. The infinitesimal method is much more sensible, and is in line with modern biological science. But its practice evidently involves the ancient, curious, and so far empirical knowledge of certain specific and unaccountably local-ized effects of vegetable and mineral substances on the vital force in animals. In such matters empirical knowledge is the ultimately scientific knowledge: syllogisms, inferences, and analogies are so extremely dangerous in dealing with the profound mystery of the vital forces that it is safer practice to dismiss them as certain to be wrong. I have never made a study of the subject, and do not know whether its facts have yet been collected and played with by first-rate investigators to the extent that would enable its empiricism to rank as the application of a science. But it has now been carried far enough in practice to reduce to barbarism the crude counteractive *materia medica* of the Harleian curri-culum. Counteractive drugging should be known to registered doctors only as an ignorant malpractice which should be penalized. Yet the impression our registered doctors receive from their training is that counteractive drugging is scientific medicine and homeopathy a disreputable quackery.

THE GAME OF CAPPING CURES

Here, if I yielded to the temptation to humbug the reader, I should give a list of the amazing cures made by our specialists in new treatments. They can all hold their own even with Sir

Herbert Barker at that game, the more gracefully as most of them are sufficiently up to date to repudiate cures and profess only to put you in a condition to cure yourself. But scientific honor obliges me to confess and even insist that stories about cures prove nothing. If they did, Harley Street would have to confess itself beaten to a frazzle by Lourdes. There is not a bottle of proprietary medicine nor a box of pills in the pharmacist's shop that is not wrapped up in a list of cures, the authenticity of which there is no reason to doubt, which puts not only the Blessed Virgin, Sir Herbert Barker, the masseurs and the osteopaths, but the whole medical register to shame. Christian Science cures. Mattei cured. Charles II cured scrofula by touching it. I endure, like many "brain-workers," periodical headaches from which doctors of all sorts, registered and unregistered, have retired baffled; but a pleasant lady who volunteered to cure one of them by sitting near me and composing herself into a bland reverie unspeakably exasperating for a suffering man to contemplate, did actually take the headache away, or provoke it to take itself away, the very scepticism she inspired, or perhaps her good looks, acting as a sort of psychological stimulant to the phagocytes who eat the headache bacillus: a theory which I leave Sir Almroth Wright to elaborate. I know of a working jeweller who cures diphtheria, pneumonia, and swine-fever by the fumes of nitric acid. I know of a registered practitioner who cures rheumatism and cognate diseases by hypodermic injections of hypochlorites. I have described how Mr Raphael Roche effected a cure on my own person. I know a successful healer who is frankly a thaumaturge of the Jesus type, and holds that his apparently miraculous gift is common enough, though few cultivate it. And I know doctors of extraordinary ability and scientific keenness who have never, as far as I have been able to ascertain, cured anyone or anything, and whose advice I should nevertheless value highly if I were unlucky enough to be in pressing need of it. The result is to convince me that there is no direct guidance to be got out of mere cure capping. Cures have as much to do with science as ghost stories, no more and no less. I return to the less romantic aspects of my subject.

We have seen that the apparently simple expedient of adding the new techniques to the old ones as conditions of qualification is impracticable economically on the score of the impossible prolongation of the qualifying period of study. But even if a ten years' period were to be made possible by a general economic reform of society—and this is not at all impossible—we should only be faced with the fact that some of the new techniques are not extensions of the old but supplantations of them. Osteopathy, for instance, is, like Kellgren massage, a no-drug system. The fact that nothing in heaven or on earth will prevent masseurs and osteopaths from taking short ways with trivial ailments like any apothecary does not alter their opposition to the whole medicinal system. The osteopath is essentially what Samuel Butler, in a flash of prophecy, called "a straightener." He does not admit any limits to his scope as a pathologist; but he is primarily a spinal surgeon. His special theory is that a very slight displacement of any vertebra will, if it nips a nerve channel or a blood vessel, contract or starve or irritate or abort that channel or vessel, with all sorts of mischievous results, direct and remote. The application of this theory to clinical practice is effected by a tactile and manipulative technique which enables the osteopath to diagnose spinal lesions by his sense of touch, and then correct them by manipulation. This tactile skill and knowledge is arduous of acquirement; and the chief American schools of osteopathy will not give a student the degree of D.O. unless he has gone through a four years' course of training. This stipulation, as we have seen, makes it equally impossible for the British L.R.C.P. or M.R.C.S. to acquire the technique or to pretend with any plausibility that the D.O. is an ignorant, unqualified quack. Indeed, the osteopathic colleges turn the tables on the old school by offering all its guarantees of general education and technical training, and improving on them.

DOCTORS' DELUSIONS

THE RITUAL OF THE GUINEA-PIG

In one respect they have even gone a step backward to get into line. One of the devices by which doctors save themselves the trouble of thinking is the convention that a clinical observation does not become scientific until it has been repeated on the body of a rabbit, guinea-pig, frog, cat, or stolen dog. I refrain from giving examples, not only because they are sickening, but because their silliness is so incredible that they make people believe I am joking. Suffice it that when Dr Still, the founder of osteopathy, alleged that certain spinal lesions would produce certain diseased conditions, and that the conditions would disappear when the lesions were corrected, and demonstrated this by curing human patients, he was met with an intellectual atrophy which involved total inability to perceive that his clinical exploits proved anything. His medical colleagues said, in effect: "Our minds have not been trained to act in your vulgar way. We attach no significance to these operations of yours on human beings. You say that you have found John Smith suffering from appendicitis; that a couple of his dorsal vertebræ were rotated; that the rotation deranged the mechanism provided by God to prevent appendicitis; that on your correcting the rotation the inflammation disappeared and the patient recovered. We do not perceive any connection between these events and your manipulation; nor is it clear to us how a man who believes in God (except in conversation to oblige old-fashioned patients) can possibly be a man of science. But if you will take a guinea-pig or a dog; dislocate its dorsal vertebræ; arrange that it shall get appendicitis; and then reduce the dislocation and allow the guinea-pig to get well and have its experience described for it by the experimenter with more or less of the brilliancy of a Sydenham or a Trousseau, then your thesis will be firmly established as science." It is pitiful to have to record that the osteopaths have under this pressure actually set up a laboratory where they solemnly damage animals and mend them again; and no doubt they take care that these imbecile put-up jobs resemble the clinical feats of Dr Still and

35

his followers at least as closely as the antics of a performing poodle pretending to feel the pulse of a toy terrier in a cradle on the stage of a variety theatre resemble a professional visit by a medical baronet to a sick bishop. The osteopaths have the grace to protest that they do not like the business, and, of course, ridicule the notion that it proves anything that they have not proved legitimately in their practice; but they declare that they have been forced to resort to it by the obsession of the medical world with the methods of the physiological laboratories. Their plea is, "If you will not believe when we cure a sick man, and will believe abjectly and credulously when we make a guinea-pig sick and then let it get well, why, we must do it, or pretend to do it, for your own silly sakes."

It is impossible not to indulge in a grim chuckle at the vivisectors thus hoist with their own petard. They tried to make science a monopoly for men of the type of St Thomas, who, with the living Fact staring him in the face and talking to him, did not consider its existence proved until he had thrust his cruel fingers into it. They forgot that they could not make a corner in folly and imposture.

The Osteopath as a Miracle Worker

The osteopath thus comes into the scientific world with not only all the prestige that the approved routine of examinations and diplomas can give him, but with the retinue of tormented rabbits and dogs that is *de rigueur* in the modern scientific ritual. He has also, by the way, an elaborate code of professional etiquette which is virtually that of the General Medical Council. Add to this what is much more effective from the lay point of view: that the osteopath's procedure in the consulting room or at the bedside leaves the registered doctors nowhere in its power of impressing the patient. Instead of saying, "And how are we today?" in the approved clinical manner (thereby asking the patient the very question he sent for the doctor to answer) and listening gravely to replies which, like Sir William Watson Cheyne's replies to Sir Almroth Wright, are all adjectives and adverbs instead of numerals, and in which the unascertained personal equation is so large a factor that one man will describe as a dreadful pain a sensation of which another would be ashamed to complain, not to mention the answers we all give to the doctor because we are afraid he will think us fools if we confess that we dont know clearly how we feel or what we feel, the osteopath seizes the patient and feels his skeleton with fingers and hands that are obviously highly skilled. If he discovers a lesion, he proceeds to wrestle with it. When the treatment is over for the day, the patient is amazed and feels considerably straightened, whilst the osteopath, having visibly had a spell of hard work, conveys an impression of having earned his money which cannot be achieved by looking wise and writing a prescription, even for a patient to whom the words *aqua, micapanus,* and *quant. suff.* suggest unutterable learning.

Even if osteopathy be as great a delusion as antiseptic surgery is according to Sir Almroth Wright, yet, like antiseptic surgery, it is not nonsense: a layman of ordinary intelligence can understand its extremely plausible theory. Besides, the most sceptical patients argue that a body of practitioners specializing on the skeleton in this way must, whether their views as to the serious consequences of spinal lesions are sound or not, inevitably acquire and refine upon all the dexterities of the bonesetter in diagnosing and correcting directly crippling dislocations. The fashionable lady, aged and crippled with rheumatism and "excess of uric acid," who has spent hundreds of guineas on doctors, and wandered over Europe from one cure-place to another until she has filled herself with every fetid water from Harrogate and Bath to Kissingen and Mont Dore, and wallowed in every sort of mud brown enough to seem worth three marks a bath, getting all the time stouter and less able to walk upstairs without creaking like her grandmother, sooner or later hears about the osteopath, and tries him in desperation, just as she has tried the famous Paris doctor who cures rheumatism with a wonderful little pill of which you take 250 a day, or as she would try anybody or anything that promised relief. The osteopath instantly diagnoses a simple displacement of "the innominate" or nameless bone. The lady says she never knew she had a nameless bone, and accuses the osteopath of laughing at her. The osteopath explains that though a British M.D. could not possibly mention it to a lady, the osteopath, having to tackle it in a manner that renders concealment impossible, does not hesitate to confess that it is the haunch bone. He reduces the dislocation in a few treatments; the lady skips downstairs twenty years younger with nothing whatever the matter with her; she proclaims the miracle; all her friends applaud her; all registered doctors are voted humbugs; and the osteopath flourishes extremely.

Such incidents as the above have been multiplied by the war. Sir Herbert Barker sets our crippled soldiers on their legs. Ladies trained in Sweden as masseuses, and preserving their professional enthusiasm after marrying and retiring from practice, visit military hospitals and are followed by cries of "Another leg saved." Necks blown awry by high explosives come straight in the hands of osteopaths whilst the Royal Army Medical Corps leaves the soldier, like the one who scandalized Macaulay in Robert Montgomery's poem, to lie on his bleeding breast and stare ghastly at the skies. The embarrassment caused to the R.A.M.C. by Sir Herbert Barker's offer to place his services at the disposal of the Army gratuitously has been capped by a similar offer of the services of a body of six osteopaths; for the D.O. cannot be staved off on the pretext that he has no academic qualification. Even if all these rumored successes consist of fairy tales to quite as great an extent as the recent obituary notices of Sir Victor Horsley (and that is conceding a good deal), it is still evident that with the whole registered profession straining every nerve to expose the failures of the unregistered and to conceal its own, there is no danger of the fairy-tale element in public opinion benefiting the unregistered more than the registered: the probabilities are quite the other way. In any case, the unregistered have gained so much credit of late that unless the profession repents and sets its house in order, Harley Street itself will shine with brass plates on which the names of bonesetters, Kellgren masseurs, psycho-therapists, and D.O.s will be followed by the reassuring words: *No connection with the General Medical Council.*

THE UNQUALIFIED QUALIFIED

If the reader is sufficiently convinced of the danger of the exclusion of new techniques from the official course of study, I must now ask him to turn his mind right round and contemplate the even more terrifying assumption that the registered practitioner is qualified to try his hand at all the new techniques and administer all the new medicines in virtue of his registration, whether he has studied them or not. If Nelson were to rise from his grave to save his country, and insisted on taking command of a submarine on the ground that once a captain always a captain, and that what a lieutenant can do an admiral can do, it would be necessary to remove him to Copenhagen Hospital. But nobody can restrain the medical Dug Out from venturing upon new techniques and medicines that are hideously dangerous. After the Wright opsonin innovation, the two that have made most noises in the medical world are the X-rays and salvarsan. To read the popular articles on the subject in the papers one would suppose that the X-raying of a patient or the administration of doses of salvarsan is as simple a matter as taking a snapshot or giving a seidlitz powder. The truth is that X-ray cautery in the hands of any but a highly trained expert produces after a few days a burn beyond all comparison worse than a brand from the hottest of red-hot pokers, and that the victim is to be heartily congratulated if, after months of atrocious pain, which only a reckless use of morphia can make bearable, the excision of the part leaves the patient boasting himself an interesting case of "dermatitis" sooner than confess that he has been simply burnt by a bungler. As to salvarsan, when it goes wrong it goes so very wrong that experts use it with their hearts in their mouths, as part of the old mercury treatment it is erroneously believed to have supplanted. To put such things into the hands of a general practitioner with a diploma perhaps forty or fifty years old is as dangerous as giving them into the hands of a man with no qualification at all. Yet the British Medical Association demanded that the Local Government Board should serve out rations of salvarsan to all general practitioners indiscriminately as if nothing more lethal than "the old mixture" were in question. Whenever it is proposed to restrict the practice of any therapeutic process to experts, the doctors cry out that the general practitioner is being degraded into "a mere signpost to the specialist." One would suppose that this was at least less degrading than the responsibility for horrible suffering and death caused by ignorant bungling: indeed, in practice no general practitioner feels any degradation when he sends his patient to an operating surgeon, and does not himself undertake even the administration of the anæsthetic. In the case of the midwife, who is now bound under penalties to send for a doctor the moment any complications present themselves in a labor, the doctors do not consider that the midwife is thereby degraded: they approve enormously of the restriction.

This tradition that once a doctor gets his name on the register he may attempt without supervision or restraint or (virtually) responsibility every operation or course of treatment known or hereafter to be known throughout the entire realm of surgery and medicine, raises the whole question of division of labor in medicine. The problem is a difficult one, because no doctor can really be an efficient Jack of All Trades; and yet a doctor may have to turn his hand to anything under certain conditions. Compare for example, the city doctor, who has a dozen specialists at the end of his telephone, with the country doctor who may have to wait from three to twenty-four hours for skilled help, not to mention the island doctor, who may have a fortnight of impassably stormy seas between him and the mainland. Men thus isolated must be prepared, within human limits, to do everything for their patients, whilst their city colleagues need never tackle a case which presents the slightest difficulty without aid. When we have a State service of sanatoria with rows of laboratories and staffs of experts throughout the land like post offices, as no doubt we shall have unless civilization turns back in its tracks first, our present system of private practice will seem insane enough. But that organized medical corporations should fiercely defend it, and resist every attempt to restrict the practice of individual doctors to those professional operations which their qualifications really cover, will appear something much less honest than insanity. The inoculator who "shoves in" tuberculin without ever having read a line of Wright; the medical amateur photographer who turns on the X-rays as lightheartedly as if he were trying a new brand of bromide paper; the apothecary to whom salvarsan is the "perfect cure": these are much more dangerous quacks than the unregistered ones, because they flourish a State guarantee that they are universal experts in all the arts of healing.

The Inevitability of Specialization

Yet this state of things is the result of a great reform only half a century old. Before 1858 there were physicians, and even therapeutic metaphysicians, barber-surgeons, surgeons, and apothecaries, learning their trade as private apprentices, and quarrelling fiercely about the overlapping of their departments. In 1858 they were all compelled to qualify themselves for general practice; and the advantage of getting rid of Figaro with his lancet, and substituting an educated and systematically trained man, was so obvious that the world breathed freely and ceased to bleed freely at last. But, as we have seen, surgery and medicine could not be kept within the limits of one-man capacity. The Act of 1858 put the medical trade union in the position of the old trade union of shipwrights. Formerly every fixture in a ship was the work of the shipwright: woe to the member of any other union who dared to lay a finger on it! But the shipbuilding industry would not "stay put." When big ships came to be made of metal, the shipwright could no more make them than a cooper can make milk-cans. Ocean liners are now nothing but steel shells containing hotels: there is hardly a shipwright's job in the whole concern except a few rudimentary organs which are mere ornamental vestiges of the evolution from the old wooden sailing ship. No shipwright now pretends that liners and battleships are his job, or that they could exist without the co-operation of scores of specialists, many of whom never saw a ship in their lives.

What has happened to the shipwrights must inevitably happen to the doctors. No doubt commercial specialism in medical practice has special dangers. Just as the barrister who can handle a particular type of case will take briefs for all sorts of cases and distort them to fit his speciality, so the specialists in a particular treatment or a particular operation will try that treatment or that operation on all sorts of complaints. They are not necessarily knaves: they delude themselves before they delude the patient. But business is business. When you go into the Rolls-Royce showroom the salesman does not say, "If I were you I should buy a Daimler"; and the throat specialist easily pesuades himself that the real source of gout in the toe is that the patient's uvula is a little too long.

Wanted: a State Medical Service

This leads us again, as almost every medical difficulty leads us, to the necessity for a disinterested medical service: that is, a State Medical Service continually subjected to the test of vital statistics. And never has there been a more favorable moment for advocating one. The war has done two very desirable things. It has taken a crowd of doctors from ill-equipped private practices in which their interest was to keep the patients as ill as they dared, as often as they dared, as long as they dared. Having broken up these practices, it has placed their struggling exploiters in a public practice in which there is the most urgent national need for restoring the patient to full efficiency in the shortest possible time; in which money does not count at all; and in which you need not compete with your neighbor in dishonest humbug. It is not too much to say that this change has thrown a new light on life not only for the doctors, but for all professional men and men of business who have had their services transferred in the same way. But here we are concerned only with the doctor. He foresees with dismay that at the end of the war he will be thrown back into civil practice to begin life over again. But by that time an unprecedented mass of public medical work will have been created by the war casualties. All through the summer of 1916, during the Somme offensive, the casualty list stayed with remarkable steadiness at 3000 a day, not counting 1000 deaths. Making even the largest allowance for "cushy" wounds, such figures represent a considerable new body of disabled pensioners; for the official tradition of throwing all war wreckage, with or without a few pence a day, into the streets to shift for itself as best it may, is not now tolerated by public opinion, which is already in active revolt against even discharging unaided the men who have broken down in training and never seen a trench, whether their illness was contracted in the ranks or not.

We are therefore going to have at the same moment a public need and a professional demand for a State medical service.

In such a service division of labor would be a matter of course. In private practice every man is both general and drummer-boy, extirpator of the most vital organs and poulticer of whitlows; but in the Army there is no such nonsense: there are majors and colonels, chiefs and subalterns, due subordination, economy of ability, and division of labor; and the war-trained doctors will fall into the necessary specialism as naturally as they have fallen out of the continual speculation as to how ill a patient can afford to be: in other words, how long he can afford to stay away from his work, and how much he can afford to pay. In the field hospitals they do not cherish a colonel in bed for six weeks for a wound which would not detain a private more than ten minutes.

Now comes the question: How can the profession set its house in order? and, if it refuses, as it most likely will, how can the Government set about the necessary repairs over its head?

43

DOCTORS' DELUSIONS

The Medical Profession and the State

Before any repairs can be intelligently planned, some knowledge of the present constitution of the profession must be acquired. The reformer finds himself face-to-face with two bodies: the State-constituted General Medical Council with incredibly oppressive powers and the usual remarkably bad middle-class manners, and a very completely organized trade union called the British Medical Association, employing all the characteristic weapons of trade unionism and syndicalism with a skill and ruthlessness impossible to our less instructed and more sentimental unions of laborers and mechanics. It was this union that, by the threat of a general strike, brought Mr Lloyd George to his knees over the Insurance Act. Virtually, the State-created powers of the General Medical Council are at the disposal of the British Medical Association, which is thus enabled to employ the weapon of the boycott against non-unionists with crushing effect, as it can have blacklegs struck off the register for "infamous professional conduct," a statutory phrase which is made to cover any sort of conduct, however laudable from the point of view of general morality, which damages the commercial interests of the profession.

Trade Unionism on Miraculous Assumptions

Here, as many educated people are still ignorant enough to suppose that trade unionism is in itself discreditable and anti-social, it must be admitted, and indeed insisted, that the professional organization of doctors in a trade union is as necessary and, on the whole, as socially beneficial as the organization of the miners or steel smelters. But what would be said if Parliament conferred on the Parliamentary Committee of the Trade Union Congress the power of discrediting and ruining any person who practised coal hewing or steel smelting without its licence, or who assisted any person so practising, or who saved any person employing an unlicensed person from acute suffering. Suppose,

44

in addition to this, none of us could go into a tool-shop and buy a hammer without paying a fee to a licensed artisan, and obtaining a paper signed by him to certify that we needed the hammer to knock in a nail and not to knock out our mother's brains! It is evident that such legislation would be impossible under existing circumstances. Why, then, has it been actually passed in the case of the doctors? Simply because we believe doctors to have miraculous powers, recondite knowledge, and divine wisdom. Now the fact is that they have no more miraculous powers than any other skilled worker has. They have no knowledge that is out of the reach of any layman who cares to acquire it: in fact, it may be doubted whether two per cent of our general practitioners know as much science as an average lay frequenter of the Royal Institution or University Extension lectures. And as to their wisdom, themselves have testified, through the mouths of Almroth Wright, Watson Cheyne, Hadwen, and many another, that their understandings have all the normal human infirmities and some specially inculcated professional ones as well. The objection to the British Medical Association is not that it is a trade union employing all the regular weapons of trade unionism and syndicalism, but that Parliament, by means of the General Medical Council, has placed within its grasp powers which are jealously and properly denied not merely to all other trade unions, but to the Church, the Throne, and even to Parliament itself. To speak of the medical profession as a priesthood is to understate the case. No priest, no Consistory, no Church has such legal powers over the lay community and over its own members as the General Medical Council. To take the simplest and most obvious instance: no priest can legally compel a citizen to have his child baptized. But the doctor can and does compel the citizen to have his child vaccinated, even when other children of his have already been killed by the operation. A British rector cannot be deprived of his living without a process so elaborate and so fenced about with provisions for his defence that no rector who has any business to be in the Church at all suffers the slightest sense of insecurity or fear of persecution; but a doctor can be unfrocked in ten minutes by a handful of other doctors sitting without legal assessors or responsibility to any but themselves. Their proceedings and their decision may in any particular case be so scandalous that articles appear in leading magazines and in The Times denouncing them, and the most distinguished persons sign public protests. The General Medical Council receives all such remonstrances with the thumb to the nose.

Lay Representation now Feasible

What is to be done? One step can be taken without any new legislation, and should have been taken from the beginning, which, by the way, is no further back than 1858. The General Medical Council should, for the protection of the laity and for the protection of the profession itself, be reinforced by a majority of laymen. The General Medical Council is a Government department subordinate to the Privy Council. It is made up of nine representatives of the medical corporations, eighteen of the Universities, five nominees of the Government, and six elected representatives of the registered practitioners. Thus the nominees of the Universities and of the Government outnumber the medical members by twenty-three to fifteen; and there is nothing in the constitution of the Council to prevent the Universities or the Government from not only nominating Sir Herbert Barker or any osteopath, masseur, or homeopath, but from making it a rule to nominate laymen only, and thus prevent the Council from being, as it as at present, virtually a committee of a trade union, and from using for commercial purposes powers so extraordinary, and indeed outrageous, that even the highest political and religious public organizations would not be trusted with them if they were so foolish as to demand them. In fact this obvious public safeguard was the unmistakeable intention of the framers of the Council; and its neglect is a grave dereliction on the part of the constituent bodies.[1]

[1] A beginning of the return to sanity has been made by the addition to the Council of Sir Edward Hilton Young. But until he is reinforced by a majority of laymen his position will not be an enviable one.

DOCTORS' DELUSIONS

What could Lay Representatives do?

But even if the General Medical Council were thus made a public body instead of a professional conspiracy, the representatives of the laity would still have to make up their minds as to a practical policy of reform. And one of the first discoveries they would make is that an adequate national medical service on the basis of private practice is a commercial impossibility. The apparently conclusive retort to this is that the alleged impossibility exists, as the private doctor is actually meeting the medical needs of the people as effectually as the baker and the butcher, and only fails where they fail equally; that is, when the patient or the customer is penniless. To which it must be at once firmly replied that the so-called medical service is, as to four-fifths of it, a delusion and a pretence, and that this is proved by the fact that when the required service is of such a nature that no pretence is possible, only about one-tenth of the population can afford to pay for it out of their private resources.

Services which cannot be simulated

To illustrate, let us take two branches of the first importance: obstetric practice and dental surgery. Childbirth is an operation as to which pretence is not feasible. The doctor cannot persuade the patient that a few minutes' conversation and a bottle of water flavored with some cheap phosphate syrup, with a payment on her part of anything from sixpence to half-a-crown, will leave her convalescing with her child safely in her arms. Nor can the same process excavate and fill up a decaying tooth and supply the elaborate dentures which are needed to take the place of lost ones. Dr Dulcamara at the fair, or the village blacksmith, or the local druggist in his back parlor may extract a tooth, violently or dexterously as the case may be, for no more than the doctor asks for doing it in his surgery *tant bien que mal*, just as the nearest pugilist may, uninvited, do it for nothing. But no civilized man, except the negligible, if not fabulous, few who celebrate their

47

ninetieth birthday without a single unsound tooth in their heads, can have their teeth kept in order without occupying so much of the time of a highly trained operator and his skilled mechanic, and using so much costly material, that the fees must be counted in guineas and not in sixpences. Even at that the temptation to take short cuts by putting in work that will not last is more than most dentists can afford to resist.

What is the consequence? Most mothers are delivered not by a registered doctor but by a midwife, as to whom the utmost that it has been possible for the law to exact is that if certain grave symptoms occur she must send for a doctor. As to dentistry, most people do not have their teeth attended to at all, and suffer much pain and evil in consequence; while of those who do, the great majority are treated by unregistered practitioners; so that the unregistered dentists are actually more powerful, because more numerous and better organized, than the registered ones. Some of them are no doubt quite as expert, and perhaps none of them are so unskilful, as the ordinary doctor who pulls out a tooth in his surgery; but still they are either collectively self-registered (like the doctors) or have no standing or training except what they pick up in practice at the expense of their patients. Even counting these last under the heading of "*bona-fide* practitioners" with the registered and unregistered dentists, the existing supply of dentists falls ruinously short of the need for them, the reason being that there is not a living in dentistry except in practices in which the patients belong to that ten per cent of the population which owns ninety per cent of the land, capital, and secondary education of the country.

Precisely the same difficulty arises with the masseur and the osteopath. Both of them have to spend at least half an hour of highly skilled and vigorous labor on each patient. Neither of them is supposed to employ drugs, though he may drop into tabloid druggery as Mr Wegg dropped into poetry, as a friend, not as an osteopath or masseur. Therefore he must also charge fees on the dental scale; and four-fifths of the population must go without his services accordingly.

DOCTORS' DELUSIONS

THE DESTINY OF THE PRIVATE SANATORIUM

Those who have already forgotten my opening pages will now ask why, because the work of the obstetric surgeon, the masseur, and the osteopath takes so much time, the work of the doctor, who can diagnose all human ailments at a glance, or, at worst, after feeling the pulse and looking at the tongue, should not be comparatively cheap and plentiful. The answer, of course, is that he cannot do anything of the sort, and, in so far as he pretends to be able to do it, is a dangerous impostor. There are, it is true, many ailments which anyone with clinical experience can recognize at a glance. A bad cold or a gumboil, an attack of smallpox or a broken arm, need not puzzle anybody, much less a doctor; and an experienced doctor can go much further than this by simply keeping his nose open. But the huge burden of pain and disablement under which the world groans is due only in small part to ailments of this class. It is the periodical or chronic indisposition due to obscure lesions that drains the vitality and lowers the productivity of a nation, and that incidentally makes fortunes for druggists and for the ground landlords of chalybeate springs, as well as incomes for doctors. All these chronic cases are simply undiagnosed cases; and they are undiagnosed because the doctor cannot afford to diagnose them. I once discussed with an expert the economic question of what an ordinary general practitioner would have to charge if he were asked to vaccinate a millionaire's child in a completely scientific manner according to the latest theory of Wrectified Immunization. We finally guessed it roughly at about £2000, which would include the provision of a properly equipped laboratory and the acquirement of the Wright technique. Yet the Wright technique is a very cheap one. If the millionaire required, instead, the diagnosis of some ailment that cost him a couple of months' *malaise* and disablement every year, and made him wish he were a healthy railway porter, the range of laboratories and experts needed (as at Battle Creek) might multiply the £2000 by ten.

Still, if the millionaire provided the necessary funds, it might be possible to keep the laboratories and experts going by treating the general public at prices within the means of moderately-well-off patients. This possibility has led in the past to the establishment by private enterprise of sanatoria of various kinds, from the tubs of Mesmer and Dr Graham's Celestial Bed (at which Nelson's Emma Hamilton was an attendant angel) to the Water Cures or Hydropathics of the nineteenth century and the Open-air Cures and Sun Baths, the Battle Creeks, Nordrachs, and Weisser Hirschs of the twentieth. But all these places are under a steady economic pressure which eventually and inevitably changes them into more or less expensive hotels. For a time the inmates are patients, and are really ill, or fancy they are. But friends who wish to visit them, and relatives who wish to stay with them, provide the proprietors with a very convenient means of making money out of empty rooms which would otherwise be eating their heads off. All the amenities so carefully arranged, including the healthy climate and the fine situation, are as attractive to the patient when he has recovered as when he is under treatment; and he returns as a simple holiday-maker to the place he discovered as an invalid. For a time a valetudinarian air may hang about the institution; but sooner or later the laboratories and surgeries and gymnasia are converted into ordinary domestic rooms; the experts find their occupation gone, as nobody requires their services; and the general craze for baths deprives such utensils of any special significance. In the end one goes to "The Hydro" exactly as one goes to The Metropole; and a demand for hydropathic treatment as part of the routine of the establishment would create as much amazement as a demand for extreme unction as part of the routine of a variety theatre. And at no stage of the process, from its inception in therapeutics to its culmination in golfing, does it come within the reach of the submerged nine-tenths.

DOCTORS' DELUSIONS

Reform of Private Practice within its Limits

Under existing economic circumstances, then, public health cannot be provided for by private practice or private enterprise of any sort as far as modern therapeutics are concerned. But it does not follow that the class which can afford to pay for adequate treatment should be left at the mercy of the medical trade union merely because it consists largely of the undeserving rich. A good deal has been done in America, the fatherland of osteopathy, and in Sweden, the fatherland of modern massage, to deliver the layman from the yoke of Dr Diafoirus. America is specially interested because of the number and variety of the State laws and the overwhelming vogue of osteopathy. The arrangements arrived at fall under two main types. Either the osteopaths have achieved the status of an independent examining and qualifying body, with a recognized register which gives the D.O. the privileges of the M.D., or they are represented on the State equivalent to our General Medical Council, and have modified the examinations so as to allow any student who so desires to drop *materia medica* altogether, and qualify in practical therapeutics as an osteopath, his examination in the osteopathic branch being conducted without hostile prejudice by osteopaths. In anatomy, physiology, and all the subjects which are common to the two systems, as well as in the preliminary general cultural qualification by an Arts examination, or by the production of certificates of a minimum of high school education, the osteopath and the ordinary traditional doctor pass the same ordeal.

The latter is obviously the wisest solution for the medical profession. It is better to be catholic, and assimilate all the sects, than exclusive, like the Church of England, and lose grip of the laity. Whether it is equally desirable for the dissenters is another question. But, on the whole, most of them would be satisfied if the existing D.O.s, like the established dentists in 1878, were admitted to the register as *"bona-fide* practitioners" without being compelled to go to school again. Some such exception is necessary at every advance in registration, and affects only one generation. The result of refusing it in the past was that the passing of an examination by old hands became a question of paying fees, answering questions about the weather, and remarking that measles are now too serious to be neglected; and this did not tend to the good repute of certain medical degrees, as those old enough to remember the first effects of the Act of 1858 can testify.

On the whole, if the General Medical Council would modernize and specialize its examination so as to provide for the registration of osteopaths, Swedish medical gymnasts, and Kellgren masseurs, without imposing economically impossible years of study on them; if it guaranteed the good faith of these arrangements by the presence of representatives of these techniques on its own body; and if it made the usual provision for qualification by "*bona-fide* practice" of those already recognized and certified by their own colleges, there need be no more troubles as between the practitioners themselves.

But how about the public? Once admitted to the medical trade union, the new directorate would be no whit less exclusive or less subject to economic pressure than the old. No M.D. speaks of a D.O. as contemptuously as the D.O. speaks of the chiropractor, or the Kellgren masseur of the nurse who has paid a doctor ten guineas to teach her massage in a month. When their own competition is admitted, the newly registered members will join in the struggle of the British Medical Association to prevent outsiders from practising as keenly as any trade union limits the number of apprentices, or bars polytechnic-trained youths as "no tradesmen." Already they are faced with a new departure which scandalizes them far more than they have scandalized the old Diafoiruses: a departure that will undertake to meet the mighty challenge of Shakespear. Macbeth asked the doctor whether he could minister to a mind diseased, or pluck from the memory a rooted sorrow. Being told that "therein the patient must minister to himself," he exclaimed, "Throw physic to the dogs: I'll none of it." But Mrs Eddy with her Christian Science, and Freud with his psycho-analysis, have taken up the challenge. Freud's system is precisely one of plucking rooted sorrows from the memory. Neither Freud nor Mrs Eddy may be quite convincing; but they are at least as likely as Farmer Jesty once was to dominate a century of medicine and have Acts of Parliament passed to compel whole nations to accept their therapeutics; and Christian Science and Mental Healing and Psycho-analysis have only to find their Jenner or their Wright or their Still or Ling or Hahnemann (what about Dr Crichton Miller?) to confront a future united General Medical Council of M.D.s and D.O.s and masseurs and homeopaths with a new heresy that will threaten them all impartially. But even in drugging itself, revolutions are threatened. The current mechanical and chemical theories of medicine are obviously irrelevant to living organisms; and Mr Raphael Roche, with his revival of specific medicine, and Professor Starling, with his "hormones," may upset the whole shelf of medicine bottles as alarmingly as Hahnemann did. In short, the whole trouble will have to be gone through periodically until we are wise enough to make the medical expert subject to the lay representative, as he would be in any political concern, and to take out of his hands decisively and on principle the keys to his own profession. Nothing in our constitution is quainter than the fact that in religion, the thing we pretend to believe in, we are so jealous of the expert that a clergyman is actually legally disqualified from sitting in Parliament, whereas in medicine, the thing as to which we are abjectly and superstitiously credulous, we do not dare to send even one layman to represent us in the medical Star Chamber, though we have full power to do so.

THE KEY OF THE STREET

On one point lay control must be supreme. All trade union experience shews that the doors of a trade or profession must not be guarded, either for entrance or exit, by the members inside. Limitation of output to keep up prices, limitation of apprentices to keep up wages or fees, specialization of qualification to keep out candidates of certain social classes and religious sects, fossilization of the curriculum to keep out new methods, abortion of new

discoveries to fit them to obsolete conditions, deliberate persecution of original, independent, or critical individuals, and all
the tricks by which moribund institutions and harassed competitive breadwinners struggle for life, are anti-social; and it
should not be in the power of any sectional body, much less one
pecuniarily interested in them, to enforce them by powers of
expulsion and professional ruin. No man's livelihood and reputation, much less the progress of science, should be at the mercy
of an irresponsible clique of autocrats. The sentence of ruin for
"infamous professional conduct" must not be passed, nor the
case tried, by the profession. On the principle of setting a doctor
to catch a doctor the medical corporations may be allowed to
indict a practitioner, though they should have no exclusive right
in the matter; but they should not have the power to lynch him;
for the law of court-medical, like the law of court-martial, is no
law at all. The College of Physicians, at a period when its examination occupied half an hour or less, insisted on membership
of the Church of England as a qualification. If the General
Medical Council had that power at present, it would probably
exclude as unscientific any profession of religious faith of any
sort.

Medical Advertizing

There is no reason to fear that a really public court would
establish a lower code of professional conduct than that now in
force: it could hardly fail to improve on it. But it would certainly
modify such traditions as that the doctor must not advertize. Not
that it would be so inhuman as to throw on the struggling general
practitioner the expense of taking an inch of the daily paper for
his professional card, nor encourage him to announce "Biggest
and Best Bottle in Bermondsey for Sixpence: Three Babies Cured
of Croup last week." But it would not strike him off the register
because his name appeared as physician to a joint-stock sanatorium with that of the solicitor, the banker, the auditor, the
engineer, and the chaplain.

It might even go a good deal further in the direction of individual liberty in this matter. If we compare the dense ignorance of the public as to the development and march of therapeutic science with its keenness and instructedness as to the development and march of automobile construction, for instance, so that doctors with hopelessly obsolete methods and theories flourish where cars with tube ignition and chain drive are unsaleable, we are compelled to ask how the public is to be as fully guided in the selection of a doctor as of a motor-bicycle. Admit that the guidance is often that which a jury gets from a conflict of special pleading in which mendacity is part of the game, nevertheless that is by no means the worst sort of guidance: we hang men on the strength of it.

Besides, advertisement is not really suppressed. The advertisements of quacks and their remedies, and of proprietary medicines, are flaunting everywhere, and must achieve a considerable total of manslaughter every year: indeed, some public restraint on these is probably inevitable in the near future. But we must not allow the obtrusiveness and ubiquity of modern advertizing to convince us that everyone advertizes nowadays in business. The majority of business firms are as innocent of advertizing as their doctors; and all wise customers know that a record of prolonged success in business without advertisement is a better guarantee than fifty full pages of the most popular newspapers or the most attractively illustrated and seductively written prospectus. The question, "Is such and such an article a good one?" is often answered by, "It must be pretty good, because it has been on the market twenty years, and I have never seen an advertisement of it." The big commercial trusts which make a regular business of crushing their poorer competitors have never done it by out-advertizing them, but always by underselling them. Therefore, while enterprises like that with which the name of Herr Eugen Sandow is associated would continue to advertize largely, and the amazing advertisements of the French firms which manufacture specifics would continue to spread from L'Illustration to the English papers, and be imitated and outdone (if possible) by British firms, it is not at all likely that a complete removal of the ban on advertizing by general practitioners would cause any appreciable number of them to advertize. It might rather induce newspaper proprietors and managers to be much less tolerant than they are at present of letters to the editor which are really advertisements in the guise of indignant defences of scientific progress. For example, an anti-vivisectionist writes to protest against some experiment which has horrified him. Immediately some astute Harley Street consultant seizes the opening to denounce the anti-vivisector, and to ask him whether he is aware that it is due to the experiments he is thoughtlessly and ignorantly denouncing that the horrors of epilepsy, of myxœdema, of diphtheria or what not, no longer exist. Naturally all the people in whose family there is a case of epilepsy or myxœdema rush to that consultant's doorstep; and he reaps a substantial harvest of guineas for many days in explaining as best he can why the charm will not work in their particular cases. Why any newspaper should insert these advertisements without being paid for them I cannot imagine. The Times has been victimized again and again in this fashion; but it never seems to lose its faith, probably because it never reads its own back numbers even when it is compiling an obituary of some medical knight who has abolished in its columns all the diseases flesh is heir to. The day will come when any person, doctor or layman, professing to cure any disease whatsoever, will be placed in the same legal category as fortune-tellers and rogues and vagabonds in general; but meanwhile it seems rather invidious to allow a doctor to write to The Times announcing himself as in possession of various elixirs of more than Renaissance nastiness, warranted to cure all the plagues of Egypt, provided he couples the announcement with contemptuous abuse of some honest and sensible layman who does not believe him, and yet forbid him, on pain of unfrocking, to adopt the more civil and straightforward method of sending a string of sandwichmen down Bond Street, or wearing a sugar-loaf hat and scattering small bills from a triumphal chariot to the music of a brass band.

DOCTORS' DELUSIONS

THE MONOPOLY OF ANODYNES

The provisions of the Acts regulating the sale of drugs have now become so monstrous that they are bearable only because the number of people seriously needing scheduled poisons for any wholesome purpose is not sufficient to create a strong public opinion on the subject. To people with their imaginations full of the horrors of morphinomania or cocaine craving, it seems at first sight no hardship at all that a man cannot go into the nearest pharmacy and purchase a dose of morphia without paying a doctor to prescribe it, even when he has no power to compel the doctor to do so at a statutory price, and can therefore be black-mailed to the utmost of his need. But let us consider possible cases. A respectable citizen has a wounded son in the hands of Sir Herbert Barker, say, or of an osteopath to whom he has re-sorted after the R.A.M.C. and the family registered doctor have failed completely to treat his wound successfully. Or he has a wife who, having been unskilfully treated with the X-rays, is suffering from the agonizing burn that these rays produce in the hands of doctors, however highly qualified otherwise, who have not been very carefully trained in their application; and the lady, after this frightful experience, has refused ever to consult a regis-tered doctor again and has placed herself in the hands of, say, a Swedish medical gymnast. Or he has himself, through overwork at the War Office, brought on the sort of neuritis, or pseudo-neuritis, which is one of the penalties of such overwork; and the sudden development of an acute phase of it has placed him at midnight in tormenting need of the twelfth of a grain of morphia to secure his night's sleep in view of having work to do next day for which he must fit himself at any cost. Or he is subject to paroxysms of asthma, which have no terrors for him if he has at hand a certain famous specific which contains a trace of cocaine, without which his existence is miserable. These are not imaginary or far-fetched cases: they occur daily in considerable numbers under pressure of the war, and would occur in still considerable numbers in a population so large as ours if there were no war.

The citizen goes to the nearest pharmacy and finds the shop full of gentlemen in khaki in urgent need of tonics. He asks for his dose of, say, morphia. The pharmacist knows him quite well, and has not the smallest doubt of the emergency and entire propriety of his demand, but he has to say, "Unless you bring me an order from a registered doctor, you or your son or your wife may agonize to death; I may not sell you the millionth of a grain." The citizen, in desperation, brings the Archbishop of Canterbury, the Prime Minister, Queen Alexandra, and the Lord Chancellor, who all testify to his good faith, and implore the pharmacist on their knees to relieve the acute suffering of the innocent patient. The pharmacist, less merciful than the apothecary in Romeo and Juliet, and intimidated by the fate of Sir Herbert Barker's anæsthetist, informs them all that he is obliged by law to regard them as either the accomplices of a murderer or the fellow-debauchees of a morphia fiend, and, on their remonstrating, hands them over to the police for inciting him to break the law. The citizen asks desperately what he is to do. The pharmacist replies that he must ring up the nearest doctor. He does so. The doctor cannot prescribe unless he sees the patient, and, before consenting to a visit, inquires whether there is anyone in charge of the case. On learning that an unregistered person is in charge of it, he refuses to prescribe, as he will himself be struck off the register if he does anything to relieve the pain of a patient who is being treated by a quack. The citizen, after expressing his opinion of the law and of the medical profession in appropriate terms, returns to the pharmacy determined to appeal to the pharmacist to connive, in common humanity, at his stealing the morphia, and to take it by violence if he refuses. In the shop, however, he is lucky enough to find an undersized gentleman, evidently not very well off, and not at all scrupulous-looking, buying hyoscin, the most dangerous poison on the schedule. The citizen asks why this shady person can buy hyoscin when he cannot buy morphia. The pharmacist introduces the stranger as a registered doctor, by name Crippen, legally entitled to buy and dispose of everything that is forbidden to those comparatively suspicious characters, Lloyd

George, Randall Cantuar, Alexandra, and Finlay aforesaid. The citizen draws this favored darling of the British Constitution aside, and offers a sovereign for a prescription of a twelfth of a grain of morphia, adding, to soften him, "It is for my wife." Dr Crippen, deeply sympathetic, whispers that a twelfth of a grain will not be enough, and that he could improve on the prescription considerably for ten pounds. The citizen has to explain that he is fond of his wife, and has no immediate occasion for getting rid of her. Dr. Crippen apologizes for a natural misunderstanding; writes the prescription; pockets the sovereign; sends the citizen away happy; and, having paid for the hyoscin out of his sovereign, goes home and murders his own wife with it, and thereby becomes the most famous doctor of his time.

Parliamentary Idolatry

I submit that the fact that Parliament was quite easily induced to create such a possibility as this is a proof that our attitude towards the medical profession is one of an infatuation as gross as any of those recorded of the witch-doctor-ridden tribes of Africa. There are some parallels to it in our temperance legislation, which lately led to a man dying of collapse within reach of all the brandy in a public-house; but the regulations of the drink traffic are at least fiercely contested, denounced, criticized, and held in some sort of reasonable check by large and powerful bodies of political opinion, backed by formidable vested interests, whereas, at the mere utterance of the word "medical profession," the House of Commons falls under a spell as complete as that of the hypochondriac paying his hundredth doctor's bill for the treatment of a complaint that grows worse with every guinea. Nobody has yet dared to make alcohol a scheduled poison, though it is just as toxic as many scheduled poisons and far more mischievous; and nobody with money to pay for it has the smallest difficulty in procuring more of it than is good for him, or indeed in unlimited quantities, even in the teeth of his doctor's protests that he is making a suicidal and ruinous use of it. And nobody has suggested, or is likely to suggest, that if references to the respectability of a whisky purchaser's character, and inferentially of his motives, are ever to be taken by the vendor, the testimony of the clergyman under whom the purchaser sits should be deemed worthless, and absolute validity granted to that of any shabby, needy stranger, too drunken for the remotest village poor law infirmary, and too degraded for the most forlorn hope on the Gold Coast, with a diploma thirty or forty years out of date. Not that people really believe that a drunken doctor is a being of a superior order to a sober bishop. But they do imagine that quinine and rectified spirits of wine are things of an order different from sago and rum: the latter being common articles which can be left to common people and their common grocers, whereas the former are magical things that only a specially ordained and instructed priesthood can touch without profanation and dire consequence of divine wrath. The oil-shops sell every day a ton of rank poison for every pound that is dispensed in the pharmacies. A criminal on his way home from serving his last sentence for manslaughter at Portland can buy a quart of muriatic acid, though the jail chaplain may not buy a spoonful of laudanum. The only reason is that muriatic acid is kitchen stuff and laudanum is doctors' stuff, which makes the laudanum taboo at once. There is much less sense in the distinction than there is in the Italian law forbidding anyone to carry a stiletto, though everybody may carry an equally lethal oyster-knife. On the lines of the Italian law a serious case might be made out for forbidding doctors to carry lancets or hypodermic syringes without a licence, or to use them except in the presence of a magistrate; but what sane Italian legislature would propose that anyone should be allowed to carry pistols and daggers if they produced a privately purchased prescription from a private doctor, written in Latin, to be made up by the gunmaker and swordsmith? To a medical officer of health, who is a responsible public official with duties, including the duty of accepting no private inducements to perform or not perform them, certain powers may reasonably be given. But to give tyrannous powers to Dr Crippen to exercise just as he pleases and sell to the first comer, is abject idolatrous doctor worship, impossible to legislatures with even the most superficial notions of science, political or medical. Even a panel doctor is not forbidden to take tips from his patients; for he may, it appears, put up a placard in his surgery which implies that panel patients will receive better advice if they hand the doctor half-a-crown than if they rely on the money they have paid the Government in insurance stamps. One does not hear of such doctors being struck off the register, though their colleague who ventured to administer nitrous oxide gas to a patient of Sir Herbert Barker's after the most eminent registered surgeons had failed to cure him, was struck off for "infamous professional conduct." Doctors are, to say the least, no worse than other men: they do a prodigious quantity of irksome work for nothing out of sheer good nature in addition to hospital work; but if Governments and juries persist in acting on the insane assumption that the doctor can do no wrong, they will finally provoke a revolt in which everybody convicted of being on the register will be guillotined.

MEDICAL HOME-MADE STATISTICS

If the consequences were not so serious, it would be impossible to present the current medical tests of the efficacy of prophylactics otherwise than as a roaring farce. Take the case of the army inoculations. These are now virtually compulsory, as the ill-treatment, the extra fatigues, and the deprivation of leave, which refusal to submit to them entails, are more dangerous than any immediately obvious effects of compliance, which is all that the statistics suggest so far. The troops are inoculated against typhoid and assured that they are safe from it. They get typhoid in the proportions usual since the introduction of ordinary sanitation without inoculation during the Russo-Japanese War, which completely prevented such ravages as this disease made in our army in South Africa, where inoculation was depended on and hygiene neglected. The bacteriologists immediately investigate these cases and announce that what the men have died of is not the work of the typhoid bacillus, but of another bacillus, which produces a new disease called paratyphoid because it is just like typhoid. They combine this new bacillus with the old one in the preparation of a new "vaccine" warranted to protect against both typhoid and paratyphoid. The troops suffer from typhoid and paratyphoid as before. A fresh investigation is made, and it is discovered that there is yet another bacillus which produces another sort of paratyphoid, called, to relieve the strain of inventing new names, Paratyphoid B. A new vaccine, compounded of the previous T and A with B, is prepared, and the soldiers are inoculated all over again, and are now proof against three deadly diseases. They suffer as before; but the indefatigable bacteriologists rise to the occasion, and the discovery of Paratyphoid C and the preparation of vaccine TABC leads to the re-inoculation of the army survivors, who now, we should imagine, consist of men able to stand anything that Nature, the R.A.M.C., or the American vaccine companies can inoculate them with. Nevertheless, they succumb in sufficient numbers to prompt fresh investigation; and in due course Paratyphoid D and vaccine TABCD is added to the triumphs of Pasteurian prophylaxis. The precise letter of the alphabet at which this process has now arrived does not matter; but it cannot reach finality, as when the alphabet is run through it can recommence with AA, BB, etc. Meanwhile, a French *savante* (the laboratory lady is beginning to play a part in modern science) announces that bacilli change from one sort into another according to the color of the light to which they are exposed, raising dreadful doubts as to whether A, B, C, AA, BB, CC, and the rest, may not, after all, be the same bacillus, in which case it will be necessary to have a new vaccine, the materials of which have been subjected to every possible sort of metamorphological ray, and a re-inoculation of the army, if the combined efforts of the worshippers of Pasteur (an unqualified person, by the way) and the hardly more lethal operations of Hindenburg have by that time left any British army in being. Meanwhile Sir Almroth Wright, whose restless activity leaves our theorists no time to breathe, seems to be driving himself, by a series of more and more closely conditioned and controlled experiments, to the conclusion, guessed at by some of the earlier and bolder vaccinators, that the tactics by which our blood combats the invasion of disease are non-specific, or, roughly, that any vaccine is as good (or as bad) as any other for rousing our antitryptic resistance to any disease.

I am conscious that the above account is comically incredible. I can only refer sceptics to the Gallipoli Expedition. It is not even new except in its development of the old "pseudo bacillus," who used to be reputed harmless and made the scapegoat for all the failures of the early antitoxins and discoveries of incriminated bacilli in healthy people, into the parabacillus who is received with all the honors of virulence and made the subject of a special prophylaxis. It illustrates the eclipse of common sense which is apt to follow an enthusiastic interest in science; for the eye that is glued to the microscope ceases to see men life-size, and ends by imagining that individuals who occupy several cubic feet of space can be played with as easily and cheaply and simply as colonies, a billion strong, which can live on a sixpence. The doctors all know and understand that hyperæsthesia (or the magnification of sensations) produces insanity. They have not yet discovered that microscopic vision, which is an artificially produced hyperæathesia, must produce the same effect (and does) unless it is either corrected by continual clinical experience, or is by sheer brain power kept constantly in scale with real magnitudes.

THE INOCULATION CHAOS

The whole inoculation craze—for the way in which it is believed in and defended shews that whatever valuable discoveries may be reached through it, it is a craze of the most extravagant kind—is obscured and confused by the variety of its applications. At one end you have the desperate empiricism of vaccination, in which you are dealing not with a discovered and identified bacillus, but with matter taken from the eruptions of a calf or a child which has been infected with smallpox or cow-pox; and this matter cannot be sterilized because the active agent in it cannot be isolated, and the operator must take his chance of what may be in the stuff besides the unknown thing that causes the inoculation to "take." Then you have anti-toxin, produced by inoculating a horse with diphtheria poison in which the bacilli have been carefully slaughtered, and, having thus cheated his vital fluids into a violent antagonism to the diphtheria poison, tapping them and injecting them into the human diphtheria patient, with startling results; some, like the sensational fall in temperature and the disappearance of the white membrane, triumphant; others, including an occasional period of paralysis, not so satisfactory, and all subject to the objection that though the figures given by the hospitals point to a miraculous conquest of the disease by this treatment, the figures of the Registrar-General do not confirm the alleged reduction in the disease. Then you have the phagocytosis-provoking vaccines of Sir Almroth Wright, produced by simply killing the bacteria and mashing them up; for even in death they claim the power of stimulating the phagocytes to multiply mightily for the attack on them: a fact which provokes from the sceptical a reminder that it has never yet been proved that the bacilli characteristic of certain diseases are the causes of the disease, and not merely victims of it and carriers of its contagion.

What the Doctors really want

It will be seen that the whole practice of prophylaxis is still crude and confused. Yet in August 1914, when every other section of the nation kept silent as to considerations that could discourage recruiting, the medical profession did not hesitate to raise an alarm as to the risk of typhoid run by soldiers on active service, when they might just as easily have reassured them by reference to the successful hygiene of the Manchurian War. The avowed object of this recklessly selfish exploit was to force on the nation the system of inoculation which has been so successful in enlarging the list of human ills by Paratyphoids A, B, C, D, etc. Even if it can be proved that a real economy in military efficiency has been the result, the assurances given by eminent medical men in communications to the Press none the less shew an unscrupulousness which indicates an extraordinary personal petulance and intellectual demoralization. It is one of the standing grievances of the profession that patients are allowed to use their own judgment as to whether their doctors' orders are carried out or not. A doctor may prescribe a bottle, and the patient may empty it down the sink with absolute impunity, although from the doctor's point of view he is guilty of insulting an honorable profession and attempting suicide at the same time, to say nothing of the occasional possibility of his starting an epidemic. Every doctor believes that he should have legal powers to compel his patients to swallow drugs, to have their limbs and breasts cut off, their internal organs extirpated, and their blood provided with exceedingly unpleasant stimulants for the phagocytes, besides dictating what they shall eat and drink and whether they shall stay at home or go out or go to bed. He believes it because he desires the good of his patients, and is convinced that he knows better than they what is good for them, as indeed no doubt he often does.

To some extent the State is compelled to yield to these monstrous pretensions. For example, if parents are to be held responsible for the care of their children's health, and the parents' notions of that care seem to the doctor to amount to criminal neglect or cruelty, and are obviously unusual, it is difficult to see what is to guide the State except the expert's evidence. Poor men who do not believe in doctors and do believe in the Epistle of St James, and rich men who leave their children naked as to the limbs and feet, and never give them cooked food or meat, occasionally come into conflict with the law as laid down by the doctors, and suffer for it, though their children may not die oftener or be less hardy than those who never escape for a week from the family doctor. With the extension of school clinics, school meals, and public as distinguished from private and particular parental care of children, the power of the doctor will

F

necessarily increase, and increase without any check from the common sense of juries, or from that mere impatience of control which makes it impossible to interfere beyond a certain point with adults.

THE REMEDY

The only real safeguard against the tyrannies of sectional science is lay scientific control. Medicine by itself is no more science with a big S than boxing is (pugilists, like doctors, talk of their art as science). The self-styled Science of the medical profession should be constantly checked by the political, the mathematical, and, generally, the sociological sciences. For instance, it is evident that the paratyphoid alphabet, if submitted to an expert statistical audit, would be referred back as a ghastly joke. If the proposals which have been made to render all diseases, and even wounds, harmless by a long string of inoculations, repeated annually or oftener, were submitted to an economic audit, the auditors would "turn them down" at once on the ground that even if they were perfectly effective, they would not pay. A sociological audit would take into account the factors that continually operate in public hygiene apart from medical treatment, producing results which the doctors ignorantly appropriate as due to their specifics by putting forward as death rates and disease rates figures which are really persecution rates and poverty rates. An historical audit would make short work of the wild assumptions as to the prevalence and mortality of disease in pre-Pasteurian times, and would press on the bacteriologists who explain so glibly the spread of the old epidemics, from plague to hospital gangrene, the question, never yet faced by them, of how, on their assumptions, those epidemics spontaneously died out and permitted the human race to survive. A mathematical audit (as part of the statistical one) would pull up the doctor when he was building on the incidence of disease without taking into account the fact that the odds against any particular individual ever catching any particular disease are so much, the odds against his catching it twice so much more, and the odds against his dying of it, doctors or no doctors, so much again. All these odds and more have to be deducted before the medical figures begin to count; yet medical statisticians generally assume that everybody who is not medically protected must catch every disease under the sun, and everybody who is not treated by a doctor, and even by a particular method, must die. From these big mistakes to such amateur crudities as striking an average of two widely different figures and supposing that it represents anything real, instances can be found in the writings of our cleverest doctors. The remedy is, not less science and more *laissez-faire*, but more science and still more. A little science is a dangerous thing, and science in science-tight compartments is worse. Bring to bear on every department the co-ordinated science of all the other departments, and the doctors will be promptly driven beyond their crudities and follies and oversights into as sound positions and as reasonable methods as humanity is capable of.

The measures immediately practicable may be roughly summed up as follows:

1. The General Medical Council to put its house in order by revising its conditions of registration so as to admit the new systems to the canon, and their practitioners to the register, the examinations in the special branches to be conducted by their own professors. This would, of course, involve the immediate admission to the register, if not to the Council, of a certain number of "*bona-fide* practitioners" without further ado; but there need be no difficulty in finding persons of unquestionable qualifications, quite as highly tested in their special institutions in Sweden or America as most registered British practitioners, to conduct the new examinations.

2. The Government and the Universities to send representatives of the public and of disinterested general science to the General Medical Council instead of doctors, leaving the medical corporations to secure a minority representation of the profession.

3. The Universities to deal with such scandals as that of the

boycotting of Sir Herbert Barker by conferring honorary degrees on clearly suitable unregistered persons, and registration to be extended to the recipients of such degrees.

All this can be done forthwith, without fresh legislation. The urgent measures for which legislation would be necessary are:

1. A revised constitution for the General Medical Council providing that—

(*a*) Medical practitioners, registered or unregistered, shall not be eligible for nomination by the Government or the Universities.

(*b*) Medical practitioners nominated by the medical corporations shall sit as assessors only, all decisions being made by the representatives of the laity.

(*c*) All decisions of a judicial character shall be considered in the presence of legal assessors, and be subject to appeal.

(*d*) The code of professional conduct shall be approved by the Privy Council and be revised at intervals of not more than five years.

(*e*) Except for wilful violation of the code the Council shall not strike any practitioner off the register except on conviction of breach of the criminal law or suffering an adverse verdict in a civil action for malpractice; and the practitioner shall be, if he or she so desires, represented by counsel.

(*f*) The proceedings of the Council shall be public; and the Council shall be as accessible to deputations as other representative public bodies.

2. The existing schedules of poisons to be supplemented by a schedule of specifics containing toxicologically negligible quantities of poison for use as anodynes, soporifics, and the like, purchasable by all customers without prescription; and freedom of purchase of all substances now scheduled to be secured to persons known to the vendor as responsible citizens or able to produce satisfactory references and credibly to allege legitimate purposes: all restrictions to apply equally to the medical profession and to the laity.

3. A public medical service, specialized, graded, and equipped with laboratories for diagnosis, conducting a full complement of school clinics, hospitals, and nursing homes, to be a compulsory part of the machinery of Public Health in every centre of population, reporting to an independent central statistical department under lay control for the collation of its results, and for the establishment of a maximum of disease and mortality beyond which the central government, by direct interference or by the withdrawal of grants-in-aid, shall not allow the figures to rise without giving the local authority cause to regret its neglect or corruption very sincerely.

VACCINATION

The Jenner Centenary
From The Nation, 3 February 1923

Edward Jenner died in 1823 in Gloucestershire, now the head-quarters of Anti-Vaccination. He is still frequently described as the extirpator of smallpox and consequently one of the greatest benefactors of our race, and will be long remembered as the successful author of the most amazing empirical stunt in medical history. Until the Americans invented the word stunt, there was no way of characterizing the vaccination craze of the nineteenth century in English without much confusing circumlocution.

Jenner had an active, curious, quick, shallow mind, and a ready though then fashionably heavy pen. To call him a man of science nowadays would be like calling Old Moore an astronomer; but we are still so completely in the dark as to the ultimate nature of disease that on that fundamental point his opinion remains as good or as bad as ours.

In his day smallpox was, and had been since Western Europe had ceased to trouble itself about leprosy, the most dreaded of diseases, partly because the bad cases were so disfiguring, and partly because the increase of population produced by the industrial revolution, and the insanitary conditions in which the new proletariat lived, had made it much commoner and more virulent. The fashionable way of dealing with it was by inoculation: that is, you deliberately contracted the disease to protect yourself from it.

This sounds insane; but there was some reason in it. People believed that they could not have the same sort of fever twice. They also saw that a fever caught spontaneously was usually much worse than a fever artificially forced on a healthy person.

Of these two articles of faith the first must always prevail among primitive rough-and-ready thinkers. They discover by simple experience that a man is unlikely to have any one disease twice. They overlook the fact that he is unlikely to have it once, and therefore *a fortiori* very unlikely to have it twice. As a matter of fact a man may have smallpox twice, and have it very badly both times, within a period of a year; but though this has actually occurred, the chances were very heavily against it, just as in a battle at sea the chances are very heavily against a ship being struck twice in the same spot. A comic character in one of Marryat's novels held that he could secure himself under such circumstances by placing his head against a plugged shot hole; and he was so far right that whereas the first shot hole would have been nothing remarkable, a second in exactly the same place would have been extraordinary. Few people are so subtle or so well instructed in the curiosities of the mathematical doctrine of chances. They infer simply and directly that one attack of a disease will protect them against a second; and it follows that if they also believe that they can insure that the first attack shall be a light one, it will seem to them very good business to contract the disease purposely when they are young, and get it over. Accordingly, it was a common practice in the country for children with measles or scarlatina to have healthy children sent to bed with them; so that they might be infected and become immune for life when they recovered. Inoculation was no worse than that.

Modern discoveries reveal some foundation for this belief that diseases intentionally acquired are lighter than those accidentally contracted. Roughly it may be said that though Man has developed a considerable power of resisting disease (otherwise he would have been extinct long ago), this power is subject to fluctuations which can be measured by modern methods. If when it is weak he catches any disease that he may be unlucky enough to encounter, he puts up a very poor fight against it, with the result that it kills him or gives him a very bad time. But if his resistance is strong, the disease has to be forced on him artificially by inoculation or contagion of some gross kind; whereupon he is able to put up a strenuous fight, his blood performing prodigies of slaughter among the infected germs, with the result that the disease has a bad time, and sheers off beaten.

This is why the old practice of deliberately inoculating small-pox and sending children to sleep with cases of measles and the like produced a mass of apparently convincing results. People inoculated with smallpox, as recommended by Voltaire and Great Catharine, mostly did as a matter of fact throw off the disease much more easily than those who had caught it accidentally; and there could be no doubt that people who had had a disease once seldom had it twice, though in chronic cases the once might last a lifetime. Jenner was misled by these facts like other people. A week ago Dr Saleeby, hanging his centenary wreath on the tomb of Jenner, exclaimed dithyrambically, "Small-pox perpetually slew hecatombs of infants; it blinded hosts; and the scarred faces of those who recovered were met at every turn. With Jenner's discovery the thing became first a memory and a tradition, and, later, a name to which not even the medical profession of today, as a whole, can attach any positive content of experience, so rare is the disease at all, and so excessively rare in its unmodified form." If Dr Saleeby ever departs from the practice of his profession so far as to read the pamphlets of Jenner, he will, I am afraid, be much taken aback on finding that Jenner said just the same about inoculation before vaccination was in practice at all. He noted a hundred and twenty-five years ago that the ravaged faces had disappeared; and though he could not claim the wonders wrought by our Public Health Acts for inoculation as Dr Saleeby claims them for vaccination, yet everything that Dr Saleeby says that does not apply equally or more to the extirpation of cholera and typhus was said by Jenner for a practice which was made a criminal offence not long after his death. And in the face of modern discoveries it is as certain as anything of the kind can be that vaccination as at present practised will share the fate of inoculation.

Just then, however, a discovery was made quite empirically by a farmer named Jesty which is now seen to be one of great importance. Although everybody believed that one attack of a specific fever protected you against a second attack of that fever, nobody supposed that one disease could protect you against another: for instance, that measles could protect you against smallpox. But Jesty was an exception to this rule. He believed that cow-pox could protect you against smallpox; and instead of allowing his family to be inoculated with smallpox he inoculated them with cow-pox. In short, he invented vaccination. Jenner got hold of this, and—herein lies his sole claim to be ranked as a genius—saw what could be done with it if it could be substantiated. He investigated it, and found evidence that it protected milkmaids and milkmen, after which he found incontestable proofs that it did not. His efforts to reconcile this contradiction led him to conclude that the protective pox was not cow-pox but horse-pox with which the cow had become infected; and his own final practice was to inoculate direct from the diseased horse: horse-pox being therefore the true Jennerian protective pox.

But in the meantime vaccination, as a relief from the terrors of inoculation, had caught on so tremendously that Parliament voted two grants of money to Jenner, amounting to £30,000. His assurance that a person once successfully vaccinated could not possibly catch smallpox even if actually inoculated with it, much less exposed to ordinary infection, was accepted in spite of all evidence to the contrary; and in the end the Governments of Western Europe, ignoring the horse-pox, made the vaccination of all infants with cow-pox compulsory. When its failure to protect for life could no longer be denied, it was alleged to last for seven years (seven is the characteristic number of magic); and revaccination was made compulsory in many cases: for instance, persons entering various public services, and, on pain of quarantine, crossing frontiers. The every seven years might have become every seven months or even days had not vaccination received its death-blow in 1871, when compulsory vaccination was at its height, from the most appalling epidemic of smallpox on record. This was followed by another great epidemic in 1881, in which, by the way, I, being a vaccinated person, caught the disease. I was more lucky than my grandfather, who was inoculated, vaccinated, and had smallpox spontaneously as well. After these two staggering epidemics the public health authorities ceased to rely on vaccination and took to isolation. This at once produced a striking advance in the mastery of the disease; and though the Jennerians promptly claimed the credit of it for vaccination, none of them dared suggest that it should be discarded as superfluous, which it would have been had vaccination been effective. Since then the nation has been coming slowly to its senses on the subject. Direct compulsion has been abolished bit by bit; the Jennerians complain that we are now an unvaccinated nation, and openly long for a terrible epidemic to punish us for our apostasy; and the centenary of Jenner's death is being celebrated amid a smallpox scare caused by 40 cases in a population of 40 millions, provoking grim smiles from those who remember the thousands of victims in the heyday of compulsion in 1871. The bubble is burst; the stunt is played out; only in those homes of lost causes which have supplanted Oxford: the medical profession, the magistracy, and the Press, is vaccination now believed in as Jenner believed in it—and Jenner was far from being as fanatical about it when he died as his followers.

It must not be supposed, however, that the statistics which imposed so effectually on the public and on Parliament were false, or the alleged experiences invented. The mischief was that people did not know how to handle statistics; and doctors not only shared this ignorance of what was practically a new science, but knew nothing of the ancient science of evidence, and never dreamed of such indispensable checks as control experiments. If smallpox began to disappear after vaccination was introduced, and disappeared faster and faster as it became more and more general, then it was clear that vaccination was abolishing smallpox. But as illumination by coal gas was introduced at the same time as vaccination, and the spread of the two was proportionate and simultaneous, it was equally clear that smallpox was being abolished by the domestic gasalier. Also, vaccination (or gas) was much more efficacious in abolishing cholera and typhus than in abolishing smallpox; for these two dreaded scourges actually did disappear completely, whilst smallpox broke out again and again, and broke out worse. Jenner himself had described eighteenth century local epidemics so light that the sufferers never went to bed, and danced every night. No such festivities attended the epidemics of the vaccination period. It was the flagrant contradiction between them and the rash guarantee of Jenner that a vaccinated person was incapable of smallpox, that made Leicester abandon vaccination; and when the expected and prophesied decimation of Leicester by smallpox did not come off, the game was up.

This, however, does not explain the intensity and even ferocity of the public feeling against vaccination that forced the Government to repeal compulsion. I have explained how it is that a patient on whom a disease is forced by inoculation or intentional contagion seldom suffers so much as one who contracts the disease spontaneously. But this does not always hold good. Diseases are not so omnipresent that the fact that a person is not suffering from them is a proof that his resistance is at its height. His resistance may be at its lowest point; and he may be well simply because the disease has not come his way. If at such a moment he be inoculated, the effect may be fatal and will certainly be very serious. To inoculate a patient without carefully measuring his resistance is to risk murdering him; and in the nineteenth century there was no known method of measuring his resistance. Children were vaccinated and adults revaccinated indiscriminately. The consequence was that shocking cases were always happening.

In spite of the determination of the doctors and the authorities to ascribe a death from vaccination to anything else from which the victim could by any sophistry be said to have suffered, a baby was admittedly killed every week by vaccination.

But this was not the worst in its effect on public opinion. The animal poxes used as vaccines produced some of the most horrible results of human venereal contagion. When these results appeared in a vaccinated child, the doctors, trained to regard "vaccinia" as a harmless and beneficent ailment, concluded that the case was not one of vaccinia, but of syphilis communicated by diseased parents; and when the parents were poor, the doctors said so openly. The feelings of the parents can be imagined. At last one couple, in spite of their poverty, managed to bring an action against their doctor. There was a trial; and the doctor defended himself by putting a very eminent medical authority, the late Jonathan Hutchinson, into the box to testify that the effects of vaccination were not distinguishable from those of syphilis. This may have excused the doctor; but it was a knock-out blow for vaccination. An attempt was made to counter it by giving up arm-to-arm vaccination and using lymph direct from the calf; but the glycerinated calf lymph differed from the arm-to-arm lymph only by acting more violently; and the Jennerian situation was not saved.

Even more exasperating than the attempts to excuse the failures of vaccination by accusing the parents of debauchery were the cases in which certain families reacted fatally to the inoculation. A laborer's first child would die of it. His second child would die of it. Naturally he and his wife objected vehemently to allowing their third child to be vaccinated: it seemed to them simple murder, as indeed it virtually was. But the law was inexorable. They were bullied by the vaccination officer; hectored by the magistrate; told that they were dangers to society; and finally forced to send their child to the slaughter by penalties at which a rich man would have laughed, but which were ruinous to couples living on thirteen shillings a week in the country and eighteen in town. In the end the revolt against vaccination became so intense that the Government, placidly convinced that vaccination was one of the permanent institutions of the country and that nobody but the most ignorant and impossible cranks could possibly object to it, or question its success, found themselves to their amazement confronted with a Parliament in which all their newly elected supporters told them that the constituencies were on fire with the madness (as they thought it) of Anti-Vaccination, and that compulsion must go. Very reluctantly a Bill was passed enabling magistrates to exempt children from vaccination if their parents conscientiously objected to it. The British magistrate, always the prince of Anarchists when the law does not happen to reflect his own personal and class prejudices, rose to the occasion by redoubling the insolence and hectoring which had given so much offence, and by flatly refusing to grant the demanded exemptions on the ground that the applicants had not asked for them in the phraseology of the Act. There was an interval of bewildered fury on the part of the baffled and insulted objectors. Then the Anti-Vaccination Society coached them in the words of the Act; and the magistrates found themselves confronted by applicants who kept doggedly repeating the exemption clause word for word in reply to all questions and all hectorings and all insolences. This checkmated the magisterial bench; and the making of a statutory declaration on unstamped paper was substituted for the ordeal of "satisfying" a magistrate. At present the most advanced Jennerians denounce infant vaccination on the ground that as sanitation makes the danger of smallpox negligible, and as vaccinated children, when attacked, resist the disease so stoutly that they remain at school spreading infection until the eruption breaks out, whereas the unvaccinated child succumbs and is sent to bed at the first onset, it is the vaccinated child and not the unvaccinated that is dangerous.

That is the history of Jennerian vaccination: that is, of vaccination as a stunt. But it has been told so often that only those who are new to the subject will be satisfied with it. What the rest want to know is whether there must not have been some prophylactic fire beneath so prodigious a smoke, and whether out of so gross an empiricism and such a colossal scale of experiment, some beginnings of a genuine science of prophylaxis have not arisen. I shall next week address myself to these questions, the answer to them being happily to some extent affirmative. And I must dismiss Jesty-Jenner and their purely empirical vaccination, and introduce our own distinguished contemporary Almroth Wright and his scientific study of immunization.

From The Nation, 10 *February* 1923

In dealing with Jenner I have carefully avoided condemning him because he was an empiric. A doctor is at best only an empiric once or twice removed; and when we touch vital forces and phenomena we are all ignoramuses. Nevertheless there are distinctions to be made. When we pass from Jenner and Pasteur to Almroth Wright we mount from one intellectual category to another and obviously a keener one. The difference between Farmer Jesty and Dr Jenner is hardly worth examining; and even the much greater difference between Jenner and Pasteur is only the difference between a bacteriologist with the training and apparatus of a chemist and physicist and a medical general practitioner who called microbes animalculæ, and knew nothing else about them. But the ready shallow wit, the keenness for cures, the levity in experimenting on the living subject, the confidence in superficial solutions of very deep questions shew the same quality of mind, and led to the same sort of quite sincere imposture. Lister was a more conscientious specimen of the type. These three men loaded their successors with a heavy burden of error and malpractice which was eagerly adopted by the General Medical Council (a body almost perfect as an example of everything that is pernicious in Trade Unionism). Our system of paying the private doctor only when we are ill, and mostly paying him very poorly, has the disadvantage of giving him a direct interest in our ill-health. In Sweden people are not so foolish: they pay their doctor by the year, and thereby give him the strongest incentive to keep them well. Prophylactic medicine, on the contrary, is a godsend to the British doctor, for it enables him to get fees from healthy patients. The strenuous and practically unanimous testimony of the medical profession that prophylactic inoculations, including vaccination and revaccination, are priceless boons to the human race, is worth as much as the equally emphatic testimony of the butcher and the meat trade generally against vegetarianism.

Listerian surgery was a terrible temptation to our surgeons, because whilst a wound, surgical or accidental, treated in the old-fashioned way, would heal in a fortnight or perhaps a month, the same wound thoroughly treated in Lister's way (if that were possible) could never heal at all; and even with the makeshift antiseptic dressings actually in use, it would often keep the doctor dressing it daily for a year or so, the patient being assured meanwhile that he was very fortunate in not having been born before Lister and perishing miserably from septic dissolution, as Nelson and all the other surgical cases before 1860 should have done according to Lister. Doctors no more dared tell us these things than a member of the Amalgamated Society of Engineers durst have told us before the war that the skill for which he demanded and received double the wages of unskilled labor could be acquired in a week by any reasonably strong and handy young woman. Not until the colossal surgery of a European war made further trifling with the question intolerable was it possible for Sir Almroth Wright to expose Listerism as impracticable, and the attempts at it as dangerous and unscientific. Even in that emergency he dare not have done it were it not that, like the Dean of St Paul's, he carries so many trophies of academic distinction, not only in his own profession, but in law and literature, that the General Medical Council, if it attempted to strike him off the register without trial for "infamous professional conduct," would reduce itself to absurdity even more disastrously to itself than would the Church of England if it ventured to unfrock the Dean.

To understand the work of Almroth Wright, it is necessary to describe what had happened between his advent and the death of Jenner a hundred years ago.

After Jenner's £30,000, and his apotheosis as a savior of mankind, it was not to be expected that attempts would not be made to repeat his success. Pasteur, born the year before Jenner died, was not a doctor. He had a genuine scientific training as a chemist and physicist; and after distinguishing himself by a good deal of work on crystals he investigated the phenomenon of fermentation. Learning that it depended on the presence and activity of microbes, he became a bacteriologist, and found that when fermented liquors, wine, beer, vinegar, and so forth, went wrong: that is, became diseased, he could always detect an intruder of strange appearance under the microscope among its microbes. It was found that this observation held good with the diseased silkworm, the sheep with anthrax, the mad dog, and the human being with tetanus and diphtheria. Had Pasteur reasoned about these discoveries as capably as he contributed to them, he would have been a trustworthy leader in therapeutics. As it was, he was only an observer like Jenner, except that Jenner observed at the bedside and Pasteur in the laboratory. When they proceeded to redeem the world from disease on the basis of their observations they got out of their depth, and indeed out of anybody's depth, at once.

Pasteur persuaded himself that every disease could be prevented by inoculating the patient with the microbe which he found invariably associated with it, opening up a quaint prospect of nations tattooed from head to foot with inoculation scars, but absolutely proof against infection. It seemed to him obvious that if a peculiarly shaped bacillus always appeared in the blood of people smitten with such and such a disease, that bacillus must be the cause of that disease. This did not follow. It was equally on the cards that the disease had attacked and modified the bacillus. It has been shewn since that bacilli are so susceptible to modification that they can be transformed by changes of colored light.

Also he was under the nineteenth century spell of statistics, which even in skilled and intellectually honest hands can establish nothing scientifically except coincidences, and are full of fallacies and illusions for amateurs. Though a Jennerian, he could not meddle with smallpox, because his "vaccines" (as he called

79

them in order to give them Jennerian prestige) were made from the characteristic bacilli associated with the particular diseases against which his inoculations were meant to protect; and this was impossible with smallpox because, as no smallpox bacillus has ever been discovered, Jennerian vaccine cannot be manufactured or even defined: you inoculate with pus from an ulcer on a calf, and just take your chance with it.

Anyhow, smallpox was already being dealt with; so some other equally dreaded disease had to be selected. An ideal one for the purpose was hydrophobia. Just as people believe that before Jenner came everyone was disfigured with smallpox, so they believe that everyone bitten by a mad dog must die of hydrophobia in torment and madness unless the bite is burnt out instantly. Charlotte Brontë has described how people actually operated on themselves with red-hot pokers in their terror of the disease; and Trousseau's description of the cases induced by pure imagination is not easily forgotten. I was early delivered from these apprehensions by a discussion which arose among doctors in Ireland when one of them declared that hydrophobia was not distinguishable from tetanus induced by any sort of lacerated wound. The disputants surprised me by putting the number of cases in which hydrophobia followed dog bite at about one per cent. Assuming that they were right, it was and is possible to set up an institute for the prevention of hydrophobia which may double the death rate from dog bite and yet convince the public that it is saving 98 per cent of its patients from a hideous death. Under such circumstances the Pasteur Institutes found it easy to make a deep impression on the public by their statistics.

In ordinary hospital practice some of the Pasteurian inoculations produced a glaring statistical contradiction. According to the medical statistics they wiped out all the diseases to which they were applied irresistibly and triumphantly. According to the returns of the Registrar-General they either produced no effect whatever or made matters rather worse. When this was pointed out, the Pasteurians were rash enough to retort that whereas the Registrar-General's returns gave only the simple mortality, the real test was the case mortality. Thus if in a community of 100 souls a single one catches diphtheria and dies, the case mortality being 100 per cent, and this leads to the introduction of inoculation with the result that the whole population is afflicted with diphtheria and eighty of them die, the reduction of the case mortality from 100 to 80 per cent must be taken to indicate an enormous advance in hygiene produced by the introduction of inoculation.

As there is no trade more lucrative than the trade in well advertized cures, capital soon woke up to the advertizing value of statistics. The manufacture of vaccines, anti-toxins, and antiseptics became a flourishing industry, always sure of a good word in the newspapers. The second half of the nineteenth century was drenched, poisoned, nauseated by carbolic acid until the trade in it must have been almost as profitable as the liquor trade.

When conscientious objection to compulsory vaccination was admitted, the vaccine business received a blow from which it could recover only by restoring absolute compulsion. It was impossible to reimpose it on the citizen, but easy to impose it on the soldier. Nothing is so profitable as army supply. Luckily for the contractors, it happened that a prodigious advance was made by the Japanese army in preserving the health of troops in the field. This was done by sanitation without any inoculation; but the press was easily persuaded that the Japanese soldiers had all been inoculated. Inoculation was established in the British army amid general acclamation, and is now made compulsory there, not by law or the articles of war, but by the simple process of marking down every soldier who exercises his legal right to object to it, and making life so intolerable to him by refusal of leave and by imposing all sorts of the most unpleasant fatigues on him, that it would be far better for him if there were legal compulsion with a definite penalty. During the late war, in which obstinate objectors in some cases went for two years without leave, Mr Chancellor was kept busy in Parliament fighting their battles. The objectors who knew their way about sufficiently to appeal to Mr Chancellor, or even to me (as if I could do anything!), were let alone; but the average soldier was and is helpless. The press would not say a word against inoculation or antiseptics. There is far too much money in them.

All this mass of statistical illusion, Press advertizing interest, shareholders' interest, Trade Union interest, and the educated ignorance and superstition on which they were all playing their very hardest, was misleading and threatening Almroth Wright when he entered on the researches and experiments by which he has established that indiscriminate inoculation is and always has been bound to produce a proportion of horrible cases such as discredited Jenner's vaccine and Koch's tuberculin; that the protective power of the blood can be tested and measured; that the assumption that every disease is caused by a specific microbe is a delusion; that almost any sort of pathogenic matter will do the work of inoculation; that all that is needed in a military field hospital is chloroform, water, salt, and surgeons with brains; and that our huge army supplies of carbolic acid are useful only for spraying the enemy.

I cannot here attempt any account of the technical procedures by which Sir Almroth made these propositions good, and incidentally blew the reputations of Jenner, Pasteur, and Lister as profound scientists and saviors of mankind into smithereens. But I had better point out that his work would not have been done by anyone who had not begun by believing all that the conventional curriculum inculcated about these famous men, and by aiming at an elaboration and completion rather than a refutation of their doctrine. As far as I know, none of the doctors who stood out stoutly all through against the inoculation craze made any positive contribution of importance to the study of bacterial prophylaxis. Dr Walter Hadwen of Gloucester, their doughtiest champion, brought clinical common sense to bear ruthlessly on the controversy, and wiped the floor with the fallacies, the spurious claims, the savage tyrannies, and the shameless mendacities, positive as well as suppressive, that produced the reaction against vaccination, to say nothing of the stupid cruelties which had made biological research and vivisection convertible terms; but his hostile criticisms and detective expeditions to Malta (the Lourdes of Pasteurism) and elsewhere left bacteriology very much where it was: that is, in the mud of the infallible cure market.

It is therefore not surprising that Wright's first big British experiment on the human subject, which was made on our army in South Africa, when he still accepted Pasteur's rule that the quantity of the inoculation did not matter, was not a success. It cannot without considerable controversial licence be said to have exterminated our devoted troops; but, like Jennerian vaccination, it did mischief enough to make it impossible to persist in practising it with Pasteurian recklessness. Incidentally, it supplied the terrible and unanswerable Hadwen with several tons of fresh fuel to throw on the smouldering fury of Labor against medical tyranny and vaccinal dividends. But Wright was not shaken in his conviction, based on the statistics, that the soldiers who were not exterminated or disabled did get some accession of protective energy from inoculation, and that there was a net gain in immunity. His conclusion was, not that inoculation was uniformly good or uniformly bad, but that when it was good it was very very good and when it was bad it was horrid. And he set to work to find out why.

In this enterprise he was hampered not only by the mistakes of Pasteur, but by a remarkable *saltus empiricus* made by a famous bacteriological acrobat in this kind named Metchnikoff. He, finding that when you studied a diseased microbe under the microscope, it was sometimes inside another microbe, jumped to the conclusion that what happens when a disease is vanquished is that the white corpuscles in the blood eat up the invading disease germs. This made a very effective fairy tale; and the process was called phagocytosis, the cannibal microbes being phagocytes. Here was another lesson for Almroth Wright to unlearn; and he had not unlearnt it when he made his first great discovery and invention. His discovery was that the protective power of the blood rises and falls like the tide. He called the flood tide the positive phase and the ebb tide the negative phase. If an inoculation caught you at low water the result might be appalling: if at high water it might be a stimulus to victory. His invention was a method of ascertaining what phase your blood was in by testing it in the laboratory. But as he was still misled by Metchnikoff, he thought he had to account for the effect of inoculation on the imaginary phenomenon of phagocytosis; and his explanation was that it produced an appetizer which made the diseased germs more palatable to the phagocytes and led to their being more greedily devoured. This appetizer he called opsonin; and the measure of the protective power of your blood as effected by his method was your opsonic index. The practical moral was that to inoculate a patient without first taking his opsonic index to make sure that he is not in a negative phase is a grave malpractice.

Then came the war of 1914. The Army Medical Service, like the General Medical Council, knew no more of Wright's discovery and technique, or of any other discovery or technique less than half a century old, than Noah knew of telephony. Our unfortunate soldiers were inoculated much as they had been in South Africa. Wright had by this time found out that Pasteur was mistaken in thinking that the quantity of pathogenic matter inoculated did not matter; and more attention may have been paid to the dosage. But he still accepted medical statistics and even army statistics as scientific evidence; and he remained convinced that indiscriminate inoculation without previous opsonic measurement, though risky, was better than no inoculation at all. Accordingly, indiscriminate inoculation raged unchecked in the trenches. It saved its face in Flanders, where some sanitation was possible, but broke down hopelessly in Gallipoli. The official excuses for its failure seem to a layman to belong to *opéra bouffe*, not to grave scientific history. When an uninoculated soldier died of typhoid it was called typhoid. When an inoculated soldier died of it, it was called paratyphoid, and made the excuse for a fresh inoculation with a paratyphoid microbe. When a soldier thus inoculated died of paratyphoid, it was called paratyphoid B; and a third inoculation was devised. But even army medicine had to stop there. It was clear that if the business were pursued to the bitter end the soldiers would have to be inoculated with a whole alphabet of microbes. Yet the procedure was perfectly scientific. Paratyphoid was visibly different from typhoid, and paratyphoid B from paratyphoid A, in respect of their characteristic microbes.

The true significance of this did not flash on Wright at once. He still believed in the specific microbe causing its specific disease; and he still worked at the compounding of specific vaccines. But at last the explanation dawned. There is no such thing in the world as a typical case of typhoid fever. What there is is an infinite number of paratyphoids, all different; and each of them impresses its difference on the otherwise undifferentiated microbe. The curtain began to lift. Already Sir Clifford Allbutt had, at a hospital bedside, said to his students, "This is what we call a case of scarlet fever; but all the cases are different." Mr Raphael Roche, a well-known figure in the group of unregistered practitioners who are now rapidly ousting Harley Street, had strenuously denied that the diseases classified under Greekish names in medical books correspond to the facts of illness: he maintained that the cases are never the same, the symptoms are never the same, the appropriate treatment is never the same. And now Wright had found that paratyphoid was not even paratyphoid, nor was paraparatyphoid (otherwise paratyphoid B) paraparatyphoid.

He continued his work in this new light; and it is still proceeding. Its results up to this date of a century after Jenner's death may be summarized as follows. 1. Phagocytosis has nothing to do with recovery from disease. A phagocyte may swallow a typhoid bacillus or a tubercle bacillus just as it may swallow anything else that comes its way; but the blood slays the bacillus by simple direct wilful bactericide without any help from the phagocytes. This bactericidal action can be stimulated or stunned, as the case may be, not only by inoculating microbes infected with the disease from which the patient is suffering, but by inoculating any microbe infected with any disease to which the patient is susceptible. 2. As a dead microbe will serve as well as a live one, just as a dead man is as infectious as a live one, it follows that the microbe, like the man, is the vehicle of the disease and not the prime cause of it. 3. Statistical evidence is not scientific evidence: a case which is proved by statistics only is not proved at all; and nothing is scientifically proved until it is explained. 4. Antiseptic surgery is impossible and would be deadly were it possible; aseptic surgery is a delusion; simple irrigation of wounds is useless; but saline irrigation is effective and bacteriologically correct. 5. In spite of an attack of disease being evidence that the patient's resistance is in the negative phase, it is not necessarily too late to inoculate when disease has set in, as a skilled operator may be able to induce a reinforced positive phase. 6. There is no rule of thumb for the dosage, as a large one may in certain circumstances be safer than a small one: an examination of the blood is always necessary. 7. Indiscriminate inoculation is indefensible, and inoculation of healthy persons living in healthy conditions a wanton and expensive manufacture of unnecessary illness; but persons already infected, or exposed to great risk of infection, may, after skilled examination of their blood, be helped or protected by a carefully measured injection of carefully selected staphylococci of not too vicious a kind. And this, which rules out ordinary vaccination as a gross malpractice, is the utmost that can yet be said, not too confidently, for therapeutic or prophylactic inoculation with pathogenic matter.

Here we have additions to our knowledge and corrections of our errors and delusions of sufficient value to place their author in the first rank as a scientific discoverer and inventor. But let not the admiring reader forget two things. The first is that we remain so completely in the dark as to the nature of disease, that Herbert Spencer's warning that when we trick our vital forces artificially we know not what we do, and should regard such tricks as desperate measures to be used only in desperate cases, is still valid. The second is that the General Medical Council and the medical profession at large is still pre-Wright, and indeed largely prehistoric. His techniques of blood testing and of the saline irrigation of wounds are little known and less practised; and the students in our medical schools have no time to learn them, because the curriculum is loaded with obsolete rubbish, the most modern part of which consists mostly of the errors which Wright has disproved: the real object of the examination being the old Trade Unionist one of restricting entry to the over-crowded profession. Doctors who have never heard of the opsonic index are still inoculating and vaccinating and revaccinating all over the place: a lady nearly connected with myself was all but slain the other day by an inoculation which caught her "beauti-fully" on the ebb; and the less lucky of those who have been recently scared into revaccination are probably sorry that they did not catch smallpox instead. Chauffeurs who have been ordered to get themselves revaccinated, and aeroplane pilots who have been inoculated, are still let loose on the third day or sooner to smash their cars or crash from a thousand feet up. All the wounds of the war are not healed yet: Pasteurized and Listerized sinuses are still discharging as if Almroth Wright were notori-ously Almroth Wrong, and 1923 were 1860. And always in the Press "the rest is silence."

From The Nation, 17 February 1923

Mr Gillison asks where it is admitted that one baby was killed every week by vaccination. When a doctor gives a death certi-ficate stating the cause of death as vaccination, he admits that the child died of vaccination. The admission becomes public in the returns of the Registrar-General. When for a long period the annual figure is fifty-two or thereabouts, as it was during the last twenty years of compulsory vaccination, the mortality is ad-mittedly one a week; and the word admittedly is used because the actual number is much greater, as it includes deaths returned under the numerous *aliases* of vaccinia. The statement, of course, applies only to deaths registered officially in this country, and not to the world at large, the figures for which, could they be ascertained, would probably horrify Herod.

I took the figure from the returns without reference to the Anti-Vaccination League, because foolish people always distrust and sneer at disinterested and public-spirited unofficial investigators, and will swallow nothing but obvious advertisements or official figures.

Mr Gillison also asks me why has no single case of smallpox been reported in the German army since 1874; the year in which compulsory revaccination was introduced? Simply because a German army doctor would lose every chance of promotion, and probably also his job and his social standing, if he dared certify the death of a revaccinated soldier as being caused by smallpox. In the army any disease can be made to disappear by putting it in another column under another heading. In the last smallpox epidemic in London, about twenty years ago, when I was a member of a public health authority, and every revaccination brought the operator half-a-crown, a revaccinated lady was sent to the Wharf as a case of smallpox in ignorance of the fact that she was "protected." Our attention was called to the fact by the indignant doctor who had revaccinated her; and she was immediately removed from the Wharf and rediagnosed as suffering from pustular eczema, or varioloids, or some other of the alternatives which we should later on perhaps have called paravaricella. We were determined that revaccination should come out with a clean sheet; and it did. It will interest Mr Gillison to learn thus how it is done. When it is not done, the country or district which does not do it naturally comes out with a comparatively heavy smallpox mortality; and Mr Gillison, deeply impressed by the contrast, rushes to get revaccinated. That is precisely what he was intended to do.

Mr Gillison is mistaken in supposing that I am a professional bacteriologist. I am not a bacteriologist at all. I doubt if I have looked at a culture through a microscope more than twenty times in my life; and I look at the pictures in the National Gallery much oftener than at the pictures of the cocci. Probably all the bacteriological statements I have made will be upset by the next generation of students; but I have to take what the bacteriologists tell me are the facts. Mr Gillison will find them all in the nearest up-to-date encyclopædia, or in Sir Almroth Wright's recent lectures. On Sir Almroth and the learned contributors to the standard textbooks let Mr Gillison's sarcasms fall: *my* withers are unwrung.

DOCTORS' DELUSIONS

From The Times, 14 *August* 1902

Will you allow me to correct an error into which the writer of your article on the Imperial Vaccination League of the 12th inst. has fallen? Glycerine is a convenient and economical vehicle for the smallpox lymph used in vaccination (or inoculation, as it would now be properly called but for the rash statute which made direct inoculation a criminal offence), but the risk of general vaccinia is just as great with glycerinated calf lymph as with the old stocks that went, and still go, from arm to arm. One of the most eminent of the signatories of the Imperial Vaccination League, Mr Jonathan Hutchinson, convinced the Royal Commission that general vaccinia is indistinguishable from syphilis, and that the alleged cases of syphilis conveyed from arm to arm by vaccination were really cases of general vaccinia. General vaccinia is also indistinguishable from smallpox itself. Case after case of a disease diagnosed as smallpox has been sent to the hospital ships during the late epidemic; but whenever the authorities at the Wharf found marks of recent revaccination on the patient the case was promptly sent back as one of general vaccinia. One of the leading metropolitan medical officers of health, himself an ardent vaccinist, asked the Wharf authorities, for the guidance of his medical referees, how they distinguished smallpox from general vaccinia. They replied that they knew of no diagnostic except that general vaccinia is not infectious. No steps, as far as I am aware, were taken to follow up the rejected cases with a view to tracing infection from them; nor indeed could such steps have been conclusive in view of the apparently hopeless incompatibility of the course and decline of the epidemic with the ordinary view of infection. As I have before pointed out, the real popular objection to vaccination is the possibility of general vaccinia ensuing; and as no known process of treating the lymph, whether by glycerine or anything else, can separate the power of inducing local vaccinia (itself sometimes a by no means inconsiderable ailment) from the possibility of inducing general vaccinia, any attempt to persuade the public that glycerinated lymph is absolutely safe must be classed with those over-sanguine assurances which, as your article very justly remarks, have done more than all the efforts of the antivaccinists to discredit the Jennerian propaganda.

Incidentally it will be noticed that, if a public body like the Metropolitan Asylums Board starts with the assumption that a recently revaccinated person cannot catch smallpox, it is quite easy to substantiate that assumption by refusing to diagnose smallpox in revaccinated cases and declaring the case one of general vaccinia or some other indistinguishable alternative. The difficulty of diagnosis is now admitted by the costly new institution of official medical referees, whose reports are very instructive as to the number of complaints which pass as small-pox until there is some strong reason for, or interest in, challenging the diagnosis.

A further significant change is the admission, after a century of sturdy resistance and denial, of the fact that many cases cannot be confidently classed as either vaccinated or revaccinated. We now have a "doubtful" column, which, as might have been ex-pected, often exceeds in number the ascertained cases. The sort of person who does not know whether he was vaccinated or not is obviously likely to suffer more from smallpox, and every other "filth" disease, than those who at least know that they were not vaccinated, not to mention the comparatively well nourished, cleanly housed, and educated people who read The Times and observe the custom of vaccination among the other customs of ladies and gentlemen. But what is to be said now of the old statis-tics which would not admit that a doctor could be in doubt about anything? Yet it is on these statistics that the faith of the founders of the Imperial League is based; for they can hardly have been newly convinced, as their manifesto so comically suggests, by the occurrence of a smallpox epidemic.

However, the Imperial Vaccination League is perfectly wel-come to do its best for the "have it and get it over" method of dealing with smallpox, provided only it does not act as an anti-sanitation league also. Of the anti-sanitation danger you allowed me to give early warning in your columns. Let me now give an example of what I feared. In the borough of St Pancras, Dr J. J. Sykes, the medical officer of health, a distinguished authority on public health, and a very pillar of vaccinism, promptly recognized that he would have to deal with "contacts" who could not afford to be revaccinated, since, though we revaccinate for nothing, we give no compensation for temporary disablement by a bad arm. Dr Sykes induced the borough council to establish a disinfecting station where people could be vigorously washed, including their teeth and nails, whilst their clothes were being baked. The process proved quite as effectual as revaccination. Meanwhile at the hospital ships moribund patients were being visited daily by relatives. One would suppose that, in view of the obvious danger of these relatives carrying infection and the certainty that some of them would refuse revaccination, the visitor would be disinfected as our contacts were in St Pancras. As nobody could reasonably object to a bath and temporary change it could be made compulsory, whereas there are circumstances under which compulsory vaccination is too atrocious to be enforced without great trouble. Yet, as far as I have been able to ascertain, nothing was done but to offer the visitors revaccination and to call attention quite triumphantly to the cases when refusal was followed by infection. Nor does it seem to have been considered that a revaccinated person's clothes are not revaccinated, and that the disease may consequently be carried by people who themselves escape. If I am wrong in assuming that disinfection was not practised, the public will be glad to have an authoritative assurance to that effect. If I am right, the public will see how untrustworthy a public health authority may become when its officials become men of one idea, and that idea vaccinism. I venture to submit that a league to discover an unobjectionable method of extirpating smallpox is much more urgently wanted than an Imperial Vaccination League, the very title of which is already an anachronism.

DOCTORS' DELUSIONS

From The British Medical Journal, 8 *November* 1902

Let me, for the sake of simplifying the argument, surrender the point of character completely. Let it be granted that Herbert Spencer, Russel Wallace, Sir William Collins, and Gladstone may be dismissed, with myself and all the other critics of vaccination, as hopeless cases of a horrible moral perversity which has for its object the disfigurement and destruction of the human race by smallpox, and for its weapon a senseless misrepresentation of the facts and documents.

This concession, complete as it is, leaves you as to vaccination (which is, after all, what we are arguing about) exactly where you were before. Was the famous case dealt with so conspicuously by the Royal Commission a case of syphilis conveyed by vaccination, as the antivaccinators contended, or was it, as Jonathan Hutchinson contended with the assent of the majority of the Commission, a case of general vaccinia resembling smallpox so closely as to have misled the doctors who diagnosed it as syphilis? You declare that no such resemblance exists between vaccinia and syphilis. I point out to you that this involves either the acceptance of the antivaccinist view of the case or the production of a third explanation hitherto overlooked by both sides.

You do not produce the required *tertium quid*. Instead you quote the following passage from the majority report of the Commission, signed by Jonathan Hutchinson: "For all practical purposes, variola and vaccinia are both wholly distinct from syphilis, and their differences are, with the rarest exceptions, easily recognized." But, pray, how does the fact that the Royal Commission contradicted itself help you out of your dilemma? Whoever has read the report of the Commission carefully must know that the Commissioners contradicted themselves repeatedly, because, instead of investigating vaccination, they set themselves to fence with the antivaccinators, with the result that they stoutly denied certain contentions when they told in favor of antivaccination in particular instances, and triumphantly affirmed them in other instances when they told the opposite way. Besides, the

contradiction does not come to much after all. It is true that the
Commissioners state that vaccinia is wholly distinct from syphilis
for all practical purposes—this, if you please, in a report which
contains a long and detailed account of a case in which for all
practical purposes, and for all political and scientific purposes as
well, they had found a case in which the diseases were indistinguishable. But this proves only what every investigator now
knows: namely, that a man may be a very eminent physician and
surgeon without having any skill in the use of language or statistics. Having made the statement, the signatories felt that it was
not satisfactory, and resorted to the usual expedient, the insertion
of the saving clause "with a few rare exceptions." What they
meant was that in the great majority of cases no confusion arises.
But who has ever asserted or implied that the confusion arises in
every case? You quote a sentence from a letter of mine to The
Times, which, taken apart, might (or might not) bear that construction. But nobody who read my letters has been misled: I
dealt with specific instances. The sentences you quote as general
propositions were references to these instances. If you wish, pray
reprint my letters in full. If a single person can be found to mis-
understand them, I shall apologize at once.

However, to save your space, I will now say what I did not
say before. I will say that the two ambiguous cases cited by me
do suggest very strongly that the smallpox and the great-pox,
the cow-pox and the horse-pox may be the same disease after all.
The fact that they are very rarely confused by medical men cannot be built upon under existing circumstances. The sort of
diagnosis which consists in "guessing eggs when you see the
shells" can prove nothing as to the unmistakeable character of
the disease. If I go to a doctor and tell him I am suffering from
the sequelæ of vaccination and exhibit the scars on my arm (which
are perhaps the work of his own lancet) he is not likely to diagnose
syphilis. And if a profligate young man goes to a doctor and tells
the sort of story that the doctor has learned to interpret, or else
confesses frankly that he has exposed himself to contagion, and
fears he has caught it, that doctor is not likely to diagnose vac-

cination. But suppose the syphilis patient were to exhibit a scar of recent vaccination, and the vaccinated patient to conceal his scar and hint at recent profligacies on his part, is it so sure that the disease would prove so "wholly distinct" for scientific purposes as they now seem to be for practical purposes? Let me point out, however, that even if a course of such experiments finally enabled physicians to discriminate with certainty between variola, vaccinia, and syphilis, this would not dispose of the possibility of their being the same disease. Asthma, hæmorrhoids, and epilepsy can hardly be mistaken for one another by the least observant practitioner: yet Trousseau, a famous clinical observer, came to the conclusion that they were manifestations of the same diathesis, and that the suppression of one involved the risk of the appearance of another. No doubt, to the ordinary private practitioner, that treatment of disease which consists in suppressing a symptom, and sending away the patient "cured," seems perfectly simple and sensible. He is not troubled by such anxieties as that expressed in Herbert Spencer's impatient but very natural remark that "the assumption that vaccination changes the constitution in relation to smallpox, and does not otherwise change it, is sheer folly." But public health authorities are not done with men when they vaccinate them. It is a very grave matter to them that even now, when in, say, 9999 cases out of 10,000 the discrimination of vaccinia and syphilis is a matter of simple information and not of true diagnosis at all, cases occur in which vaccinia is diagnosed as syphilis, and that the identity of vaccinia with variola and of vaccination with inoculation, long denied, is now admitted. If there is eminent authority for the proposition that hæmorrhoids may be suppressed at the cost of their replacement by epilepsy, it is impossible not to ask whether the suppression of smallpox may not be achieved at the cost of its replacement by a fatal form of measles, by modern diphtheria, by cancer, by leprosy, or by anything that an antivaccinist may select as most terrifying to the public imagination.

I am, as you rightly remind your readers, ignorant on these subjects. I am even dangerously ignorant, since I take part in the administration of the Public Health Acts. So are you; and if you are not anxiously aware of the fact you are not yet at the beginning of a suspicion of what public responsibility means. I challenge you to produce a single man of any weight in your profession who will say more for himself than you have said for me. We are all alike ignorant of the nature and reciprocal action of variola and vaccinia. The omniscience which the superstition of the public forces even the most intellectually conscientious doctor to assume, or at least allow his patient to credit him with, will not pass with a genuinely scientific audience, and ought not to be tried on a merely professional one.

I can only thank you for so neatly smashing your own contention that the Imperial Vaccination League does not advocate revaccination beyond the school period. As you point out, the immunity of the German women, who do not undergo the army adult revaccination, knocks the bottom out of the contention that it is to this adult revaccination that Germany owes its comparative immunity from smallpox epidemics. But, as you will recollect, it was the Imperial Vaccination League and not I who advanced this contention. The birth throes of the League were announced by a manifesto which held up the German army, not the German women, as an example to England. So you see I was precisely right in assuming that the League went the full modern length as to the necessity for adult revaccination. And I am afraid I must urge that this carries with it, according to Dr Stewart, that decennial expenditure of seventy millions which seems to you so monstrous that you declare you will take care not to let it be forgotten. As to that, you may rely on my assistance. I am fully alive to the importance of this new fact that the report of an official vaccinator gives the social cost of an experiment in modern adult revaccination, carried out by him under practical conditions on patients of the class to which four-fifths of the population belong, at 35s. a head. Revaccinate every ten years a population of about forty millions at 35s. a head, and you get seventy millions per decade, without allowing anything for the establishment of night nurses for the revaccinated, as Dr Stewart humanely suggests. And yet they say vaccination is cheaper than sanitation! If this statement is, as you assert, "utterly and absolutely untrue," you must settle that with Dr Stewart. You may be quite right: medical statistics often are worthless. But if, after throwing over the German army, adult revaccination, and the Imperial League, you now throw over medical statistics, I doubt whether I can any longer claim you as a sound vaccinist; so I shall gain nothing by carrying my point against you. I note that you believe that children do not suffer so much from revaccination as adults, and that if they do it does not matter, as they are not at work for wages. Again, you may be right; but my calculation was founded not on your beliefs, but on Dr Stewart's figures.

I shall worry you no further about the statistics of doubtful cases. I offer, for what it is worth, my strong impression that the documents that have created the bulk of vaccinist opinion, professional and lay, are the tables in which vaccinated cases are compared with unvaccinated, no intermediate class being mentioned. You believe, on the contrary, that the documents which give more elaborate classifications were the main factor. We must agree to differ. The matter is one of opinion, and we cannot settle it by throwing the two types of document at one another's heads.

May I suggest, finally, that vaccinism, like antivaccinism, has as much to fear from the intemperately virtuous indignation of its advocates as from its opponents. There are two weak points in your position, quite apart from its scientific validity. The first is that as you are defending a vested interest of enormous pecuniary value, whilst the antivaccinist is facing very serious persecution without any prospect of personal gain, you are bound to get the worst of it the moment you begin to impute discreditable motives. The second is that the vaccinists are themselves so divided in opinion that if you once give way to the temptation to retort instead of arguing, you can always do so with fatal facility by denying, on the authority of some leading vaccinist, whatever an antivaccinist asserts to be vaccinist doctrine on the authority of some other leading vaccinist. Nay, as in the present case, when he quotes an authority by name, you can generally find something that the very same authority has written or signed which seems to contradict the antivaccinist flatly. For a week or a fortnight you enjoy the triumph of having apparently exposed your opponent. Then comes the explanation; and you lose your public exactly as you lost Gladstone. People grow tired of these perpetual recriminations that end in nothing, these tremendous impeachments of men who have committed no crime, these implications that Herbert Spencer was an obscure notoriety hunter, and that Sir William Collins is a sixth-rate practitioner who ought to be struck off the Register. This sort of thing is beyond human patience; and all the time you are doing it, you are bewildering the public with contradiction after contradiction instead of throwing the contradictions overboard and sticking to the positions which can still be defended. You are tempting me to prolong this correspondence, not because there is nothing serious to be said on your side, but because you will not say it: you prefer to express your resentment at my venturing to disagree with you, to disparage my personal character, and to deny my good faith. And in doing so you sacrifice your cause recklessly. Any man with sufficient public practice to debate impersonally and keep his temper (especially if he has a slight sense of humor to help him out) can, without knowing more than the commonplaces of the subject, tie you up in your own admissions. I am sorry to be driven to take you to task thus in your own columns: but since you insist in treating the discussion as a conflict of personalities, you must allow me to do your cause the justice of admitting that I am perfectly aware that the ease with which I am able to stand your case on its head every time you lose your temper with me must be more amusing than scientifically convincing to your readers.

From The Times, 12 May 1925

A Fleet surgeon states that the wrecking of women's complexions and appearance through smallpox was "almost universal" in the eighteenth century. This amazing assertion is supported by a quotation from one of Captain Marryat's novels in

1829, after thirty years of vaccination. It is perhaps appropriate that our Fleet surgeons should study Marryat rather than Jenner: but Marryat was merely echoing Jenner, who made exactly the same remark before vaccination was introduced, and attributed the alleged phenomenon to inoculation, which is now a criminal practice.

Dr Home's lectures to bluejackets appear to have reflected the teaching of our newspapers on vaccination very faithfully. He exhibited terrifying pictures of cases of confluent smallpox, but omitted the pictures (now in extensive circulation) of cases of that equally hideous and more deadly disease, generalized vaccinia. He "told of the scourge smallpox was before vaccination came in in 1800, and how it lessened thereafter," but said nothing of cholera, typhus, and the other scourges, which had practically disappeared during that period, whilst smallpox marched to its climax in the appalling epidemic of 1871, which gave vaccination, then ruthlessly compulsory, its death-blow. He contrasted arm-to-arm vaccination with vaccination by "good and safe" calf lymph, but omitted to explain in what sense undefined pathogenic matter scraped from an ulcer on a calf infected with vaccinal syphilis can be good and safe for any other purpose than that of infecting anyone inoculated with it with the calf's disease.

As the doctor had to go off to China without waiting to see what happened to the 120 victims of the operation, possibly the "week or fortnight of slight illness" prescribed for them may have been the worst that ensued. But I remember an experiment made by the Metropolitan Asylums Board, in which the men working on a certain job during an epidemic were induced to submit to revaccination, not by lectures and pictures of confluent smallpox, but by a bribe of 5s. per man. The resultant "slight illnesses" included some that were much worse than any ordinary case of smallpox. The medical report was never published.

I have two reasons for inflicting these commonplaces of the vaccination controversy once more on your readers. The first is that the Press and the administrative departments seem to be relapsing into that infatuated ignorance of the strength of the popular and scientific opposition to vaccination which received such a shock when the compulsory clauses had to be repealed by a scared House of Commons in 1898. If the departments and the Press persist in ignoring and suppressing the case against vaccination until there is another explosion, the result may possibly be that vaccination will be made a crime, as inoculation (equally well accredited) has been.

My second reason is that, although smallpox is now a comparatively negligible disease—so much so that in the little outbreaks which seem so trumpery to those of us who remember 1871 and 1881, we sometimes find no deaths, and the whole affair dismissed by old hands as chicken-pox—yet the shortage of houses has produced so much overcrowding that there is a serious danger that Nature may strike again, and strike hard, as she does always when she is too long defied. It is an established fact that adequate housing and sanitation can avert the blow. It is an equally established fact that revaccination cannot. Anything that leads us to rely on vaccination and neglect housing and sanitation is therefore most mischievously inopportune at the present time.

But for these considerations nothing would have induced me to take up my pen again in argument with a profession which has surrendered itself to a fixed idea. I fear it is now too late for it to put its house in order; but when the laity—the consumers and victims—take it in hand, as they presently must, at least it will not be able to plead that nobody warned it of the wrath to come.

From The Times, 22 January 1904

Let it be granted that by taking out our smallpox in periodic inoculations instead of in epidemics we can save the whole cost of smallpox hospitals. The question still remains, which plan is the cheaper? The cost of inoculation, both in lymph and in fees to the operator, is heavy and constant; its cost in indisposition and disablement is heavier still, not to mention the chances of serious disease. The tendency of modern inoculation practice is to insist on greater severity in the operation, and consequently in its immediate and inevitable consequences. The tendency of modern sanitary regulation is to mitigate and confine smallpox epidemics, and all other epidemics as well. It is therefore quite possible, without the smallest scepticism as to the possibility of preventing smallpox epidemics by inoculation, to prefer the disease to that particular remedy, both on economic and hygienic grounds.

From *The Dublin Evening Telegraph*, 14 *January* 1916

I regret that I shall be unable to attend the meeting of the Maryborough Society, which is doing good work in calling attention not only to the general question of vaccination, but in exposing the unteachable stupidity which permits the Local Government Board at such a moment as this to strain one of the worst powers of coercion which distinguishes English law in Ireland from English law in England.

After a long agitation the House of Commons was forced to release the English people from compulsion to throw their babies into a lottery in which one of them was killed every week, and many of them seriously injured, with the additional outrage that parents who complained of the injuries were accused by the doctors of having themselves infected their children with disgraceful disease. The climax was reached when the doctors who were proceeded against by parents for this abominable sort of libel were forced to defend themselves by admitting that the results of vaccination could not always be distinguished from the diseases in question. When it came to that, compulsory vaccination had to go in England; but the English Government retained it for the Irish on the general principle, doubtless, that compulsion of any sort is good for the Irish.

You will be able to give the meeting startling figures as to how the English people immediately threw off the yoke by availing themselves of the Act. I hope, however, you will also impress on them that owing to the infamous ignorance and credulity of the English magistrates the poor were most shamefully bullied and tricked out of the relief they were entitled to under the Act; and it was a common thing to see a laborer treated more offensively than a criminal in the Police Courts when he applied for exemption, and finally refused it, on the grounds that he had not used the exact words of the clause, whilst the next applicant would be a University man of good standing, who would receive his certificate without the least demur, the magistrate knowing well that they dare not treat a gentleman able to command legal aid and capable of arguing the scientific question as they treated poor men who knew nothing except that their last two children had died of vaccination and that an Act of Parliament had been passed to make such horrors impossible. Therefore, the audience may take it as certain that those who have demanded and obtained the benefit of the Act consist largely of highly educated people who had carefully studied the subject with the full knowledge that their children's lives and health might depend upon their coming to a sound conclusion. In saying this I am not forgetting the good work that has been done by the National Anti-Vaccination League in helping poor men to have their claims justly dealt with and in shaming and intimidating those magistrates whose anarchism seemed incorrigible and who set the example of evading and ridiculing the law they were sworn to administer.

Vaccination is, unfortunately, a powerful vested interest. It is the only ground on which a parent can be forced to call in a doctor to a perfectly healthy child and, naturally, the doctors defend it desperately, because the healthier we all are the harder it is for private doctors to live. They have seen for years past now that Ireland is no longer full of fever as it used to be, and death-rates and disease-rates are falling in all directions, that doctors must find some means of getting fees from healthy people. Prophylactic inoculations not only supply such means but make the inoculated persons so ill that they have to call the doctor in again to cure the illness the doctor himself has produced. Besides this, the firms who manufacture the serums and lymphs with which the inoculations are made represent extensive commercial interests. Put the professional and the commercial interests together, and the meeting will be able to understand why it is the Local Government Board keeps driving the Guardians to insist on vaccination, whilst at the same time it neglects to make them enforce the Public Health Acts and allows the slums of Dublin and Belfast to be one of the scandals of the civilized world.

Irish Boards of Guardians

If the Irish Boards of Guardians have any doubt as to the right way to get to work to maintain the health of the community, let them send a deputation to Leicester, or to any other town which has been sensible enough to discard vaccination and substitute cleanliness and careful sanitation, and they will come back determined that there will never be another child vaccinated in Ireland if they can help it.

Incantation with a Lancet

Sanitation requires much greater knowledge, ability, and industry than paying a doctor to perform a magical incantation with a lancet, but it does its work.

I cannot conclude without a reminder that the last great war in the West of Europe—the Franco-Prussian War of 1870–71— occurred when compulsory vaccination was at its height and in its glory, and when the world was promised that there could never again be an epidemic of smallpox. The result was the most appalling epidemic of smallpox on record. That was what killed vaccination; and if the members of the Irish Local Government Board have not found out that yet, the sooner they hurry up with their information the better, for it is sanitation and sanitation alone that will save us from a similar visitation as a result of the present war.

From The Liverpool Echo, 5 October 1926

In the report of Mr Viereck's interview with me it is stated that when I was attacked by smallpox in the epidemic of 1881, "my body, not tainted by vaccination, conquered."

Mr Viereck misunderstood me, as his own statement that it was through this attack that I became interested in the subject shews. I was a fully vaccinated person, guaranteed immune from smallpox for the whole of my natural life. When compulsory vaccination, ruthlessly enforced, had culminated in two of the worst smallpox epidemics on record, the guarantee was contracted to seven years. It is now probably seven minutes.

Believers in vaccination must have been led by Mr Viereck's mistake to attribute the attack to the fact that I was unvaccinated. Now that they know better, they will attribute my recovery to my vaccination. They like to have it both ways; and they are quite welcome as far as I am concerned.

THE ALLEGED MILITARY CONQUEST OF TYPHOID FEVER

From The New Statesman, 25 November 1916

THE figures given by Dr Saleeby as to the relative susceptibility to disease and mortality of inoculated and uninoculated soldiers are much more serious than he perceives. What he takes to be merely a typhoid rate looks uncommonly like a murder rate.

Dr Saleeby imagines that he is comparing an otherwise constant quantity called a British soldier under two simple conditions which he calls protection and unprotection. What is he really doing? He is comparing a body of soldiers worried with threats, bullied, harassed with extra fatigues, denied leave for two years at a stretch, illegally imprisoned, persecuted in every way that military ingenuity can devise and military tyranny execute, with another body enjoying popularity, the relief of leave and jollification, and every alleviation of their lot compatible with their effectiveness in the field. Even if the persecuted section were not in any way selected to start with, their disease rate and mortality rate would be much higher than that of the others: quite sufficiently so to account for differences of 7.7 and 1.54 per thousand. "These cold figures," says Dr Saleeby, "express a triumph which is glorious almost beyond belief." No doubt the cold figures of the persecuted dead express a triumph; but it is clearly the triumph of the persecutor and not of the T.V. or T.A.V. It represents so many soldiers killed by deliberate and intentional ill-usage.

But even if there were no persecution, the experience represented by the figures would not pass with any scientifically trained mind as a conclusive control experiment. The non-protected are self-picked men, not normal unselected soldiers. The ordinary soldier in robust health does not trouble himself about inoculation controversies or make a fuss about a pin-prick: he gets inoculated because he is told by the doctor that it is the right thing, as far as he is consulted at all. Who are the objectors? The comparatively sedentary men who read and think, the hypochondriacs, the weaklings who know by experience that they suffer exceptionally from the slightest touch of fever, the men whose relatives have succumbed to vaccination, the men who have an unreasoning dread of the lancet or the hypodermic syringe, the nervously cantankerous men who have the diathesis of the born objector, the independent spirits who chafe under army conditions at all times, and are never in perfect physical or moral health in a military environment. If men selected in this fashion are compared with unselected soldiers they will come out at a disadvantage, not only as to health and vitality, but as to discipline, steadiness in action, tidiness, sociability, and almost everything military except general apprehensiveness.

If Dr Saleeby wants a real control experiment, he should propose the one I suggested long ago: that is, placing in the field under similar conditions two regiments, one inoculated by order, whether they like it or not, and the other uninoculated, also by order whether they like it or not. Even that would be badly vitiated by the attitude of the men towards the experiment; for so much has been done by Dr Saleeby and others to persuade soldiers that the neglect of inoculation means certain death, that the majority of the compulsorily uninoculated might die of anxiety whilst, the compulsorily inoculated who were equally persuaded that inoculaton was hideously dangerous would be in a negligible minority. Even in the figures Dr Saleeby quotes there is probably a factor representing the misgivings of the objector whom Dr

Saleeby has half-convinced that he is running a terrible risk for the sake of a principle. But as trial with two regiments would shew at least a glimmering sense of what really constitutes a control experiment, the figures would not be conclusive; but their worthlessness would not hit us in the face as the worthlessness of Dr Saleeby's figures does.

When will Dr Saleeby take to science in earnest? When will he acquire a wholesome sense of the irresistible comicality of such a sentence as "Typhus and typhoid have nothing in common but their clinical similarity," or of the ghastly cheerfulness which consoles us for the inoculated dead of Gallipoli by assuring us that it was all a mistake: it was only the wrong bacillus. We remember how devoutly Dr Saleeby believed in that wrong bacillus and how he encouraged its victims to believe that they were protected, sanitation or no sanitation. And he is now as "gloriously" certain as ever that he has got hold of the right one this time, especially since Madame Victor Henri has convinced him that there is no difference.

I hasten to say that I have no conclusion of my own to announce or advocate. But when I see men of Dr Saleeby's general powers of mind and skill with the pen producing as "glorious beyond belief" evidence that would not impose on the Statistical Society's cat, and conclusions that carry their oversights blazing in front of them like motor headlights, I am compelled in common humanity to ask that the public should be treated a little more seriously, as it is probably sincerely anxious to be well-informed on a very difficult subject.

OUR PECULIAR PEOPLE AND CHRISTIAN SCIENTISTS

From The Daily Chronicle, 29 October 1898

I MUST utter a word of warning to the public and to the Press as to the risk they run in commenting on the Peculiar People case and the Harold Frederic inquest. Such comments, if favorable to the medical profession, are, by the law of England, blasphemy, exposing those who make them to criminal prosecution and exemplary punishment. For example, a juryman at the Frederic inquest said in open court that Mrs Mills, the Christian Scientist, had been talking nonsense for an hour. As the lady had been simply declaring the supreme authority of the Bible and the sovereign efficacy of faith in the healing of diseases, that juryman may think himself fortunate if he escapes the sentence of a year's imprisonment suffered not so very long ago by the President of the National Secular Society for his outspokenness on the same point. Your own position is not free from danger. Your leaderette on the Peculiar People case flatly contradicts the doctrine that "it is faith, and not the doctor, that cures." I see that you claim the authority of Mr Justice Bigham for this denial of the creed established by law in this country; but on turning to your report of this judge's utterances, I can find nothing but reiterated statements that it is a breach of law not to call in a doctor to a case of illness. From anybody but a judge these statements would be surprising. Since the judge in this case was fortunately a humane one, they may be passed over in consideration of the benevolence of their intention.

It is impossible not to be struck by the completeness with which medical science has now usurped the dominion over the public mind formerly exercised by priestcraft. In dealing with the Peculiar People it does not occur to anyone even to suggest that the case against them must, from the point of view of genuine science, stand or fall by a statistical inquiry into the comparative mortality of those who call in doctors and those who do not. Some years ago the Colonial Office issued an interesting report on the condition of the Virgin Islands, from which it appeared that only one of the islands had a doctor on it, and that people died faster on that island than on any of the others. It may be, of course, that the island was a specially unhealthy one; but there was nothing in the report to that effect. Suppose it should turn out that the Peculiar People have the same advantage over their neighbors as the undoctored Virgin Islanders had over the doctored one, what would become of the case against them? Nay, would it not then be our duty to prosecute the people who call in doctors?

Again, if we make it a crime not to call in a doctor, we must equally make it a crime not to do what the doctor orders. If he prescribes brandy for a teetotaller, meat for a vegetarian, marriage for an ascetic, he must be obeyed. If he is a believer in bleeding, in the universal efficacy of mercury as a medicine, in any or all of the various anti-toxins now fashionable, or in unlimited drugging with poisons, the patient must undergo all these, although he may be perfectly aware that eminent medical authorities who are out of his reach regard these things as infinitely worse than prayer and anointing, which can at least do no harm. I leave out of account that the medical profession, like all other professions, has its proportion of drunkards, fools, and scoundrels (a doctor has just been sentenced to death), and that very eminent medical men publicly defend the position that the pursuit of knowledge justifies what many of us regard as the most abhorrent cruelty. Yet out of sheer credulity as to the infallibility of the medicine man, we are drifting into a legal procedure which relieves them from all necessity to gain our confidence by the good they do us, and gives them a legal power over our bodies which would overthrow any Government which would venture to claim it for the Throne, the Church, the House of Commons, or any other authority in the land.

I should add that I am not a Peculiar Person: at least, not in the technical sense. I am at present in the hands of doctors whose surgical skill, clinical experience, good sense and humanity I know how to value. But then I can choose my doctors, which laboring folk very often can not, and I am not so poor as to have to employ those failures and drunkards of the profession upon whom our wage-workers so often have to rely in great cities, and whose ministrations can hardly be more efficacious than those of an honest and decent minister, who, after all, probably learns a little by clinical experience, too. However, I wish to guard myself against prejudging the results of any really scientific tests as to various methods of treatment of disease. I only insist on the fact that in the absence of such tests the pietistic method is just as authoritative as the medical method. For the present, I merely suggest that when the next legal onslaught is made on the Peculiars, four witnesses shall be called; to wit, the anointer who has attended the case, and three doctors, aged respectively sixty-five, forty-three, and twenty-four, who shall be examined as to the way in which they would have treated the deceased. I venture to predict that the jury, having to choose between three different and contradictory versions of the infallibility of science, and one version of the infallibility of the Bible, will probably come to the sensible conclusion that people must be left to choose for themselves between the pretensions of the four rival orthodoxies.

From The Daily News, 18 December 1923

A Mr Henry Norman Purkiss, who believes the Bible to be the word of God, has just been sent to prison for six months as the murderer of his own child by the Recorder, who believes that diphtheria is not a fatal disease when treated by a doctor.

I wish to point out two consequences which should follow this decision. First, every doctor whose patient dies of diphtheria should be indicted for wilful murder. Second, the Recorder should be indicted for a breach of the statute against blasphemy, which prescribes severe penalties for anyone who denies the validity of the Epistle of St James, in which it is laid down in the most precise terms that cases of illness should be treated exactly as Mr Purkiss's child was treated. The Recorder repudiates St James, and pins his faith on anti-toxin.

Perfectly respectable evidence was called to shew that the treatment of St James has proved effective in many cases. It transpired also that in the case of another child of Mr Purkiss which was taken to hospital with pneumonia and medically treated, the child died.

Evidence of the most unquestionably qualified medical practitioners might have been called to shew that anti-toxin, as a cure for diphtheria, is not to be depended on, and that there are grave objections to it on other grounds.

Had Mr Purkiss called in a doctor, and the doctor proposed anti-toxin, Mr Purkiss would have had ample authority for refusing to allow its use.

Under these circumstances, perhaps the most sensible course would be for the Home Secretary to release Mr Purkiss, and for the Recorder to apologize. It is true that nobody expects a judge to believe in St James nowadays, in spite of the statute. But a judge who is disregarding the law himself should not lecture another gentleman for obeying it, and certainly should not sentence him to six months' imprisonment for refusing to transfer all the attributes of God to the late Dr Crippen and his surviving colleagues on the medical register.

The case illustrates the folly of slipping into an Act of Parliament (in this case the Children's Act of 1908) such a specific expression as "medical aid." The object of the Act was to protect children against neglect. Mr. Purkiss did not neglect his child: he carefully did what the Bible, which he is legally obliged to accept as the Word of God, instructs him to do.

Yet because the words "medical aid" occur in the 1908 Act, he is imprisoned for six months under the pretext that his putting faith in prayers, rather than in prescriptions, constitutes an act of criminal neglect. And he is told repeatedly by judge and counsel, who cannot in this connection be called learned, that if he had called in a doctor, the doctor could have cured his child, an assumption for which there is not the smallest warrant in law, science, or common experience.

Even a judge might be expected to know that though doctors' patients sometimes recover, they also sometimes die, as Mr Purkiss's other child did.

Perhaps I should add that I am not myself a Peculiar, save in my refusal to credit the trade union known as the General Medical Council with the power to confer Omniscience and Infallibility on its registrees.

THE AMAZING CASE OF THE GENERAL MEDICAL COUNCIL VERSUS THE LATE DR AXHAM

From The Times, 23 *October* 1925

THE difficulty about Dr Axham does not seem to be understood. Dr Axham, when he acted as anæsthetist for the patients of Sir Herbert Barker, did his clear duty as a member of a profession devoted to the relief of human suffering by every means within the competence of a physician, and to the encouragement and aid of every extension of those means. The public has benefited by his action and owes him its protection. Yet it has allowed him to be stigmatized for his services as guilty of infamous professional conduct and struck off the register. The striking-off will not hurt him nowadays, when unregistered practitioners are at a heavy premium because they have mastered the modern techniques of which registration guarantees ignorance; but at eighty-seven he is past practising, and the stigma is deeply felt and justly resented by him.

Meanwhile, Sir Herbert Barker, whom he was one of the first to recognize as a great manipulative surgeon, has been knighted in public recognition of his eminence at the instance of four famous surgeons, who petitioned the Prime Minister on the subject. The G.M.C. holds that they were guilty of infamous professional conduct, in which they were abetted by the King; but it does not act on its view, because the King and his advisers are not so helpless as Dr Axham was. Only by continuing the victimization of Dr Axham can it make its opinion quite clear, and intimidate every registered practitioner who would like to follow his admirable example.

Obviously it is useless to appeal to the G.M.C. But what about the really responsible bodies who are supposed to represent the nation in the matter—the Privy Council and the universities and the Government? It is they who, in gross neglect of their duty, and in spite of the plain provisions in the Act for public and scientific representation, have thrown the control of the profession, including powers which no political ruler in the civilized world now enjoys or would dream of claiming, into the hands of practising doctors, with the inevitable result that the Council has become a trade union of the worst type—namely the type in which the entry to the trade and the right to remain in it are at the mercy of the union. Not only is the type the worst, but in this particular instance it is at the crude stage of preoccupation with professional earnings and sullen defiance of public opinion, which produced the Manchester and Sheffield outrages in working-class trade unionism in the last century. Within the last month or two a distinguished doctor has written to the Press declaring naïvely that the first duty of the G.M.C. is to protect the livelihood of the registered practitioners. He would be quite right if the G.M.C. were a trade union *de jure* as well as *de facto*; but as it is, on the contrary, a constitutional authority, its first duty is to protect the public and secure to it the advantages of all the latest developments in medicine and surgery. It has become in effect a trade union solely through the carelessness or superstition of the controlling bodies representing us poor laymen who are so vitally interested as patients, as well as disinterested science.

It seems hopeless, however, to make people understand this. My own efforts to call attention to it result only in what I must call editorial imbecilities to the effect that I have "a down on doctors," and that every quack would have to be registered if Sir Herbert Barker were registered, which is about as sensible as saying that because Brahms was made a Doctor of Music without doing the curricular exercises in counterpoint the universities are logically bound to confer degrees on all our street piano men. As a matter of fact, few persons can have had more or better doctor friends than I; indeed, that is why my utterances have been so well informed; but they may not speak for themselves, whereas I, being free to open my mouth without being ruined and stigmatized as infamous, can act occasionally as the mouthpiece of a gagged profession. Leaving that aside, I have my own interests and grievances as a citizen. My wife suffered from a laming traumatic dislocation for eight years. Thanks to the obsolete training maintained by the G.M.C., the registered surgeons were unable to correct it. They did not pretend to: the final verdict was: "You must go to Barker." But the G.M.C. said: "If you go to that black-leg, you shall howl for it, as we will ruin any man who dares ad-minister an anæsthetic." And, in fact, the operation, which was completely successful, was performed without an anæsthetic, though I hasten to add that this was an effect of my wife's curiosity rather than of any serious difficulty in circumventing the trade union.

Later on, in an accident, I displaced one of my own bones rather badly; and again, though nothing could exceed the kind-ness of the registered medical gentlemen on the spot, they were unable to replace it for want of a perfectly well-known technique which every qualified surgeon should have at his fingers' ends. It took me ten days to get to Birmingham, where an American D.O. (doctor of osteopathy), also classed as a blackleg by the G.M.C., set me right after seventy-five minutes' skilled manipu-lation. Had the process been an unbearably painful one, which it fortunately was not, any anæsthetist saving me the pain would have done so under penalty of being rattened (as the term went in Sheffield) to the extent of being deprived of his livelihood.

No wonder, I am overwhelmed with requests from the medical societies in all the medical schools in London to lecture to them on the situation. But I have nothing more to say than I have al-ready said often and clearly enough; and I simply dare not use the language that the ablest leaders of the profession pour out on it. All I assert is that if the constitutional authorities will only do their duty by getting rid of the practitioners from the G.M.C. (save as assessors in case of need), and replace them with repre-sentatives of the public and of disinterested hygienic science, Dr Axham will be reinstated almost automatically, and the conquest of Harley Street by the unregistered, now in active progress, may be checked. For there is really nothing that the unregistered practitioners do that cannot be done by registered ones if only they are apprenticed to the techniques of today instead of to those of a century ago.

DOCTORS' DELUSIONS

From The Times, 12 *November* 1925

Dr Axham has not been "covering," nor was it for covering that he was struck off the register. I happen to know what covering means: my uncle was a doctor. Real covering, which is not uncommon, and, in the cases which have come under my observation or to my knowledge, has been practised with impunity and with hardly a pretence of concealment, arises in the following way:

A registered doctor—usually a country doctor—finds that he is getting more patients than he can attend to. Obviously he should take another registered doctor into partnership. But this means inviting a rival on to his ground, and sharing fees with him. It is better business to engage an unregistered assistant, who will work as an employee at a modest salary, and who can never capture the practice and set up for himself. It is not difficult to find such assistants. There are always men in the market with a taste for doctoring, who, through poverty, age, or lack of the necessary sort of application and memory, are unable to pass examinations. Some of them, by superior clinical instinct and dexterity, are better doctors than their registered employers, and are preferred by the patients. Employment of such unregistered assistants is "covering." I have never heard it defended in principle, and I should be surprised if I heard Dr Axham or Sir Herbert Barker defend it either in practice or principle.

Covering is always the maintenance under false colours of an unregistered practitioner by a registered one, and cannot in its own nature be the converse. If Dr Axham, being a registered practitioner, and being called in as such to perform a surgical operation, had handed over the patient to "one Herbert Atkinson Barker," unregistered, but assumed by the patient on the strength of his connection with Dr Axham to be registered, then Dr Axham would have been guilty of covering.

What actually happened was just the opposite. A patient with a dislocated knee, finding, after many expensive experiments, that neither Dr Axham nor any other available registered surgeon could set it right, and that one Herbert Atkinson Barker, un-registered, and not pretending to be registered, had become famous by his success in such cases, naturally called in the said Herbert to cure him, as he had a perfect right to do without molestation or intimidation from the G.M.C. or anyone else. He asked—Would it hurt? On learning that it would, he called in Dr Axham to anæsthetize him, which again he had a perfect right to do. Dr Axham, having convinced himself that the operation, though neither he nor any of his registered colleagues could perform it, was a surgical one in the technical sense, and that Herbert Atkinson Barker had mastered it, was under the most sacred professional obligation to give the desired relief. There was no covering whatever in the transaction.

To make this clear, let us suppose that the victim of a railway collision lies pinned down beneath the wreckage in such a way that he can be released only by a skilled breakdown gang using compressed air drills, oxy-acetylene jets, cranes, and so forth, and that its operations are so unbearably painful that it is doubtful whether the victim can survive them. Let us suppose further that Dr Graham Little and Sir Bryan Donkin are present, rendering what aid they can. The distracted wife of the victim asks Dr Graham Little to anæsthetize him. Dr Graham Little is sympathetic, but regrets that, as the members of the breakdown gang are not on the medical register, he would be guilty of covering, and would be struck off the register for infamous professional conduct, if he relieved the sufferer in any way. If, however, his registered friend Sir Bryan Donkin will be good enough to undertake the salvage operations, he will be happy to act. Sir Bryan Donkin says that he would be only too delighted to be of use, but that, as he does not know how to handle compression drills and oxy-acetylene jets, the first effect of his interference would probably be to disembowel the patient and burn his head off. In these circumstances both gentlemen are very sorry, but nothing can be done, as it is evident that if eminent registered doctors were allowed to "cover" railway mechanics wholly ignorant of anatomy the nation must presently perish.

I must apologize to Dr Graham Little and Sir Bryan Donkin for this monstrous supposition. I have not the slightest doubt that when it came to the point they would act precisely as Dr Axham acted. Perhaps they will forgive me in consideration of my having cleared up their minds on the subject of covering.

I am quite opposed to real covering, and wish the G.M.C. would stop it. Take a typical case. A patient, suffering from the very distressing pain called neuritis, calls in a registered doctor. It is clearly a case for some sort of manipulation rather than for the bottle. Possibly massage, the doctor thinks. As he knows nothing about massage, his duty is to call in a skilled Kellgren masseur. If he did, the masseur would at once tell him that massage is contra-indicated in such cases and would only aggravate the illness and give intense pain. But as, if the doctor called in a Kellgren masseur (who has to put in two years of finger training before he is considered manually qualified), he would share the fate of Dr Axham, he hands the patient over to a nurse who has spent a few hard-earned guineas on twelve lessons in massage from the local apothecary, with results that may be imagined. This procedure is tolerated by the G.M.C.; yet, if it is not covering, what is covering? The official answer is, apparently, any offence against the trade union. Offences against the patients are not only winked at, but in some of the worst instances practically imposed on the practitioner by forbidding him to call in competent assistance. Incompetent assistance is privileged.

May I say that I do not hold any brief for osteopathy, or Kellgren massage, or naturopathy or homeopathy, or Christian Science, or herbalism, or peculiarism, or for the few gifted individuals who, like Sir Herbert Barker, have developed and cultivated, by a course of intensive self-training which could not be imposed on any student, a personal technique which is practically incommunicable, and which they therefore do not pretend to teach to all comers any more than I pretend to teach all comers to write plays. My brief is for the public, the patient, the consumer, the victim who pays the piper in purse and person without being allowed to call the tune. My case is that the G.M.C. has been suffered to become a trade union of the most anti-social type, whereas it was meant to be, and if the constituent authorities will only do their plain duty can become, a public body protecting us against medical trade unionism (which is quite permissible in its proper place and under proper control by the community) as well as giving us a trustworthy guarantee that a practitioner who can produce its credentials has had a certain minimum of instruction and training, kept carefully up to date by representatives interested in scientific hygiene and not in the spread of lucrative hypochondria. Instead of this, the G.M.C. deliberately and openly addresses itself to the anti-social task of preventing the public from calling in any unregistered practitioner who is in competition with those on the register, whilst at the same time allowing the qualification for that register to remain in many respects not merely useless and out of date, but positively poisonous and murderous.

I have plenty of medical support for this view; but it will not appear in your columns, because a doctor cannot join in a Press campaign over his own name and address except at the risk of being struck off the register for "advertizing." If a doctor wishes to add to his income by writing critical articles in the lay Press, as some of our most eminent Churchmen do, he has to remove his name from the register and renounce clinical practice to secure freedom of utterance. I am not defending medical advertisement, registered or unregistered; I am simply explaining why any appeal for the reform of the General Medical Council must be conducted by laymen without avowed medical support. The situation is intolerable, and the remedy obvious.

SHALL THE ENGLISH MEDICAL COUNCIL CONQUER IRELAND?

From The Irish Times, 2 September 1925

THE Free State Government will, I hope, resolutely carry through its announced intention of rescuing Ireland from the disastrous control of that despised and self-disgraced trade union, the British Medical Council. At present, unregistered practitioners in London charge, and are willingly paid, higher fees than registered doctors, because they have acquired the modern techniques which the Council boycotts and persecutes. The most famous manipulative surgeon in England, knighted for his services, being unregistered, is denounced and ostracized as a quack by men of whom some, though registered as competent surgeons, are hardly dexterous enough to manipulate their own shoe-laces.

The Council avenges itself for the public slight of the knighthood by threatening to repeat its old exploit of striking off the register, as guilty of "infamous professional conduct," any registered doctor who acts as anæsthetist to the knight; for its members are determined that, if he dares to perform operations which are outside their technique, his patients (the public) shall howl for it. Students going up for examination have to conclude their preparation by being coached in obsolete surgical and clinical procedures, because their examiners are hopelessly out of date. This is the body which is described in your columns as possessing "the world's supreme medical charter," as having "a high and international standard," and as conferring on Ireland "our present scientific eminence."

The General Medical Council has about as much to do with science as the Miners' Federation (a much more enlightened and up-to-date body) has to do with geology and mineralogy. Even in the medical world, which is not the scientific world, it has no pre-eminence. In Europe and America it is a laughing-stock. The medical profession in Ireland will lose no prestige by dissociating themselves from it.

But now comes the very serious question: Will an Irish Medical Council prove any better? The answer is: Certainly not, if the Irish Government act as stupidly and ignorantly in this matter as the English Government. In President Cosgrave's otherwise reassuring and sensible announcement there is one terrifying phrase —"a self-controlled medical profession." A self-controlled profession is a conspiracy against the laity. Of all professions on earth the medical profession, consisting mainly of private medical and surgical practitioners, who have a direct pecuniary interest in making us ill, keeping us ill, and mutilating us, is the one that needs the sternest disinterested control not only in the common interest of the general body of citizens but in that of science.

Private practice should disqualify inexorably for any share in the control of the medical profession. The whole-time Medical Officer of Health, whose beneficent efficiency is tested by vital statistics alone, and whose chance of a knighthood depends on the disappearance of preventable disease from his district, and not on the number of fashionable death-beds at which he has assisted, is the only sort of doctor who should be trusted by a properly constituted Council. The Privy Council and the universities, though under no obligation to place a single professional doctor on the Council, have thoughtlessly betrayed their trust by handing the whole control over to the doctors, as if there were no such thing in the world as a patient. The result has been the very worst possible type of trade union—the type in which the union controls the entry into the profession and can at any moment ruin any member of it by throwing him out without any appeal, or any reason given except "infamous professional conduct," which soon comes to mean anything that is not good for doctors' incomes, or any clinical procedure that is outside the curriculum and has been introduced by unregistered discoverers.

The remedy is quite simple. Let the new Irish Medical Council be accessible to practising doctors in the capacity of consultants ("assessors") only, and consist exclusively of representatives of disinterested scientific culture, and of the laity; that is, of the unfortunate patients and those to whom they are dear. If this condition be complied with, an Irish degree will soon stand higher than an English one; and the nonsense that is being talked about Irish students deserting our schools for foreign ones (travelling expenses are no object nowadays, it seems) will be succeeded by complaints of our being crowded out of our own schools by English youths in search of Irish qualifications.

THE LISTER SUPERSTITION

From The Nation, 19 January 1918

As Mr Joseph Rowntree has started a quarrel with your re-viewer on the ground that he has not been sufficiently impressed by the reputation manufactured by the medical profession and its literary dupes for Lister, perhaps I may be allowed to attack him from the other side by asking him why, seeing that there is no widow to be wounded by perfect frankness in this matter, he did not seize the opportunity to bring out the really significant facts as to the now completely exploded blunder that made Lister famous. Let me summarize the case as briefly as possible.

Lister's theory of antiseptic surgery was so shallow and stupid in its conception, and so disastrous in its practice, that the only excuse for his rash acceptance of it was that it seemed at first to produce good results owing to the astonishing improvement wrought by its incidental introduction of cleanliness and common decency into surgery. In spite of this, antiseptically treated sin-uses refused to heal; surgeons like Lawson Tait, who would have nothing to do with Lister's antiseptics, and declared that the best "antiseptic" was pipe water, were conspicuously successful as operators; and Spencer Wells made an operation that had previ-ously been a desperate one comparatively safe by keeping the patient under temperature conditions which had nothing to do with antisepticism, Lister's method was soon dropped in hospital practice, and replaced by what was called the aseptic treatment. Lister himself dropped it. In the Medical Press and Circular of the 26th December last, the editor, apparently under the impres-sion that he is defending Lister's reputation, states that Lister nearly killed Queen Victoria by his treatment of an abscess, and saved her by an empirical anticipation of the treatment of Colonel Sir Almroth Wright, the success of whose work during the war has not only given the *coup de grâce* to Listerism in up-to-date practice, but enabled him to give a colossal experimental verifica-tion of his view that the antispetic sterilization of wounds, surgical or other, is not only impossible, but would be fatal if it were possible; and that the attempts at it retard or prevent healing instead of accelerating it.

Unfortunately, the generations of medical students and nurses now passing away, who were trained to believe in the antiseptic theory and coached in its practice, were never warned of its breakdown. Even during this war it has been necessary to get rid of asepsis-mad fanatics in whose wards soldiers were dying whilst their nurses were wasting invaluable time on unnecessary rites of sterilization, or protesting that soldiers were being murdered because everything they touched, or that a nurse touched, or that the doctor touched, was not passed through boiling water or carbolic acid, or some other sterilizer. They have been doing that sort of thing all their working lives and the doctors of their period have been stuffing sinuses with iodoform gauze, keeping them suppurating for months and years, and, at extraordinary trouble and expense, killing a considerable number of people who would have recovered in a few weeks in the hands of a doctor old enough to have qualified before Lister and Pasteur came into fashion, or young enough to have learnt his business from Sir Almroth Wright. The suffering, the invalidity, the pecuniary loss and even ruin their patients must have undergone are incalculable.

On the other hand, the profit to doctors and pharmacists has been immense. And I am sorry to say that, with a few honorable and much reviled exceptions, the doctors have kept Lister's secret, and bolstered up his reputation even whilst discarding his practice. He was certainly not ungrateful to them. The time came when they, too, needed some testimony that would not bear examination. At a moment when the opponents of vivisection, who were almost to a man sceptics as to Listerism, had all but roused the public conscience against the stupid cruelties of the physiological laboratories, Lister came forward, and, on the credit of his great reputation, saved the situation by assuring the public that, owing to the use of anæsthetics, no animal suffered a moment's pain at the hands of the experimenters. It was a heroic

sacrifice to make for what Lister ignorantly imagined to be
science; but I do not think it was one of those which the Recording Angel blots out with a tear after entering it in his book. He
probably underscored it in red ink.

Lister's powers of reasoning were of the usual simple brass-
plate order. Having learnt from Pasteur that pus was produced
by microbes, he argued that the thing to do was to clear them out,
as you clear out blackbeetles from a kitchen, by poisoning them.
To him living tissue was a mode of "matter," like a kitchen flag-
stone, just as living bone was like the leg of a kitchen chair. To
his generation, anyone who made a metaphysical distinction
between a live cell and a dead one was "superstitious," and on the
wrong side in "the conflict between religion and science." To
put it in another way, Lister was much further off the track of
genuine science than Mrs. Eddy, and did a great deal more harm.

As to the condition of hospitals before they were cleaned up,
the statements quoted by all the reviewers miss the most significant point. The mortality was not constant. It came and went by
plagues, as mortality due to neglect of sanitation always does.
When gangrene set it, it was fatal to scratch a finger in the
hospital, much less operate. Now, if Lister's theory had been
sound, these visitations would never have passed away: they
would have spread until the human race was wiped off the earth.
Yet they did pass away as mysteriously as they came. If you
asked why, you were told that only a certain number of people
are susceptible to plague, and when they are killed off, the rest
carry on. But this will not wash in the case of a hospital. There
the patients under treatment in July are a mixed lot, just like
those under treatment in January. But if, in January, everyone of
them who suffers the most trivial wound, whether from the
surgeon's knife, or from a razor, or a needle, dies, and in July
nobody suffers any unusual consequences, you have had a "control experiment," which proves that the plague has somehow
exhausted itself without reference to susceptibility. A surgeon
of today may be excused for not noticing this, because it does not
present itself to him, our hospitals having been rescued from out-

breaks of gangrene by soap-and-water, sunshine, and common decency. But in Lister's time the outbreaks were staring every hospital surgeon in the face. I am not a surgeon; but they puzzled me when, more than forty years ago, I discussed science hopefully with the doctors and medical students of that day. For the fading out of the epidemics knocked the whole germ theory, as the doctor applied it, on the head.

There are very evident reasons why the medical profession, as at present constituted in this unhappy country, and the huge commercial interests which have grown up round the blackbeetle theory of pathogenic germs, including the newspapers, to which they pay a huge annual revenue in advertisements, should shout with one voice that Lister was a great man, and persist in calling his disastrous blunder a great discovery, even at the very moment of its final exposure and banishment from the military surgical ward by Sir Almroth Wright, who denies even normal mental competence to its last desperate defenders. But why should I enter into this conspiracy? Why should your reviewer? Why should Mr Rowntree? Even if biology were the crudely simple matter Lister took it to be, and his naïve notion that you had only to poison microbes with carbolic acid to abolish disease, and make surgery as safe as carpentry, were sound, we should still refuse to class him with Plato, with Copernicus, with Descartes, with Newton and Kant, with Shakespear and Goethe, Ibsen and Bergson, or even with Darwin. Our Governmental Honors Lists are bad enough in all conscience; but when it comes to having manufacturers of "perfect cures," and practitioners who recommend them, imposed on us as great men as a matter of commercial business (for example, Ehrlich and his salvarsan), the time cannot be far off when men of genuine worth will repudiate the Great Man label as indignantly as Mr John Galsworthy repudiated the knighthood they tried to plant on him the other day.

Let us by all means give Lister his meed of ability as a mechanical surgeon. It is only fair to him to admit that his hands were better than his head.

DOCTORS' DELUSIONS

From The Nation, 2 *February* 1918

I will not trespass on your space for more than a few words on the attempts made by your three medical correspondents to convict me of ignorant misrepresentation by the odd method of repeating all my statements in their own words. I am not surprised: it is only a fortnight since the editor of a medical paper offered to his readers a crushing example of one of my alleged "howlers," and added "Unfortunately, this is perfectly true." Your correspondents have adopted the same tactics; and naturally, it is not for me to object.

In justice to Mr Fairlie, I must admit that he sticks to the Listerian guns. He still believes that a wound can be made "to heal rapidly and cleanly" by "sterilizing the part to be operated on." He denies that Sir Almroth Wright's treatment of wounds has had any convincing results. And he says that the statement that the antiseptic treatment of sinuses not only did not heal them, but prevented them from healing (Sir Almroth has now provided the explanation of this clinical fact), is "simply not true." Against such devoted conviction I am powerless. I leave Mr Fairlie to Sir Almroth, and wish him better luck than Sir William Watson Cheyne had when he led what I supposed would be the last forlorn hope of Listerism against the experience of the war. But for the rest, there is nothing in the three letters but paraphrases of my own letter and desolating blindness to their bearing and importance. As a sample of the sort of thing that passes for scientific controversy in the medical profession, I may cite the fact that whereas every one of the reviews of Lister's life which extolled him as a great man claimed that his antiseptic theory of surgery had been suggested by the researches of Pasteur, the moment I repeat this statement I am immediately told that Pasteur did not study pus and its production in wounds. Who ever said he did?

In conclusion, let me remind your readers that I did not seek this controversy. I kept silence when reviewer after reviewer, including even so keen and advanced a spirit as Miss Rebecca West,

allowed themselves to be bluffed into joining this medical conspiracy to foist on the country a professional reputation at ten times
its real value, and to conceal a disastrous blunder in the interests
of the trade in antiseptics. But when, not content with this, the
conspirators attacked your reviewer because his estimate of
Lister's intellect fell slightly short of the enthusiasm with which
he might have written about Newton, Shakespear, or St Francis,
I thought it my public duty to effect a readjustment. In doing so
I took on credit the current statement that Lister was at least a
dexterous surgeon. On this point I must withdraw and apologize, as I cannot hold out against the authority of Dr Greville
McDonald. "I was one of Lister's first dressers in London," he
says, "and later, his colleague; and I knew him better than was
possible to most students. He was, perhaps, as Mr Bernard Shaw
suggests, not a great intellectual; and he certainly was, in his
manipulations, not a great surgeon." This must, I think, be regarded as the *coup de grâce* to poor Lister's reputation. I shall
always give him the same credit for the revolution in surgery as
I give to the Tsar for the Russian Revolution. And, as a humane
man, I am glad that the final blow came from one of his defenders
and not from me.

Perhaps I had better finish by adding a simple explanation of
the whole dispute. It may have been noticed that when I deal
with any controversial question, which I never do without making as sure of my ground as possible (for my reputation is at stake
every time: I am not registered as infallible and omniscient, as
doctors are), I am invariably attacked furiously for being mali-
ciously, pervertedly, and infamously wrong by the people I am
trying to set right, and equally invariably it turns out presently
that I was carefully, laboriously, scientifically right in all essential
particulars. But do you suppose that those whom I have dis-
interestedly rescued from error and delusion are capable of seeing that their reconsideration of the point at issue involves a reconsideration of their opinion of me? Not a bit of it. When they
are all echoing my views and even making catchwords of my
phrases, they still think of me as the man who is always wrong.

Just so in the case of Lister, they were told as students that Lister was a great man; and though his practice has been discarded and his theory exploded, they are none the less amazed and scandalized when anyone suggests that as his reputation stood by that practice and theory, so it must fall by it. Even Sir Almroth Wright, in the very act of demonstrating that the chief of the old Listerian guard is ignorant of the simple facts established by experiment in the bacteriological laboratory and has no notion of scientific reasoning, will casually allude to Lister as a great man. I wish I could be judged by my mistakes: I should have a first-rate scientific reputation by this time. Unfortunately for myself, though I make plenty, I do not make them in public.

It is understood, I hope, that this discussion is quite platonic. If I thought for a moment that any wounded soldier was being treated Listerically, I should have to take the matter very seriously indeed.

SANITATION VERSUS INOCULATION

From the New Statesman, 10 *July* 1915

Is not Lens's article on the above subject rather unreasonable? Lens believes in two alternative methods of dealing with disease. In one of them, the method of sanitation, he takes a mild interest. The other is a passion with him: he writes of those who are sceptical about it as "murderous mouths," and speaks of the proofs of it which are not yet to hand as "final, overwhelming, damning." The last epithet will probably be justified.

Then why, in the name of common sense, does he advocate the sanitary method of clean farmyards and exterminated flies? It is unpopular. It is tedious. It involves a continual vigilance of the most unsavory sort over the most repulsive kinds of filth. It sets us hunting the most elusive of all sorts of game: flies, mosquitoes, lice, which have defied for centuries the most powerful monarchs. Nobody of any social consequence can make any money out of it; nor can sixth-rate minds get first-rate reputations through it. It is only cleaning up, after all; and who can be expected to be enthusiastic about cleaning up?

On the other hand, the inoculation method is simple and practicable. Instead of ridiculously chasing flies and mosquitoes, and grubbing for their eggs, you catch men and women. These are about to be nationally registered, and can easily be compelled to submit to the operation, as such compulsion is already in force in the case of vaccination. A national register of flies is impossible. Every disease which is associated with a microbe can be dealt with by a "vaccine." You take a child; you inoculate him with all the vaccines known to pathology, or, better still, you compound a single vaccine out of them all; and the whole population is then protected against all the zymotic diseases at no greater cost than vaccination now imposes on us. We can be as dirty as we please. Our costly and troublesome drainage systems can be abolished. House sewage can be allowed simply to soak into the subsoil of our towns; farmyards can be left to the beneficent hand of Nature; we need not worry about the milk: in short, we shall enjoy the blessed relief of getting rid of sanitary questions altogether. At the same time, enormous profits will be made by the commercial establishments (German and American mostly, it is true; but why not English?) which manufacture these vaccines; and the theory is so simple that any idiot will be able to discourse about it, and write monographs on it, with a lucrative air of learning. Already it has won for Pasteur, from the enthusiastic Lens, the title of "greatest Frenchman of all time." Poor Descartes! Poor Molière! Diafoirus: thou art avenged!

Now, why should we waste our time and money on the poisoning of our old friend the fly, and on the slaughter of innocent mosquitoes, if the proofs of the inoculation method are final and overwhelming?

The objections to inoculation may be scientific; but they are not practical, and not popular. I will state them quite candidly and shew that they need not be taken into account by public authorities.

1. Inoculation makes people ill, sometimes very ill, and occasionally kills them. But this is exactly what impresses people.

Doctors who do the same thing are always popular with their patients.

2. There is no evidence that inoculation has ever had the slightest success. The flat facts of the case at present are that the extraordinary improvement in the health of troops in the field which has taken place of late years was achieved by the Japanese in the war with Russia by the sanitary method, without resort to inoculations. Lord Kitchener, rising the other day in the House of Lords to testify to the efficiency of anti-typhoid inoculation, was carried by his enthusiasm into giving the whole show away by adding that the health of the troops was excellent not only as to enteric, but as to every other disease.

But what of all that? The Japanese sanitation was relevant only as "a control experiment"; and only those who really know something about science understand the value and need for control experiments, or would consent to their being made in the British army at present by inoculating, say, half a regiment, and seeing whether the other half were any more subject to the disease aimed at than the inoculated half. On the contrary, when enlisted men offered themselves for this purpose, they were ruthlessly persecuted and bullied and put on disagreeable duties and denied privileges until they submitted to inoculation. Besides, who is to know that the Japanese army was not inoculated? People dont want to know. They even boldly alleged that it *was* inoculated until the evidence came to hand, when further references to it were quietly suppressed. As to Lord Kitchener's statement, it is all to the good, because it proves that the anti-typhoid vaccine prevents not only typhoid, but all diseases whatsoever.

Lens need not hesitate. The inoculation system has been placed in an impregnable position by the war. Belief in it has become a recognized part of patriotism. London editors in all directions have given it the countenance of their scientific authority, going out of their way to say "I believe" with special solemnity. When I wrote to The Times to ask Sir William Osler, without a hint of scepticism as to inoculation, simply to make it clear that he was not declaring against sanitation, the editor refused to insert my letter. When a medical man wrote to the same paper to point out that the statistics which had been offered to its readers were apparently quoted from the advertisements of an American serum firm, his letter was also suppressed. When the vital statistics of the campaign come to be published, there is not the slightest fear than any deaths from enteric fever, or from any disease against which the troops may have been inoculated, will appear in them. No doubt the disappearance of typhoid, in so far as it is not due to sanitation, will be balanced by entries in other columns. The classification of disease is largely a method of diagnosis. Already we hear of an unaccountable outbreak of virulent measles and meningitis; but in no case can these discredit a prophylactic addressed to typhoid fever. Anybody who attempts to connect the two will simply not be listened to.

The truth is, people like inoculation. Doctors love it, naturally enough, because it has solved the great economic problem of how to extract fees from people who have nothing the matter with them. And the people believe the doctors. Besides, it is so much easier to believe in inoculation. It is so comfortable, so dirty, so thoroughly unscientific, so magical and romantic, and so satisfactory as a means of disciplining the troublesome and detestable people who insist on poking their noses into refuse heaps and insisting on more inspectors and more sanitation: above all, who brutally tell people that there are no cheap short cuts to health and long life. How delightful it is to seize these people by bodily force and just shove the serum into their blood and say, "Now, if you want to prove that it is no good, you must die; for if you survive we shall say that you would have died if we hadnt inoculated you." With such inducements as these, who can doubt that inoculation is bound to win?

As for me, I believe in getting rid of the flies and mosquitoes and filth; but that is merely because these measures have done something. I am delighted with Major Hurlstone Hardy's book. Even Lens admits that the Panama Canal was "a colossal proof" of the efficacy of the sanitary policy, though he thinks the whole business was a silly mistake due to a murderous-mouthed ignorance of the ease with which the same result could have been obtained by inoculation with anopheles vaccine and stegomyia emulsion. In short, I happen to have a scientific mind, some notion of the nature of evidence, and some practical experience of public health work, including the tricks by which the failures of prophylactic measures are concealed. That puts me out of court. Lens need not fear my "murderous mouth": its dry warnings will not prevail against the triumphs of the gentlemen who promise immunity from disease for the ridiculous sum of eighteen pence or less. My contempt for all this Cheap Jack pseudoscience, enormous as it is, will not wither it. And, like Lens, I enjoy fairy tales. But I wish he would learn some new ones. And I am a little disappointed. I do not know who Lens is; but at first I had hopes that The New Statesman was going to let a real live genuine man of science loose on the intolerable quackeries of the old-fashioned newspaper "science column." But I now see that Lens is not a man of science. I even suspect him of being, on the contrary, a doctor. Perhaps genuine science was too much to ask for; but need the paper have gone to the opposite extreme?

Suppressed Letter to The Times, from The Vaccination Inquirer,
1 February 1915

Are we to understand from the letter from Sir William Osler in The Times of the 15th that persons protected against typhoid by inoculation may safely discontinue all the troublesome and expensive precautions and strict sanitary discipline by which the Japanese achieved their famous hygienic success in the Manchurian war? The strain and cost of this sanitary discipline is considerable; and if we now have, in inoculation, "a method of protection in the efficiency of which those who have studied the question have confidence," had we not better at once make inoculation compulsory not only for soldiers but for everybody, and go back to our old happy carelessness, and save plumbers' bills as well as doctors' bills? I cannot imagine how we can hesitate if Sir William is right. And as he is distinguished by no less than twenty-seven medical qualifications, including those of the highest class, to suspect him of being wrong would involve the conclusion that medicine, as officially studied, acts as a disablement rather than as a qualification in science. At all events the conclusion is so obvious that Sir William had better make himself quite clear if he does not mean it to be drawn.

Sir William's division of the human race into two great groups of Misguided Cranks (playing into the enemies' hands), and Men Who have Devoted Their Lives To The Service Of Humanity, and his discovery that these groups coincide exactly with the two other groups of those who do not believe in typhoid inoculation and those who do, is really epoch making if it be scientifically sound; and I suggest that if it stands investigation the London University should recognize it by a gold medal.

It will be observed that I am taking Sir William with the most exact scientific seriousness on the assumption that his letter to you was on that plane; and I am doing so in order that he may have an opportunity of disclaiming, if, as seems possible, he has simply been letting himself go in an ordinary friendly human fashion, without any pretence to more than a common degree of clinical authority.

By the way, do any of the protected inoculated men become "carriers"? For if so, all the more reason for universal compulsory inoculation. I presume Sir William is in favor of compulsory universal inoculation of every possible kind in any case.

WHAT IS A SCIENTIFIC JOURNAL?
From The Nation, 6 March 1923

SIR ALMROTH WRIGHT has started a new and very important subject. He says that the proper place for the publication of his discoveries and inferences is "the scientific journals," implying that The Nation is not a scientific journal.

What is a scientific journal? Is it a wadge of advertisements of every pill, potion, appliance, instrument, and utensil that can be used in the bedroom of an invalid, with a few medical lectures in the middle to help the sales? Clearly not: that is a trade paper; and the medical contributors to such papers have, ere now, deigned to supply testimonials of wholesomeness to brands of whisky, to the atmosphere in the old underground railway before it was electrified, and apparently to anything whose proprietors were willing to pay fees for scientific analyses provided the result were reassuring to the consumer.

Ruling out these flourishing commercial speculations, what is left in the way of technical journals? There is Science Progress, which I take in piously because Sir Ronald Ross is as entertaining a heretic as Sir Almroth Wright. There is Biometrika, of which I can understand about one page out of every thousand. It is safe in the hands of Professor Karl Pearson, whose views of Sir Almroth's excommunication of statistics would be interesting. But publication in highly technical quarterlies is a contradiction in terms, because they do not reach the public; and if Sir Almroth resorts to them, I shall still have to act as his megaphone and sow what he calls the tares of my extremely frank remarks about the General Medical Council and general medical practice among the wheat of his bacteriological discoveries. As a matter of fact, Sir Almroth does not contribute to these quarterlies, and does perforce contribute to the trade papers. Result: in the multitude of Jenner-Pasteur celebrations by speeches and articles this year, his name, as far as I could follow them, was not mentioned once. This ignorance is deplorable; but can we blame it?

Why in the name of common sense does not Sir Almroth contribute to The Times Supplements, The Nation, The Spectator, The New Statesman, The Saturday Review, and the rest of the serious weeklies? Dean Inge gives himself no airs of condescension when he contributes the weekly sermon which makes all serious people buy The Evening Standard every Thursday. Mathematicians, philosophers, physicists, biologists, sociologists, economists, historians, poets communicate directly with the public through the general Press without reserve. Why is it that Sir Almroth Wright, because he is on the register of a profession practising an art (not a science) which is clotted with tribal superstitions, is forced to plead that the Press which is scientific enough for all the classical sciences is not scientific enough for medical science? Why is it that Dr Saleeby has actually had to remove his name from that register to secure his freedom to tell his fellow citizens that sunshine is better than poultices? Just because their trade union could and would strike them off the register for "advertizing" if they said a word to the laity that would discredit the obsolete methods and notions of the elderly Vehmgericht at whose mercy their livelihoods and good names lie.

Sir Almroth Wright cannot say these things: his loyalty to his professional colleagues forbids him. Fortunately for the public I can, and do. My sense of responsibility, not being limited to any profession, obliges me to do so; and I shall go ahead until the Government purges the General Medical Council of its trade unionist doctors and makes it representative of contemporary science and of the consumer, or patient-public, putting the doctors in their proper places as assessors only. Then it will at last be safe for Sir Almroth to explain his work to the public instead of having to depend on me. It is true that I seem to have done it faithfully enough; for nobody has ventured to demur to a single item in my statement of it; but Sir Almroth can handle a pen as well as I can; and there is a certain quality in first-hand description that no reporter can attain, as everyone could see for himself if Sir Almroth's monographs were within everyone's reach. And if in a transport of sentimentality he wished to express "reverence for the work of Pasteur, and gratitude for that of Jenner and Lister" (emotions to which Science is stonily insensible), how much better he would do it than the gentlemen who hurl selected statistics at me, and declare that the successes of the new Wright and Carrel methods in wound surgery have convinced them that the discarded and disastrous methods of fifty years ago must have been perfect and immortal!

But there is not much vogue for reverence and gratitude in science. Copernicus and Galileo were grossly ungrateful to Ptolemy; and Einstein's irreverence for Newton has lacerated many sensibilities; so poor old Jenner must take his turn, and Pasteur be reviled for a second-rate sciolist by young lions trained by Sir Almroth himself. Even I, who have conferred benefits on the world less questionable than inoculating three generations of infants with cow syphilis, have my infallibility challenged quite often, and most disrespectfully.

VIVISECTION

From *The Sunday Express*, 7 *August* 1927

WE have got it at last from my friend Mr H. G. Wells. The vivisector experiments because he wants to know. He is driven by a will for abstract lucidity. On the straight question whether it is right and permissible to cut even a single animal, or indeed to hurt any living creature at all for the sake of knowledge, he claims to be free to do it; and the anti-vivisectionist labors strenuously to prevent him. He wants knowledge because he wants knowledge: it is his characteristic good. He regards animals as illuminating inferiors, and can conceive no better or more profitable use for their lives than to serve the ends of mental growth.

That is how Mr Wells puts it. The advantage of having it put clearly is that we now see that the vivisector is distinguished from the ordinary run of limited scoundrels by being an infinite scoundrel. The common scoundrel who does not care what pain he (or she) inflicts as long as he can get money by it can be satiated. With public opinion and a stiff criminal code against him he can be brought to a point at which he does not consider another five-pound note worth the risk of garrotting or sandbagging or swindling anybody to get it. But the vivisector-scoundrel has no limit at all except that of his own physical capacity for committing atrocities and his own mental capacity for devising them. No matter how much he knows there is always, as Newton confessed, an infinitude of things still unknown, many of them still discoverable by experiment. When he has discovered what boiled baby tastes like, and what effect it has on the digestion, he has still to ascertain the gustatory and metabolic peculiarities of roast baby and fried baby, with, in each case, the exact age at which the baby should, to produce such and such results, be boiled, roast, fried, fricasseed, etc., etc. You remonstrate with him, especially if you are the mother of one or two of the babies. You say "What good is all this? You do not eat babies. Neither do I. England is not a cannibal island." He replies contemptuously, "Do you think, then, that I have any practical end in view? Not at all. I merely desire to learn something I do not know at present. Like Cleopatra I have immortal longings on me. When I know all these things about babies I shall know more than Wells, more than Einstein, more than Solomon. As Wells puts it, the babies will have served the ends of mental growth. I shall have eaten one more apple from the tree of knowledge of good and evil. I—" "You will have eaten your own damnation, as Paul said to the Corinthians" is as good a reply as another to such monstrous twaddle, if you condescend to reply to it at all. The proper place in organized human society for a scoundrel who is prepared to seek knowledge or anything else without conscience is the lethal chamber.

There was once a gentleman who wanted to know how many times he could chop a paw off a dog who was very fond of him before the dog would lose confidence in his adored master and discover that he was only a moral imbecile. He got a dog; gained its affection; and proceeded to chop off a paw whenever it came to him for a caress. As the dog had only four paws its confidence may have survived the four betrayals of it; but after all even this fact was an interesting addition to the sum of inhuman knowledge. Why was there no law to chop that experimenter's head off?

Obviously not because of any enthusiasm for "abstract lucidity" on the part of our excessively dog-loving public. Put that experimenter into any normal British crowd, or even into a rabbit coursing crowd, and tell what he did; and this experiment of yours (which he will probably deprecate strenuously in spite of his principles) will probably be the last in which he will figure as a principal. And all the doctors in the crowd, though "massively in support of vivisection," will take a hearty hand in securing that result, not in the least as a contribution to knowledge, but solely for the satisfaction of their feelings.

When the Anti-Vivisection agitation began, Queen Victoria wrote to Lister asking him to give the support of his great reputation as a surgeon to a public repudiation of the claim to the vivisectors to be exempt from humane law and duty and decency in their experiments. Lister failed lamentably to grasp the situation or rise to it. In his early days, when he was beginning to study what he then called inflammation (suppuration of surgical wounds), he had poured boiling water on the foot of a frog, and thereby discovered what happened to a frog's foot when boiling water was poured on it. When he realized that there were people, including Queen Victoria, who were actually proposing to treat a surgeon in respect of pouring boiling water on frogs exactly as a farmer's boy is treated, he lost his head, and opposed the attack on cruelty as an attack on science. From that time forth medical students were taught to advocate and defend vivisection as an essential tenet of scientific faith (precisely as Baptists are taught to advocate and defend total immersion) and to repudiate and abhor Anti-Vivisection as Roman Catholics are taught to repudiate and abhor Birth Control. Consequently the medical profession is, as Mr Wells puts it, massively in support of vivisection. They do not massively practise it; and when you mention any of its more revolting excesses to one of them he generally manifests a normal loathing of it; but as long as you avoid coming down to tin tacks he preserves his inculcated attitude of contempt for Anti-Vivisection as bad form.

Lister's reply to the Queen fell away into shallow petulances and *tu quoques* which have remained part of the vivisector's stock of debating points ever since. They are summed up by Mr Wells in a couple of sentences. "Far more pain, terror, and distress is inflicted on the first day of pheasant shooting every year, for no purpose at all except the satisfaction of the guns, upon the wounded and mutilated birds which escape, than is inflicted by all the scientific investigators in the world vivisecting for a year." Clearly this, though a terrific indictment of pheasant shooting, is no defence of vivisection. And again, "There is a residuum of admittedly painful cases; but it is an amount of suffering infinitesimal in comparison with the gross aggregate of pain inflicted day by day upon sentient creatures by mankind."

The advantage of this defence is that its scope is so magnificent that it fits every possible crime from pitch-and-toss to manslaughter. Its drawback is that it is not good enough to impose on the simplest village constable. Even Landru and the husband of the Brides in the Bath, though in desperate peril of the guillotine and gallows, had not the effrontery to say, "It is true that we made our livelihood by marrying women, and burning them in the stove or drowning them in the bath when we had spent their money; and we admit frankly and handsomely that the process may have involved some pain and disillusionment for them; but their sufferings (if any) were infinitesimal in comparison with the gross aggregate of pain inflicted day by day upon sentient creatures by mankind." Landru and Smith knew what Lister ought to have known: that scoundrels who have no better defence than that have no defence at all.

As a matter of fact we do not tolerate vivisection on these absurd grounds: we cling to it dishonorably because we are repeatedly assured that it has led to the discovery of cures for our diseases; and we are prepared to snatch at any dirty receipt for immortality rather than face death like ladies and gentlemen. Now I am the last man alive to deny that vivisection has led to discoveries. I could fill columns with an account of all the mare's nests it has discovered during my own lifetime. Much has been learnt during the same period from war, from earthquakes, from plague, pestilence, and famine; battle, murder, and sudden death. But if any class of persons devoted themselves to the artificial production of such calamities on the offchance of learning something from them I should advocate their painless but prompt extirpation. They would no doubt denounce me as an enemy of Science. They would be mistaken: I know the difference between science and scoundrelism: that is all.

Unfortunately people know so little about science, and are so saturated with tribal superstitions which connect supernatural powers with appalling cruelties and terrors, that they are easily persuaded that truth cannot be divined without horrible rites and sacrifices. When a vivisector says, in effect, "I have a dread secret to wrest from Nature: so you must license me to sacrifice a guinea pig," the Sambo in us assents; and the more hideously the guinea pig is sacrificed the more we feel the importance of the secret and the success of its extraction. And the magician can sell us any-thing as a cure next day, even without telling us the secret. And we feel that the Anti-Vivisector is trying to rob us of the elixir of life, and to keep our dear doctors' minds in darkness.

Anyone who knows the ABC of Science, which includes political science as well as physiological science, knows that this is all Hottentot superstition. He does not say that physiologists must not seek knowledge and make experiments. He says that they must not seek knowledge by criminal methods, just as they must not make money by criminal methods. He does not object to Galileo dropping cannon balls from the top of the leaning tower of Pisa; but he does object to his shoving off an American feather-weight and heavy-weight athlete simultaneously to see which will reach the ground first. He knows that there are fifty ways of ascertaining any fact; that only the two or three worst of them are dirty ways; that those who deliberately choose the dirty ways are not only morally but intellectually imbecile; that the "clean-handed man with the scalpel" is a humbug who has to buy his brains from the instrument maker; that it is ridiculous to expect that an experimenter who commits acts of diabolical cruelty for the sake of what he calls Science can be trusted to tell the truth about the results; that no vivisector ever accepts another vivi-sector's conclusions nor refrains from undertaking a fresh set of vivisections to upset them; that as any fool can vivisect and gain kudos by writing a paper describing what happened, the labora-tories are infested with kudos hunters who have nothing to tell that they could not have ascertained by asking a policeman except when it is something that they should not know (like the sensations of a murderer); and that as these vivisectors crowd humane research workers out of the schools and discredit them, they use up all the endowments and bequests available for their purposes, leaving nothing for serious physiological research. When one thinks of the Rockefeller funds, the Cancer Research funds, and the rest of the money that has gone down the vivisectors' sinks during the past quarter century, and compare its worse than negative results with the amazing series of discoveries made during that period by physicists doing sheer brain work within the strictest limits of honor, it is difficult to resist the conclusion (not that any normal person wants to resist it) that only imbeciles can be induced to practise vivisection, and glory in it. We give them huge sums to discover why we are dying of cancer at such an alarming rate, and how we can avoid it. They seize the money and buy innumerable mice with it to play with in their laboratories. After years of developing in themselves the mouse mind, they tell us that they have found out how to give a mouse cancer, and that they have found a microbe which is quite harmless, but which, when associated with other conditions which they cannot define, seems to be characteristic of cancer. Who would pull the whiskers of a single mouse for the sake of so pitiful a result? If these experimenters still think that playing with mice is better than using their brains nothing will persuade me that they have any brains to use.

As to the bearing of all this on general medical and surgical practice, it is hard to speak of it with good temper. Here is the surgeon under a strain of temptation which only the highest standards of honor and devotion can resist. We are helpless in his hands: we must deliver our bodies and those of our husbands and wives and children up to him to be mutilated on his simple assurance that if we refuse, the penalty is death. He can make sums of money ranging from tens to hundreds and even thousands of guineas in a few hours by imposing useless operations on us; assuring us that long and serious operations are trifling and brief; persist in treatments that prevent natural curing instead of hastening it; tempt us to call him in by promises of cures or intimidate us when we despair of his broken promises by threats of death: in short, exercise powers over us for claiming which kings have lost their heads and Popes and Inquisitors their dominion over half the world. Against the abuse of such powers we have no security except the surgeon's humanity and magnanimity; for it must not be forgotten that as we leave him to qualify himself at his own expense, and then to live on what he can extract from us in our illnesses, we have no claim whatever on his gratitude or even his forbearance. The more conscientious he is, socially and scientifically, the surer he is to have twenty years of genteel poverty before his circumstances become reasonably comfortable. When he comes through unspotted we do not even make him a Saint: we throw him a commonplace knighthood.

And this, if you please, is the man to whom the vivisectors and their champions would have us say: "Dont worry about humanity. Dont hamper yourself with a conscience. As a Man of Science you are beyond good and evil. No matter what you do, you can learn something from it; and the increase in your knowledge justifies your deed. Let yourself rip. Have a good time. Superstition is on your side. Ignorance is on your side. The dread of death is on your side. The Press is on your side. Parliament is on your side. Only a few notorious cranks are against you. And if you join the cranks you are a lost man, and will be prosecuted for malpractice by your colleagues, as Dr Hadwen was." Can anything be madder?

For my part I urge the doctors to flee from the wrath to come. Dr Hadwen's case was an unpleasant surprise for his prosecutors. To their amazement and subsequent confusion and ignominious defeat, the general public instantly subscribed money enough to enable Dr Hadwen to retain an overwhelming bar for his defence. The jury turned the vivisectors down and gave the famous anti-vivisector a triumph. Who were the subscribers who saw Dr Hadwen through so handsomely? Not the cranks who barely keep in existence a few little "anti" leagues with their scanty shillings. That ill-advised prosecution roused a section of the big public to active hostility to the doctors. It is not in the lump an instructed scientific hostility. It is largely the resentment of the rich for their enormous expenditure on treatments that do not cure, and operations that do not save; for our doctors and surgeons are forced to live like Robin Hood, doing endless work for the poor for nothing, and fleecing the rich unmercifully. And the poor do not enjoy the footing they are on with the doctors. Both rich and poor are disquieted by the sinister background of vivisection, not knowing that the doctors are mostly quite innocent of it, and have no time to study its dull and occasionally revolting oracles or to acquire its suggested clinical techniques on the rare occasions when it has anything to suggest. The resentment and mistrust are accumulating at a rate which the cancer scare is accelerating. They are partly absorbed by the resort to the unregistered practitioners of the new techniques and professors of modern vitalistic theories who now flourish all over the West End. But there are not enough of these to supersede the regulars; and their fees are too high to open the safety valve widely enough. We are heading for an explosion of popular wrath which will not discriminate between genuine science and obsolete trade unions like the General Medical Council with the dismal survivals of augury and witch-doctoring which it supports. It may for a time become impossible to obtain a penny of public or private money for honorable research; and the serious physicists and biologists may find themselves starving alongside the bogus physiologists and sadists.

I hope it is not too late to avert this catastrophe. I hope to learn some day that one of the best of our London hospitals is no longer dedicated to St Thomas, the apostle of the vivisectors. One can never forget the story of that amazing half-wit, with his friend and master, the risen Christ, standing before him saying, "Well, here I am," and Thomas replying, "Pardon me, but I cannot consider your existence scientifically established unless you will permit me to thrust my fingers through the holes in your hands and my fist into the hole in your side. It will hurt you, of course; but what is your pain compared to the impetus

I shall give to Christian science by absolutely proving the fact of your resurrection?" Possibly—though it is not recorded—downright Peter said, "Cant you open your eyes and look at Him, you fool, or shake His hand without hurting Him?"

At all events, this is what I should have said.

From The Nation, 10 May 1913

Mr Stephen Paget, secretary of the Research Defence Society, like most defenders of vivisection, is an exceedingly simple-minded man. He thinks that what the jury had to decide in the recent action taken by Miss Lind-af-Hageby was whether vivisection is a justifiable practice. He is quite mistaken. What the jury had to decide was whether the parties were abusing one another or slandering one another, and, if abusing, whether Dr Saleeby had said anything worse of Miss Lind-af-Hageby than Miss Lind-af-Hageby had said of Dr Saleeby. And as it was clear, in spite of all the pseudo-scientific dust that was raised, that poor Dr Saleeby had got as good as he gave and a good deal to spare into the bargain, the jury very properly gave the Doctor the verdict. My utter intellectual contempt for vivisection prejudices me in the plaintiff's favor as much as my natural abhorrence of cruelty; but had I been on the jury I should have agreed with the verdict, which, as it happened, I declared to be inevitable before the case was tried, on reading the pleas. The commonsense distinction in English legal practice between vulgar abuse and serious slander escaped Miss Lind-af-Hageby because, though a highly intelligent person, she is a foreigner. It is far too subtle to be understood by vivisectors, who are by definition ethical and legal imbeciles. The case leaves the vivisection controversy exactly where it found it. It reaffirms the unwritten law that if you blacken your opponent's eye you must not complain if he makes your nose bleed. It does not suggest that the assault was not deserved, but simply that what is sauce for the gander is also sauce for the goose.

I think there can be no doubt that Mr Paget is sincere even to indignation in his belief that every practice out of which any sort of good has come is thereby justified, and that its opponents are enemies of the human race. Thus Dynamitardry, having effected the Disestablishment of the Irish Church, is a humane practice which should be endowed by the State. The collision of the Victoria and the Camperdown having effected an invaluable demonstration of the dangers of ramming as a method of naval warfare, it is our duty to regard insanity as the first qualification of an admiral, and to maintain the system by which it is very generally secured at present. The Titanic disaster having led to the equipment of the Olympic with a double bottom, all good captains should run full steam ahead through ice fields. The cholera epidemics of the first half of the nineteenth century having produced our code of Public Health, let us use our tubes of microbes to produce an epidemic whenever the authorities shew any slackness in sanitary work. Coleridge wrote an immortal fragment of verse under the influence of opium; so let all our poets take opium freely, and let us continue to force opium on the Chinese lest they should have to live without poetry. The Crucifixion having resulted in the establishment of the Christian religion and European civilization, why not impress the gospel of the Research Defence Society on all nations by executing its secretary with horrible torments; for the blood of the martyrs is the seed of the Church. I can supply Mr Paget with pages and pages of such additions to his stock of arguments in favor of vivisection. He will find them quite convincing to vivisectors, criminals, imbeciles, and children under the age of three.

We all hope that Mr Paget will not allow his mind to be preyed on by "the dark side, the ugly side of Anti-Vivisection; its untruthfulness, its shameless uncharitableness, its cruelty." He should turn away resolutely to the bright side of Research: for example, to the inspiring recollection of Neisser inoculating children with gonorrhœa, and being received with great honor by Research Defenders for it.

"How otherwise could the thing have been proved?" cries Mr Paget, referring to a thing which, as it happens, has been most ignominiously disproved. How otherwise, indeed, by men without brains enough to devise better methods of proof? "How else am I to live?" cries the swindler, the pickpocket, the adulterator, the brothel-keeper. Hear Mr Paget: "Take the testing of digitalis. Of two samples on the market, one may be three times as strong as the other. Very well. The two samples are tested on the hearts of frogs. By this simple test their strength is ascertained." Quite so. You can even, when frogs are not convenient, test it on the hearts of your babies or your grandparents, and remark, complacently, "Very well. The two samples are tested on the hearts of infants (or octogenarians). By this simple test, their relative strength is ascertained." After all, the great thing is that you should know the strength of your samples of digitalis. What is a murder or two compared to the acquisition of knowledge? And it would be so troublesome to find out another test, especially if you are not very clever at devising tests.

For my part, I recommend the Report of the Royal Commission on Vivisection to Mr Paget as more relevant than the recent trial. The vivisectors had it all their own way on that Commission: it was so frankly packed in their interests that the anti-vivisectors refused to give evidence. If ever a report in favor of vivisection could have been obtained, that Commission would have made it. And all it dared to say was that it approved of experiments on animals, as if anybody ever disapproved of experiments on animals, or on men, or on vegetables, or minerals, or anything else. All persons of normal mental capacity who read the Report saw that the question at issue—the question whether the pursuit of scientific knowledge is exempt from the moral laws that restrict all human activity from degenerating into villainy—was never touched, and appreciated the pages of clumsy prevarication by which the Commissioners succeeded in persuading the vivisectors that they were finding a verdict in their favor: no very difficult task with an invincibly stupid audience. Would anybody but a vivisector be such a hopeless noodle as to try to conciliate public opinion by declaring that, though animals never suffer the slightest pain from vivisection and though the special provision made in the Vivisection Legalization and Protection Act for vivisecting without anæsthetics does not mean anything, yet dogs and horses should not be vivisected? The spectacle of comic stupidity imposing itself on a nation as impressive learning and profound science would be amusing if one could forget how frightfully cruel stupid people always are.

From The Nation, 24 *May* 1913

I am afraid I cannot deal with Mr Paget point by point as he asks me to. As he has not dealt with me in that way, or indeed at all except for three flat contradictions, as to which I can assure him he has been imposed on as usual, he will forgive me. Let me say comprehensively of his thirteen articles that, as far as they are relevant to the controversy (which is not saying much), they are—as far as I may say so without incivility, malice, or identification of Mr Paget personally with his academic opinions —erroneous, abominable, damnable, abhorrent, and excommunicable. That, I think, meets the case very clearly and fairly.

As to Neisser, I leave Mr Paget to tell the story himself in his own way, since he does not consider that I told it accurately. But what really interests us all is not in the least whether I have told three lies in sixteen words, as Mr Paget avers, but whether Mr Paget takes my sixteen words, true or false, as a calumny of Neisser or a compliment to him. From Mr Paget's point of view there can be no possible objection to inoculating children with gonorrhœa. Yet Mr Paget seems to object. Is Saul, then, also among the prophets?

I said that the official theory of Malta fever has been most ignominiously disproved. Mr Paget says I will not find, in all the world, one man of common sense who will agree with me. This is rather hard on the medical profession, considering that the man who exploded the theory by the trite expedient of going to Malta and making a few simple inquiries on the spot is described in Who's Who, in addition to the surgical qualifications held by Mr Paget and the diplomas of doctor and physician, as First

Prizeman in Physiology, Operative Surgery, Pathology, and Forensic Medicine, Clarke scholar, Suple prizeman, and double gold medallist in surgery and medicine. Mr Paget's contention that a man can be all this without having any common sense is interesting. I suppose there is no use in my offering to fill the large Queen's Hall with people who agree with me, or to suggest that the rapid subscription of £4000 to pay Miss Lind-af-Hageby's costs may indicate that the British nation is not quite so wholly prostrate at the feet of Mr Paget as he thinks; for Mr Paget would simply deny that the parties have any common sense. I am therefore content with his admission that professors of physiology and pathology may suffer from the same very common disability. Note, by the way, how Mr Paget, confronted with Miss Beatrice Kidd's clear and circumstantial account of how the Maltese mare's nest was converted into a British cocked hat, does not venture to challenge a single particular of it.

Now for Mr Paget's new statements. "The life and health of children come before the life and health of guinea-pigs and rabbits." But that is a very bald example of this sort of arithmetic. The life and health of some children come before the life and health of others. The speed of communication on which our modern civilization turns comes before the life and health of a few children playing carelessly in the street. The life and health of a starving child come before Mr Paget's need for seeing a musical comedy. If the Research Defence Society is right, the life and health of Mr Paget come before the life and health of Dr Hadwen. Therefore, let motor mail-vans drive at fifty miles an hour through village streets. Let every man whose child is hungry pick Mr Paget's pocket of half a guinea. Let the rickety child in the hospital be sacrificed to test a drug or a treatment or an operation before trying it on a sturdy little boy whose parents can afford to feed him and educate him properly. If vivisection is science, and science is to be the salvation of the world, and Dr Hadwen is discrediting vivisection, "it is expedient that one man should die for the people"; so let Mr Paget prescribe an overdose of his favorite drug, digitalis, for Dr Hadwen. This is what comes of tomfooling with logic. I advise Mr Paget to drop it. It is not his job.

Anyhow, it has nothing to do with the controversy. Mr Paget is like the old critics of the Puritan who objected to bearbaiting. They called him a sentimentalist. "You are mistaken," he said. "You think I object to the pain inflicted on the bear. This does not concern me at all. What I object to is the pleasure the bearbaiting gives to the spectators." I am not fussing about the rabbit's feelings, greatly as I dislike cruelty to rabbits. What I do object to is turning a decent medical student into a scoundrel by teaching him the arguments that are used by all scoundrels. I had rather let our children take their chance of surviving without the help of vivisection (after all, children used occasionally to survive their ailments before the Research Defence Society was founded) than destroy the souls of the men whose consciences are the living body of science. After this it would be an anticlimax to point out that a man who believes that the existence of the human race depends on the vivisection of rabbits and guinea-pigs is so obviously mad on this particular subject that it is hardly charitable to argue with him.

Says Mr Paget, "Animals, for certain experiments under anæsthesia, are tied down, for this reason, and for this reason alone, that they cannot lie on their backs, as we can, when they are under anæsthesia." I did not know that animals, when vivisected, are always placed on their backs. Is Mr Paget quite sure that they are? It must be inconvenient when the spinal cord has to be investigated. Besides, we humans do not have it all our own way. It is true that animals do not share with men and turtles the honors of the supine position. But then an animal can lie on its side more solidly than any man; and a turtle cannot lie on its side at all. Are men strapped down and gagged during operations which require them to lie on their sides? Are animals vivisected without straps and gags when the same position is convenient? Dr Saleeby almost implied that all operations are conducted on tables similar to the one exhibited in the antivivisection shop in Bond Street. I am personally concerned in this, because I have been twice operated on; and I was not provided with a table or with gags or straps; and if this was an improper and unusual omission, I must ask Sir Anthony Bowlby what he meant by depriving me of my rights. The whole thing is very mysterious. And yet there can be no question as to what Mr Paget means. "Animals are tied down for this reason, and for this reason alone, that they cannot lie on their backs as we can when we are under anæsthesia." Now that I think of it, I cannot lie on my back when I am under anæsthesia. I have to lie just as they put me.

"Tuberculin, in suitable cases, gives good results." Certainly it does. There was a quite celebrated case of a woman who had a tuberculous ulcer on her arm. On treatment with Koch's tuberculin, the arm promptly rotted off; and the woman, who was poor, was enabled to make a very welcome addition to her little income by exhibiting herself at the hospitals as an object-lesson. This was unquestionably a good result; and yet it led to the disuse of tuberculin until Sir Almroth Wright, instead of inoculating rabbits and guinea-pigs on the ground that their lives are less important than those of children, unexpectedly mixed tuberculin with a little of his own brains, and immediately made important discoveries which might just as easily have been made by the vivisectors if they had had any time to spare for really scientific work from their silly ancient Roman superstitions of groping in the entrails of animals for magical revelations.

"The efficacy of the protective treatment against typhoid fever has been proved," etc., etc. Of course it has—to the satisfaction of vivisectors. You can prove anything to the satisfaction of vivisectors, provided it is something improbable and disgusting. The efficacy of the treatment was proved to their satisfaction before the South African War broke out. That was why our troops were inoculated on the way out, with the result that for several months they were ignominiously vanquished by the Boers. And they died of typhoid in heaps after all.

"The suggestion that the Indian Government has killed six and a half millions of people with a serum treatment is, to say the least of it, false." Well, come! How does Mr Paget know any more than I know? I did not make the statement; but I know that plague, which used to ravage London, has been extirpated without any serum treatment by common sanitation. And in the face of that fact, I am prepared to say that if any Government is credulous enough to trust to serums instead of to sanitation as a safeguard against plague, a statement that the serums (or, rather, the people who advocate them and deny that ignorance, poverty, and dirt have anything to do with disease) are responsible for the deaths by plague, is much less sporting than the one I shall now quote from Mr Paget's letter.

"No operation, more than the lancing of a vein just under the skin, is allowed to be done on any animal in this country unless the animal, throughout the whole of the operation, is under some anæsthetic strong enough to prevent it from feeling pain." I am glad Mr Paget has committed himself to this statement, because it confirms what I suspected: that he knows practically nothing about vivisection, and has never read the Act of Parliament by which vivisection was made legal when the vivisectors were threatened with prosecution for cruelty to animals. Anyone referring to the Act will find that in order to perform vivisection without anæsthetics, all that is necessary is to get two vivisectors to certify that the object of the operation would be defeated by the use of an anæsthetic. The Act is not difficult or obscure on this point: there is special provision and a special certificate; and every proposal to repeal this special provision is fiercely opposed by the vivisectors. They know, of course, that some of the most interesting experiments, those devised to investigate the physiology of emotion and of pain, would be illegal without this deliberate legalization of torture.

Mr Paget, after telling us that the great majority of experiments on animals are inoculations, adds that "the great majority of these inoculations may truly be said to be painless." To which I may add that the great majority of cases of syphilis are inoculated; and that the inoculation is not only painless, but highly pleasurable. Nothing more need be said, I presume, to reconcile

Mr Paget to the practices and social conditions which are accountable for the prevalence of syphilis, and to persuade him that it causes no suffering to its victims.

As to Mr Paget's peroration in the style of the temperance orators of bygone years, I will quote only the opening: "If the Anti-Vivisection Societies, some thirty years ago, had been able to stop all experiments on animals, they would be guilty, by this time, of all the pain, disease, and deaths which have been averted from mankind and the higher animals during these years, by the methods discovered through experiments on animals." Let me tell Mr Paget for his comfort that they would in that case have very little, if anything, on their consciences; and they would be free of the guilt of banishing conscience from research. Those of us who have had cherished friends and relatives attacked by the diseases which the vivisectors claim to be able to cure, know best what value we have had for the guineas their announcements have drawn from our pockets into theirs. Those who are more fortunate have only to look at the Registrar-General's returns to see the rate at which we are still dying of the cures. If the men who have been stultifying themselves over vivisections for the last thirty years had been working in the paths of honor and mercy, and using their brains instead of carving living animals and calling it "Research," who shall say what they might not have discovered?

To which Mr Paget will reply, as usual, with the old cry of the proprietary medicine vendor: "Another leg saved!" and will consider it cheap at the cost of another soul damned. And to think that the leg is generally not saved after all, but rots off, and is exhibited in hospitals for money!

From *The Nation*, 3 *May* 1919

Sir Edward Schafer's letter in your issue of the 17th is so reassuring that I, for one, can see no reason why Sir John Rose Bradford should not confirm his kidney experiment by at once repeating it on a human subject. I have now the authority of Sir Edward Schafer for declaring that the subject "would suffer no

pain whatever during, or as the immediate result of, the operation," and that "the healing of the operation wound would also
be unattended with pain." When Sir Edward says that "no other
animal could have been used by Sir John Rose Bradford in his
investigation," he clearly means no other animal except Man, on
whom alone the experiment can be really conclusive. Sir Edward
is no doubt aware that several other animals possess kidneys;
and he will be the first to admit that if a cat's kidneys can prove
nothing about a dog's, a dog's can prove nothing about a man's:
hence we may infer that until the experiment is performed on a
man it cannot be held to be finally convincing.

The only question that remains is who the man shall be. My
first natural impulse is to offer myself; for if I can spare a wedge
of my kidney without suffering any pain, and thereby "alleviate
human suffering and advance medical knowledge," how can I
be so selfish as to hesitate because of an indirect possibility of "a
certain amount of chronic discomfort"? But I feel that if anything went wrong in my case it might be attributed to foul play
on my own part; for I am notoriously not merely an ordinary
humanitarian anti-vivisectionist, but one so arrogantly contemptuous of the intellectual imbecility and gross scientific ignorance of the vivisectionists that I am quite sure my bias would
affect my kidneys and hopelessly vitiate the experiment.

There is another reason why the subject must be a convinced
vivisectionist. As he will have to sacrifice a wedge of his kidney
on the strength of Sir Edward Schafer's assurances, he must have
an absolute faith in those assurances. This faith cannot be found
in any anti-vivisectionist. The anti-vivisectionist sees too plainly
that a man who argues that science is above or below the moral
law against cruelty will also argue that it is above or below the
moral law against lying, and that when science is at stake in a
public controversy he will no more dare to tell us the truth about
a dog than Viscount French, when the *moral* of our troops at Le
Cateau was at stake, dared to tell us the truth about General
Smith-Dorrien. The anti-vivisectionist will also note Sir Edward
Schafer's claim that he has at his back "the whole medical pro-

fession." As everybody knows that the anti-vivisectionist movement is at present led by a doctor with a string of letters after his
name, and a list of gold medals and prizes for physiology, operative surgery, pathology, medicine, and so forth, which should
surely reduce even Sir Edward Schafer to silent awe, it is impossible to repress a misgiving that Sir Edward's conviction that
his own brain is completely insensitive and might be cut about
"without the least sign of pain being produced" may be a symptom of some lesion in that organ which has already produced
the delusion about the whole medical profession being at his
back.

The conclusion is irresistible. There is only one man who can
submit to the operation with complete faith in Sir Edward
Schafer's assurances, and complete assumption of his responsibilities; and that is Sir Edward Schafer himself. I call upon him
to sacrifice a wedge of his kidney as "necessary to the progress
of medical knowledge [hitherto assumed by medical men to be
already complete] and the alleviation of human suffering." He
will not, I feel sure, allow himself to be outdone by a dog.

When he has thus placed himself in a position to apply his
gloriously gained knowledge in practice, he will find thousands
of cases of kidney disease waiting for him to treat; and it will be
interesting to us all to see whether he will be able to do anything
more or anything else than Christison could have done for them
a century ago.

VEGETARIANISM

From The Daily Chronicle, 1 *March* 1918

It is my patriotic boast that from the day the war began until
the present hour, I have abstained rigidly from consuming flesh,
fish, fowl, alcohol, and tobacco. Those envious detractors whose
yelp follows every utterance of mine like an obscene echo have
objected that as I had abstained equally for the thirty-three years
preceding the war, I deserve no credit for my conduct. This is
obvious nonsense: they might as well say that as I did not pick

pockets in the year 1900, the fact that I did not do so in August 1914 does not make me to that extent an honest man. But even they must admit that it entitles me to speak with some authority on the subject of meatless days.

Let me first reassure the aforesaid detractors on one point. They may fear that if they are compelled to abstain from meat they may all become Bernard Shaws: the most terrible fate, if their professions are to be believed, that could overtake them. Let them dismiss all anxiety on this score. There are millions of vegetarians in the world, but only one Bernard Shaw. A century ago there were millions of vegetarians and only one Shelley. Twenty-six centuries ago there were millions of them and only one Pythagoras. You do not attain eminence quite so cheaply as by eating macaroni instead of mutton chops. The country is safe as far as the danger of a population of Bernard Shaws is concerned. Otherwise I should perhaps think twice before destroying my own monopoly.

The second apprehension is more general, though less excusable. There is so much misinformation spread nowadays under cover of education, that many carefully taught people—doctors for example—think they must starve unless they eat meat. They probably attribute my own survival to a regrettable miracle. They are so ignorant of how the world lives that they do not know that the British people are now trading on the vitality they have inherited from generations of men and women who did not eat meat, for the conclusive reason that they could not afford it, and lived on bread and cheese, or potatoes and buttermilk, with an occasional scrap of bacon by way of relish. Cæsar's soldiers had no bully beef. The meat eaters have not conquered the world, nor peopled it: they have expiated their cannibalism in the mud baths of Kissingen and Mont Dore, and are now beleaguered in Harrogate and Bath.

It is a curious fact that if you meddle with meat at all, you cannot eat too little and can hardly eat too much. From the Tartar and the Gaucho we learn that 9 lb. of horseflesh a day is a healthy diet for an equestrian. From the Turkish porter and

the Chilian miner we learn that the champion weight lifters of
the world eat no meat at all. But this generalization needs a very
important qualification. An underfed man is not a man who gets
no meat, or gets nothing but meat. He is one who does not get
enough to eat, no matter what he eats. Consequently the civilian
who is ignorant enough to believe that his nourishment depends
on meat is now in a horrible dilemma. He sees that the soldier is
given a much larger meat ration than the civilian. He infers that
either the soldier is being overfed or the civilian starved. And
as the soldier shews no signs of overfeeding, and is even strong
in his testimony that he could often do with a little more, the
civilian sees death from inanition staring him in the face, and in-
clines towards an early and dishonorable peace.

Now I am by no means sure that his apprehensions may not
presently be justified. Although I can say nothing about the
text-book estimates of how much food we need except that they
are all wrong, I affirm with confidence that the civilian who
attempts to live on his meat ration will presently find himself an
invalid, whilst the more sensible person who boldly gives up
meat altogether, and makes it his business to get his fill of un-
rationed or less stinted food may be none the worse and possibly
a good deal better. Only, it must be understood that this cannot
be done by eating cabbage instead of beef. A vegetarian is not a
person who lives on vegetables, any more than a Catholic is a
person who lives on cats. Of what are commonly and usefully
distinguished as "greens" the meatless man needs no more than
the human carnivor. If you try to live on Brussels sprouts and
rice pudding, you will be as poor a specimen as the woman who
tries to live on rashers and tea. If you buy a vegetarian cookery
book, do not concentrate on the tomato and breadcrumb dish
because it happens to be easy to make. Above all, do not go to
the other extreme, and having ascertained that dates and lentils
are more nutritious than beefsteaks, attempt to swallow them on
a large scale. If you do, your sensations will convince you that
death from starvation is pleasanter than death from overfeeding.
The sedentary civilian who can eat more than two dates without

losing all desire ever to eat again, or can ingest a mass of brown lentils, with its usual attendant ration of pebbles and clay, without losing even his desire to live, must be another Daniel Lambert.

Remember, therefore, that almost all meatless beginners eat too much under the erroneous and very dangerous impression that they have to make up in quantity for an imaginary loss in quality. Novices in vegetarianism have been known to starve themselves by eating too much. These gluttons, when reduced to a mutton chop and a potato, suddenly get well, and spend the rest of their lives in describing how they once tried vegetarianism and were nearly killed by it. Men, to win bets, have been known to eat three legs of mutton, a turkey, six pounds of sausages, and 100 oysters at a sitting, with beer *ad lib*. The man who will dispose of fifty dates and a Dutch cheese has yet to be discovered. The vegetarian books are loud in their praise of cheese, oatmeal, wheatmeal, wholemeal, hominy, lentils, haricots, pease pudding, rice, and so forth. The enthusiastic vegetarian will go into the woods; strip from the bole of a tree a loathsome blanket of livid fungus, which proclaims itself to every sense as rank poison; and broil and eat it with beaming relish and flourish on it; but what I say is, be careful. Scientifically nutritious meals are, in the quantities prescribed by "metabolists" who have never eaten them, deadly. The real secret of meat is that it is two-thirds water, and not very clean water at that. If instead of serving you a steak they give you the water in a tumbler and the nitrogen on a plate, you would not only refuse them on their palatable merits, but absolutely refuse to believe them a sufficient meal for an adult. Fortunately Lord Rhondda and Mr Clynes do not know this; so they dare not ration cereals and pulses and piths and the rest as severely as they ration meat. On the other hand, they allow too little meat. It will, therefore, pay you to eschew the meat ration. By abstaining from it you can combine an air of patriotic self-sacrifice with as much repletion as is good for you. No cheaper and pleasanter way of getting on with the war can be suggested.

One general caution is important. If you are accustomed to

eat or drink any particular substance, whether it be meat, potatoes, beef, brandy, or morphia, you will find, when you first discontinue it, that you will miss it, and that you will mistake the sensation of unfulfilment for hunger. You must therefore ration yourself and live by faith until you get used to the new dietary; for if you go on eating until you feel you have had enough you will burst. A second caution is that you be not misled by tradition as regards modern foods. Soup once consisted of boiled bones. Except for the unpleasant flavor, it might as well have consisted of boiled cricket bats. You can still get bone infusion served in Ireland for soup; and very horrible it is. But thick soups have long since ceased to depend on stewed skeleton for their quality. Nobody who is not a superstitious fool ever puts a bone into thick soup nowadays. Margarine is another example. It began as a contemptible imposture produced by torturing animal fat into an imitation of butter. It still has the evil reputation it gained in those days. But today it is made from nuts and vegetable oils; and it is probable that after the war butter will be sold as inferior margarine, and that no gentleman will consent to be seen eating it. Thus do people become vegetarians without knowing it.

I will not pretend that there may not be grave drawbacks. Abstention from the practice of feeding on dead bodies seems to produce a peculiar ferocity, which is perhaps why all the great conquerors of antiquity worked with meatless soldiers. And it is the worst form of ferocity: that is, virtuous indignation. Compare, for example, Byron with Shelley! Byron made fun of George III and Southey; but he did not want to kill them. Shelley thought killing too good for Eldon and Castlereagh, and would probably have polished off every man in the kingdom above the age of sixty if he had had the power. It is all very well for weakly amiable characters like my own to be stoked up to a passable manliness by these terribly vital foods; but people with a normal quantity of sand in them will be made pugnacious, and the naturally pugnacious intensified into positive Huns, when the water is taken out of their diet. Think of the fierce energy concentrated in an acorn! You bury it in the ground, and it explodes into a giant oak. Bury a sheep, and nothing happens but decay. If the Government, instead of leaving the English people to bury sheep in their insides, compels them to bury beans, I will not answer for the consequences. The vegetarian of today may be the Bolshevik of tomorrow. The bull is a vegetarian; and if the John Bull takes to the same diet, it may tax all the resources of the Government to put a ring through his nose.

THE KING AND THE DOCTORS

An Improbable Fiction

From Time and Tide, 22 February 1929

ONCE upon a time, in the country of the Half Mad, which was cut off from the western end of Europe in prehistoric times to prevent the inhabitants from injuring any but themselves, the King fell ill. As he had always been well spoken of, and had established very kindly relations with his subjects, his illness caused a great increase of their affection for him and for his family. All the married women saw in the Queen a wife anxious about her husband, with a sick-bed to provide for. All the men saw in the King a fellow-man suffering as they themselves had suffered or might at any moment have to suffer. For sickness is a Great Leveller, and consequently a great breeder of sympathy, unlike that Impostor Death, who gives a pompous eminence to even the humblest. And thus, with sympathy added to loyalty, the nation was in such a state of concern about the King as had never before arisen within living memory. Naturally, the case being one of dangerous illness, it was to the doctors that the nation turned for help and reassurance.

Now in the country of the Half Mad the doctors had long before this taken the place of the medieval Church. There was a law that when a man was ill he must on pain of punishment send for his parish priest; but this law had been so long disregarded that only a few specialists in Church history knew of its existence. Its place had been taken by a law that when there was sickness in the house the doctor must be sent for, and that if the doctor said that any part of a sick child's body must be cut out its parents must have that done at once whether they approved or not, or else be haled before a magistrate and heavily fined, or, should the child have died, committed for trial for having killed it.

To such powers as this were added extraordinary privileges. For instance, doctors were licensed to commit murder with impunity, provided they did it either by administering poison or by using knives of a particular shape in such a manner that the victim did not die until he or she had been put to bed. Not only was no inquest held and no indictment brought against the doctor, but he was actually paid for his labor, and sometimes invited to the funeral.

As the Half Mad were so jealous of their liberties that a priest could not even order a father to have his child baptized, it will be seen that this strange people, though half sane on the subject of priests, were wholly mad on the subject of doctors, willingly granting them powers which they had denied to their Kings at the cost of revolution and civil war.

Now the doctors, being no worse than other people, did their best to prove worthy of their extraordinary trust by using it for the relief of the sick, and making it impossible for anyone to become a doctor except by years of study to qualify him for his duties. But as the Half Mad, whilst bowing down with the deepest reverence to the condition of omniscience which they supposed these studies to confer, would not pay a doctor anything until they were actually ill and threatened with death, the doctors were mostly poor, and would have starved altogether if the nation had been in a reasonably healthy condition. Thus their duty to themselves and their wives and children was to keep their patients ill as long and as often as possible; to persuade them that they were dangerously ill when there was nothing the matter with them that their own recuperative powers could not cure; and even to deprive them of as many of their limbs and organs as they could without killing the goose that laid the golden eggs. On the other hand, their duty to their patients and their country was to do exactly the contrary, and strive to their utmost to produce a state of things in which doctors would starve.

Now in the kingdom of the Half Mad, people always ended by believing what they wanted to believe, no matter how much it might be contradicted by facts; and so it had come about that the doctors, though they were as kindly and honorable as could reasonably be expected, and sometimes very clever, had built up an elaborately reasoned and ingenious series of mechanical explanations of all the diseases, giving them impressive names, and setting forth the treatments and operations and medicines proper to them, until at last they could do almost anything with a patient except cure him or even allow him a fair chance of curing himself. Thus the calling of a doctor to the sick-bed was rather a pious ceremony enforced by law than a proceeding from which any relief to the patient could be expected. But the doctors were wonderfully accurate in predicting the time at which the patient would die in their hands; and this was very necessary for the settlement of the affairs of patients who had any affairs to settle.

With a Faith (for such it was) in this condition, naturally there were Heresies in all directions. New methods of treating disease were discovered; but the doctors took so long to learn the old ones that they had no time for the new ones. Even the surgeons had to do without any manual training, and picked up their art as the father of a family picks up the art of carving a turkey. So, instead of adopting the new methods, they excommunicated the new practitioners and all their accomplices. Only, as the heretics either cured their patients or at least did not kill them by obsolete and barbarous treatments, the doctors, when they were ill themselves, often resorted to the heretics for treatment.

This was the state of things when the King fell ill. He had twelve doctors to attend him; and when there was no sign of his being cured, his people became anxious, and said, "A single doctor is generally sufficient to kill one of us, so how can the King survive twelve doctors?"

Then the King's son, who was at the other side of the world among the black savages (for he was very tired of the white ones), came flying, sailing, and express-training at an amazing speed back to his father, and spoke with the King's chief physician, who was so delightful a person that his patients were often cured by his mere appearance in the bedroom. The Prince knew that his father's case must be most serious since it resisted the presence of this great healer and the influence of the King's faith in him. And the Prince said to him: "Doc, the King my father does not seem to be getting any better. Is it not possible to get a move on?"

"In what direction, sir?" replied the chief physician.

"In the direction of getting him up and about," said the Prince.

"Everything is being done that can properly be done," said the physician. "If your Royal Highness has not confidence in our knowledge and devotion—"

"Stow that," said the Prince. "Your devotion is all right; but your knowledge is bunk."

"Bunk!" exclaimed the chief physician, highly scandalized.

"Well, perhaps not all of it," said the Prince, feeling that he had gone a little too far; "but I cannot help knowing what everyone knows, and that is that according to your own best men nine-tenths of your official notions are fit only for the dustbin. I have a heap of letters, books, pamphlets, and magazines here which have been sent me; and they have disturbed me very much."

"I have not read these documents," said the physician. "If your Royal Highness can suggest any measure we have omitted, my opinion is at your service."

"Drugs, now?" said the Prince. "Drugs are bunk, are they not?"

"Undoubtedly, from a purely secular point of view, drugs are bunk," said the physician; "but in the case of a royal patient I could not possibly take the responsibility of withholding from His Majesty the official remedies from our *materia medica*."

"But," said the Prince, "there is a way of giving drugs in infinitesimal quantities to which all the latest discoveries and scientific speculations point as the right way."

"Infinitesimals," replied the physician, "are used only by homeopaths: that is, by empirics who, being ignorant of the nature of disease, merely treat its symptoms. If you bring a Chinese patient to a homeopath, he will treat him for yellow fever."

"Do you really know the nature of disease any more than a homeopath does?" said the Prince.

"Certainly," said the physician. "I have passed an examination in pathology, and written books about it. What a strange question!"

"What is the nature of my father's complaint?" said the Prince.

"It is what we call pleurisy," said the physician.

"I know that," said the Prince. "I know its name; and I know its symptoms. What is its nature?"

"If I knew that," said the physician, "perhaps I could cure it."

"Then pathology is bunk," said the Prince, who had picked up this expression from a famous motor-car manufacturer, who had applied it to History. "Let us call in a homeopath."

"Unfortunately," said the physician, "the only one in London whose reputation and success would satisfy public opinion has not been admitted to our communion; and if I discussed the case with him I should be excommunicated."

"Well," said the Prince, "they say a lot of trouble comes from spinal displacements. What about my father's spine?"

"It looks all right," said the physician.

"But there are chaps who are trained to feel whether it is all right or not," said the Prince. "There is a machine that will register on a galvanometer displacements that nobody can feel."

"I never heard of it," said the physician. "I can assure you that these people who feel spines are almost all ignorant Americans who have spent two years in mere manual training instead of in the study of pathology."

"All the same," said the Prince, "they bring off cures occasionally; so why not call one in?"

"I should be excommunicated if I were seen speaking to one," said the physician.

"Why not do it yourself?" said the Prince. "You are a surgeon."

"I have not had the two years' training," said the physician:

"it is not part of our official surgery."

"Official surgery is a wash-out," said the Prince. "What about testing my father's blood for radiations? That can be done by a rheostat, cant it? And there is some method of neutralizing the rays that sometimes cures, isnt there?"

"But it was discovered by an American," said the physician.

"I am prepared to overlook that if my father's health can be restored by his method," said the Prince.

"Impossible," said the physician. "He was not only an American, but a Jew."

"I understand he was a proper doctor all the same," persisted the Prince.

"No doubt," said the physician; "but the treatment would involve attaching His Majesty to the electric light switch; and public opinion would never tolerate that."

"Public opinion be blowed!" said the Prince. "Do you suppose I am going to let my father lose a chance because people are fools? Besides, we can use a private battery."

"It may not be," said the physician. "This discovery reached us only about a dozen years ago, and is not yet recognized by our Vatican. I dare not take the responsibility of experimenting on the King with a treatment that has not been proved by at least fifty years' experience."

"Proved to do what?" said the Prince. "To cure the disease?"

"To have stood the test of being taught in our medical schools as the logical and appropriate treatment," said the physician.

"Do the patients recover under your logical and appropriate treatments?" said the Prince.

"Sometimes," said the physician. "Quite frequently."

"They might do that if they had no treatment at all," said the Prince.

"That is true," said the physician. "The recuperative power of the human organism is marvellous. Quacks take advantage of that, I am sorry to say."

"I am not satisfied about all this," said the Prince. "It seems to me that my father, just because he is a king, is cut off from the benefit of all the new discoveries and treatments that are available for the meanest of his subjects."

"I exhort your Royal Highness to be patient," said the physician. "Your royal father is in the hands of God."

"You mean that we should call in a Christian Science practitioner?" said the Prince.

"Most certainly not," said the physician. "I and my colleagues would be obliged to withdraw at once if such a person were admitted to the palace."

"Another wash-out," said the Prince.

"Not at all," said the physician. "We should not object to a visit from His Majesty's domestic chaplain; though of course we could not allow him to treat the case; and anything in the nature of a consultation would be out of the question."

"In short," said the Prince, "my poor father is in the hands of your confounded Vatican. However, I suppose we must make the best of it. I should like to call in your Pope for a consultation."

"We should have to tell him what to say beforehand," said the physician. "You see, he was qualified more than half a century ago, and may not be quite up to date."

"But I have looked him up in Who's Who," said the Prince; "and he has ninety distinctions and qualifications, entitling him to a dozen medical letters after his name. I attach great importance to a lot of letters because I have nothing else to go by."

"As I myself have only six, you naturally consider his opinion twice as valuable as mine," said the physician.

"Well, if the letters dont mean that, they dont mean anything," said the Prince.

"Precisely," said the physician.

"Then your Pope is another wash-out," said the Prince. "Are there any laymen on your Vatican council to represent my father and all the other patients?"

"A notorious enemy of our profession has succeeded, after years of agitation, in having one layman appointed," said the physician.

"Well, dont you agree with that?" said the Prince.

"Officially, no," said the physician.

"But unofficially—as between man and man?" pleaded the Prince.

"Since your Royal Highness is good enough to admit me to that footing," said the physician, "I am bound to say, as between man and man, that the exclusion of laymen from a body whose business it is to safeguard the general interests of the laity against the sectional interests of the medical profession is only one out of the many instances of the almost incredible incapacity of the Half Mad for taking care of themselves. In respect of the art of life, our people must be set aside as unqualified practitioners."

"This is a world of bunk," said the Prince; "and the boasted capacity of my father's subjects for self-government is the biggest bunk of the lot. But my father's life is in danger. I appeal to you to throw over your silly Vatican and be a friend to us in our need. If they give you the sack you shall have a dukedom and a pension of a hundred thousand a year. Tell me what is the most up-to-date scientific treatment for my father?"

"I have already ordered it," said the physician. "And you will be glad to hear that it will involve no conflict on my part with my colleagues."

"Splendid!" said the Prince. "I will never forget this proof of your sympathy and devotion. What is the treatment?"

"The seaside," said the physician.

"The seaside!" cried the Prince. "You call that the latest! Why, it is what my great-grandmother would have recommended."

"Yes," said the physician, "but not for the true scientific reason. She thought that the benefit arose from change of air."

"Then what does it arise from?" said the Prince.

"That," said the physician, "is a professional secret which I can impart to you only under a solemn pledge that it shall go no further."

"I give you my word of honor," said the Prince. "What will the seaside really do to cure my father?"

The physician stooped to the Prince's ear, and whispered: "It will get him away from the doctors."

Shortly afterwards, the King recovered.

CRUDE CRIMINOLOGY

CRUDE CRIMINOLOGY

IMPRISONMENT

Foreword

WHEN I was a boy in my teens in Dublin I was asked by an acquaintance of mine who was clerk to a Crown Solicitor, and had business in prisons, whether I would like to go through Mountjoy Prison, much as he might have asked me whether I would like to go through the Mint, or the cellars at the docks. I accepted the invitation with my head full of dungeons and chains and straw pallets and stage gaolers: in short, of the last acts of Il Trovatore and Gounod's Faust, and of the Tower of London in Richard III. I expected the warders to look like murderers, and the murderers like heroes. At least I suppose I did, because what struck me most was that the place was as bright and clean as whitewash and scrubbing and polish could make it, with all the warders looking thoroughly respectable, and all the prisoners ruffianly and degenerate, except one tall delicate figure tramping round in the exercise ring, a Lifer by the color of his cap, who had chopped up his family with a hatchet, and been recommended to mercy on account of his youth. I thought, and still think, imprisonment for life a curious sort of mercy. My main impression of the others, and the one that has stuck longest and hardest, was that as it was evidently impossible to reform such men, it was useless to torture them, and dangerous to release them.

I have never been imprisoned myself; but in my first years as a public speaker I had to volunteer for prison martyrdom in two Free Speech conflicts with the police. As my luck would have it, on the first occasion the police capitulated on the eve of the day on which I had undertaken to address a prohibited meeting and refuse to pay a fine; and on the second a rival political organization put up a rival martyr, and, on a division, carried his election over my head, to my great relief. These incidents are not very impressive now; but the fact that my acquaintance with the subject of the following essay began with the sight of an actual prison, and that twice afterwards I was for a week or so firmly convinced that I was about to spend at least a fortnight and possibly a month in the cells, gave me an interest in the subject less perfunctory than that of the ordinary citizen to whom prison is only a reference in the police news, denoting simply a place where dishonest and violent people are very properly locked up.

This comfortable ignorance, by the way, is quite commonly shared by judges. A Lord Chief Justice of England, grieved at hearing from a lady of social importance that her son had been sent to prison as a Conscientious Objector, told her that he hoped she would get to see him often, and keep up his spirits with frequent letters, and send him in nice things to eat. He was amazed to learn from her that he might just as well have suggested a motor ride every afternoon and a visit to the opera in the evening. He had been sentencing people all through his judicial career to terms of imprisonment, some of them for life, without knowing that it meant anything more than being confined to the house and wearing a dress with broad arrows all over it. No doubt he thought, quite rightly, that such confinement was bad enough for anybody, however wicked.

I had no such illusions about prison life. My political activities often brought me into contact with men of high character and ability who had been victims of modern forms of persecution under the very elastic headings of treason, sedition, obstruction, blasphemy, offences against press laws, and so forth. I knew that Karl Marx had declared that British prisons were the cruellest in the world; and I thought it quite probable that he was right. I knew Prince Peter Kropotkin, who, after personal experience of the most villainous convict prisons in Siberia and the best model prison in France, said that they were both so bad that the difference was not worth talking about. What with European "politicals" and amnestied Irish Fenians, those who, like myself, were in the way of meeting such people could hardly feel easy in their consciences about the established methods of handling criminals.

Also I was in occasional touch with certain efforts made by the now extinct Humanitarian League, and by a little Society called the Police and Public Vigilance Society, to call attention to the grievances of prisoners. The League dealt with punishments: the Society, which was really an agitation conducted by one devoted man with very slender means, the late James Timewell, tried to obtain redress for people who alleged that they had been the victims of petty frame-ups by the police. But the witnesses on whose testimony these two bodies had to proceed were mostly either helpless creatures who could not tell the truth or scoundrels who would not tell it. The helpless creatures told you what they wanted to believe themselves: the scoundrels told you what they wanted you to believe.

Anyone who has tried to find out what war is like from our demobilized soldiers will understand. Their consciousness is limited and utterly uncritical; their memory is inaccurate and confused; their judgment is perverted by personal dislikes and vanities; and as to reflection, reason, self-criticism, and the rest of the intellectual counterchecks, they have no more of them than a mouse has of mathematics. If this is the case with normal men like soldiers, even less is to be expected from subnormal men like criminals. Neither the Humanitarian League nor Mr Timewell could rouse general public compunction with such testimony, or attract special subscriptions enough to enable them to conduct a serious investigation. And John Galsworthy had not then arisen to smite our consciences with such plays as The Silver Box and Justice.

This situation was changed by the agitation for Votes for Women and the subsequent war of 1914–18, both of which threw into prison an unprecedented number of educated, critical, public-spirited, conscientious men and women who under ordinary circumstances would have learnt no more about prisons than larks learn about coal mines. They came out of prison unembittered by their personal sufferings: their grievance was the public grievance of the whole prison system and its intense irreligiousness. In prison they had been capable of observing critically what they saw; and out of prison they were able to describe it. The official whitewash of the Prison Commissioners could not impose on them. They and their friends had money enough to take an office and engage a secretarial staff, besides supplying some voluntary educated labor. They formed a committee with Lord Olivier as chairman, which investigated the condition of English prisons and incidentally read some interesting reports of American ones. Eventually they issued their report as a volume entitled English Prisons Today, edited by Stephen Hobhouse and Fenner Brockway, who had both been in prison during the war.

I was a member of that committee; and the essay which follows was written as a preface to the report. But I did not find it possible to keep a thorough sifting of the subject within the limits of the sixth commandment, on which Mr Hobhouse took an uncompromising stand. Fortunately my friends Sidney and Beatrice Webb were just then reinforcing the work of the committee by issuing the volume of their monumental history of English Local Government which deals with prisons. By transferring my preface to their book I was able to secure the intended publicity for it, and to please everybody concerned, myself included.

I give this history of the essay lest it should be taken as a fanciful exercise by a literary man making up the subject out of his own head. I have not made a parade of facts and figures because my business is to change the vindictive attitude towards criminals which has made the facts possible; but I know the facts better, apparently, than the Prison Commissioners, and relevant figures quite as well.

However, the matter did not stop with the issue of Mr and Mrs Webb's Prisons Under Local Government. That work, though read throughout the civilized world by serious students of political science, has a specialized circulation. Fortunately, my preface to it attracted the attention of the Department of Christian Social Service of the National Council of the Protestant

Episcopal Church in the United States. That body put it into general circulation in America.

[It now appears among my own works for the first time in the British Isles, 1931.]   G. B. S.

Madeira, January 1925.

THE SPIRIT IN WHICH TO READ THIS ESSAY

Imprisonment as it exists today is a worse crime than any of those committed by its victims; for no single criminal can be as powerful for evil, or as unrestrained in its exercise, as an organized nation. Therefore, if any person is addressing himself to the perusal of this dreadful subject in the spirit of a philanthropist bent on reforming a necessary and beneficent public institution, I beg him to put it down and go about some other business. It is just such reformers who have in the past made the neglect, oppression, corruption, and physical torture of the old common gaol the pretext for transforming it into that diabolical den of torment, mischief, and damnation, the modern model prison.

If, on the contrary, the reader comes as a repentant sinner, let him read on.

THE OBSTACLE OF VINDICTIVENESS

The difficulty in finding repentant sinners when this crime is in question has two roots. The first is that we are all brought up to believe that we may inflict injuries on anyone against whom we can make out a case of moral inferiority. We have this thrashed into us in our childhood by the infliction on ourselves of such injuries by our parents and teachers, or indeed by any elder who happens to be in charge of us. The second is that we are all now brought up to believe, not that the king can do no wrong, because kings have been unable to keep up that pretence, but that Society can do no wrong. Now not only does Society commit more frightful crimes than any individual, king or commoner: it legalizes its crimes, and forges certificates of righteousness for them, besides torturing anyone who dares expose their true character. A society like ours, which will, without remorse, ruin a boy body and soul for life for trying to sell newspapers in a railway station, is not likely to be very tender to people who venture to tell it that its laws would shock the Prince of Darkness himself if he had not been taught from his earliest childhood to respect as well as fear them.

Consequently we have a desperately sophisticated public, as well as a quite frankly vindictive one. Judges spend their lives consigning their fellow-creatures to prison; and when some whisper reaches them that prisons are horribly cruel and destructive places, and that no creature fit to live should be sent there, they only remark calmly that prisons are not meant to be comfortable, which is no doubt the consideration that reconciled Pontius Pilate to the practice of crucifixion.

THE OBSTACLE OF STUPIDITY

Another difficulty is the sort of stupidity that comes from lack of imagination. When I tell people that I have seen with these eyes a man (no less a man than Richard Wagner, by the way) who once met a crowd going to see a soldier broken on the wheel by the crueller of the two legalized methods of carrying out that hideous sentence, they shudder, and are amazed to hear that what they call medieval torture was used in civilized Europe so recently. They forget that the punishment of half-hanging, unmentionably mutilating, beheading, and quartering, was on the British statute book within my own memory. The same people will read of a burglar being sentenced to ten years' penal servitude without turning a hair. They are like Ibsen's Peer Gynt, who was greatly reassured when he was told that the pains of hell are mental: he thought they cannot be so very bad if there is no actual burning brimstone. When such people are terrified by an outburst of robbery with violence, or Sadistically excited by reports of the

White Slave traffic, they clamor to have sentences of two years' hard labor supplemented by a flogging, which is a joke by comparison. They will try to lynch a criminal who illtreats a child in some sensationally cruel manner; but on the most trifling provocation they will inflict on the child the prison demoralization and the prison stigma which condemn it for the rest of its life to crime as the only employment open to a prison child. The public conscience would be far more active if the punishment of imprisonment were abolished, and we went back to the rack, the stake, the pillory, and the lash at the cart's tail.

Blood Sports disguised as Punishment are less cruel than Imprisonment but more demoralizing to the Public

The objection to retrogression is not that such punishments are more cruel than imprisonment. They are less cruel, and far less permanently injurious. The decisive objection to them is that they are sports in disguise. The pleasure to the spectators, and not the pain to the criminal, condemns them. People will go to see Titus Oates flogged or Joan of Arc burnt with equal zest as an entertainment. They will pay high prices for a good view. They will reluctantly admit that they must not torture one another as long as certain rules are observed; but they will hail a breach of the rules with delight as an excuse for a bout of cruelty. Yet they can be shamed at last into recognizing that such exhibitions are degrading and demoralizing; that the executioner is a wretch whose hand no decent person cares to take; and that the enjoyment of the spectators is fiendish. We have then to find some form of torment which can give no sensual satisfaction to the tormentor, and which is hidden from public view. That is how imprisonment, being just such a torment, became the normal penalty. The fact that it may be worse for the criminal is not taken into account. The public is seeking its own salvation, not that of the lawbreaker. For him it would be far better to suffer in the public eye; for among the crowd of sightseers there might be a Victor Hugo or a Dickens, able and willing to make the sight-seers think of what they are doing and ashamed of it. The prisoner has no such chance. He envies the unfortunate animals in the zoo, watched daily by thousands of disinterested observers who never try to convert a tiger into a Quaker by solitary confinement, and would set up a resounding agitation in the papers if even the most ferocious maneater were made to suffer what the most docile convict suffers. Not only has the convict no such protection: the secrecy of his prison makes it hard to convince the public that he is suffering at all.

How we all become inured to Imprisonment

There is another reason for this incredulity. The vast majority of our city populations are inured to imprisonment from their childhood. The school is a prison. The office and the factory are prisons. The home is a prison. To the young who have the misfortune to be what is called well brought up it is sometimes a prison of inhuman severity. The children of John Howard, as far as their liberty was concerned, were treated very much as he insisted criminals should be treated, with the result that his children were morally disabled, like criminals. This imprisonment in the home, the school, the office, and the factory is kept up by browbeating, scolding, bullying, punishing, disbelief of the prisoner's statements and acceptance of those of the official, essentially as in a criminal prison. The freedom given by the adult's right to walk out of his prison is only a freedom to go into another or starve: he can choose the prison where he is best treated: that is all. On the other hand, the imprisoned criminal is free from care as to his board, lodging, and clothing: he pays no taxes, and has no responsibilities. Nobody expects him to work as an unconvicted man must work if he is to keep his job: nobody expects him to do his work well, or cares twopence whether it is well done or not.

Under such circumstances it is very hard to convince the ordinary citizen that the criminal is not better off than he deserves to be, and indeed on the verge of being positively pampered. Judges, magistrates, and Home Secretaries are so commonly under the same delusion that people who have ascertained the truth about prisons have been driven to declare that the most urgent necessity of the situation is that every judge, magistrate, and Home Secretary should serve a six months' sentence incognito; so that when he is dealing out and enforcing sentences he should at least know what he is doing.

Competition in Evil between Prison and Slum

When we get down to the poorest and most oppressed of our population we find the conditions of their life so wretched that it would be impossible to conduct a prison humanely without making the lot of the criminal more eligible than that of many free citizens. If the prison does not underbid the slum in human misery, the slum will empty and the prison will fill. This does in fact take place to a small extent at present, because slum life at its worst is so atrocious that its victims, when they are intelligent enough to study alternatives instead of taking their lot blindly, conclude that prison is the most comfortable place to spend the winter in, and qualify themselves accordingly by committing an offence for which they will get six months. But this consideration affects only those people whose condition is not defended by any responsible publicist: the remedy is admittedly not to make the prison worse but the slum better. Unfortunately the admitted claims of the poor on life are pitifully modest. The moment the treatment of the criminal is decent and merciful enough to give him a chance of moral recovery, or, in incorrigible cases, to avoid making bad worse, the official descriptions of his lot become so rosy that a clamor arises against thieves and murderers being better off than honest and kindly men; for the official reports tell us only of the care that is taken of the prisoner and the advantages he enjoys, or can earn by good conduct, never of his sufferings; and the public is not imaginative or thoughtful enough to supply the deficiency.

CRUDE CRIMINOLOGY

What sane man, I ask the clamorers, would accept an offer of free board, lodging, clothing, waiters in attendance at a touch of the bell, medical treatment, spiritual advice, scientific ventilation and sanitation, technical instruction, liberal education, and the use of a carefully selected library, with regular exercise daily and sacred music at frequent intervals, even at the very best of the Ritz Hotels, if the conditions were that he should never leave the hotel, never speak, never sing, never laugh, never see a newspaper, and write only one sternly censored letter and have one miserable interview at long intervals through the bars of a cage under the eye of a warder? And when the prison is not the Ritz Hotel, when the lodging, the food, the bed, are all deliberately made so uncomfortable as to be instruments of torture, when the clothes are rags promiscuously worn by all your fellow-prisoners in turn with yourself, when the exercise is that of a turnspit, when the ventilation and sanitation are noisome, when the instruction is a sham, the education a fraud, when the doctor is a bully to whom your ailments are all malingerings, and the chaplain a moral snob with no time for anything but the distribution of unreadable books, when the waiters are bound by penalties not to speak to you except to give you an order or a rebuke, and then to address you as you would not dream of addressing your dog, when the manager holds over your head a continual threat of starvation and confinement in a punishment cell (as if your own cell were not punishment enough), then what man in his senses would voluntarily exchange even the most harassed freedom for such a life, much less wallow luxuriously in it, as the Punch burglar always does on paper the moment anyone suggests the slightest alleviation of the pains of imprisonment?

Giving them Hell

Yet people cannot be brought to see this. They ask, first, what right the convict has to complain when he has brought it on himself by his own misconduct, and second, what he has to complain of. You reply that his grievances are silence, solitude, idle-

176

ness, waste of time, and irresponsibility. The retort is, "Why call that torture, as if it were boiling oil or red hot irons or something like that? Why, I have taken a cottage in the country for the sake of silence and solitude; and I should be only too glad to get rid of my responsibilities and waste my time in idleness like a real gentleman. A jolly sight too well off, the fellows are. I should give them hell."

Thus imprisonment is at once the most cruel of punishments and the one that those who inflict it without having ever experienced it cannot believe to be cruel. A country gentleman with a big hunting stable will indignantly discharge a groom and refuse him a reference for cruelly thrashing a horse. But it never occurs to him that his stables are horse prisons, and the stall a cell in which it is quite unnatural for the horse to be immured. In my youth I saw the great Italian actress Ristori play Mary Stuart; and nothing in her performance remains more vividly with me than her representation of the relief of Mary at finding herself in the open air after months of imprisonment. When I first saw a stud of hunters turned out to grass, they reminded me so strongly of Ristori that I at once understood that they had been prisoners in their stables, a fact which, obvious as it was, I had not thought of before. And this sort of thoughtlessness, being continuous and unconscious, inflicts more suffering than all the malice and passion in the world. In prison you get one piled on the other: to the cruelty that is intended and contrived, that grudges you even the inevitable relief of sleep, and makes your nights miserable by plank beds and the like, is added the worse cruelty that is not intended as cruelty, and, when its perpetrators can be made conscious of it at all, deludes them by a ghastly semblance of pampered indulgence.

THE THREE OFFICIAL AIMS OF IMPRISONMENT

And now comes a further complication. When people are at last compelled to think about what they are doing to our unfortunate convicts, they think so unsuccessfully and confusedly that they only make matters worse. Take for example the official list of the results aimed at by the Prison Commissioners. First, imprisonment must be "retributory" (the word vindictive is not in official use). Second, it must be deterrent. Third, it must be reformative.

THE RETRIBUTION MUDDLE

Now, if you are to punish a man retributively, you must injure him. If you are to reform him, you must improve him. And men are not improved by injuries. To propose to punish and reform people by the same operation is exactly as if you were to take a man suffering from pneumonia, and attempt to combine punitive and curative treatment. Arguing that a man with pneumonia is a danger to the community, and that he need not catch it if he takes proper care of his health, you resolve that he shall have a severe lesson, both to punish him for his negligence and pulmonary weakness and to deter others from following his example. You therefore strip him naked, and in that condition stand him all night in the snow. But as you admit the duty of restoring him to health if possible, and discharging him with sound lungs, you engage a doctor to superintend the punishment and administer cough lozenges, made as unpleasant to the taste as possible so as not to pamper the culprit. A Board of Commissioners ordering such treatment would prove thereby that either they were imbeciles or else they were hotly in earnest about punishing the patient and not in the least in earnest about curing him.

When our Prison Commissioners pretend to combine punishment with moral reformation they are in the same dilemma. We are told that the reformation of the criminal is kept constantly in view; yet the destruction of the prisoner's self-respect by systematic humiliation is deliberately ordered and practised; and we learn from a chaplain that he "does not think it is good to give opportunity for the exercise of Christian and social virtues one towards another" among prisoners. The only consolation for such contradictions is their demonstration that, as the tormentors instinctively feel that they must be liars and hypocrites on the subject, their consciences cannot be very easy about the torment. But the contradictions are obvious here only because I put them on the same page. The Prison Commissioners keep them a few pages apart; and the average reader's memory, it seems, is not long enough to span the gap when his personal interests are not at stake.

Plausibility of the Deterrence Delusion

Deterrence, which is the real object of the courts, has much more to be said for it, because it is neither simply and directly wicked like retribution, nor a false excuse for wickedness like reformation. It is an unquestionable fact that, by making rules and forcing those who break them to suffer so severely that others like them become afraid to break them, discipline can be maintained to a certain extent among creatures without sense enough to understand its necessity, or, if they do understand it, without conscience enough to refrain from violating it. This is the crude basis of all our disciplines: home discipline, school discipline, factory discipline, army and navy discipline, as well as of prison discipline, and of the whole fabric of criminal law. It is imposed not only by cruel rulers, but by unquestionably humane ones: the only difference being that the cruel rulers impose it with alacrity and gloat over its execution, and the humane rulers are driven to it reluctantly by the failure of their appeals to the consciences of people who have no conscience. Thus we find Mahomet, a conspicuously humane and conscientious Arab, keeping his fierce staff in order, not by unusual punishments, but by threats of a hell after death which he invented for the purpose in revolting detail of a kind which suggests that Mahomet had perhaps too much of the woman and the artist in him to know what would frighten a Bedouin most. Wellington, a general so humane that he sacrificed the exercise of a military genius of the first order to his moral horror of war and his freedom from its illusions, nevertheless hanged and flogged his soldiers mercilessly because he had learnt from experience that, as he put it, nothing is worse than impunity. All revolutions have been the work of men who, like Robespierre, were sentimental humanitarians and conscientious objectors to capital punishment and to the severities of military and prison discipline; yet all the revolutions have after a very brief practical experience been driven to Terrorism (the proper name of Deterrence) as ruthless as the Counter-Revolutionary Terror of Sulla, a late example being that of the Russian revolution of 1917. Whether it is Sulla, Robespierre, Trotsky, or the fighting mate of a sailing ship with a crew of loafers and wastrels, the result is the same: there are people to be dealt with who will not obey the law unless they are afraid to disobey it, and whose disobedience would mean disaster.

Crime cannot be killed by Kindness

It is useless for humanitarians to shirk this hard fact, and proclaim their conviction that all law-breakers can be reformed by kindness. That may be true in many cases, provided you can find a very gifted practitioner to take the worst ones in hand, with unlimited time and means to treat them. But if these conditions are not available, and a policeman and an executioner who will disable the wrongdoer instantaneously are available, the police remedy is the only practicable one, even for rulers filled with the spirit of the Sermon on the Mount. The late G. V. Foote, President of the English National Secular Society, a strenuous humanitarian, once had to persuade a very intimate friend of his, a much smaller and weaker man, to allow himself to be taken to an asylum for lunatics. It took four hours of humanitarian persuasion to get the patient from the first floor of his house to the cab door. Foote told me that he had not only recognized at once that no asylum attendant, with several patients to attend to, could possibly spend four hours in getting each of them downstairs, but found his temper so intolerably strained by the unnatural tax on his patience that if the breaking point had been reached, as it certainly would have been in the case of a warder or asylum attendant, he would have been far more violent, not to say savage, than if he had resorted to force at once, and finished the job in five minutes.

From resorting to this rational and practically compulsory use of kindly physical coercion to making it so painful that the victim will be afraid to give any trouble next time is a pretty certain step. In prisons the warders have to protect themselves against violence from prisoners, of which there is a constant risk and very well founded dread, as there are always ungovernably savage criminals who have little more power of refraining from furious assaults than some animals, including quite carefully bred dogs and horses, have of refraining from biting and savaging. The official punishment is flogging and putting in irons for months. But the immediate rescue of the assaulted warder has to be effected by the whole body of warders within reach; and whoever supposes that the prisoner suffers nothing more at their hands than the minimum of force necessary to restrain him knows nothing of prison life and less of human nature.

Any criticism of the deterrent theory of our prison system which ignores the existence of ungovernable savages will be discredited by the citation of actual cases. I should be passed over as a sentimentalist if I lost sight of them for a moment. On any other subject I could dispose of the matter by reminding my critics that hard cases make bad law. On this subject I recognize that the hard cases are of such a nature that provision must be made for them. Indeed hard cases may be said to be the whole subject matter of criminal law; for the normal human case is not that of the criminal, but of the law-abiding person on whose collar the grip of the policeman never closes. Only, it does not follow that the hardest cases should dictate the treatment of the relatively soft ones.

The Seamy Side of Deterrence

Let us now see what are the objections to the Deterrent or Terrorist system.

1. It necessarily leaves the interests of the victim wholly out of

account. It injures and degrades him; destroys the reputation without which he cannot get employment; and when the punishment is imprisonment under our system, atrophies his powers of fending for himself in the world. Now this would not materially hurt anyone but himself if, when he had been duly made an example of, he were killed like a vivisected dog. But he is not killed. He is, at the expiration of his sentence, flung out of the prison into the streets to earn his living in a labor market where nobody will employ an ex-prisoner, betraying himself at every turn by his ignorance of the common news of the months or years he has passed without newspapers, lamed in speech, and terrified at the unaccustomed task of providing food and lodging for himself. There is only one lucrative occupation available for him; and that is crime. He has no compunction as to Society: why should he have any? Society having for its own selfish protection done its worst to him, he has no feeling about it except a desire to get a bit of his own back. He seeks the only company in which he is welcome: the society of criminals; and sooner or later, according to his luck, he finds himself in prison again. The figures of recidivism shew that the exceptions to this routine are so few as to be negligible for the purposes of our argument. The criminal, far from being deterred from crime, is forced into it; and the citizen whom his punishment was meant to protect suffers from his depredations.

Our Plague of Unrestrained Crime

It is, in fact, admitted that the deterrent system does not deter the convicted criminal. Its real efficacy is sought in its deterrent effect on the free citizens who would commit crimes but for their fear of punishment. The Terrorist can point to the wide range of evil-doing which, not being punished by law, is rampant among us; for though a man can get himself hanged for a momentary lapse of self-control under intolerable provocation by a nagging woman, or into prison for putting the precepts of Christ above the orders of a Competent Military Authority, he can be a quite infernal scoundrel without breaking any penal law. If it be true, as it certainly is, that it is conscience and not the fear of punishment that makes civilized life possible, and that Dr Johnson's

> How small, of all that human hearts endure,
> That part that laws or kings can cause or cure!

is as applicable to crime as to human activity in general, it is none the less true that commercial civilization presents an appalling spectacle of pillage and parasitism, of corruption in the press and in the pulpit, of lying advertisements which make people buy rank poisons in the belief that they are health restorers, of traps to catch the provision made for the widow and the fatherless and divert it to the pockets of company promoting rogues, of villainous oppression of the poor and cruelty to the defenceless; and it is arguable that most of this could, like burglary and forgery, be kept within bearable bounds if its perpetrators were dealt with as burglars and forgers are dealt with today. It is, let us not forget, equally arguable that if we can afford to leave so much villainy unpunished we can afford to leave all villainy unpunished. Unfortunately, we cannot afford it: our toleration is threatening our civilization. The prosperity that consists in the wicked flourishing like a green bay tree, and the humble and contrite hearts being thoroughly despised, is a commercial delusion. Facts must be looked in the face, rascals told what they are, and all men called on to justify their ways to God and Man up to the point at which the full discharge of their social duties leaves them free to exercise their individual fancies. Restraint from evil-doing is within the rights as well as within the powers of organized society over its members; and it cannot be denied that the exercise of these powers, as far as it could be made inevitable, would incidentally deter from crime a certain number of people with only marginal consciences or none at all, and that an extension of the penal code would create fresh social conscience by enlarging the list of things which law-abiding people make it a point of honor not to do, besides calling the attention of the community to grave matters in which they have hitherto erred through thoughtlessness.

CRUDE CRIMINOLOGY

Deterrence A Function of Certainty, not of Severity

But there is all the difference in the world between deterrence as an incident of the operation of criminal law, and deterrence as its sole object and justification. In a purely deterrent system, for instance, it matters not a jot who is punished provided somebody is punished and the public persuaded that he is guilty. The effect of hanging or imprisoning the wrong man is as deterrent as hanging or imprisoning the right one. This is the fundamental explanation of the extreme and apparently fiendish reluctance of the Home Office to release a prisoner when, as in the Beck case, the evidence on which he was convicted has become discredited to a point at which no jury would maintain its verdict of guilty. The reluctance is not to confess that an innocent man is being punished, but to proclaim that a guilty man has escaped. For if escape is possible deterrence shrinks almost to nothing. There is no better established rule of criminology than that it is not the severity of punishment that deters, but its certainty. And the flaw in the case of Terrorism is that it is impossible to obtain enough certainty to deter. The police are compelled to confess every year, when they publish their statistics, that against the list of crimes reported to them they can set only a percentage of detections and convictions. And the list of reported crimes can form only a percentage, how large or small it is impossible to say, but probably small, of the crimes actually committed; for it is the greatest mistake to suppose that everyone who is robbed runs to the police: on the contrary, only foolish and ignorant or very angry people do so without very serious consideration and great reluctance. In most cases it costs nothing to let the thief off, and a good deal to prosecute him. The burglar in Heartbreak House, who makes his living by breaking into people's houses, and then blackmailing them by threatening to give himself up to the police and put them to the expense and discomfort of attending his trial and giving evidence after enduring all the worry of the police enquiries, is not a joke; he is a comic dramatization of a process that is going on every day. As to the black sheep of respectable families who blackmail them by offering them the alternative of making good their thefts and frauds, even to the extent of honoring their forged cheques, or having the family name disgraced, ask any experienced family solicitor.

Besides the chances of not being prosecuted, there are the chances of acquittal; but I doubt whether they count for much except with very attractive women. Still, it is worth mentioning that juries will snatch at the flimsiest pretexts for refusing to send people who engage their sympathy to the gallows or to penal servitude, even on evidence of murder or theft which would make short work of a repulsive person.

Some Personal Experiences

Take my own experience as probably common enough. Fifty years ago a friend of mine, hearing that a legacy had been left him, lent himself the expected sum out of his employers' cash; concealed the defalcation by falsifying his accounts; and was detected before he could repay. His employers angrily resented the fraud, and had certainly no desire to spare him. But a public exposure of the affair would have involved shock to their clients' sense of security, loss of time and consequently of money, an end to all hope of his ever making good the loss, and the unpleasantness of attendance in court at the trial. All this put any recourse to the police out of the question; and my friend obtained another post after a very brief interval during which he supported himself as a church organist. This, by the way, was a quite desirable conclusion, as he was for all ordinary practical purposes a sufficiently honest man. It would have been pure mischief to make him a criminal; but that is not the present point. He serves here as an illustration of the fact that our criminal law, far from inviting prosecution, attaches serious losses and inconveniences to it.

It may be said that whatever the losses and inconveniences may be, it is a public duty to prosecute. But is it? Is it not a Christian duty not to prosecute? A man stole £500 from me by a trick. He speculated in my character with subtlety and success; and yet he ran risks of detection which no quite sensible man would have ventured on. It was assumed that I would resort to the police. I asked why. The answer was that he should be punished to deter others from similar crimes. I naturally said, "You have been punishing people cruelly for more than a century for this kind of fraud; and the result is that I am robbed of £500. Evidently your deterrence does not deter. What it does do is to torment the swindler for years, and then throw him back upon society, a worse man in every respect, with no other employment open to him except that of fresh swindling. Besides, your elaborate arrangements to deter me from prosecuting are convincing and effective. I could earn £500 by useful work in the time it would take to prosecute this man vindictively and worse than uselessly. So I wish him joy of his booty, and invite him to swindle me again if he can." Now this was not sentimentality. I am not a bit fonder of being swindled than other people; and if society would treat swindlers properly I should denounce them without the slightest remorse, and not grudge a reasonable expenditure of time and energy in the business. But to throw good money after bad in setting to work a wicked and mischievous routine of evil would be to stamp myself as a worse man than the swindler, who earned the money more energetically, and appropriated it no more unjustly, if less legally, than I earn and appropriate my dividends.

I must however warn our thieves that I can promise them no immunity from police pursuit if they rob me. Some time after the operation just recorded, an uninvited guest came to a luncheon party in my house. He (or she) got away with an overcoat and a pocketful of my wife's best table silver. But instead of selecting my overcoat, he took the best overcoat, which was that of one of my guests. My guest was insured against theft; the insurance company had to buy him a new overcoat; and the matter thus passed out of my hands into those of the police. But the result, as far as the thief was concerned, was the same. He was not captured; and he had the social satisfaction of providing employment for others in converting into a strongly fortified obstacle the flimsy gate through which he had effected an entrance, thereby giving my flat the appearance of a private madhouse.

On another occasion a drunken woman obtained admission by presenting an authentic letter from a soft-hearted member of the House of Lords. I had no guests at the moment; and as she, too, wanted an overcoat, she took mine, and actually interviewed me with it most perfunctorily concealed under her jacket. When I called her attention to it she handed it back to me effusively; begged me to shake hands with her; and went her way.

Now these things occur by the dozen every day, in spite of the severity with which they are punished when the thief is dealt with by the police. I daresay all my readers, if not too young to have completed a representative experience, could add two or three similar stories. What do they go to prove? Just that detection is so uncertain that its consequences have no really effective deterrence for the potential offender, whilst the unpleasant and expensive consequences of prosecution, being absolutely certain, have a very strong deterrent effect indeed on the prosecutor. In short, all the hideous cruelty practised by us for the sake of deterrence is wasted: we are damning our souls at great expense and trouble for nothing.

Judicial Vengeance as an Alternative to Lynch Law

Thus we see that of the three official objects of our prison system: vengeance, deterrence, and reformation of the criminal, only one is achieved; and that is the one which is nakedly abominable. But there is a plea for it which must be taken into account, and which brings us to the root of the matter in our own characters. It is said, and it is in a certain degree true, that if the Government does not lawfully organize and regulate popular vengeance, the populace will rise up and execute this vengeance lawlessly for itself. The standard defence of the Inquisition is that without it no heretic's life would have been safe. In Texas today the people are not satisfied with the prospect of knowing that a murderer or ravisher will be electrocuted inside a gaol if a jury can resist the defence put up by his lawyer. They tear him from the hands of the sheriff; pour lamp oil over him; and burn him alive. Now the burning of human beings is not only an expression of outraged public morality: it is also a sport for which a taste can be acquired much more easily and rapidly than a taste for coursing hares, just as a taste for drink can be acquired from brandy and cocktails more easily and rapidly than from beer or sauterne. Lynching mobs begin with negro ravishers and murderers; but they presently go on to any sort of delinquent, provided he is black. Later on, as a white man will burn as amusingly as a black one, and a white woman react to tarring and feathering as thrillingly as a negress, the color line is effaced by what professes to be a rising wave of virtuous indignation, but is in fact an epidemic of Sadism. The defenders of our penal systems take advantage of it to assure us that if they did not torment and ruin a boy guilty of sleeping in the open air, an indignant public would rise and tear that boy limb from limb.

Now the reply to such a plea, from the point of view of civilized law, cannot be too sweeping. The government which cannot restrain a mob from taking the law into its own hands is no government at all. If Landru could go to the guillotine unmolested in France, and his British prototype who drowned all his wives in their baths could be peaceably hanged in England, Texas can protect its criminals by simply bringing its civilization up to the French and British level. But indeed the besetting sin of the mob is a morbid hero worship of great criminals rather than a ferocious abhorrence of them. In any case nobody will have the effrontery to pretend that the number of criminals who excite popular feeling enough to provoke lynching is more than a negligible percentage of the whole. The theory that the problem of crime is only one of organizing, regulating, and executing the vengeance of the mob will not bear plain statement, much less discussion. It is only the retributive theory over again in its most impudent form.

CRUDE CRIMINOLOGY

THE HARD CASES THAT MAKE BAD LAW

Having now disposed of all the official theories as the trash they are, let us return to the facts, and deal with the hard ones first. Everyone who has any extensive experience of domesticated animals, human or other, knows that there are negatively bad specimens who have no consciences, and positively bad ones who are incurably ferocious. The negative ones are often very agreeable and even charming companions; but they beg, borrow, steal, defraud, and seduce almost by reflex action: they cannot resist the most trifling temptation. They are indulged and spared to the extreme limit of endurance; but in the end they have to be deprived of their liberty in some way. The positive ones enjoy no such tolerance. Unless they are physically restrained they break people's bones, knock out their eyes, rupture their organs, or kill them.

Then there are the cruel people, not necessarily unable to control their tempers, nor fraudulent, nor in any other way disqualified for ordinary social activity or liberty, possibly even with conspicuous virtues. But, by a horrible involution, they lust after the spectacle of suffering, mental and physical, as normal men lust after love. Torture is to them a pleasure except when it is inflicted on themselves. In scores of ways, from the habitual utterance of wounding speeches, and the contriving of sly injuries and humiliations for which they cannot be brought to book legally, to thrashing their wives and children or, as bachelors, paying prostitutes of the hardier sort to submit to floggings, they seek the satisfaction of their desire wherever and however they can.

POSSIBILITIES OF THERAPEUTIC TREATMENT

Now in the present state of our knowledge it is folly to talk of reforming these people. By this I do not mean that even now they are all quite incurable. The cases of no conscience are sometimes, like Parsifal's when he shot the swan, cases of unawakened conscience. Violent and quarrelsome people are often only energetic people who are underworked: I have known a man cured of wife-beating by setting him to beat the drum in a village band; and the quarrels that make country life so very unarcadian are picked mostly because the quarrelers have not enough friction in their lives to keep them goodhumored.

Psycho-analysis, too, which is not all quackery and pornography, might conceivably cure a case of Sadism as it might cure any of the phobias. And psycho-analysis is a mere fancy compared to the knowledge we now pretend to concerning the function of our glands and their effect on our character and conduct. In the nineteenth century this knowledge was pursued barbarously by crude vivisectors whose notion of finding out what a gland was for was to cut it violently out and see what would happen to the victim, meanwhile trying to bribe the public to tolerate such horrors by promising to make old debauchees young again. This was rightly felt to be a villainous business; besides, who could suppose that the men who did these things would hesitate to lie about the results when there was plenty of money to be made by representing them as cures for dreaded diseases? But today we are not asked to infer that because something has happened to a violently mutilated dog it must happen also to an unmutilated human being. We can now make authentic pictures of internal organs by means of rays to which flesh is transparent. This makes it possible to take a criminal and say authoritatively that he is a case, not of original sin, but of an inefficient, or excessively efficient, thyroid gland, or pituitary gland, or adrenal gland, as the case may be. This of course does not help the police in dealing with a criminal: they must apprehend and bring him to trial all the same. But if the prison doctor were able to say "Put some iodine in this man's skilly, and his character will change," then the notion of punishing instead of curing him would become ridiculous. Of course the matter is not so simple as that; and all this endocrinism, as it is called, may turn out to be only the latest addition to our already very extensive collection of pseudo-scientific mares' nests; still, we cannot ignore the fact that a considerable case is being made out by eminent physiologists for at least a conjecture that many cases which are now incurable may be disposed of in the not very remote future by inducing the patient to produce more thyroxin or pituitrin or adrenalin or what not, or even administering them to him as thyroxin is at present administered in cases of myxœdema. Yet the reports of the work of our prison medical officers suggest that hardly any of them has ever heard of these discoveries, or regards a convict as anything more interesting scientifically than a malingering rascal.

The Incorrigible Villains

It will be seen that I am prepared to go to lengths which still seem fantastic as to the possibility of changing a criminal into an honest man. And I have more faith than most prison chaplains seem to have in the possibilities of religious conversion. But I cannot add too emphatically that the people who imagine that all criminals can be reformed by setting chaplains to preach at them, by giving them pious books and tracts to read, by separating them from their companions in crime and locking them up in solitude to reflect on their sins and repent, are far worse enemies both to the criminal and to Society than those who face the fact that these are merely additional cruelties which make their victims worse, or even than those who frankly use them as a means of "giving them hell." But when this is recognized, and the bigoted reformers with their sermons, their tracts, their horrors of separation, silence, and solitude to avoid contamination, are bundled out of our prisons as nuisances, the problem remains, how are you to deal with your incorrigibles? Here you have a man who supports himself by gaining the confidence and affection of lonely women; seducing them; spending all their money; and then burning them in a stove or drowning them in a bath. He is quite an attractive fellow, with a genuine taste for women and no taste at all for murder, which is only his way of getting rid of them when their money is spent and they are in the way of the next woman. There is no more malice or Sadism about the final operation than there is about tearing up a letter when it is done with, and throwing it into the waste paper basket. You electrocute him or hang him or chop his head off. But presently you have to deal with a man who lives in exactly the same way, but has not executive force or courage enough to commit murder. He only abandons his victims and turns up in a fresh place with a fresh name. He generally marries them, as it is easier to seduce them so.

Alongside him you have a married couple united by a passion for cruelty. They amuse themselves by tying their children to the bedstead; thrashing them with straps; and branding them with red-hot pokers. You also have to deal with a man who on the slightest irritation flings his wife under a dray, or smashes a lighted kerosene lamp into her face. He has been in prison again and again for outbursts of this kind; and always, within a week of his release, or within a few hours of it, he has done it again.

Now you cannot get rid of these nuisances and monsters by simply cataloguing them as subthyroidics and superadrenals or the like. At present you torment them for a fixed period, at the end of which they are set free to resume their operations with a savage grudge against the community which has tormented them. That is stupid. Nothing is gained by punishing people who cannot help themselves, and on whom deterrence is thrown away. Releasing them is like releasing the tigers from the Zoo to find their next meal in the nearest children's playing ground.

THE LETHAL CHAMBER

The most obvious course is to kill them. Some of the popular objections to this may be considered for a moment. Death, it is said, is irrevocable; and after all, they may turn out to be innocent. But really you cannot handle criminals on the assumption that they may be innocent. You are not supposed to handle them at all until you have convinced yourself by an elaborate trial that they are guilty. Besides, imprisonment is as irrevocable as hanging. Each is a method of taking a criminal's life; and when he prefers hanging or suicide to imprisonment for life, as he sometimes does, he says, in effect, that he had rather you took his life all at once, painlessly, than minute by minute in long-drawn-out torture. You can give a prisoner a pardon; but you cannot give him back a moment of his imprisonment. He may accept a reprieve willingly in the hope of a pardon or an escape or a revolution or an earthquake or what not; but as you do not mean him to evade his sentence in any way whatever, it is not for you to take such clutchings at straws into account.

Another argument against the death penalty for anything short of murder is the practical one of the policeman and the householder, who plead that if you hang burglars they will shoot to avoid capture on the ground that they may as well be hanged for a sheep as for a lamb. But this can be disposed of by pointing out, first, that even under existing circumstances the burglar occasionally shoots, and, second, that acquittals, recommendations to mercy, verdicts of manslaughter, successful pleas of insanity and so forth, already make the death penalty so uncertain that even red-handed murderers shoot no oftener than burglars— less often, in fact. This uncertainty would be actually increased if the death sentence were, as it should be, made applicable to other criminals than those convicted of wilful murder, and no longer made compulsory in any case.

THE SACREDNESS OF HUMAN LIFE FROM THE WARDER'S SIDE

Then comes the plea for the sacredness of human life. The State should not set the example of killing, or of clubbing a rioter with a policeman's baton, or of dropping bombs on a sleeping city, or of doing many things that States nevertheless have to do. But let us take the plea on its own ground, which is, fundamentally, that life is the most precious of all things, and its waste the worst of crimes. We have already seen that imprisonment does not spare the life of the criminal: it takes it and wastes it in the most cruel way. But there are others to be considered beside the criminal and the citizens who fear him so much that they cannot sleep in peace unless he is locked up. There are the people who have to lock him up, and fetch him his food, and watch him. Why are their lives to be wasted? Warders, and especially wardresses, are almost as much tied to the prison by their occupation, and by their pensions, which they dare not forfeit by seeking other employment, as the criminals are. If I had to choose between a spell under preventive detention among hardened criminals in Camp Hill and one as warder in an ordinary prison, I think I should vote for Camp Hill. Warders suffer in body and mind from their employment; and if it be true, as our examination seems to prove, that they are doing no good to society, but very active harm, their lives are wasted more completely than those of the criminals; for most criminals are discharged after a few weeks or months; but the warder never escapes until he is superannuated, by which time he is an older gaolbird than any Lifer in the cells.

The Price of Life in Communities

How then does the case stand with your incurable pathological case of crime? If you treat the life of the criminal as sacred, you find yourself not only taking his life but sacrificing the lives of innocent men and women to keep him locked up. There is no sort of sense or humanity in such a course. The moment we face it frankly we are driven to the conclusion that the community has a right to put a price on the right to live in it. That price must be sufficient self-control to live without wasting and destroying the lives of others, whether by direct attack like a tiger, parasitic exploitation like a leech, or having to be held in a leash with another person at the end of it. Persons lacking such self-control have been thrust out into the sage-brush to wander there until they die of thirst, a cruel and cowardly way of killing them. The dread of clean and wilful killing often leads to evasions of the commandment "Thou shalt not kill" which are far more cruel than its frank violation. It has never been possible to obey it un-reservedly, either with men or with animals; and the attempts to keep the letter of it have led to burying vestal virgins and nuns alive, crushing men to death in the press-yard, handing heretics over to the secular arm, and the like, instead of killing them humanely and without any evasion of the heavy responsibility involved. It was a horrible thing to build a vestal virgin into a wall with food and water enough for a day; but to build her into a prison for years as we do, with just enough loathsome food to prevent her from dying, is more than horrible: it is diabolical. If no better alternatives to death can be found than these, then who will not vote for death? If people are fit to live, let them live under decent human conditions. If they are not fit to live, kill them in a decent human way. Is it any wonder that some of us are driven to prescribe the lethal chamber as the solution for the hard cases which are at present made the excuse for dragging all the other cases down to their level, and the only solution that will create a sense of full social responsibility in modern popula-tions?

The Sixth Commandment

The slaughtering of incorrigibly dangerous persons, as dis-tinguished from the punitive execution of murderers who have violated the commandment not to kill, cannot be established summarily by these practical considerations. In spite of their cogency we have not only individuals who are resolutely and uncompromisingly opposed to slaying under any provocation whatever, we have nations who have abolished the death penalty, and regard our grim retention of it as barbarous. Wider than any nation we have the Roman Catholic Church, which insists literally on absolute obedience to the commandment, and con-demns as murder even the killing of an unborn child to save the mother's life. In practice this obligation has been evaded so grossly—by the Inquisition, for example, which refused to slay the heretic, but handed him over to the secular arm with a formal recommendation to mercy, knowing that the secular arm would immediately burn him—that the case of the Church might be cited to illustrate the uselessness of barring the death penalty. But it also illustrates the persistence and antiquity of a point of conscience which still defies the argument from expediency. That point of conscience may be called a superstition because it is as old as the story of Cain and Abel, and because it is difficult to find any rational basis for it. But there is something to be said for it all the same.

Killing is a dangerously cheap way out of a difficulty. "Stone dead hath no fellow" was a handy formula for Cromwell's troops in dealing with the Irish; still, that precedent is not very reassuring. All the social problems of all the countries can be got rid of by extirpating the inhabitants; but to get rid of a problem is not to solve it. Even perfectly rational solutions of our problems must be humane as well if they are to be accepted by good men: otherwise the logic of the inquisitor, the dynamiter, and the vivisectionist would rule the world for ever as it unfortunately does to far too great an extent already. It may also be argued that if society were to forgo its power of slaying, and also its practice of punishment, it would have a stronger incentive to find out how to correct the apparently incorrigible. Although whenever it has renounced its power to slay sane criminals it has substituted a horribly rigorous and indeed virtually lethal imprisonment, this does not apply to homicidal lunatics, the comparatively lenient treatment of whom could obviously be extended to sane murderers. The Oxford Dictionary owes several of its pages to a homicide who was detained at Broadmoor (the English Asylum for Criminal Lunatics) during the pleasure of the Crown. As to the cases which, when not disposed of by the lethal method, involve caging men as tigers are caged, can they not be dealt with by the padded room? Granted that it is questionable whether the public conscience which tolerates such caging is really more sensitive or thoughtful than that which demands the lethal solution, and that at the present time executions, and even floggings, do not harden the authorities and lower the standard of humanity all through our penal system as much as continuing penalties do, yet the reluctance to kill persists. The moment it is pointed out that if we kill incurable criminals we may as well also kill incurable troublesome invalids, people realize with a shock that the urge of horror, hatred, and vengeance is needed to nerve them—or unnerve them—to slay. When I force humane people to face their political powers of life and death apart from punishment as I am doing now, I produce a terrified impression that I want to hang everybody. In vain I protest that I am dealing with a very small class of human monsters, and that as far as crime is concerned our indiscriminate hanging of wilful murderers and traitors slays more in one year than dispassionate lethal treatment would be likely to slay in ten. I am asked at once who is to be trusted with the appalling responsibility of deciding whether a man is to live or die, and what government could be trusted not to kill its enemies under the pretence that they are enemies of society.

GOVERNMENTS MUST PRESUME OR ABDICATE

The reply is obvious. Such responsibilities must be taken, whether we are fit for them or not, if civilized society is to be organized. No unofficial person denies that they are abused: the whole effect of this essay is to shew that they are horribly abused. I can say for my own part as a vehement critic and opponent of all the governments of which I have had any experience that I am the last person to forget that governments use the criminal law to suppress and exterminate their opponents whenever the opposition becomes really acute, and that the more virtuous the revolutionist and the more vicious the government, the more likely it is to kill him, and to do so under pretence of his being one of the dangerous persons for whom the lethal treatment would be reserved. It has been pointed out again and again that it is in the very nature of power to corrupt those to whom it is entrusted, and that to God alone belongs the awful prerogative of dismissing the soul from the body. Tolstoy has exhausted the persuasions of literary art in exhorting us that we resist not evil; and men have suffered abominable persecutions sooner than accept military service with its chief commandment, Thou shalt kill.

All this leaves the problem just where it was. The irresponsible humanitarian citizen may indulge his pity and sympathy to his heart's content, knowing that whenever a criminal passes to his doom there, but for the grace of God, goes he; but those who have to govern find that they must either abdicate, and that promptly, or else take on themselves as best they can many of the attributes of God. They must decide what is good and what evil; they must force men to do certain things and refrain from doing certain other things whether individual consciences approve or not; they must resist evil resolutely and continually, possibly and preferably without malice or revenge, but certainly with the effect of disarming it, preventing it, stamping it out, and creating public opinion against it. In short, they must do all sorts of things which they are manifestly not ideally fit to do, and, let us hope, do with becoming misgiving, but which must be done, all the same, well or ill, somehow and by somebody. If I were to ignore this, everyone who has had any experience of government would throw these pages aside as those of an inexperienced sentimentalist or an Impossibilist Anarchist.

Nevertheless, certain lines have to be drawn limiting the activities of governments, and allowing the individual to be a law unto himself. For instance, we are obliged (if we are wise) to tolerate sedition and blasphemy to a considerable extent because sedition and blasphemy are nothing more than the advocacy of changes in the established forms of government, morals, and religion; and without such changes there can be no social evolution. But as governments are not always wise, it is difficult enough to secure this intellectual anarchy, or as we call it, freedom of speech and conscience; and anyone who proposed to extend it to such actions as are contemplated by the advocates of lethal treatment would be dismissed as insane. No country at peace will tolerate murder, whether it is done on principle or in sin. What is more, no country at war will tolerate a refusal to murder the enemy. Thus, whether the powers of the country are being exercised for good or evil, they never remain in abeyance; and whoever proposes to set to those powers the limit of an absolute obedience to the commandment "Thou shalt not kill," must do so quite arbitrarily. He cannot give any reason that I can discover for saying that it is wickeder to break a man's neck than to cage him for life: he can only say that his instinct places an overwhelming ban on the one and not on the other; and he must depend on the existence of a similar instinct in the community for his success in having legal slaying ruled out.

THE RUTHLESSNESS OF THE PURE HEART

In this he will have little difficulty as long as the slaying is an act of revenge and expiation, as it is at present: that is why capital punishment has been abolished in some countries, and why its abolition is agitated for in the countries which still practise it. But if these sinful elements be discarded, and the slaying is made a matter of pure expediency, the criminal being pitied as sincerely as a mad dog is pitied, the most ardent present advocate of the abolition of capital punishment may not only consent to the slaying as he does in the case of the mad dog, but even demand it to put an end to an unendurable danger and horror. Malice and fear are narrow things, and carry with them a thousand inhibitions and terrors and scruples. A heart and brain purified of them gain an enormous freedom; and this freedom is shewn not only in the many civilized activities that are tabooed in the savage tribe, but also in the ruthlessness with which the civilized man destroys things that the savage prays to and propitiates. The attempt to reform an incurably dangerous criminal may come to be classed with the attempt to propitiate a sacred rattlesnake. The higher civilization does not make still greater sacrifices to the snake: it kills it.

I am driven to conclude, that though, if voluntary custodians can be found for dangerous incorrigibles, as they doubtless can by attaching compensating advantages to their employment, it is quite possible to proceed with slaying absolutely barred, there is not enough likelihood of this renunciation by the State of the powers of life and death to justify me in leaving lethal treatment out of the question. In any case it would be impossible to obtain any clear thinking on the question unless its possibilities were frankly faced and to some extent explored. I have faced them frankly and explored them as far as seems necessary; and at that I must leave it. Nothing that I have to say about the other sorts of criminals will be in the least invalidated if it should be decided that killing is to be ruled out. I think it quite likely that it may be ruled out on sentimental grounds. By the time we have reached solid ground the shock of reintroducing it (though this has been effected and even clamored for in some countries) may be too great to be faced under normal conditions. Also, as far as what we call crime is concerned, the matter is not one of the first importance. I should be surprised if, even in so large a population as ours, it would ever be thought necessary to extirpate one criminal as utterly unmanageable every year; and this means, of course, that if we decide to cage such people, the cage need not be a very large one.

I am not myself writing as an advocate one way or the other. I have to deal with European and American civilization, which, having no longer than a century ago executed people for offences now punished by a few months or even weeks of imprisonment, has advanced to a point at which less than half a dozen crimes are punishable by death: murder, piracy, rape, arson, and (in Scotland) vitriol throwing. The opponents of capital punishment usually believe, naturally enough, that the effect of abandoning the notion of punishment altogether as sinful (which it is) will sweep away the scaffold from these crimes also, and thus make an end of the death penalty. No doubt it will; but I foresee that it will reintroduce the idea of killing dangerous people simply because they are dangerous, without the least desire to punish them, and without specific reference to the actions which have called attention to their dangerousness. That extremity may be met with an absolute veto, or it may not. I cannot foresee which side I should take: a wise man does not ford a stream till he gets to it. But I am so sure that the situation will arise, that I have to deal with it here as impersonally as may be, without committing myself or anyone else one way or the other.

The Soft Cases that we turn into Hard Ones

Now let us look at the other end of the scale, where the soft cases are. Here we are confronted with the staggering fact that many of our prisoners have not been convicted of any offence at all. They are awaiting their trial, and are too poor and friendless to find bail; whilst others have been convicted of mere breaches of bye-laws of which they were ignorant, and which they could not have guessed by their sense of right and wrong; for many bye-laws have no ethical character whatever. For example, a boy sells a newspaper on the premises of a railway company, and thereby infringes a bye-law the object of which is to protect the commercial monopoly of the newsagents who have paid the company for the right to have a bookstall on the platform. The boy's brother jostles a passenger who is burdened with hand luggage, and says "Carry your bag, sir?" These perfectly innocent lads are sent to prison, though the warders themselves admit that a sentence of imprisonment is so ruinous to a boy's morals that they would rather see their own sons dead than in prison.

But let us take the guilty. The great majority of them have been convicted of petty frauds compared to which the common practices of the commercial world are serious crimes. Herbert Spencer's essays on the laxity of the morals of trade have called no trader successfully to repentance. It is not too much to say that any contractor in Europe or America who does not secure business by tenders and estimates and specifications for work and materials which he has not the smallest intention of doing or putting in, and who does not resort to bribery to have the work and materials he actually does do and put in passed by anybody whose duty it is to check them, is an exceptional man. The usage is so much a matter of course, and competition has made it so compulsory, that conscience is awakened only when the fraud is carried to some unusual length. I can remember two cases which illustrate what I mean very well. A builder of high commercial standing contracted to put up a public building. When the work began he found that the clerk of the works, whose business it was to check the work on behalf of the purchaser, lived opposite the building site. The contractor immediately protested that this was not part of the bargain, and that his estimate had been obtained on false pretences. The other is the case of the omnibus conductors of London when the alarum punch was invented and introduced. They immediately struck for higher wages, and got them, frankly on the ground that the punch had cut off the percentage they had been accustomed to add to their wages by peculation, and that it should be made up to them.

Both these cases prove that dishonesty does not pay when it becomes general. The contractor might just as well estimate for the work he really does and the material he actually uses; for, after all, since his object is to tempt the purchaser by keeping prices down, he has to give him the benefit of the fraud. If the purchaser finds him out and says, for example, "You estimated for galvanized pipes; and you have put in plain ones," the contractor can reply, "If I had put in galvanized pipes I should have had to charge you more." In the same way, the bus conductors might just as well have struck for an increase of wage as stolen it: the event proved they could have got it. But they thought they could secure employment more easily by asking for a low wage and making it up to their needs surreptitiously. It is one of the grievances of clerks in many businesses that they have to connive at dishonest practices as part of the regular routine of the office; but neither they nor their employers are any the richer, because business always finally settles down to the facts, and is conducted in terms not of the pretence but of the reality.

CRUDE CRIMINOLOGY

Most Prisoners no worse than Ourselves

We may take it, then, that the thief who is in prison is not necessarily more dishonest than his fellows at large, but mostly only one who, through ignorance or stupidity, steals in a way that is not customary. He snatches a loaf from the baker's counter and is promptly run into gaol. Another man snatches bread from the tables of hundreds of widows and orphans and simple credulous souls who do not know the ways of company promoters; and, as likely as not, he is run into Parliament. You may say that the remedy for this is not to spare the lesser offender but to punish the greater; but there you miss my present point, which is, that as the great majority of prisoners are not a bit more dishonest naturally than thousands of people who are not only at liberty, but highly pampered, it is no use telling me that society will fall into anarchic dissolution if these unlucky prisoners are treated with common humanity. On the contrary, when we see the outrageous extent to which the most shamelessly selfish rogues and rascals can be granted not only impunity but encouragement and magnificent remuneration, we are tempted to ask ourselves have we any right to restrain anyone at all from doing his worst to us. The first prison I ever saw had inscribed on it CEASE TO DO EVIL: LEARN TO DO WELL; but as the inscription was on the outside, the prisoners could not read it. It should have been addressed to the self-righteous free spectator in the street, and should have run ALL HAVE SINNED, AND FALLEN SHORT OF THE GLORY OF GOD.

We must get out of the habit of painting human character in soot and whitewash. It is not true that men can be divided into absolutely honest persons and absolutely dishonest ones. Our honesty varies with the strain put on it: this is proved by the fact that every additional penny of income tax brings in less than the penny preceding. The purchaser of a horse or motor-car has to beware much more carefully than the purchaser of an article worth five shillings. If you take Landru at one extreme, and at the other the prisoner whose crime is sleeping out: that is to say, whose crime is no crime at all, you can place every sane human being, from the monarch to the tramp, somewhere on the scale between them. Not one of them has a blank page in the books of the Recording Angel. From the people who tell white lies about their ages, social positions, and incomes, to those who grind the faces of the poor, or marry whilst suffering from contagious disease, or buy valuable properties from inexperienced owners for a tenth of their value, or sell worthless shares for the whole of a widow's savings, or obtain vast sums on false pretences held forth by lying advertisements, to say nothing of bullying and beating in their homes, and drinking and debauching in their bachelorhood, you could at any moment find dozens of people who have never been imprisoned and never will be, and are yet worse citizens than any but the very worst of our convicts. Much of the difference between the bond and the free is a difference in circumstances only: if a man is not hungry, and his children are ailing only because they are too well fed, nobody can tell whether he would steal a loaf if his children were crying for bread and he himself had not tasted a mouthful for twenty-four hours. Therefore, if you are in an attitude of moral superiority to our convicts: if you are one of the Serve Them Right and Give Them Hell brigade, you may justly be invited, in your own vernacular, either to Come Off It, or else Go Inside and take the measure you are meting out to others no worse than yourself.

Good Soldiers often Bad Citizens, and Bad Citizens Good Prisoners

The distinction between the people the criminal law need deal with and those it may safely leave at large is not a distinction between depravity and good nature: it is a distinction between people who cannot, as they themselves put it, go straight except in leading strings, and those who can. Incurable criminals make well-behaved soldiers and prisoners. The war of 1914–18 almost emptied our prisons of able-bodied men; and in the leading strings of military discipline these men ceased to be criminals.

Some soldiers who were discharged with not only first-rate certificates of their good conduct as soldiers, but with a Victoria Cross "For Valor," were no sooner cast adrift into ordinary civil life than they were presently found in the dock pleading their military services and good character as soldiers in mitigation of sentences of imprisonment for frauds and thefts of the meanest sort. When we consider how completely a soldier is enslaved by military discipline, and how abhorrent military service consequently is to civically capable people, we cannot doubt, even if there were no first-hand testimony on the subject, that many men enlist voluntarily, not because they want to lead a drunken and dissolute life (the reason given by the Iron Duke), or because they are under any of the romantic illusions on which the recruiting sergeant is supposed to practise, but because they know themselves to be unfit for full moral responsibility, and conclude that they had better have their lives ordered for them than face the effort (intolerably difficult for them) of ordering it themselves.

This effort is not made easier by our civilization. A man who treated his children as every laborer treated them as a matter of course a hundred years ago would now be imprisoned for neglecting them and keeping them away from school. The statute book is crammed with offences unknown to our grandfathers and unintelligible to uneducated men; and the list needs startling extension; for, as Mr H. G. Wells has pointed out, its fundamental items date from the Mosaic period, when modern Capitalism, which involves a new morality, was unknown. In more obvious matters we notice how the standard of dress, manners, and lodging which qualifies a man socially for employment as a factory hand or mechanic has risen since the days when no person of any refinement could travel, as everybody now travels, third-class.

REMEDIES IN THE ROUGH

We may now begin to arrange our problem comprehensively. The people who have to be dealt with specially by the Government because for one reason or another they cannot deal satisfactorily with themselves may be roughly divided into three sections. First, the small number of dangerous or incorrigibly mischievous human animals. With them should be associated all hopeless defectives, from the idiot children who lie like stranded jellyfish on asylum floors, and have to be artificially fed, to the worst homicidal maniacs. Second, a body of people who cannot provide for or order their lives for themselves, but who, under discipline and tutelage, with their board and lodging and clothing provided for them, as in the case of soldiers, are normally happy, well-behaved, useful citizens. (There would be several degrees of tutelage through which they might be promoted if they are fit and willing.) Third, all normal persons who have trespassed in some way during one of those lapses of self-discipline which are as common as colds, and who have been unlucky enough to fall into the hands of the police in consequence. These last should never be imprisoned. They should be required to compensate the State for the injury done to the body politic by their misdeeds, and, when possible, to compensate the victims, as well as pay the costs of bringing them to justice. Until they have done this they cannot complain if they find themselves distrained upon; harassed by frequent compulsory appearances in court to excuse themselves; and threatened with consignment to the second class as defectives. It is quite easy to make carelessness and selfishness or petty violence and dishonesty unremunerative and disagreeable, without resorting to imprisonment. In the cases where the offender has fallen into bad habits and bad company, the stupidest course to take is to force him into the worst of all habits and the worst of all company: that is, prison habits and prison company. The proper remedies are good habits and good company. If these are not available, then the offender must be put into the second class, and kept straight under tutelage until he is fit for freedom.

CRUDE CRIMINOLOGY

DIFFICULTY OF THE UNDISCIPLINED

The difficulty lies, it will be seen, in devising a means of dealing with the second class. The first is easy: too easy, in fact. You kill or you cage: that is all. In the third class, summoning and fining and admonishing are easy and not mischievous: you may worry a man considerably by badgering him about his conduct and dunning him for money in a police court occasionally; but you do not permanently disable him morally and physically thereby. It is the offender of the second class, too good to be killed or caged, and not good enough for normal liberty, whose treatment bothers us.

THE INDETERMINATE SENTENCE

Any proposal to place men under compulsory tutelage immediately raises the vexed question of what is called "the indeterminate sentence." The British parliament has never been prevailed on to create a possibility of a criminal being "detained preventively" for life: it has set a limit of ten years to that condition. This is inevitable as long as the tutelage is primarily not a tutelage but a punishment. In England there is a law under which a drunkard, politely called an inebriate, can voluntarily sentence himself to a term of detention for the sake of being restrained from yielding to a temptation which he is unable to resist when left to himself. Under existing circumstances nobody is likely to do that twice, or even once if he has any knowledge of how the unfortunate inebriates are treated. The only system of detention available is the prison system; and the only sort of prisoner the officials have any practice in dealing with is the criminal. Every detained person is therefore put through the dismal routine of punishment in the first place, deterrence in the second place, and reform in the very remote third place. The inebriate volunteer prisoner very soon finds that he is being treated as a criminal, and tries in vain to revoke his renunciation of his liberty.

Otherwise, say the authorities very truly, they would be overwhelmed with volunteers. This reminds us of the Westminster Abbey verger who charged a French gentleman with brawling in church. The magistrate, inquiring what, exactly, the foreigner had done, was told that he had knelt in prayer. "But," said the magistrate, "is not that what a church is for?" The verger was scandalized. "If we allowed that," he said, "we should have people praying all over the place." The Prison Commissioners know that if prisons were made reasonably happy places, and thrown open to volunteers like the army, they might speedily be overcrowded. And this, with its implied threat of an enormous increase of taxation, seems a conclusive objection.

The Economy Aspect

But if its effect would be to convert a large mass of more or less dishonest, unproductive or half productive, unsatisfactory, feckless, nervous, anxious, wretched people into good citizens, it is absurd to object to it as costly. It would be unbearably costly, of course, if the life and labor of its subjects were as stupidly wasted as they are in our prisons; but any scheme into which the conditions of our present system are read will stand condemned at once. Whether the labor of the subject be organized by the State, as in Government dockyards, post offices, municipal industries and services and so forth, or by private employers obtaining labor service from the authorities, organized and used productively it must be; and anyone who maintains that such organization and production costs the nation more than wasting the labor power of able-bodied men and women either by imprisonment or by throwing criminals on the streets to prey on society and on themselves, is maintaining a monstrous capitalistic paradox. Obviously it will not cost the nation anything at all: it will enrich it and protect it. The real commercial objection to it is that it would reduce the supply of sweatable labor available for unscrupulous private employers. But so much the better if it does. Sweating may make profits for private persons here and there; but their neighbors have to pay through the nose for these profits in poor rates, police rates, public health rates (mostly disease rates), and all the rest of the gigantic expenditure, all pure waste and mischief, which falls on the ratepayer and taxpayer in his constant struggle with the fruits of the poverty which he is nevertheless invited to maintain for the sake of making two or three of his neighbors unwholesomely and unjustly rich.

It is not altogether desirable that State tutelage should be available without limit for all who may volunteer for it. We can imagine a magistrate's court as a place in which men clamoring to be literally "taken in charge" are opposed by Crown lawyers and court officials determined to prove, if possible, that these importunate volunteers are quite well able to take care of themselves if they choose. Evidence of defective character would be sternly demanded; and if these were manufactured (as in the not uncommon case of a poor woman charging her son with theft to get him taken off her hands and sent to a reformatory) the offender would be ruthlessly consigned to my third division, consisting of offenders who are not to be taken in charge at all, but simply harried and bothered and attached and sold up until they pay the damages of their offences.

But as a matter of experience men do not seek the avowed tutelage of conditions which imply deficiency of character. Most of them resent any sort of tutelage unless they are brought up to it and therefore do not feel it as an infringement of their individuality. The army and navy are not overcrowded, though the army has always been the refuge of the sort of imbecile called a ne'er-do-well. Indeed the great obstacle to the realization of the Socialist dream of a perfectly organized and highly prosperous community, without poverty or overwork or idleness, is the intense repugnance of the average man to the degree of public regulation of his life which it would involve. This repugnance is certainly not weaker in England and America than elsewhere. Both Americans and Englishmen are born Anarchists; and, as complete Anarchism is practically impossible, they seek the minimum of public interference with their personal initiative, and overshoot the mark so excessively that it is no exaggeration to say that civilization is perishing of Anarchism. If civilization is to be saved for the first time in history it will have to be by a much greater extension of public regulation and organization than any community has hitherto been willing to submit to. When this extension takes place it will provide the discipline of public service for large masses of the population who now look after themselves very indifferently, and are only nominally free to control their own destinies; and in this way many people of the sort that now finds itself in prison will be kept straight automatically. But in any case there is no danger of a tutelary system being swamped by a rush of volunteers qualifying themselves for it by hurling stones through shop windows or the like.

All this does not mean that we must have indeterminate sentences of tutelage. The mischief of the present system is not that the criminal under preventive detention must be released at the end of ten years, but that if he relapses he is sent to penal servitude instead of being simply and sensibly returned to Camp Hill. What it does mean is that if the tutelage be made humane and profitable, the criminal, far from demanding his discharge, will rather threaten the authorities with a repetition of his crime if they turn him out of doors. The change that is needed is to add to the present power of the detaining authorities to release the prisoner at any time if they consider him fit for self-responsibility, the power of the prisoner to remain if he finds himself more comfortable and safe under tutelage, as voluntary soldiers feel themselves more comfortable in the army, or enclosed nuns in a convent, than cast on the world on his own resources.

WHITHER THE FACTS ARE DRIVING US

So much for the difficulty of the indeterminate sentence, which is quite manageable. Its discussion has led us to the discovery that in spite of the unchristian spirit of our criminal law, and the cruelty of its administration, the mere logic of facts is driving us to humane solutions. Already in England no judge or magistrate is obliged to pass any sentence whatever for a first offence except when dealing with a few extraordinary crimes which have affected our imagination so strongly that we feel bound to mark our abhorrence of them by special rigor not only to those convicted of them, but to those accused of them: for example, persons accused of high treason were formerly not allowed the help of counsel in defending themselves. And when the account of the English system of preventive detention at Camp Hill is studied in connection with the remarkable series of experiments now being made in America, it will be seen that nothing stands between us and humanity and decency but our cruelty, vindictiveness, terror, and thoughtless indifference.

CRIME AS DISEASE

It must not be imagined that any system will reach every anti-social deed that is committed. I have already shewn that most crime goes undetected, unreported, and even unforbidden; and I have suggested that if our system of dealing with crime were one with which any humane and thoughtful person could con-scientiously co-operate, if we compensated injured persons for bringing criminals to justice instead of, as at present, making the process expensive and extremely disagreeable and even terrify-ing to them, and if we revised our penal laws by striking out of their list of criminal acts a few which ought not to be there and adding a good many which ought to be there, we might have a good many more delinquents to deal with than at present unless we concurrently improved the education and condition of the masses sufficiently to do away with the large part of law-break-ing which is merely one of the symptoms of poverty, and would disappear with it. But in any case we should diligently read Samuel Butler's Erewhon, and accustom ourselves to regard crime as pathological, and the criminal as an invalid, curable or incurable. There is, in fact, hardly an argument that can be ad-vanced for the stern suppression of crime by penal methods that does not apply equally to the suppression of disease; and we have already an elaborate sanitary code under which persons neglecting certain precautions against disease are not only prosecuted but in some instances (sometimes quite mistaken ones, as the history of vaccination has proved) persecuted very cruelly. We actually force parents to subject their children to surgical operations, some of which are both dangerous and highly questionable. But we have so far stopped short of making it a punishable offence to be attacked by smallpox or typhus fever, though no legal assumption is more certain than that both diseases can be extinguished by sanitation more completely than crime by education. Yet there would be no greater injustice in such punishment than there is in the imprisonment of any thief; and the sanctimonious speech in which the judge in Erewhon, sentencing a man for phthisis, recapitulated the career of crime which began with an accident in childhood, and ended with pulmonary tuberculosis, was not a whit more ridiculous than the similar speeches made at every session by our own judges. Why a man who is punished for having an inefficient conscience should be privileged to have an inefficient lung is a debatable question. If one is sent to prison and the other to hospital, why make the prison so different from the hospital?

But I make the parallel here because it brings out the significance of the fact that we admit without protest that we have to put up with a good deal of illness in the world, and to treat the sufferers with special indulgence and consideration, instead of turning on them like a herd of buffaloes and goring them to death, as we do in the case of our moral invalids. We even punish people very severely for neglecting their invalids or treating them in such a way as to make them worse instead of better: that is, for doing to them exactly what we should do ourselves if instead of doing wrong in body and losing health they had gone wrong in mind and stolen a handkerchief. There are people in the world so incredibly foolish that they expect their children to be always perfectly truthful and perfectly obedient; but even these idiots do not expect their children to be perfectly well always, nor thrash them if they catch cold. In short, if crime were not punished at all, the world would not come to an end any more than it does now that disease is not punished at all. The real gist of the distinction we make is that the consequences of crime, if unpunished, are pleasant, whereas the consequences of catching a chill are its own punishment; but this will not bear examination. A bad conscience is quite as uncomfortable as a bad cold; and though there are people so hardily constituted in this respect that they can behave very selfishly without turning a hair, so are there people of such hardy physical constitution that they can abuse their bodies with impunity to an extent that would be fatal to ordinary persons. Anyhow, it is not proposed that abnormal subjects should be unrestrained.

On the other hand avoidable illnesses are just like avoidable crimes in respect of being the result of some form of indulgence, positive or negative. For all practical purposes the parallel between the physical and moral invalid holds good; only, we may have to reconsider the absolute sacredness of the physical invalid's life. I shall not here attempt to prejudge the result of that consideration; but it is clear that if we decide that this sacredness must be maintained at all costs, and that the idiot in Darenth, who lies there having food poured into it so that its heart may continue to beat and its lungs to breathe automatically (for it can do nothing voluntarily), must be preserved from death much more laboriously than Einstein, then we must hold the criminal equally fetish unless we are to keep the whole subject in its present disastrous confusion.

Reforming Our Consciences

The change in the public conscience which is necessary before these considerations can take effect in abolishing our villainous system of dealing with crime will never be induced by sympathy with the criminal or even disgust at the prison. The proportion of the population directly concerned is so small that to the great majority imprisonment is something so unlikely to occur—indeed, so certain statistically never to occur—that they cannot be persuaded to take any interest in the matter. As long as the question is only one of the comfort of the prisoner, nothing will be done, because as long as the principle of punishment is admitted, and the Sermon on the Mount ridiculed as an unpractical outburst of anarchism and sentimentality, the public will always be reassured by learning from the judges (none of whom, by the way, seems to know what really happens to a prisoner after he leaves the dock) that our prisons are admirable institutions, and by the romances of Prison Commissioners like Du Cane and Sir Evelyn Ruggles-Brise, who arrange prisons as children build houses with toy bricks, and finally become so pleased with their arrangements that they describe them in terms which make us wonder that they do not commit serious crimes to qualify themselves for prolonged residence in their pet paradises. I must therefore attack the punitive position at another angle by dealing with its psychological effect on the criminal.

Expiation and Moral Accountancy

No ordinary criminal will agree with me for a moment that punishment is a mistake and a sin. His opinions on that point are precisely those of the policeman who arrests him; and if I were to preach this gospel of mine to the convicts in a prison I should be dismissed as a hopeless crank far more summarily than if I were to interview the Chief Commissioner at Scotland Yard about it.

Punishment is not a simple idea: it is a very complex one. It is not merely some injury that an innocent person inflicts on a guilty one, and that the guilty one evades by every means in his power. It is also a balancing of accounts with the soul. People who feel guilty are apt to inflict it on themselves if nobody will take the job off their hands. Confessions, though less common than they would be if the penalties were not so soul-destroying, are received without surprise. From the criminals' point of view punishment is expiation; and their bitterest complaints of injustice refer, not to their sentences, but to the dishonesty with which society, having exacted the price of the crime, still treats the criminal as a defaulter. Even so sophisticated a man of the world as Oscar Wilde claimed that by his two years' imprisonment he had settled accounts with the world and was entitled to begin again with a clean slate. But the world persisted in ostracizing him as if it had not punished him at all.

This was inevitable; but it was dishonest. If we are absurd enough to engage in a retributive trade in crime, we should at least trade fairly and give clean receipts when we are paid. If we did, we should soon find that the trade is impracticable and ridiculous; for neither party can deliver the goods. No discharge that the authorities can give can procure the ex-prisoner an eligible situation; and no atonement that a thief or murderer can make in suffering can make him any the less a thief or murderer. And nobody shirks this demonstration as much as the thief himself. Human self-respect wants so desperately to have its sins washed away, however purgatorially, that we are willing to go through the most fantastic ceremonies, conjurations, and ordeals to have our scarlet souls made whiter than snow. We naturally prefer to lay our sins on scapegoats or on the Cross, if our neighbors will let us off so easily; but when they will not, then we will cleanse ourselves by suffering a penalty sooner than be worried by our consciences. This is the real foundation of the criminal law in human superstition. This is why, when we refuse to employ a discharged prisoner, he invariably pleads that what he did is paid for, and that we have no right to bring it against him after he has suffered the appointed penalty.

As we cannot admit the plea, we should consider whether we should exact the penalty. I am not arguing that the plea should be admitted: I am arguing that the bargain should never have been made. I am more merciless than the criminal law, because I would destroy the evildoer's delusion that there can be any forgiveness of sin. What is done cannot be undone; and the man who steals must remain a thief until he becomes another man, no matter what reparation or expiation he may make or suffer.

A punishment system means a pardon system: the two go to-gether inseparably. Once admit that if I do something wicked to you we are quits when you do something equally wicked to me and you are bound to admit also that the two blacks make a white. Our criminal system is an organized attempt to produce white by two blacks. Common sense should doggedly refuse to believe that evil can be abolished by duplicating it. But common sense is not so logical; and thus we get the present grotesque spectacle of a judge committing thousands of horrible crimes in order that thousands of criminals may feel that they have balanced their moral accounts.

Familiar Frauds of the Trade in Sin

It is a game at which there is plenty of cheating. The prisoner pleads Not Guilty, and tries his best to get off, or to have as light a sentence as possible. The commercial brigand, fining himself for his plunderings by subscribing to charities, never subscribes as much as he stole. But through all the folly and absurdity of the business, and the dense mental confusion caused by the fact that it is never frankly faced and clearly stated, there shines the fact that conscience is part of the equipment of the normal man, and that it never fails in its work. It is retributive because it makes him uncomfortable; it is deterrent because detection and retribution are absolutely certain; and it is reformative because reformation is the only way of escape. That is to say, it does to perfection by divine methods what the Prison Commissioners are trying to do by diabolical methods without hope or even possibility of success.

Revenge the Destroyer of Conscience

The effect of revenge, or retribution from without, is to destroy the conscience of the aggressor instantly. If I stand on the corn of a man in the street, and he winces or cries out, I am all remorse, and overwhelm him with heartfelt apologies. But if he sets about me with his fists, the first blow he lands changes my mind completely; and I bend all my energies on doing intentionally to his eyes and nose and jaw what I did unintentionally to his toes. Vengeance is mine, saith the Lord; and that means that it is not the Lord Chief Justice's. A violent punishing, such as a flogging, carries no sense of expiation with it: whilst its effect lasts, which is fortunately not very long, its victim is in a savage fury in which he would burn down the gaol and roast the warders and the governor and the justices alive in it with intense satisfaction if he could.

Imprisonment, on the other hand, gives the conscience a false satisfaction. The criminal feels that he is working off his crime, though he is doing it involuntarily, and would escape at any moment if he could. He preserves his sense of solvency without ceasing to be a thief, as a gambler preserves it by paying his losses without ceasing to be a gambler.

The Sentimentality of Revenge

There is a mysterious psychological limit to punishment. We somehow dare not kill a hopelessly diseased or dangerous man by way of punishment for any offence short of murder, though we chloroform a hopelessly diseased or dangerous dog by way of kindness without the least misgiving. Until we have purged our souls of malice, which is pure sentiment, we cannot get rid of sentimentality; and the sentimentality which makes us abominably cruel in one direction makes us foolishly and superstitiously afraid to act sternly in others. Homicidal lunatics say in their asylums "They cannot hang *us*." I could give here, but refrain for obvious reasons, simple instructions by carrying out which any person can commit a murder with the certainty, if detected, of being sent to an asylum instead of to the gallows. They ought to have just the contrary effect; for the case of the homicidal lunatic is the clearest case for judicial killing that exists. It is the killing of the sane murderer that requires consideration: it should never be a matter of course, because there are murders which raise no convincing presumption that those who commit them are exceptionally likely to commit another. But about a chronically homicidal lunatic there should be no hesitation whatever as long as we practise judicial killing at all; and there would not be if we simply considered without malice the question of his fitness to live in society. We spare him because the gallows is a punishment, and we feel that we have no right to punish a lunatic. When we realize that we have no right to punish anybody, the problem of disposing of impossible people will put itself on its proper footing. We shall drop our moral airs; but unless we rule killing out absolutely, persons who give more trouble than they are worth will run the risk of being apologetically, sympathetically, painlessly, but effectually returned to the dust from which they sprung.

MAN IN SOCIETY MUST JUSTIFY HIS EXISTENCE

This would at least create a sense of moral responsibility in our citizens. We are all too apt to take our lives as a matter of course. In a civilized community life is not a matter of course: it can be maintained only on complicated artificial conditions; and whoever enlarges his life by violating these conditions enlarges it at the expense of the lives of others. The extent to which we tolerate such vital embezzlement at present is quite outrageous: we have whole classes of persons who waste, squander, and luxuriate in the hard-earned income of the nation without even a pretence of social service or contribution of any kind; and instead of sternly calling on them to justify their existence or go to the scrap heap, we encourage and honor them, and indeed conduct the whole business of the country as if its object were to produce and pamper them. How can a prison chaplain appeal with any effect to the conscience of a professional criminal who knows quite well that his illegal and impecunious modes of preying on society are no worse morally, and enormously less mischievous materially, than the self-legalized plutocratic modes practised by the chaplain's most honored friends with the chaplain's full approval? The moment we cease asking whether men are good or bad, and ascertain simply whether they are pulling their weight in the social boat, our persistent evildoers may have a very unpleasant surprise. Far from having an easy time under a Government of soft-hearted and soft-headed sentimentalists, cooing that "to understand everything is to pardon everything," they may find themselves disciplined to an extent at present undreamed of by the average man-about-town.

CIVILIZED MAN IS NOT BORN FREE

And here it will occur to some of my readers that a book about imprisonment should be also a book about freedom. Rousseau said that Man is born free. Rousseau was wrong. No government of a civilized State can possibly regard its citizens as born free. On the contrary, it must regard them as born in debt, and as necessarily incurring fresh debt every day they live; and its most pressing duty is to hold them to that debt and see that they pay it. Not until it is paid can any freedom begin for the individual. When he cannot walk a hundred yards without using such a very expensive manufactured article as a street, care must be taken that he produces his share of its cost. When he has paid scot and lot his leisure begins, and with it his liberty. He can then say boldly, "Having given unto Cæsar the things that are Cæsar's I shall now, under no tutelage or compulsion except that of my conscience, give to God the things that are God's." That is the only possible basis for civil liberty; and we are unable to attain it because our governments corruptly shirk the duties of Cæsar; usurp the attributes of God; and make an unholy mess of which this horrible prison system of ours is only one symptom.

OUR NATURE NOT SO BAD AS OUR PRISON SYSTEM

We must, however, be on our guard against ascribing all the villainy of that system to our cruelty and selfish terrors. I have pointed out how the operation of the criminal law is made very uncertain, and therefore loses the deterrence it aims at, by the reluctance of sympathetic people to hand over offenders to the police. Vindictive and frivolous as we are, we are not downright fiends, as we should be if our modern prison system had been deliberately invented and constructed by us all in one piece. It has grown upon us, and grown evilly, having evil roots; but its worst developments have been well meant; for the road to hell is paved with good intentions, not with bad ones. The history of it is too long to be told here in detail; but a word or two of it is needed to save the reader from closing the volume in despair of human nature.

The History of our Prisons

Imprisonment was not originally a punishment any more than chaining up a dog, cruel as that practice is, is a punishment. It was simply a method of detention. The officer responsible for the custody of an offender had to lock or chain him up somewhere to prevent him from running away, and to be able to lay his hand on him on the day of trial or execution. This was regarded as the officer's own affair: the law looked to him for the delivery of the offender, and did not concern itself as to how it was effected. This seems strange nowadays; but I can remember a case of a lunatic on a battleship, who had one man told off to act as his keeper. The lunatic was violent and troublesome, and gave his keeper plenty of severe exercise; but the rest of the crew looked on with the keenest enjoyment of the spectacle, and gave the lunatic the strictest fair play by letting his keeper fight it out with him unaided. And that is what the law did mostly in England until well into the nineteenth century. To this day there is no prison in some of the Virgin Islands. The prisoner is tied by the leg to a tree, and plays cards with the constable who guards him.

The result was that the provision of lock-ups became a private commercial speculation, undertaken and conducted for the sake of what could be made out of it by the speculator. There was no need for these places to be lock-ups: the accused could be chained up or gyved or manacled if no safe prison was available; and when lock-ups came to be provided as a matter of business, the practice of chaining was continued as a matter of tradition, and formed a very simple method of extorting money from prisoners by torture. No food was provided by the State: what the prisoner ate was charged against him as if he were in a hotel; and it often happened that when he was acquitted he was taken back to prison as security for his bill and kept there until he had paid it.

Under these circumstances the prison was only a building into which all classes and sorts of detained persons were thrown indiscriminately. The rich could buy a private room, like Mr Pickwick in the Fleet; but the general herd of poor criminals, old and young, innocent and hardened, virgin and prostitute, mad and sane, clean and verminous, diseased and whole, pigged together in indescribable promiscuity. I repeat: nobody invented this. Nobody intended it. Nobody defended it except the people who made money by it. Nobody else except the prisoners knew about it: they were as innocent as Mr Pickwick of what went on inside the prison walls. And, as usual in England, nobody bothered about it, because people with money could avoid its grossest discomforts on the negligibly rare occasions when they fell into the hands of the officers of the law. It was by the mere accident of being pricked for sheriff that John Howard learned what the inside of a gaol was like.

HOWARD'S GOOD INTENTIONS

As a result of Howard's agitation prisons are now State prisons: the State accepts full responsibility for the prisoner from the moment of his arrest. So far, so good. But in the meantime imprisonment, instead of being a means of detention, has become not only a punishment, but, for the reasons given at the outset of this essay, *the* punishment. And official shallowness, prevailing against the poet Crabbe's depth, has made it an infernal punishment. Howard saw that the prisoners in the old gaol contaminated one another; and his remedy was to give them separate cells in which they could meditate on their crimes and repent. When prisons with separate cells were built accordingly, the prison officials soon found that it saved trouble to keep the prisoners locked up in them; and the philanthropists out-Howarded Howard in their efforts to reform criminals by silence, separation, and the wearing of masks, lest they should contaminate one another by the expression of their faces. Until 1920 the convicts in Belgian prisons wore iron masks. Our own convicts wore cloth masks for some time, and would probably be wearing them still had not our solicitude for their salvation killed and driven them mad in such numbers that we were forced to admit that thorough segregation, though no doubt correct in principle (which is just where it is fatally incorrect), does not work. Frightful things in the way of solitude, separation, and silence, not for months, but for many years at a time, were done in American prisons.

The reader will find as much as he can stand in English Prisons Under Local Government, by Sidney and Beatrice Webb, and a good deal more in English Prisons Today, edited by Stephen Hobhouse and Fenner Brockway, in which the system is described from the prison cells, not by common criminals, but by educated and thoughtful men and women who, as agitators for Votes for Women or as Conscientious Objectors to military service, have been condemned to imprisonment of late years. Our horror at their disclosures must not blind us to my immediate point, which is that our prison system is a horrible accidental growth and not a deliberate human invention, and that its worst features have been produced with the intention, not of making it worse, but of making it better. Howard is not responsible: he warned us that "absolute solitude is more than human nature can bear without the hazard of distraction and despair." Elizabeth Fry saw nothing but mischief in prison silence and prison solitude. Their followers were fools: that is all.

The So-called Criminal Type

Perhaps the most far-reaching service done by the Brockway-Hobhouse report is the light it throws on the alleged phenomenon of a Criminal Type. The belief in this has gone through several vicissitudes. At first a criminal was supposed to be a beetle-browed, bulldog-jawed person for whom no treatment could be too bad. This suited the prison authorities, as nothing is so troublesome to them as waves of public sympathy with criminals, founded on imaginative idealizations of them. But the authorities changed their note when a scientific account of the type was put forward by Lombroso and a body of investigators calling them-selves psychiatrists. These gentlemen found that criminals had asymmetrical features and other stigmata (an effective word). They contended that the criminals were the victims of these con-genital peculiarities, and could not help themselves. As the ob-vious conclusion was that they were not morally responsible for their actions, and therefore should not be punished for them, the prison authorities saw their occupation threatened, and denied that there was any criminal type, always excepting the beetle-brows and bulldog-jaws which the criminal was assumed to have imposed on his naturally Grecian features by a life of villainy. They were able to point out that everybody has asymmetrical features, and that the alleged stigmata of the Lombrosic criminal are as characteristic of the Church, the Stock Exchange, the Bench, and the Legislature as of Portland and Dartmoor. That settled the matter for the moment. The criminal type was off.

But nobody who has ever visited a prison has any doubt that there is a prison type, and a very marked one at that. And if he is saturated with the teachings of the Natural Selectionists, accord-ing to which changes of type are the result of the slow accumula-tion of minute variations, and therefore cannot be visibly pro-duced in less than, say, a million years, he will conclude, like Lombroso, that the criminal is a natural species, and therefore incorrigible.

How Types are Manufactured

But twentieth century observation has lately been knocking nineteenth century science into a cocked hat by shewing that the types that were said to take a million years to produce can be produced in five. I have in my hand number seventy-four of the privately printed opuscula issued by the Society which calls itself the Set of Odd Volumes. It is entitled The Influence Which Our Surroundings Exert On Us, and is the work of Sir William Arbuthnot Lane, one of our most distinguished surgeons. In it he shews that by keeping a man at work as a deal porter, a coal trimmer, a shoemaker or what not, you can, within a period no longer than that spent in prison by typical criminals, produce a typical deal porter, coal trimmer and so on, the changes involved being visible grotesque skeletal changes for which Huxley or Owen would have demanded a whole evolutionary epoch. No Bolshevik has yet written so revolutionary a pamphlet as this little record of a recent after-dinner speech.

What it means is that the criminal type is an artificial type, manufactured in prison by the prison system. It means that the type is not one of the accidents of the system, but must be produced by imprisonment no matter how normal the victim is at the beginning, or how anxious the authorities are to keep him so. The simple truth is that the typical criminal is a normal man when he first enters a prison, and develops the type during his imprisonment.

PSYCHIATRISTS AND ENDOCRINISTS

This does not mean that no other types are to be noted in prison. By all means let the endocrinists go on dividing abnormal people, in prison and out, into hyper and sub pituitaries and thyroidics and adrenals. They need not, as the habit of the scientific world is, quarrel furiously with me for remarking that another type can be externally imposed on their pituitaries and thyroidics and adrenals impartially. The fact that a man has an excessive adrenal secretion may be a reason for trying to check it instead of punishing him. It does not alter the fact that if you keep one adrenal in penal servitude and another in the House of Lords for ten years, the one will shew the stigmata of a typical convict, and the other of a typical peer, in addition to the stigmata of adrenalism.

CRUDE CRIMINOLOGY

To realize the importance of this, we must recall the discredit into which Lombroso fell when it was pointed out that by his diagnosis everybody was more or less a criminal. I suggest that this was not quite so complete a *reductio ad absurdum* as it seemed. I have already accounted for the curious insensibility of the public to the misery they are inflicting on their prisoners by the fact that some of the most mischievous and unhappy conditions of prison life are imposed on all respectably brought-up children as a matter of course. It is arguable that what Lombroso took to be criminal stigmata were genuine prison stigmata, and that their prevalence among respectable people who have never been in gaol is due to the prison conditions to which such people are conventionally subjected for the first twenty years of their life.

The Case of Queen Victoria

I take up another much discussed and most readable modern book: Queen Victoria, by Lytton Strachey. It contains some shocking pages, made bearable by the comedic power of the author, but still ghastly reading. Queen Victoria was very carefully brought up. When she was eighteen they came to her and told her that she was Queen of England. She asked whether she could really do what she liked; and when this was reluctantly admitted by her careful mother, Victoria considered what wonderful and hitherto impossible happiness she could confer on herself by her new powers. And she could think of nothing more delightful than an hour of separate solitary confinement. She had never been alone before, never been unwatched by people whose business it was to see that she behaved herself, and to rebuke her and punish her if she did anything they disapproved of. In short, she had been treated as a dangerous criminal, unfit to be trusted with any initiative or moral responsibility.

It would carry me too far to trace the effects of this monstrous bringing-up on the course of history. The book should be given to every prisoner who finds his solitary confinement every day from half-past four in the afternoon to next morning more than he can bear. He will find that there are worse things than solitude when the only company available is that of the warders and governor. And he will understand why the next thing the queen did was to turn her mother practically out of the house. She was, as he would put it, getting a bit of her own back. Let him then, if he is an intellectually curious prisoner, and has not been long enough in prison to have his intellect atrophied, make a list of the miseries that are common to the lot of our little Queen Victorias out of prison and our thieves and murderers in prison. Confinement, obedience, silence at associated work, continual supervision by hostile guardians reporting every infraction of rule for punishment, regulation of every moment of one's life from outside, compulsory exercise instead of play, systematic extirpation of initiative and responsibility, uncongenial and sometimes impossible tasks, and a normal assumption that every original and undictated action will be a wrong action. This is the lot of the well-brought-up child, whether heiress to a throne or heir to a country rector, like Samuel Butler, who was beaten by his father until he acquired and retained until his death some of the stigmata of a chained dog. The British statesman Mr Winston Churchill, a duke's grandson, tells us in his reminiscences that when he was a child of seven he was sent to an expensive school where the discipline was more ferocious than would be permitted in a Reformatory for young criminals of twice that age.

PREVALENCE OF CRIMINAL CHARACTERISTICS IN POLITE SOCIETY

Butler, a man of exceptionally strong character which reacted violently against his training, would have been what the Prison Commissioners call a bad prisoner, and therefore does not illustrate the normal social effect of the system. Even Queen Victoria, with all her characteristic prison transitions from tutelage to tyranny, and her inability to understand or tolerate any other conditions, was too energetic, uneducated, and original, not to react vigorously against her circumstances. It is when we look at modern civilization in bulk that we are forced to admit that child training (or rather taming), as we practise it, produces moral imbecility. About a dozen millions of persons, on whose education enormous sums had been spent publicly and privately, went like sheep to the slaughter in 1914–18; and the survivors are making elaborate arrangements to go again. A glance at the newspapers which cater specially for the classes which go through the respectable routine of preparatory school, public school, and university, will shew that the ideals of those classes, their points of honor, their sense of humor, their boasts, their anticipations of future exploits, are precisely those of criminals. They always are ready (Steady, boys, steady) to fight and to conquer again and again. Ned Kelly, Charles Peace, Dick Turpin and Claude Duval, the Black Prince, Harry the Fifth, Robin Hood, Paul Jones, Clive, Nelson and Captain Kidd, Cortez and Lord Roberts, were not all on the side of the law; but their morality was the same: they all held that pugnacity, the will to conquer, and the sort of courage that makes pugnacity and the will to conquer effective, are virtues so splendid that they sanctify plunder, devastation, and murder in direct proportion to the magnitude of these operations. The relaxations of the operators are love affairs and luxurious banquets. Now pray what else is the romance of the thieves' kitchen and of the surreptitious conversations of the prison exercise ring and associated labor shop? The difference is no more essential than that between whiskey and champagne, between an ounce of shag and a box of Havanas, between a burglary and a bombardment, between a jemmy and a bayonet, between a chloroformed pad and a gas shell, between a Browning pistol bought at a pawnbroker's and a service revolver. Gild the reputable end of it as thickly as we like with the cant of courage, patriotism, national prestige, security, duty, and all the rest of it: smudge the disreputable end with all the vituperation that the utmost transports of virtuous indignation can inspire: such tricks will not induce the divine judgment, by which all mankind must finally stand or fall, to distinguish between the victims of these two bragging predatory insects the criminal and the gentleman.

CRUDE CRIMINOLOGY

The gentleman beats the criminal hollow in the magnitude of his operations and the number of people employed in them. For the depredations of the criminal are negligibly small compared to the military holocausts and ravaged areas, the civic slums, the hospitals, the cemeteries crowded with the prematurely dead, and the labor markets in which men and women are exposed for sale for all purposes, honorable and dishonorable. These are the products of criminal ideas imposed on the entire population. The common thief and burglar, miserably sweated by the receiver to whom he has to sell his plunder, steals a few spoons or diamonds at a monstrous risk, and gets less than a tenth of their value from a rascal who runs no risk worth considering; and the poor wretch is content with the trumpery debauch his hard-earned percentage brings him. The gentleman steals a whole country, or a perpetual income for himself and his descendants, and is never satisfied until he has more conquests and more riches to boast of. What is more, the illicit thief does not defend his conduct ethically. He may cry "To hell with the parsons and with honesty and white-livered respectability!" and so forth; but he does so as a defier of God, a public enemy, a Satanic hero. The gentleman really believes that he is a creator of national prestige, a defender of the faith, a pillar of society; and with this conviction to strengthen him he is utterly unscrupulous in his misplaced pride and honor, and plays the wholesaler in evil to the criminal's petty retail enterprises.

THE ROOT OF THE EVIL

And what is at the bottom of it all? Just the belief that virtue is something to be imposed on us from without, like the tricks taught to a performing animal, by the whip. Such manufactured virtue has no ethical value whatever, as appears promptly enough when the whip is removed. All communities must live finally by their ethical values: that is, by their genuine virtues. Living virtuously is an art that can be learnt only by living in full responsibility for our own actions; and as the process is one of trial and error even when seeking the guidance of others' experience, society must, whether it likes it or not, put up with a certain burden of individual error. The man who has never made a mistake will never make anything; and the man who has never done any harm will never do any good. The disastrous people are the indelicate and conceited busybodies who want to reform criminals and mould children's characters by external pressure and abortion. The cowards who refuse to accept the inevitable risks of human society, and would have everybody handcuffed if they could lest they should have their pockets picked or their heads punched, are bad enough; and the flagellomaniacs who are for ever shrieking the exploded falsehood that garotting was put down by flogging, and that all crimes, especially the sexually exciting ones, can be put down by more flogging, are worse; but such obvious cases of phobia and libido soon make themselves ridiculous if they are given a free platform. It is the busybody, the quack, the pseudo God Almighty, the Dr Moreau of Mr H. G. Wells's ghastliest romance, continually lusting to lay hands on living creatures and by reckless violation of their souls and bodies abort them into some monster representing their ideal of a Good Man, or a Model Citizen, or a Perfect Wife and Mother: he is the irreconcilable enemy, the ubiquitous and iniquitous nuisance, and the most difficult to get rid of because he has imposed his moral pretensions on public opinion, and is accepted as just the sort of philanthropist our prisons and criminals should be left to, whereas he (or she) is really the only sort of person who should never be admitted to any part of a prison except the gallows on which so many less mischievous egotists have expired. No one who has not a profound instinctive respect for the right of all living creatures to moral and religious liberty: that is, to liberty of moral and religious experiment on themselves, limited only by their obligations not to become unduly burdensome to others, should be let come within ten miles of a child, a criminal, or any other person in a condition of tutelage. Indelicacy on this point is the most conclusive of social disqualifications. When it is ignorant and short-sighted it produces criminals. When it is worldly-wise and pompous it produces Prison Commissioners.

CRUDE CRIMINOLOGY

Recapitulation

For the reader's mental convenience, I recapitulate the contentions presented above.

1. Modern imprisonment: that is, imprisonment practised as a punishment as well as a means of detention, is extremely cruel and mischievous, and therefore extremely wicked. The word extremely is used advisedly because the system has been pushed to a degree at which prison mortality and prison insanity forced it back to the point at which it is barely endurable, which point may therefore be regarded as the practicable extreme.

2. Although public vindictiveness and public dread are largely responsible for this wickedness, some of the most cruel features of the prison system are not understood by the public, and have not been deliberately invented and contrived for the purpose of increasing the prisoner's torment. The worst of these are (a) unsuccessful attempts at reform, (b) successful attempts to make the working of the prison cheaper for the State and easier for the officials, and (c) accidents of the evolution of the old privately owned detention prison into the new punitive State prison.

3. The prison authorities profess three objects: (a) Retribution (a euphemism for vengeance), (b) Deterrence (a euphemism for Terrorism), and (c) Reform of the prisoner. They achieve the first by simple atrocity. They fail in the second through lack of the necessary certainty of detection, prosecution, and conviction; partly because their methods are too cruel and mischievous to secure the co-operation of the public; partly because the prosecutor is put to serious inconvenience and loss of time; partly because most people desire to avoid an unquestionable family disgrace much more than to secure a very questionable justice; and partly because the proportion of avowedly undetected crimes is high enough to hold out reasonable hopes to the criminal that he will never be called to account. The third (Reform) is irreconcilable with the first (Retribution); for the figures of recidivism, and the discovery that the so-called Criminal Type is really a prison type, prove that the retributive process is one of uncom-

230

pensated deterioration.

4. The cardinal vice of the system is the anti-Christian vice of vengeance, or the intentional duplication of malicious injuries partly in pure spite, partly in compliance with the expiatory superstition that two blacks make a white. The criminal accepts this, but claims that punishment absolves him if the injuries are equivalent, and still more if he has the worse of the bargain, as he almost always has. Consequently, when absolution on his release is necessarily denied him, and he is forced back into crime by the refusal to employ him, he feels that he is entitled to revenge this injustice by becoming an enemy of society. No beneficial reform of our treatment of criminals is possible unless and until this superstition of expiation and this essentially sentimental vice of vengeance are unconditionally eradicated.

5. Society has a right of self-defence, extending to the destruction or restraint of lawbreakers. This right is separable from the right to revenge or punish: it need have no more to do with punishment or revenge than the caging or shooting of a man-eating tiger. It arises from the existence of (A) intolerably mischievous human beings, and (B) persons defective in the self-control needed for free life in modern society, but well behaved and at their ease under tutelage and discipline. Class A can be painlessly killed or permanently restrained. The requisite tutelage and discipline can be provided for Class B without rancor or insult. The rest can be treated not as criminals but as civil defendants, and made to pay for their depredations in the same manner. At present many persons guilty of conduct much viler than that for which poor men are sent to prison suffer nothing worse than civil actions for damages when they do not (unhappily) enjoy complete impunity.

6. The principle to be kept before the minds of all citizens is that as civilized society is a very costly arrangement necessary to their subsistence and security they must justify their enjoyment of it by contributing their share to its cost, and giving no more than their share of trouble, subject to every possible provision by insurance against innocent disability. This is a condition pre-

cedent to freedom, and justifies us in removing cases of incurable noxious disability by simply putting an end to their existence.

7. An unconquerable repugnance to judicial killing having led to the abolition of capital punishment in several countries, and to its reservation for specially dangerous or abhorrent crimes in all the others, it is possible that the right to kill may be renounced by all civilized States. This repugnance may be intensified as we cease to distinguish between sin and infirmity, or, in prison language, between crime and disease, because of our fear of being led to the extirpation of the incurable invalid who is excessively troublesome as well as to that of the incurable criminal.

On the other hand, the opposite temperament, which is not squeamish about making short work of hard cases, and which is revolted by the daily sacrifice of the lives of prison officials, and of relatives and nurses, to incurable criminals and invalids, may be reinforced by the abandonment of ethical pretentiousness, vengeance, malice, and all uncharitableness in the matter, and may become less scrupulous than at present in advocating euthanasia for all incurables.

Whichever party may prevail, punishment as such is likely to disappear, and with it the ear-marking of certain offences as calling for specially deterrent severities. But it does not follow that lethal treatment of extreme cases will be barred. On the contrary, it may be extended from murder to social incompatibility of all sorts. If it be absolutely barred, sufficient restraint must be effected, not as a punishment but as a necessity for public safety. But there will be no excuse for making it more unpleasant than it need be.

8. When detention and restraint are necessary, the criminal's right to contact with all the spiritual influences of his day should be respected, and its exercise encouraged and facilitated. Conversation, access to books and pictures and music, unfettered scientific, philosophic, and religious activity, change of scene and occupation, the free formation of friendships and acquaintances, marriage and parentage: in short, all the normal methods of creation and recreation, must be available for criminals as for other persons, partly because deprivation of these things is

severely punitive, and partly because it is destructive to the victim, and produces what we call the criminal type, making a cure impossible. Any specific liberty which the criminal's specific defects lead him to abuse will, no doubt, be taken from him; but if his life is spared his right to live must be accepted in the fullest sense, and not, as at present, merely as a right to breathe and circulate his blood. In short, a criminal should be treated, not as a man who has forfeited all normal rights and liberties by the breaking of a single law, but as one who, through some specific weakness or weaknesses, is incapable of exercising some specific liberty or liberties.

9. The main difficulty in applying this concept of individual freedom to the criminal arises from the fact that the concept itself is as yet unformed. We do not apply it to children, at home or at school, nor to employees, nor to persons of any class or age who are in the power of other persons. Like Queen Victoria, we conceive Man as being either in authority or subject to authority, each person doing only what he is expressly permitted to do, or what the example of the rest of his class encourages him to consider as tacitly permitted. The concept of the evolving free man in an evolving society, making all sorts of experiments in conduct, and therefore doing everything he likes as far as he can unless there are express prohibitions to which he is politically a consenting party, is still unusual, and consequently terrifying, in spite of all the individualist pamphlets of the eighteenth and nineteenth centuries. It will be found that those who are most scandalized by the liberties I am claiming for the convict would be equally scandalized if I claimed them for their own sons, or even for themselves.

The conclusion is that imprisonment cannot be fully understood by those who do not understand freedom. But it can be understood quite well enough to have it made a much less horrible, wicked, and wasteful thing than it is at present.

AYOT ST LAWRENCE,
   Dec-Jan. 1921–22.

THE UNPROTECTED CHILD AND THE LAW

From Time and Tide, 23 February 1923

IT is a curious feature of British civilization that our police arrangements, though they enable the adult male citizen to face his fellow-men unarmed and the adult female to walk abroad unescorted, fail to protect children from the most detestable forms of molestation. The woman who goes shopping with a sense of complete security, and never has a moment's anxiety as to the safe return of her husband from his work, cannot feel that her children, even at the smallest age compatible with independent locomotion, are safe in broad daylight in a London park, much less in the *camera obscura* of the picture theatre. When her worst apprehensions are justified, she finds that her legal remedy, as far as it affects the child, is an aggravation of its wrong by the addition of a series of legal psychological outrages to the illegal physical outrage; so that she resorts to it only when she does not fully know what she is doing. When she realizes too late that the law, professing to deter the criminal, is really calculated to deter the prosecutor, she is sometimes moved to suspect that this effect is not wholly unintended.

There is something more than motherly indignation to support that suspicion. The few publicly articulate people who concern themselves about the matter, and who form the so-called public opinion that finds expression on the bench, seem to fall into two extremes with no middle. Either they are psychopathically excited by psychopathic outrages, and frankly demand that the offenders be flogged or emasculated, or they regard the offence as an amiable weakness, and the notion that its consequences to the victim are necessarily serious as sentimental nonsense. They shew their reluctance to punish it by very light sentences, and by a resolute opposition to the raising of the age at which the consent (and by inference the enjoyment) of the child can be pleaded in defence. Thus between the flagellomaniacs who are making the offender's vice an excuse for gratifying their own peculiar form of it on the one hand, and the sympathetic amorists on the other, the children have to thank their luck rather than the law when they escape molestation.

The matter is further complicated by men's dread of false charges, blackmail, and conspiracies between mother and child to "put away" an inconvenient father. Such apprehensions seem ridiculous to people who have no experience of the subject; but practical acquaintance with it modifies that view considerably. Sir Basil Thomson, in his very entertaining book on police experiences entitled Queer People, humorously suggests that all girls should be locked up until they are eighteen to save the police the trouble of investigating the stories they invent. The late Frank Podmore, an author who, as a very active member of the Psychical Research Society, became an expert in haunted houses, told me that he had become so skilled in the detective side of his hobby that he could walk into any haunted house and almost in every case lay his finger instantly on the ghost, who was always a girl and often quite a little one. In fact the younger the girl the more unrestrained the imaginative liar. Further, differences between child and child in precocity are so incalculable that we have Oscar Wilde giving sixteen as the age at which conscience of sex begins, and Rousseau, in his autobiography, giving the date in his own case at his birth: the net conclusion being that in the case of any individual child it is impossible either to accept any story on the ground that the teller is too young to have invented it, or to reject it as too grotesque to be credible. Anything that is thinkable and much that is unthinkable may be true; but also it may be invented, especially by a child with such prompting as it must necessarily get when it is spoken to on the subject at all, to say nothing of deliberate suggestion from adults interested in establishing a charge.

In view of these facts, it is impossible to exempt a child from the most searching cross-examination when criminal proceedings are taken; yet from every point of view other than that of establishing or refuting a charge, cross-examination is as undesirable as its necessarily bad effect on the child can make it. In short, the remedy offered by the criminal law may easily be worse than no remedy at all. It rubs violently into the child's mind an impression that had much better be obliterated, or, as that is hardly possible, minimized. It associates the impression with the morbid terrors of a criminal court, or, worse still, with its unwholesome interest. Like so many of our procedures, it is rather a concession to the feeling that something must be done than a serious attempt to do the right thing. And it encourages the inveterate superstition that an evil is satisfactorily dealt with and done with when somebody has been taken up by the police and punished for it.

The danger to children is at its gravest when popular ignorance and superstition on matters of sex are left undispelled because of the taboo which forbids their being mentioned. Take, for example, the case of venereal disease. Few people realize that children are in special danger of being infected by it: they regard them as specially exempt from it because of their innocence. They do not know that there is a belief, widespread in our most ignorant classes, that a man suffering from such disease can be cured by intercourse with a virgin: and that because childhood seems the surest guarantee of virginity, children are violated as a therapeutical measure, the only result, of course, being that the child is infected too. And the only provision we make for this quite common horror (as far as horrors can be said to be common at all) is to punish the man with one month or twenty-four months' imprisonment, as the judge or magistrate may feel disposed, and to send the child to the Lock Hospital to associate with prostitutes and discuss its experiences with them. As far as I know, there is only one attempt being made to provide, by private subscription, a hospital for innocently infected children to which any sane mother would consent to send her child. That staggering fact illustrates the sort of consideration children get from our public authorities and from the public conscience behind them.

The cultivated reader will perhaps doubt whether so gross a superstition can really have any hold in any class of modern society. I shall not refer such sceptics to the police statistics, because these do not really cover all the ground. I prefer to point to the fictions which delight civilized people in the theatre, the picture house, and the novel. Is there a theme more threadbare with repeated use than that of the rake redeemed by the love of a beautiful and virtuous maiden? Yet this is a less excusable superstition than the other by just so much as a moral miracle is less credible than a physical cure. And the superstition in this form is no more confined to fiction than in its grosser one. The evil wrought by girls marrying men with the intention of reforming them is no doubt much mitigated by the fact that the superiority on which the woman is banking is only an illusion created by her vanity; but the fact remains that though the greatest blackguards are cut off by their characters from many opportunities open to well-conducted men, no blackguard ever seems to have the smallest difficulty in inducing a comparatively respectable girl to marry him, even when she knows that she must reform him to the extent of a rebirth if her life with him is to be endurable. The result is precisely what it is in the physical case with the child: she does not reform him, and is herself morally infected. When the tragedy of the morally infected and ruined wife supplants in popularity the comedy of the reformed rake who makes the best husband, and Thackeray's Barry Lyndon figures in the movies as prominently as Charles Surface, it will be time enough to marvel at the ignorance of the peasant child ravisher.

When we come to the remedies, we are forced to admit that what cannot be prevented cannot be remedied. Some of the preventive remedies are obvious enough. Wherever you have overcrowding and overwork both of children and adults, you get a high rate of incest with children as certainly as a high rate of zymotic disease. People who have bedrooms all to themselves as a matter of course, and who have plenty of sport and music and reading and pictures to divert them, cannot conceive a life in which young girls boast of being the mothers of their fathers' children; yet this is an established modern industrial phenomenon; and the comfortable people may as well know that it exists and is part of the price of their comfort. Here there is no question about the remedy. Civilization progresses from one roof with no beds for the whole family to one room with one bed; then to one room with more beds, until finally there is a separate room and a separate bed for everybody. One room for husband and wife, one room for the girls, and one room for the boys is still considered a very reasonable provision; and even in the well-to-do middle class a married man or woman demanding a separate room is still sometimes looked on as unreasonable, fastidious, and even irreligious. If the question of how much population the country can bear is ever faced as it should be, the first point to be settled will be not one of heads per acre divided into wheat per acre, but of space available for separate bedrooms (not to say bathrooms) per head.

When incest and promiscuity have been cut off at their source in poverty and drudgery, there will still be an irreducible minimum of criminal assault for which society at large is not responsible. For the decent and as far as possible harmless investigation of such cases we need special courts, women police, women jurors, judges, magistrates, advocates, and doctors alongside the male ones, with none of them in any uniform recognizable by a child as a police uniform. The examination of the child should be completely detached from the rest of the proceedings, about which the child should know nothing. The publication of the child's name, or of portraits of it, should be made a serious offence; and the publication of the name of the accused person unless and until convicted should also be prohibited. There are many things shamelessly featured in our newspapers which are forbidden by French law, and should be forbidden in every decent country. I must add that the advocates of complete licence for the Press have one argument which cannot be ignored. I can remember a case in which the husband of a famous beauty sought to divorce her on the ground of misconduct by her in London on a certain date. The late Dr Furnival read a newspaper report of the case, and remembered that he had met her in the country on that date: a fact she had herself forgotten. This enabled her to establish a complete alibi. Cases of this kind may occur, and lead both to convictions and acquittals; but their remote possibility does not outweigh the certainty of the mischief done in every case where children and wrongly accused persons are now pilloried in the papers.

As to punishments, when they are simply vindictive they are also simply wicked; and their effect on the imagination increases crime: indeed as I write these lines I have before me a case of a young man who, after reading the accounts of the execution of a woman for the murder of her husband, was so morbidly fascinated that he actually hanged himself. Deterrent punishments do not deter unless they are certain; and nothing can make exposure, prosecution, and conviction certain in cases of this sort. Cases vary extremely in gravity from those in which, extraordinary as it may seem, an adult is practically hypnotized and seduced by a child, to those of pests who spend their lives pursuing and molesting children and young persons. It would be no harm to suggest to these human nuisances that as the community cannot afford to detach adults from productive industry merely to shadow them (which would seem to be the only adequate safeguard) it must regretfully dispense with their continued existence and dispose of them with due apologies in a lethal chamber. In cases which are not chronic the appropriate course would be to make the offender pay heavy damages to the Public Trustee for the child's benefit at maturity, a reservation which would not tempt the parents to provoke the offence for the sake of the penalty. It goes without saying that if a cure for the propensity be possible, it should be employed. Disablement of the offender is often suggested nowadays. The objection is that it is abominable, dishonorable, "not surgical" in the opinion of the best surgeons by whom I have heard it discussed, and not a cure, as some of the people accused of the less serious forms of assault are already incapable of the more serious ones.

It will be seen from these few notes that the question is difficult practically and complicated psychologically. Both the opposition to legal protection and the advocacy of it are carried to rabid lengths by people who see either a prowling pest in every elderly gentleman who smiles at a child in the park or a prurient Mrs Pardiggle in every policewoman or welfare worker. Both must be bundled out of any sane discussion of the matter; but this is difficult as long as they are practically the only people who will concern themselves with it at all.

REASONABLE MURDER

From The Sunday Express, 13 *May* 1928

I HAVE been asked to give my opinion "on the popular point of view that a particularly brutal and callous murder of this kind [the reference is to the murder of Police Constable Gutteridge] is one of the cases in which capital punishment is justified."

Now the first thing I have to observe is that the adjectives "brutal and callous" are wildly inappropriate, and represent simply the popular loss of temper over the murder, and the customary English resort to vituperation to relieve the strain.

The murder of Constable Gutteridge was an entirely reasonable one; the work, apparently, of an out-and-out Rationalist. Further, the person who committed it was one of those sensitive people to whom the condition of a criminal under punishment is unbearable.

Also it was the work of someone who was credulous as to "the marvels of science," which take the same place in modern life as miracles did in that of the Ages of Faith.

Reasonable murders practically all fall into the same class: they are murders committed by criminals to escape detection and capture. The reasoning is simple. Our police statistics shew the number of murders committed every year, and the proportion of them that are never brought to justice. That is, they shew the odds for and against impunity for the murderer.

A robber surprised in the act by a police officer or a householder has to consider that if he surrenders he will certainly spend several years in penal servitude. If he shoots, this certainty is replaced by a risk of being hanged, and a chance of escape.

Such was the situation created by the encounter with the unfortunate Constable Gutteridge, who, though very likely an amiable and humane person, confronted his murderer not as a man, but as a representative of all the terrors and cruelties of the law. The criminal was rational enough to decide to shoot. There is no ground for suspecting him of any animosity to the man: he shot the law.

He had a sufficient smattering of physiology to know that the last picture that was focussed on the constable's retina was a picture of himself; and his modern superstitious credulity as to the possibility of this picture, or rather these two co-ordinated pictures, being photographed in the laboratory and used to identify him led him to destroy the dead man's eyes with two more careful shots.

These shots were not an outrage: they were a precautionary operation. They complete the impression of the murderer's character. He (or she) was most certainly not the Bill Sikes of the popular imagination.

He (I will assume the male sex) was a murderer not from malice, but solely in the way of business, and therefore conceivably a good husband and a kind father. He was sensitive and imaginative, because only sensitive and imaginative people risk hanging to avoid penal servitude.

He had brains enough to be able to calculate his chances, and strength of mind enough to act on his calculation. He was an habitual criminal, because such calculations are not made on the spur of the moment: he must have thought it all out before he armed himself with a loaded revolver.

He had lost the ordinary squeamishness about bloodshed and death that disables the man of peace in such emergencies; but this gives no special clue to him, because the war has left millions of men in that condition.

These reasonable murders are very dangerous, partly because they serve us right for making our criminal law more "brutal and callous" (if we must sling adjectives) than any criminal ever was or could ever possibly be; so that the criminal feels a natural right to do his worst to us to prevent us from doing our worst to him; and partly because they threaten not only the police force, but the whole body of citizens whose only resource when confronted with a criminal is to call in the police.

Their peculiarity has also an important bearing on the question of the death penalty. There is only one excuse for the official slaughter of a man (or woman) in cold blood; and that is that he gives more trouble to the community than he is worth. The same excuse, that is, that we have for killing a tiger or a mad dog.

If we could get this into our heads, and get the wicked and stupid idea of retaliative punishment (murdering the murderer) and the superstitious idea of expiatory punishment (the blood sacrifice) out of them, we should spare some murderers and kill quite a number of intolerable nuisances whom we now only torment in a cowardly and spiteful way, because, let us say, instead of murdering women they pass their lives in entrapping them into bogus marriages and deserting them after spending all their money.

In Scotland they hang people very properly for throwing vitriol: in England the vitriol thrower is sacred because vitriol blinds but does not kill. Such a distinction is absurd. We should calculate as coolly as the murderer of Constable Gutteridge, and refuse to sacrifice the lives of useful people to caging and guarding mischievous ones, simply turning on our convenient domestic gas when it becomes apparent that any individual is not suited for life in a civilized community. There should be no vindictiveness nor punishment nor any other sort of sentimentality in the matter: our attitude at the execution should be apologetic and regretful.

Now a criminal who shoots to escape detection as a matter of business may be no more homicidal by nature than any soldier. The remedy in his case may be to give up our cruel punishments, and to give him a better chance for the honest employment of his talents than our present system offers.

I have dealt with the general subject pretty fully elsewhere, and must leave it at this. But as somebody is pretty sure to fall back on the official theory that punishment is deterrent—I call it official because it is the judicial theory, and the recent impudent attempts to revive the vindictive theory have not yet had any judicial confirmation—I may as well remind my readers that there are two conclusive objections to it.

The first is that no severity of punishment deters when detection is uncertain, as it must always be.

When pickpockets were hanged pockets were picked under the gallows. Now that the penalty is comparatively trifling, pockets are still picked, but never when a policeman is looking on.

The second is that the deterrence theory leads to the conclusion that somebody must be punished for every crime to deter others from committing it. Whether that somebody has committed the crime or not is of no consequence: an innocent person will do as well as a guilty one for the purpose.

As the gentleman in Bleak House said, "Much better hang wrong feller than hang no feller."

ON REWARDS FOR CONVICTIONS AND "SCIENTIFIC" EVIDENCE

From the Daily News, 8 *May* 1928

A VETERAN journalist, who has never had time to think twice before he writes, is obsessed with the nineteenth century conception of me as a paradox monger.

I am as well aware as he can possibly be of the value of the enormous extension of publicity in criminal proceedings by Press reporting. I am not likely to overlook it when it has just been the means of calling my attention, and through me that of the public, to a very dangerous innovation and a very serious abuse.

But when he contends that the right of a newspaper to give the fullest publicity to criminal proceedings, to circulate descriptions of suspected or missing persons, and even to offer rewards for their apprehension or identification, or for the discovery of missing evidence (provided no condition as to the effect of the evidence be attached to the reward), includes a right to offer a reward for a conviction or acquittal, then it is clear that he has never given five minutes serious consideration to the point at issue.

If I were to offer a reward of £2000, which would have the practical effect of creating an interest to that amount in getting my critic hanged, he would be converted to my opinion without further argument.

"Is it not open to any person or persons to assist out of their purses the progress of justice?"

It is; but it is not open to anyone to bias the progress of justice. You may contribute two thousand pounds, or two millions, to the expense of bringing a case to trial, and be applauded for your public spirit; but if you offer twopence for a conviction and nothing for an acquittal, or twopence for an acquittal and nothing for a conviction, then you are plainly not assisting justice, but corrupting it.

If there is, as suggested, any such thing as a private detective agency which works on the terms of no divorce no payment, who defends it? Would anyone support a proposal to pay our judges only when they are trying successful prosecutions? If not, why support the payment of witnesses for evidence provided it results in a conviction? Surely the extent to which justice is already corrupted by command of money on either side is sufficient without such a preventable and flagrant increase of it.

As to the heading, "Mr Shaw's Charges," I do not say that the police faked the cartridge evidence; but I do say that if I were Mr Browne I should plead that the fact that they might easily have done so made that evidence inadmissible against me, especially as the official theory of our punishment system is that the punishments are not vindictive but deterrent, which carries the less reassuring conclusion that it does not really matter who is punished provided somebody is punished.

But I need not quibble about the word "charges." Let us admit, to save time, that I am a "very angry" person "aiming shots at the police and the Press." As the article is a fairly point blank shot at me, and its tone was not noticeably dispassionate, we may cry quits as to that. But what have our tempers to do with the questions I have raised? A leading Sunday paper has just published an article by a well-known writer, who says "I have the highest authority for saying that without the revolver Browne could not have been convicted."

If that is so then Mr Browne should have been acquitted, not because he is necessarily innocent, or because his country needs him very urgently, but because no innocent man's life or liberty will be safe if he can be "put away" upon evidence that could be easily fabricated not only by any ruthless scoundrel, but by any indignantly virtuous person so convinced of his guilt that he felt it to be his duty to make sure of his conviction. Mr Browne admits that he will be sequestered, anyhow, so there is no question of "letting a murderer loose on society," though that would be a trifle compared to letting unsound evidence loose on society.

Side by side with Sir Alfred Robbins's communication you print an account of the ex-convict who testified that Mr Browne said to him, "The police are not so fond of pulling up motors on the road after what we did to Gutteridge." Not for worlds would I suggest that this gentleman was not telling the truth and nothing but the truth; but as, when he gave that evidence, he knew that he stood to receive £2000 for giving it, and has now actually received that sum, very welcome to him as a married man with seven children, I do most strenuously contend that his testimony should be left entirely out of account, and that such bribes should be made illegal in future.

Now if his testimony is to be disregarded it is difficult to see how any testimony favoring the prosecution can be admitted. Thus not only does that £2000 nullify the whole trial; but it makes it impossible to re-try the case, because the witnesses would have to choose between sticking to their former testimony or being prosecuted for perjury.

In short this no doubt well-meant attempt to assist justice has produced a situation so completely subversive of it that there seems nothing for it but to release Mr Browne, with apologies for having detained him, and wait until his impulsive and adventurous temperament renews his present intimate relations with the police.

From the Sunday Times, 6 May 1928

As Mr Browne prefers death to penal servitude (a choice for which there is much to be said), it is not for me to attempt to thwart him.

But, on public grounds, a strong protest should be made against three features of the case. One is the publication of biographies of persons whose cases are still subject to appeal, especially when such biographies cannot possibly be authentic, and are published only because they are made sensational.

The second is the use of a method of identification by coincidences which anyone can manufacture with the greatest ease. We were assured that the Bertillon measurements were infallible until the fingerprint method was substituted. There was this to be said for both of them: No person anxious to secure a conviction could tamper with the dimensions or skin markings of the accused. But anyone with access to a discharged cartridge case and to a revolver can tamper with the revolver so that by simply putting the cartridge case into one of the chambers and snapping the hammer on it a mark made on the hammer or cylinder can be reproduced on the cartridge case, and a jury deeply impressed by a manufactured coincidence.

"TRIAL BY NEWSPAPER"

The third is the fact that a reward of £2000 was offered to any person who secured a conviction. It is amazing that we should still tolerate such a survival from the childhood of legal civilization, in which it seemed the most natural thing in the world for litigants and their friends to make presents to the judge. It certainly was more sensible to allow the judge to be bribed by both sides than to allow, as we are doing, anyone to approach the evenly balanced scales of justice and impudently fling £2000 into one of them.

If Mrs Browne had offered to bet the Chief Commissioner of Police £2000 that her husband would be hanged, she would have gone to prison for it. If I had offered that sum to anyone who should secure an acquittal, I suppose I should have been prosecuted for subornation. Yet in what do these three methods of creating a pecuniary interest in a certain desired verdict differ?

No judge would try the most trivial case, nor any citizen sit unchallenged on the jury, with £2000 at stake on the verdict. Why, then, is a newspaper allowed to bribe every person alive to procure a conviction on a capital charge?

A case in which a reward for £2000 for a conviction is combined with a novel method of identification by easily manufactured coincidences is an extremely serious one for all of us.

I hold no brief for Mr Browne; and, if nothing worse were involved in his case than in that of Stinie Morison, who died in penal servitude for a murder for which he would most certainly have been hanged if his guilt had been really established, solely because the jury thought with good reason that he had better be locked up than left at large, I should not take the trouble to write this letter.

But when I see Mr Browne's unpopularity made an excuse for slipping into our criminal procedure a method obviously open to appalling abuse, and for developing "trial by newspaper" into something like a blood sport, I am reminded of the fact that I have been in certain quarters unpopular myself, and may feel it my duty to make myself so again.

In that case I should be sorry to be hanged because somebody spent five minutes tampering with a pistol and a cartridge with the prospect of thereby securing a couple of thousand pounds and at the same time ridding the country of so troublesome a character as myself.

P.S. [1931]. It is proper to add here that the fabrication of evidence by reproducing pistol marks is by no means so easy as it seems; for the markings relied on are too subtle to be forged. The pistol cannot be adapted to the cartridge; but there is no apparent reason why the cartridge cannot be adapted to the pistol by recharging it and firing it again. I was assured by an expert that if he could get both pistol and cartridge into his hands for half an hour he could do the trick.

At all events it was (and is) urgently necessary to warn a generation which is boundlessly credulous as to the infallibility of any method calling itself scientific, whether it be Bertillon measurement, fingerprint identification, or, as in this case, "forensic ballistics," that pretences to infallibility are exceedingly unscientific, and that the temptation to suppress or fabricate evidence is terribly strong-in-righteousness when the prosecution (or the defence) is so firmly convinced of the justice of its case that it seems positively wicked to omit any means of establishing it. For it is a serious mistake to suppose that cooked cases are always the work of rascals bent on misleading juries into unjust verdicts. It is the virtuous resolution to obtain a true verdict at all costs that makes it so unsafe to assume that the high character of the police guarantees fair play for the criminal. It sometimes does just the opposite.

Frederick Guy Browne was hanged in due course. His craze for collecting revolvers led to a disclosure of the fact that in the war of 1914–18 our officers were sent to the front with flatnosed bullets in their pistol cartridges. The Germans thereupon gave us notice that they would shoot every officer captured with this sort of ammunition on his person. The cartridges were then sent back and replaced by the correct kind, with an explanation that the flatnosed bullets had been left over from the South African War, and that their despatch to Flanders was an oversight. Those who recollected how the Boers were denounced as fiends during that war for using flatnosed bullets must have smiled grimly at this revelation. They may have known that it is practically impossible to prevent soldiers from tampering with bullets that will not stop an enemy promptly; but that flatnosed bullets were served out as official ammunition to British troops was painful news to those who still supposed that the morals of peace can ever prevail against the horrors of war when the battle is joined.

PLUNDERING THE PENSIONER

From the Evening Standard, 20 December 1927

In your issue of the 17th you rightly feature as "appalling" the consequences to a postman aged sixty of having been convicted at the Marylebone Police Court of a theft of 10s.

This man has earned by thirty-six years' public service a State insurance of £300 and a pension of £2 15s. a week. The "appalling consequences" to which you call attention are not the ordinary punishment incurred by the theft of ten shillings, but the assumed intention of the Government to confiscate the insurance. May one ask under what law the Government has power to commit this monstrous outrage?

When eminent financiers, criminally negligent company directors, fraudulent trustees, income-tax evaders, and other gentlemanly culprits pass from the dock to penal servitude, are their insurances confiscated? I have never heard of any such practice.

In the days of Judge Jeffries it was still the law that the property of a person convicted of treason or felony went to the Crown, as his clothes went to the hangman; but this was so revolting to the general sense of justice that the question was always put to the jury "Any property?"; and the jury always answered "None," no matter how well off the criminal might be.

What I want to know is why, after this confiscation has been abolished, and forgotten in the case of the propertied classes, it is still calmly continued, without a word of protest, as if it were the most natural and obvious course on earth, in the case of poor men like postmen, police constables, and weekly wage workers generally.

What divine or earthly right has the Crown to seize the Kilburn postman's hard-earned provision for his old age? He has committed a theft, and thereby incurred the penalty decreed by the law for theft. But he has incurred no other penalty. If some indignant moralist were to kick him as he left the dock that zealot would be punished for assault. When a postman is sentenced to be hanged, the Postmaster-General may not draw and quarter him as well.

Is there any warrant (except a thoughtless usage at the expense of men too poor to appeal to the courts for a declaration of the law) for this Kilburn infamy, which will not only inflict on the postman a punishment savage enough for the most brutal crime, but reduce his innocent dependents to penury as well?

You report the magistrate as saying "I am very sorry for you. I can do nothing for you." But surely he could have sentenced him to a suitable period of imprisonment, and at the same time warned the authorities that they have not the ghost of a legal or moral right to steal his money or add to the penalty in any way.

From The Evening Standard, 11 *January* 1928

The Postmaster-General's remark that there is no precedent for treating delinquent postmen with common honesty can suggest nothing except that the present is an excellent opportunity for him to create one. After the death of Abel there was no precedent for brothers refraining from killing one another; but even Cain, in his celebrated discussion of the case with his Divine Judge, was not brazen enough to stand upon the precedent he had himself set.

The Postmaster-General, having prosecuted his postman for stealing ten shillings, now alleges that he stole a great deal more. If so, surely the prosecutor should himself be prosecuted for compounding the rest of the felony. But the size of the theft has nothing to do with the justice of the case.

Let me assume for the purpose of illustration, and with due apologies to the postman, that he never in the course of his thirty-seven years' service was entrusted with a letter containing money without stealing it. Let me assume furthermore that he forged postage stamps to the value of £50,000; that he rifled the post office safe regularly once a fortnight and set fire to the premises to conceal his crime; and that he polygamously married dozens of telephonists and deserted them after spending their hard-earned savings in riotous living.

Let us assume, in short, that he put up such a record in postal crime that the very lightest sentence that could decently be passed on him was one of twenty years' penal servitude. In that case, if he went into prison clad in his shabbiest suit, with an old clay pipe in its pocket, that suit and pipe would be solemnly preserved and handed back to him at the expiration of his term to shew the respect of the law for property.

Now what we want to know is, if the governor of a prison may not steal a pipe from the most abandoned felon, why may a Postmaster-General steal a pension? Who made the Postmaster-General judge, jury, and executioner, concurrently with and independently of our courts of law?

If he charges his postman with the full extent of the newly alleged thefts, and a judge, after a jury's verdict of guilty, sentences him to a ruinous fine which will crush his dependents equally with himself, then there will be nothing more to be said: the law will have taken its course, and the accused enjoyed his right of trial by jury. But when the head of a department whose powers were given to him for the provision of a postal and telegraph service cries "Off with his pension!" in the manner of Cibber's Richard crying "Off with his head!" it is time to remonstrate.

I hope some underworked Member of Parliament—if there be such a person—will take up the whole question of public service pensions. A communication from the War Office just sent to me by its unfortunate recipient seems to suggest that this department not only cancels allowances and pensions at its pleasure (or displeasure), but does so retrospectively and demands repayment without regard to the Statutes of Limitation on the principle that to him that hath shall be given, and from him that hath not shall be taken even that which he hath.

SIX MONTHS IN CHAINS

From The Daily News, 23 June 1922

In celebration of Midsummer Day, and in compliment to Queen Alexandra (a conspicuous humanitarian) and to the Prince of Wales, the authorities of Parkhurst Prison announce that they have taken a man who convicted them of negligence in allowing him to escape, and put him into an iron belt and fetters, connected with 6 lb. chains, and that they propose to leave him in this form of the torture known as the Scavenger's Daughter night and day for six months.

This is their reply to the challenge of the history just published by Sidney and Beatrice Webb, and of the Prison Inquiry edited by Fenner Brockway and Stephen Hobhouse, which have just exposed our prison system in all its cruelty, stupidity, and senseless mischief. What does the public think of it?

If the two hanged murderers who have occupied so much public attention recently had been put in chains during the three weeks between their trial and execution by order of the judges who tried them, the judges would have been transferred from the bench to a lunatic asylum amid a general howl of execration.

But to the governor of a prison such a breach of routine as an escape is far worse than a murder. To humane public opinion an escape from prison is no crime at all. Take the unfortunate convict out of his chains and put him on his trial for escaping, and no jury in the world can, without manifest perjury, apply the word guilty to an escape from prison.

The man was sentenced to be imprisoned, not to imprison himself. The commonest instinct of decent sportsmanship, to put it no higher, insists on the sacred right of the prisoner to escape if he can.

The odds on the side of the prison authorities are overwhelming: all that public money, bolts and bars, sentinels and rifles, walls and spikes, and the unmistakeable brand of the prison dress can do to baffle a single destitute and unaided man are leagued against him. Were he the worst of criminals, public opinion must applaud the feat when he wins even for a few days,

If the prison authorities had a scrap of human feeling, they would take their momentary defeat as the public thought they would take it: goodhumoredly, and be more careful next time. But no: they must take a savage revenge on him for their own carelessness, and put him in chains for six months "to larn him."

A more disgusting episode could hardly have spoilt a national festival.

Be it noted that there are some people who have a real grievance. It is stated, and must evidently be true, that during his thirteen days at large the convict stole his food. Why is he not prosecuted for these thefts? Obviously because there is no Englishman mean enough to grudge a meal to a starving fugitive.

The lad could not have begged for food without forcing the person begged from either to give him up or become his accomplice. He had to steal. Nobody asks for vengeance except the prison authorities, who, indeed, take it without asking judge or jury.

So much for our prison system and its effect on those who administer it! I invite the gentlemen who have been defending it against my denunciation to try wearing a set of chains for the next six months, and then tell us whether their official optimism is in any way modified by the experience.

P.S. [1931]. This outburst served its purpose. A few days after its appearance the public was officially assured that chains for simple escape are abolished.

THE ETERNAL STRIFE BETWEEN JUDGE AND JURY

From The Times, 27 September 1898

Two recent cases of severity in the operation of the criminal law have produced the usual outcry against the cruelty of the Home Secretary, with the accompaniment, now quite common, of letters from members of the jury protesting that they returned a verdict of guilty only because they did not believe that the Home Secretary would permit it to be acted upon.

It is clear that neither the average juryman nor the average humanitarian journalist understands the constitutional function of a jury or the meaning of a verdict. A jury has two separate and perfectly distinct points to decide. First, whether the accused did or did not perform the action in respect of which he is alleged to be guilty; and second (if they conclude that he has performed it), whether the circumstances were such as to make the action a guilty one. For example, a man is indicted for murder. Obviously the jury must first be satisfied that somebody has been killed, and then that the man in the dock is the slayer; otherwise the case falls to the ground, and, in fact, ceases to be a case at all. But suppose the jury fully convinced on those two points, a verdict of guilty by no means follows. The jury may consider that in slaying his victim the prisoner was not only not guilty, but was performing an innocent, beneficent, and highly laudable action the omission of which would have deserved capital punishment: for instance, the prevention of a murder by shooting the assassin in the act. If under such circumstances the jurors were to bring in a verdict of guilty, and then write to the papers declaring, in effect, that they did not mean guilty, but used that word improperly to express their conclusion, in itself void of moral significance, that the alleged slaying had actually taken place at the hands of the prisoner, and that they trusted to the judge or the Home Secretary to save him from the consequences of their verdict, then the reasonable course would be to prosecute every one of the twelve for perjury.

I need hardly point out that every attempt to conceal this distinction, and to save our Courts trouble by working our criminal law mechanically upon facts instead of upon the moral interpretation of human intention, tends to make government by law inhuman, abhorrent, and finally impossible. The practice so prevalent of late years of putting a string of questions of fact to the jury, and then permitting the judge to interpret their replies as a verdict, is disgraceful to our constitutional lawyers, by whom it should have been rebuked instead of connived at, as it has been. That it should have been encouraged by judges is only natural, since its effect is to transfer the really eminent part of the jury's function and power to the judge, who, with his wide experience of jurymen, can hardly help believing himself to be better fitted to exercise it than they are. The result is now before us. Jurymen have lost all sense of moral responsibility; ninety-nine citizens out of a hundred, if examined as to the meaning of guilty or not guilty, will explain without hesitation that it means did he do it or did he not do it. In dealing with the lighter offences, the judge, having induced the jury to leave their duty to him, practically does as he pleases by his power of determining the sentence. But the gravest crimes involve fixed penalties which the judge has no power to reduce or modify. When the charge is one of wilful murder and the verdict is Guilty he must sentence the prisoner to death. Certain other crimes are punishable by not less than ten years' penal servitude. In such cases the jury cannot transfer their responsibility to the judge. Consequently it passes on to the Home Secretary. This is how we have reached a state of things in which jurymen openly and shamelessly avow that in murder cases they leave the whole question of guilt to this unfortunate Minister and content themselves with deciding the facts.

Consider the situation of Sir Matthew White Ridley today. It has been proved that a man has taken his children out on a marsh and there slaughtered them. A woman has thrown her child into a pond and drowned it. If all this slaying was guiltily and wilfully done, the culprits are guilty of wilful murder and can claim no further consideration from any official whose duty it is to administer the law. If, on the other hand, they were crazy when they killed the children, and are in their normal state harmless and reputable people, then they are not guilty of wilful murder at all; and it was the duty of the jury to say so. Instead of doing their duty the jury return a verdict of wilful murder, coupled with a recommendation to the Home Secretary not to believe it. Can any constitutional situation more absurd, more unsound, more anarchical than this be imagined? Yet it has become quite the usual upshot of a murder trial. Twenty years ago, in the Penge case, a jury found several persons guilty of wilful murder. They were condemned to death. The Home Secretary released one of them immediately, whilst another remained in prison until the other day. Possibly that may have met the justice of the case as justice is commonly conceived; but it brought the law and the jury system into contempt. What would be said if a jury acquitted a prisoner and the Home Secretary insisted on hanging him? Yet there have been cases in which that would have been quite as satisfactory a solution as some reprieves have been.

I venture to urge, then, that whilst we retain the jury system juries should be taught to act as jurors and not merely as investigators. I am quite aware that those who know most about jurymen will see in this proposal nothing but a *reductio ad absurdum* of the whole institution of trial by jury as now practised, and that a judicial conspiracy to neutralize the jury is inevitable under present conditions. But it is time to face that conclusion, even if it leads us to tear up Magna Charta. If a juryman were an elected person, if he incurred even as much responsibility as the publication of his name and address would carry, if any sort of qualification, however slender, were exacted from him, something might be said for putting him in the enormously responsible position which he detests and abuses. As it is, I should be glad to hear what any rational person has to say in his defence.

From The Daily News, 24 May 1919

In the Daily News report of the Raymond case the following passage occurs:

Mr Justice Darling, in summing up, said the only question for the jury was whether the defendant took the girl out of the possession and against the will of her father. If he did that, no matter whether he did it for a good motive or a bad one, their duty would be to find that he was guilty.

Surely there is some mistake here. Mr Justice Darling must

have said exactly the opposite. It is part of the A B C of jury law that the jury must find on the question of guilt and not of fact. To direct a jury to find a prisoner guilty after ascertaining that his motive was good would be to direct them to commit perjury. I can as easily conceive a judge telling a jury that if they ascertained that a prisoner had actually killed someone, even by the most unavoidable accident, their duty would be to find that he was guilty of murder.

It is true that in the eighteenth century judges made an attempt to usurp the power of deciding the question of guilt by persuading juries that all they had to do was to decide the question of fact, and that in effect guilty or not guilty meant only was an alleged act committed or not committed; but an Act of Parliament was passed expressly to put an end to this abuse (the Libel Act), and since then there has been no excuse for such gross misdirection.

I have been so often reported as having said in public precisely the opposite of what I actually did say that I have no doubt that what Mr Justice Darling did was to impress on the jury that they had first to satisfy themselves as to what the prisoner actually did and then return their verdict on the question whether the nature and intention of his action constituted him a guilty person. Otherwise the institution of trial by jury would have no value.

From The Daily News, 28 May 1919

The legal expert from King's College is quite right in saying that the judge decides questions of law and the jury questions of fact. If the jury did not decide the question of fact it could not possibly deliver a verdict. It is no use discussing whether a prisoner is guilty in respect of a homicide, for instance, until the jury decides whether it was actually committed and whether the prisoner committed it. But having ascertained these indispensable facts the jury then proceeds to consider its verdict, which is not a declaration of fact but of guilt or innocence.

As to the case cited by the expert of a gentleman who took a girl away without her father's consent to save her from being

CRUDE CRIMINOLOGY

placed in a convent (a highly questionable project on the father's part if the girl was unwilling), are we to take it as a precedent in the case of a fireman who takes a girl out of her father's house (actually through the window and down a ladder) without first obtaining his consent?

Not even the popular passion for contradicting me justifies a legal expert in pontificating from King's College to create an impression that I am misdirecting the jury when my law is perfectly sound.

From The Daily News, 31 *May* 1919

I had better not leave your latest correspondent's letter unanswered, because the British juryman will snatch at the thinnest pretext for evading his responsibility to the prisoner, and judges will encourage him in order to get the real verdict into their own hands. Thus we have just seen a judge direct a jury to find a prisoner Guilty and then himself deliver a verdict of Not guilty by setting the prisoner free.

The most effectual reduction to absurdity of the view that the jury must find the prisoner Guilty if he has in fact committed the act in respect of which he is indicted, is the case of an unintentional, or even unconscious, act. Because I used this method your correspondent says I am confusing the question of motive with the question of intention, implying that the jury must find a verdict of "Guilty" when the act is intentional, no matter how good the motive. Yet it is only a few weeks since a soldier intentionally shot and killed another soldier near Waterloo Station with impunity. If a man runs amok with a hatchet, and I see him pursuing a child or my wife or any other innocent person with the evident intention of burying the hatchet in that innocent person's skull, and I am lucky enough to be able to shoot him before he reaches his victim, would any sane jury find me guilty of murder because my act was extremely intentional?

The question the jury has to decide is not whether the act is intentional or unintentional, but whether it is a guilty action or an innocent one. It may be a guilty one even when it is unintentional, as in the case of a criminal who brings about the death of some person in the commission of a crime which had no such object. Neither intention nor motive furnish any rule of thumb for arriving at verdicts.

Jurymen may feel some remorse in finding a man guilty of the bad qualities he was born with, and cannot resist. They perceive that the jury in Erewhon, which found a man guilty of pulmonary consumption, was not more unjust than one of our juries finding a man guilty of murder. They are so far right that the cruelties inflicted on prisoners as consequences of a verdict of guilty are not really deserved: guilt means only moral invalidism. Hence we find that when the jury does its duty by finding a considered verdict instead of shirking its responsibility by doing what the judge tells it, and leaving the rest to him, the question which really decides its verdict is whether the prisoner is a dangerous person or not. What concerns it is not so much whether the prisoner killed a man yesterday as whether he is likely to kill another tomorrow.

There is at present in prison a man convicted of a murder so ferocious that he would certainly have been hanged ten times over had that been necessary if the Home Office and the judge could have convinced themselves that he had really committed it. No respectable and normally harmless man would have been convicted on the evidence. As far as I know, nobody who has examined the case believes that he committed the murder. But the case established the fact that he was a dangerous man; and on that the jury gave society the benefit of the doubt and found him guilty. I do not defend the verdict any more than I defend certain recent acquittals of murderers under what is called "the unwritten law": I merely cite both as illustrations of the way our jury system works when it works at all, and is not simply side-tracked by the judge.

From *The Daily News*, 3 *March* 1923

The Daily News article on the case of Dr Marie Stopes is headed A Verdict And A Ruling. May I point out that there was no verdict? Instead of finding a verdict the jury allowed itself to be drawn into answering questions, which was not its business. Juries should never answer questions and never argue. What has just happened in a case quite as important in its way as the famous trial of the seven bishops makes it unnecessary to say anything more, except that if jurymen are not better instructed in their rights and duties than they are at present, the continuous pressure of the Bench to usurp their function will end in nothing being left to the jury but the responsibility for the judge's decision.

FLOGGING IN THE FIGHTING SERVICES

From The Saturday Review, 26 *August* 1897

I TRUST that The Saturday Review is not too preoccupied with the subject of Military Prisons to spare a word for the latest exploit of that heroically popular service, the Royal Navy. A court-martial of representative naval officers has just sentenced a lad who struck his officer to imprisonment, dismissal from the service, *and twenty-four cuts with a cane*. The corporal punishment was added in pure wantonness. It is not prescribed by law. If the court-martial had been able to muster a single officer of ordinary longshore moral courage, intelligence, and humanity, such a sentence could not have been passed; for twenty-four cuts with the tongue of such a man would have shamed the rest into public decency. Apparently, however, the British naval officer is still cruel in his fear of the men under his command, and viciously sensual in the severities by which he secures their obedience. I am perfectly acquainted with the arguments used by persons who believe that discipline cannot be maintained in the Services without making every man-of-war and every barracks a much more barbarous place than a public school fifty years ago. But I am not aware that discipline is more important in the army and navy than it is in the arsenal, the police force, the hospital, the laboratory, the mine, or the many factories in which negligence or insubordination may produce ruinous waste or devastating calamity;

and yet it is maintained in such places without passionate cruelty by civilians who can be defied with impunity as far as the law is concerned, and who can be assaulted without exceptional penalties. This is attained quite simply and sensibly by visiting a breakdown of discipline on the officer whose business it is to maintain it. The man who cannot acquire sufficient influence over his subordinates to command their obedience without a cane or a cat is superseded by a man who can, that is all; whereas in the navy a man who cannot give an order without provoking its recipient to strike him is propped up in the position for which he has proved his unfitness by barbarities which degrade the Service and disgust the whole nation.

There was a time—the age of the wooden walls—when naval warfare required only seamanship and ferocity. Victories could then be won with men kidnapped by the pressgang, fed on filthy scorbutic food, flogged like badly driven horses, and shot down on occasion by a rival force—the Marines—kept on board expressly for that purpose. The villainy of the system was defended, then as now, by representations of the supreme importance of discipline in times of war, and despised, then as now, by men of heart and character who knew that in action necessary discipline is maintained by the common danger and the common humanity, and that unnecessary discipline goes by the board in spite of all its sanctity at Portsmouth. In modern naval warfare the conditions—far more terrible—are also far more exacting as to the quality of the combatants. A fleet manned by beaten men, by petty officers who will cane their shipmate (provided he be tied up securely) for half-a-crown, by chief officers who will order such outrages and will go into action with men who submit to and inflict them, may rule the waves as long as all the other fleets are equally bankrupt in manhood and more so in seamanship. But if a foreign fleet should arise, generously nourished by its nation and manned by free self-respecting men commanded and valued by the sort of officer that never gets struck or defied, then our Royal Navy, with its twenty-four cuts of a cane across its back, will take a second place.

I am aware that many people have not yet learnt to distinguish between punishments which are severe and punishments which are cruel. A cruel punishment is one which gratifies a passion in those who inflict it, witness it, or imagine it. Imprisonment and dismissal from the service are severe punishments; but they can afford no gratification whatever to officers who have no personal grudge against the sufferer. They are purely troublesome; and the fewer of them we are forced to inflict the better for everybody concerned. But corporal punishment is a completely different matter. It is capable of being used as a sport, a debauch, masquerading as a deterrent or as "justice." There is a flagellation neurosis, well known to psychiatrists and some less reputable persons. A public flogging will always draw a crowd; and there will be in that crowd plenty of manifestations of a horrible passional ecstasy in the spectacle of laceration and suffering from which even the most self-restrained and secretive person who can prevail on himself to be present will not be wholly free. Even the anger, disgust, and contempt of the humane people who avoid such spectacles and protest against them is passionate, and is probably degrading. It is for this reason that humane people object to have such experiences forced on them by cruel people, and that corporal punishment is going the way of duelling and all other survivals from uncivilized conditions. To make the matter vividly clear, I ask those who regard the sentence of the court-martial with indifference to imagine for a moment that the sentence of twenty-four cuts with a cane had been passed on a young woman instead of a young man. There would have been a shriek of hysterical horror and fury from the entire Press at once; and not an officer of that court would have dared to shew his face in society until the case was forgotten. And yet women bear pain better than men and are not more susceptible to disgrace and humiliation: indeed, the injury to the victim, whether male or female, might be disregarded as a trifle in comparison with the moral injury to the crew of the fleet and to the nation. But the passionate character of the sentence would be so emphasized in the case of a girl sentenced by men, that it would be at once seen that the corporal part of the sentence had been added by the judges for their own satisfaction and not for public ends. The actual case, being that of a lad, suggests nothing to superficial people but the common violent vindictiveness which is still tolerated by public opinion when it is regularized by legal forms, or by parental or pedagogic authority, or shielded by the extra licence in vice which we allow to soldiers and sailors. But it is none the less a cruel and passionate sentence, and therefore none the less repulsive and immoral.

I hope we shall hear no more of such cases. It will be a long time before I shall be able to look at a Union Jack without a shudder of disgust.

From The Saturday Review, 10 *September* 1897

I wish we could prevail on our Knights of the Cane to be a little more explicit as to what their actual opinions are on this subject. I gather from their letters that they are self-consistent on one point only: namely, that the punishment of an offender is a piece of retaliation pure and simple and must be judged as such. This view is very generally entertained by intelligent elephants. Among civilized men it need not be further discussed.

Sir Benjamin Bolt quotes, as a conclusive refutation of my assertion that discipline can be maintained without cruelty, the remark of the French admiral a few weeks ago: "I cannot understand how it is that your officers can play cricket with the men, and yet preserve discipline." What the French admiral could not understand is precisely what Sir Benjamin cannot understand. What he meant was that if the French officers were to play cricket with their men, necessary discipline could not be maintained in the French navy. What Sir Benjamin means is that if officers were to stop flogging their crews, necessary discipline could not be maintained in the British navy. Sir Benjamin Bolt can see the folly of the French admiral's error. He holds it up to insular contempt, and in the same breath offers it as an unanswerable refutation of me. This shews that Sir Benjamin is not, on this subject, a brilliantly lucid thinker.

Mr Wackford says, "To send these boys to prison instead of awarding them a few cuts with the cane is the cruellest of mercies." After explaining that the mercy in question is not to the boys, but to the shipmates on whom their work would fall if they were imprisoned, he adds: "I am aware that the two Royal Sovereign culprits have been dismissed the service, in addition to the punishment of caning or imprisonment [Mr Wackford should have written caning *and* imprisonment] awarded." Precisely. He is aware that his argument does not apply. Then why does he apply it?

Mr Wackford caps Sir Benjamin's French admiral with a French general. This warrior has told us that democratic ideas of equality are one of the chief difficulties in the French army. An English general would have added that the army was going to the dogs. The remark is old enough to have become the totem of the particular grade of intelligence and humanity which Mr Wackford has come forward to defend.

Mr Wackford attributes the French naval defeats of 1793–1815 to discipline democratically undermined by the Revolution and confronted by "a squadron beaten into shape by the iron discipline and severity of St Vincent." The theory that it was the cat-o'-nine-tails of St Vincent instead of the genius of Nelson that won the Nile and Trafalgar would be more convincing if it accounted with equal neatness for the defeat of Prussian, Austrian, and Russian discipline during the same period by the French troops led by Napoleon, whose soldiers cursed him openly when their luck was bad.

Both Mr Wackford and Sir Benjamin agree in maintaining, first, that our sailors are never corporally punished, and that it is a wicked and hysterical libel to say that they are; second, that discipline cannot be maintained in the fleet without corporal punishment; third, that the boys recently flogged for so heinous an offence as striking an officer richly deserved the pain they suffered; and fourthly, that the flogging hurts them so little that they would hardly suffer more if they were birched at Eton. I should myself be guilty of inclemency if this chain of reasoning inspired me with any sentiment but one of pity. Of my inclination to laugh I am ashamed.

Sir Benjamin is specially indignant with me for attacking naval captains who cannot defend themselves. I am aware that they cannot defend themselves, their conduct being indefensible; but if Sir Benjamin thinks that they are not as free to write letters to the Press as I am, he must be even a more innocent gentleman than the rest of his letter suggests. The Times has no more active correspondents than our commanders of the Royal Navy, whose explosions in its columns have created a distinct public opinion as to the value of quarter-deck publicism. But I would ask Sir Benjamin what he would think of me if I objected to his letter on the ground that he is attacking young seamen who are much more effectually precluded from replying to him than any captain. He would probably form an estimate of my intelligence deeply wounding to my vanity. Nevertheless the point was worth notice—on my side. The fact that courts-martial will not bear the publicity which attends every step of civil criminal procedure is one of the heaviest counts against them. It is monstrous that degradation, ruin, and physical cruelty should be inflicted on soldiers and sailors by despotic tribunals of officers prejudiced by social class and official *esprit de corps* against the prisoners. Sir Benjamin's reply to this is that "captains in the navy are men of mature age, and, especially when serving on a court-martial, they act under a very grave sense of responsibility." Good: then let us extend their powers to giving Sir Benjamin twenty-four cuts with a cane on the hand or back (he attaches deep importance to the difference), depriving him of his means of livelihood, and imprisoning him. It will be interesting to see whether his confidence in them, or even in the fact that Mr Wackford "counts many officers among his personal friends," will make him quite easy under such circumstances. I positively find myself blushing at having to reduce such trivialities to absurdity.

As to my "entire inaccuracies," I wish my two unfortunate critics joy of such consolation as they can find in them. I confess I thought the twenty-four cuts of a cane were to be administered on the lad's back: it did not occur to me that anything so fiercely cruel and likely to cause permanent injury as twenty-four cuts on the hand were contemplated. But the sentence of twenty-four cuts with a birch, reported as passed on one of the Jupiter boys, should have dispelled Sir Benjamin's illusions as to the sanctity of the seaman's back, and saved him from crushing refutation by the later case of the flogged sailor who has just turned out to be a lunatic. Pray observe that the Jupiter sentence was expressly ordered to be carried out in the presence of the other boys. The object of that was to intimidate them by a deliberate exhibition of cruelty; and if Mr Wackford and Sir Benjamin think otherwise, they must either believe the officers who ordered the punishment to be fools, or else submit to be placed in that humiliating category themselves. Their notion that the boatswain's mate, under orders to make an example of a mutineer, handles a birch as an Eton master does, is entirely worthy of their credulity.

I am sorry I paid the British seaman the compliment of assuming that, like a prison warder, he expected some compensation for the degradation of doing the work which formerly belonged to the common hangman. But I will not insult him by implying, as Sir Benjamin does, that he does it of his own free will. He does it because he would be court-martialled himself if he refused.

I am sorry to waste your space over these childish cavils, which leave my argument against corporal punishment untouched. But when a newspaper of the standing of The Globe disposes of an important public subject like this by a few puerile comments by the side of which even the observations of Sir Benjamin and Mr Wackford seem sensible and dignified, it is really necessary to do something to maintain discipline on shore.

As to your correspondent the Lieutenant, who reminds me that Her Majesty's ships fly the White Ensign and not the Union Jack, he may depend on it that I know that, but that I also know my business as a journalist. The public do not care a straw about the White Ensign. When journalists write about gallant officers nailing the Union Jack to the masthead, or wrapping themselves in its folds to die, the Service does not write to the papers to correct the mistake. If the Union Jack is good enough to celebrate the heroism of the navy, it is also good enough to expose its stupid barbarism.

From The Saturday Review, 2 October 1897

Unless I again beg for some of The Saturday Review's space, it is clear that I shall go virtually unanswered, and that the correspondence will end with nothing more satisfactory than an ex-naval officer setting me an example of dignified composure by gnashing his teeth at me. There is nothing for it but to help my opponents out of their difficulty by answering myself.

The real reason why civilians can maintain discipline in factories without martial law is that the employees, being free to leave if they choose, would not be in the factory at all if they did not wish to stay there. Consequently the fear of "getting the sack" restrains them from insubordination. When they are dismissed, they are dismissed against their will. The case of a sailor is different. A considerable number of persons get seastruck in their boyhood, and commit themselves to a sailor's life only to find it intensely tedious and disagreeable to them when they find out what it really means in comparison with life on shore. If we did not catch our officers very young, and make it clear to them, by the time they have realized their position as grown men, that they had better go through with their term of service for the sake of the comparatively early retirement, the pension, the secure livelihood, and the social rank involved, we should be seriously hampered by the extreme dislike which many of our naval officers have, not so much for their profession, as for the sort of life it involves. It is just the same with the men. If the pecuniary inducements were not even greater in their case, relatively to the standard of their class, than in that of the officers, we should soon be reminded of the fact that in every ship in the fleet there are plenty of steady, good men who are looking forward eagerly to the moment when they will see the last of her.

In the army there is less disappointment of this kind, because the man who enlists nowadays seldom expects anything very romantic, though he probably hardly ever foresees how humiliatingly impecunious he will be. Borrowing money from domestic servants is but a precarious means of keeping yourself in pocket-money, even if it were quite to the taste of a high-spirited young man. But the want of pocket-money is too pressing for pride. A young soldier with a vigorous appetite seldom feels that he has had as much to eat as he would like; and he always want more amusement than he can afford to pay for.

Under these circumstances, we are bound to have a certain number of cases of lads in the navy striking their officers in order to escape from the service by dismissal. It is argued that the only way to prevent this is by savage sentences of flogging and imprisonment. Even if the sentences did this, they would not be justified any more than burning the lads alive would be justified if it not only prevented mutiny but guaranteed to England the absolute and eternal supremacy of the sea into the bargain. But the fact that the case which provoked this correspondence has produced fresh cases instead of preventing them shews that they do not prevent it.

With soldiers another class of cases gives trouble. The soldier, to get pocket-money, sells his kit, or some other part of his equipment. Formerly it was argued, on precisely the grounds which have been urged by the anti-humanity party in this correspondence, that if soldiers were not flogged for this offence, the whole army would instantly sell kit, weapons, and ammunition, leaving our country defenceless before the soundly lashed soldiers of the Continental Powers. Fortunately we are all reading Lord Roberts now, and have freshly in mind his story of the two soldiers who were flogged for selling their kits, and immediately and manfully sold them again to shew that they would not be subdued by such dishonorable means, with the result that their officers, to their tardy honor, were ashamed to flog them again. Lord Roberts does not mention that this surrender of discipline sent all the kits of the regiment into the market, because of course nothing of the sort happened; what he does mention is the trouble he had afterwards with soldiers demoralized by the intimidation system, and how he got rid of all that trouble by taking precisely that view of the case which has convinced the gentlemen who have been posing in your columns as authorities on the art of governing men that I know nothing about discipline.

Here, then, though we have no justification of corporal punishment, we have a difference between the conditions under which a factory is governed and those which prevail in a regiment or a ship. The solution, however, is not to dissimilate the fighting industry from the civil industry, but to assimilate them by civilizing the services.

If a soldier or a sailor is a blackguard, the proper remedy is, not for his officers to outblackguard him by torturing him, but simply to turn him out of the service. If he desires nothing better, then his dismissal is a benefit both to himself and the service. If he does not desire it, then he will do his best to mend his ways so as to be allowed to stay in it. If an officer is a blackguard, a tyrant, or an incompetent nuisance, the proper remedy is for the soldier to refuse to serve under him. This means that the soldier should be as free to leave the army as I am to leave the staff of this journal. To retain a well-conducted soldier in the army against his will is to make a slave of a man who has done nothing to deserve it. Some day, when we get the better of our national cowardice, we shall give up the system of having our fighting done by slaves, and boldly make the soldier and sailor as free as the policeman. The lads who want to leave the fleet so badly that they will strike their officers and face flogging and imprisonment for the sake of the dismissal will be provided with an honorable means of retreat. I look forward to the time when the army will be reformed by a powerful trade union of the rank and file, which shall drive incompetent officers out of the army as effectually as the cotton operatives of Lancashire drive incompetent managers out of the trade. I would have soldiers perfectly free to strike for higher pay or better conditions in time of war if they chose. For example, I would trust them unhesitatingly with an undisputed legal right to receive an order to charge on the field of battle itself by striking then and there for another twopence a day, if that struck them as a favorable moment. I am perfectly aware that with every demand made and enforced on behalf of the men, the standard of ability among officers would go up, and whole batches of stiff-necked dolts who now blunder their way along, making infinite trouble for the Robertses, and costing the country huge sums for "discipline," would be retired as useless. I am also aware that the army and navy under such circumstances would withdraw from civil activity a much higher class of men than they do at present, and that these would cost more money per man per day than mere "cannon fodder." But if a conflict arose between such an army and cannon fodder, I know on whose side I should feel most comfortable.

I beg Sir Benjamin Bolt's pardon for not knowing that when he paid naval officers the compliment of claiming for them, on the ground of their perfection of character, powers which we have made revolutions sooner than entrust to our kings, he was indulging in what he calls "a self-presented testimonial." But I still think him as ludicrously unfit to have any such powers entrusted to him as I am myself. I am sorry he thinks my style "insinuating": I really thought I had been blunt to the verge of rudeness. Of course I was annoying: anybody but a naval officer would have seen at once that I was purposely provoking him to make an exhibition of himself which should carry conviction to our readers. I am afraid I must admit that my naval "shop" is deplorably behind his: I got the boatswain's mate out of Captain Marryat when I was a boy; and I can only ask Sir Benjamin to convey my heart-felt apologies to the ship's corporal. I was told by The Times that the birch was a cane, and by Sir Benjamin that the cane was a birch. Sir Benjamin contradicted The Times, contradicted me, contradicted himself, contradicted me again, rebuked me for "relying on my imagination" in spite of "perfectly plain language," and finally says I ought to apologize. I do; but I protest that the incident leaves me in utter bewilderment as to where and how that boy was beaten. I am naturally somewhat alarmed by the news from Algiers confirming Sir Benjamin's statement (which I was far from questioning) that French mutineers are shot; for, if Sir Benjamin's views of the effect of discipline are correct, the British army, owing to its comparatively lax discipline, will infallibly succumb to the French in the event of an international conflict. As to his advice to me for my guidance in my profession, it is excellent; and I shall do my best to profit by it. If I can return his kindness at any time by giving him a few hints on navigation, my advice on that subject is cheerfully at his service.

From The Saturday Review, 13 *November* 1897

Mr Rosepath misunderstands me when he takes me to wish that the army were "manned" like the police force. For all the practical purposes of my argument, the army *is* manned like the police force. We keep on foot in London alone a force of sixteen thousand constables at twenty-four shillings a week. Mr Rosepath's contention amounts to this: that if you take a police constable representing the average of these sixteen thousand, and place beside him a soldier representing the average of any sixteen thousand men of our infantry battalions, the difference in civilization and moral character between them will be so great that the policeman may be trusted with all the rights of an ordinary English citizen, whereas the soldier must be outlawed, enslaved, and subjected to cruel punishments at the will of his officers, exactly as if he were a vicious elephant. Does Mr Rosepath expect me or any sensible person to believe that? Or take the bad characters alone. Mr Rosepath contends that if we take the blackest sheep in the London police force and the blackest sheep in the London barracks, the policeman's case can be met by simply shewing him the door or charging him before the nearest civil magistrate with whatever breach of the ordinary law he has committed, with a right to trial by jury if he demands it, whilst the military *mauvais sujet* must, in addition to dismissal from the service, suffer special retaliatory sentences inflicted by court-martial composed of officers who openly cite the instance of a soldier swearing at them as a convincing proof of a hardened brutality in him which only the cat-o'-nine-tails can correct, and then go into Hyde Park and themselves swear like costermongers at the first amateur blunder made by a Volunteer corps. Again I ask, does Mr Rosepath expect me to believe that such differences in treatment correspond to any possible difference in character between constables and soldiers? Does he believe it himself now that his ideas are sorted out and arranged comprehensibly before him?

Mr Rosepath may make his mind easy about "the undisputed legal right to strike on the field of battle." The use of putting the rights of soldiers in that way is that it gets rid at once of all the foolish people who thrust themselves into public controversies without the necessary qualifications for dealing with them. Appalled at the prospect of strikes occurring all over the next battle-field on which the destiny of the nation may depend, and convinced of the insanity of the man who sees no necessity for making such strikes criminal, they rush screaming away, and the controversy is well rid of them. It is, of course, physically possible that a regiment might strike on the field of battle. It is also physically possible that the whole army might simultaneously commit suicide, or become suddenly converted to Christianity and throw down their arms, or realize that they had no quarrel with the enemy and fraternize with them: any of these contingencies being much more probable than a strike. They might even run away, supports, officers and all. We must take our chance of that, though Mr Rosepath will no doubt think the risk very grave with a class of scoundrels so abandoned that he is able to cite two exceptionally atrocious cases in which one villain washed in the tea-can, whilst the other, lost to all sense of propriety, abused the general who had confirmed the sentence of the court-martial, refused to perform his shot-drill, and "destroyed as much public property as possible." Mr Rosepath, with apparent seriousness, asks me what I would do with these men? On Mr Rosepath's principles I should burn them alive, since if you are going in for retaliation and intimidation you may as well go in for them thoroughly. But on the principle of dispassionately making the best of a difficulty, I think I should be content in the case of the miscreant who washed in the tea-can to simply mention that fact to his comrades; and as to the other gentleman, I should do exactly what a publican would do: that is, drop him outside the barrack door and leave him to the police; unless indeed, in consideration of the possibility of applying his talent for destroying public property to the property of other nations, and the identity of his most salient qualities (including his aptitude in the use of profane and obscene language) with those displayed by many eminent military heroes, I decided to offer him the command of a frontier expedition.

I am sorry, however, that Mr Rosepath did not follow up the family history of this man. He would probably have found that, so far from his habits and character being the result of too humane a discipline, he had been kicked and cuffed and knocked about and sworn at on the most extreme retaliatory principles from the time he could feel anything until he was big enough to retaliate effectively himself. The orderly blackguardism of the parade ground and the anarchic blackguardism of the slum are the same thing, and produce the same results.

From The Saturday Review, 27 November 1897

The following extract from The Westminister Gazette of the 24th will probably excite keen indignation among those who, like The Globe, think that a lad who would strike his officer must be "such a blackguard at heart" that no punishment can be too cruel for him.

"An eye-witness states that a singular scene was witnessed yesterday morning at a parade of one of the Scots regiments now quartered at Aldershot. The sergeant of a company bullied and swore at the men, complaining of the manner in which they were drilling, and individualizing the men against whom his remarks were specially directed. At last a young soldier, who had been several times referred to, lost control of himself, and sprang out of the ranks and prodded the sergeant with his rifle, which he then clubbed. But on the sergeant stepping out of the way, he hurled the weapon at him. It was fortunate that the company had no bayonets fixed. The man then threw himself into a fighting attitude, but was seized and marched off by a file of men to the guard-room, and a second man was ordered to take off his belt and put down his rifle, and was sent off to the guard-room. The scene caused considerable excitement."

I presume this young soldier will be sent by a tribunal of officers to a military prison where there is plenty of flogging, *pour encourager les autres* (the other sergeants).

From The Times, 14 June 1904

The letter of "In Partibus Maris," inspires a hope that the Government will lose no time in abolishing corporal punishment in the navy unconditionally and at once, before there is any chance of our finding our seamen under the strain which the Japanese and Russian fleets are now enduring.

According to "In Partibus Maris," whose letter bears the stamp of that combination of direct practical knowledge and straightforward statement with unsuspicious simplicity which survives only in remote villages and *in partibus maris*, the effect of corporal punishment in the navy is to retain in the service a percentage of ill-conditioned youths, lazy, dirty, foul-mouthed, incapable of subordination, deaf to exhortation, callous to rebuke, and consequently useless to the ship until the incentive of earning their wages, serving their country, and taking their share with their comrades is replaced by the terror of being cut across the back with the corporal's cane. The birch has an even more important function. Without it, it seems, we should have to expel from our ships all the liars, the thieves, and the offenders against decency and common morality. Thanks to its application, we have now in our navy, as your correspondent vouches from his personal knowledge, a member who was habitually filthy, one whose leisure was given to telling foul stories to his mates, and one who had been grossly cruel to a monkey who was the pet of the ship. And to keep these heroic tars in countenance we use the same instrument to secure for them the congenial society of the unfortunate wretches who, being too weak morally to refrain from mean and low offences, are too weak physically to refrain from "howling like curs" when they are birched for them. Finally, we have the cat, which some of us supposed to have been abolished, but which we now find to be still a cherished institution of the British Navy. Its use is to enable us to retain the services of persons addicted to mutiny, to brutal assault on their officers, and to unnatural crime.

It is for the sake of these persons that the respectable and manly men and boys in the navy are paraded to contemplate their bare breeches (I quote the regulations) whilst the ship's police administer not more than 24 cuts with a birch. And the medical officer, a humanitarian by profession, and presumably a gentleman of culture and delicate habits, is compelled to superintend this indecency.

"If a vote," says "In Partibus Maris," "were taken for and against the retention of the cat as a possible punishment for crimes against country and humanity, the British sailor would uphold the custom of the service and the regulations of his King." I do not quite see why the King should be dragged into this unsavory business. If the matter were in his hands its settlement might possibly take "In Partibus Maris" aback quite as much as the vote of the seamen most assuredly would. But suppose it be true that the spectacle of a flogging is popular in the navy! Could a better reason be given for abolishing it? One of the most popular entertainments in London in former times was the public fustigation of the street-walker by the beadle. The defence of the practice was precisely the defence now offered by "In Partibus Maris" of its remnant in the navy. It was abolished not because it was unpopular, and not because it hurt the women (imprisonment is much crueller), but because it was degrading to the spectators and dishonorable to the nation. If our seamen really enjoy flogging and caning parades, and would vote for their continuance, the sooner we discharge them all and replace them by really manly men without any percentage of ill-conditioned, lazy, foul-mouthed, insubordinate liars, thieves, etc., the safer I, for one, shall feel, if we are ever unhappily engaged in a business that makes so tremendous a demand on the character of the combatants as a modern naval war.

In the police force, in signal cabins, and in cordite factories, where the least breach of discipline may entail consequences no less disastrous than on a battleship, discipline is maintained by making the employment worth the while of men of good character, and promptly discharging them if they do not do their duty. I do not believe for a moment that the British Fleet is manned by a horde of intimidated blackguards who cannot be trusted with the liberties of a tramp in a casual ward; but I am, of course, aware that in ships, as on shore, a man's character, like his constitution, may break down and leave him practically a criminal. This might occur on a battleship clearing for action as easily as in a liner overtaken by a typhoon. The same remedy is available for both cases; put the man in irons until it becomes possible to put him ashore at the nearest port. The only difficulty peculiar to the navy is the case of the man who refuses his duty, or the boy who strikes his officer, because he hates the service and wants to be discharged. It is held that, if the man or boy were free to go when he liked on reasonable notice, as in civil employment, and the commander equally free to sack a man who was not worth his salt, the officers would lose all their authority, and the men would instantly give a month's notice and leave England at the mercy of her enemies. The most charitable explanation of this delirious absurdity is that the isolation which discipline imposes on the higher grades of naval officers produces some of the familiar effects of solitary confinement on land, and makes them morbidly apprehensive of results which the common experience of civil life shews to be wildly impossible.

I am sincerely sorry that "In Partibus Maris" thinks me "a well-intentioned but mischievous person." At the same time, I am resolved that he shall never have an opportunity of reforming me by the hands of the ship's police. Not that I have any overwhelming dread of being flogged; I have survived worse physical sufferings than that. But nothing would induce me to enter a service in which I could be either compelled to flog another man or paraded to see it done by anyone else. I am not prepared to argue about it; it is an elementary point of honor with me, just as it is an elementary point of honor with me not to pick "In Partibus Maris's" pocket, though I could give a column and a half of excellent reasons for believing that I could spend his money much more beneficially to the nation than he could himself. In short, there are certain practices which, however expedient they may be, are instinctively barred by the humanity of the highest races; and corporal punishment is one of them. I should blush to offer a lady or gentleman mere reasons for my disgust at it.

From *The Times*, 2 September 1904

In a recent correspondence on this extremely disagreeable subject, I pointed out that the effect of flogging in the navy, on the shewing of its advocates, was to retain in the service lads of weak or vicious character, who had much better be put out of it.

Accordingly, it appears from a recent report that a boy of the first class in the cruiser Berwick, having stolen a letter containing two postal orders from the ship's post-box, has been dismissed from the service "as an objectionable character."

Nobody with any sense and knowledge of the world will fail to appreciate the severity of this proper and inevitable result of the boy's dishonesty. It bars all public employment to him, and all responsible private employment. It condemns him to the grade of labor in which character is not important enough to be worth inquiring into, or in which the absence of it is taken as a matter of course. It hits him harder than a sentence of imprisonment for petty pilfering hits an office boy; for many people would give the office boy "another chance" who would be merciless to a person dismissed from the Royal Navy for stealing a comrade's money.

Now here one can conceive a sentimentalist, moved by the boy's hard case, pleading that he should be let off with a flogging sound enough to keep his hands from picking and stealing for the rest of his life. Such a plea would shew little regard for the honor of the service and the dignity of English manners and customs, and still less enlightenment on the general question of crime and its treatment; but it would at least shew a sort of rough and ready consideration for the boy.

Will it be believed by any person, not a member of the Royal Navy or an inmate of a lunatic asylum, that the actual sentence passed by the court-martial was dismissal from the service as aforesaid and the most severe flogging that the regulations permit: namely, 24 strokes of the birch, the ship's company being compulsorily paraded to witness the flaying of the unfortunate wretch's "bare breech" (see regulations), and the ship's police, or the ship's corporal, or whoever the official executioner may be, being compelled to flay it.

Let us, as our custom is in England, leave out of the question the possibility of this being a case of flogging for the mere lust of flogging, not forgetting, however, that we do not leave that view out in our own judgment of Russian and Oriental floggings, and that those of us who travel enough to value Continental public opinion are painfully aware of the popular European belief that all Englishmen are addicted to physical cruelty and to the coarse vices which are usually associated with it: a belief for which our public schools are even more largely responsible than our naval courts-martial.

What reason, then, can there be for this apparently senseless heaping of physical torture on social ruin for a theft of 40s. by a lad? The old plea of reformation of the offender, of a sharp punishment that will be a lesson to him not to do it again, is here frankly given up; for if the flogging is to reform the boy, why dismiss him from the service, and, if not, why flog him? Is it not clear that the object of the flogging is to intimidate the other boys, and that this constitutes an admission that the brutalities which they are called on to witness week after week, the stupid, ill-tempered canings on the most trivial provocation—canings for such offences as smoking and backwardness in learning to swim (why not flog the instructors, by the way?)—have so destroyed their self-respect and *esprit de corps* that they have come to regard dismissal from the service as a stroke of good luck instead of a punishment, and have no conception of loss of character as a disadvantage at all? And the only remedy proposed is more flogging. The real remedy is more brains. When the quarter-deck is adequately supplied with this commodity the cane and the birch, which are essentially a fool's implements, are not tolerated.

But really, when we have the Government itself justifying the caning of backward swimmers on the ground that it is better that boys should be caned than drowned—which is a false issue, would not be true if it were the right issue, and would be just as good a reason for caning every yachtsman in the House of Commons as for caning lads in the navy—it seems a heartbreaking waste of time to struggle against the flagellant epidemic. The intellectual contrast between Mr Balfour at the British Association and some of his colleagues on the front bench is so stupefying that I have hardly sufficient courage or hope left to ask you to insert this protest. It seems as though the determination with which the Humanitarian League is forcing these naval floggings on the notice of the public will end, not in the abolition of corporal punishment in the navy, but in the refusal of every decent and high-spirited lad to enter the service, and consequently an actual increase of mere brute coercion as a means of driving refuserecruits through their duties. Which, I submit, is not the way to rule the waves.

From The Times, 14 September 1904

I thank Admiral Prugle Fustigum for his invaluable letter on this question. It is conclusive both as to the temper in which corporal punishment is administered in the navy and the fitness of our naval commanders for powers which civilians in situations of equal and sometimes much greater difficulty have discarded as unnecessary and barbarous. It will no doubt be vigorously circulated by the Humanitarian League, with what effect on our naval recruiting may be imagined.

On the admiral's kind recommendation, I have gone carefully through the history of Solomon and his presumably well-birched son. I find that Solomon himself was the son of David, a successful warrior and ruler, who spoiled his children, as the case of Absalom shews. Solomon introduced the flogging system, which grew more severe in the family until scorpions were substituted for whips. And, as might have been expected, Solomon's children lost the kingdom his father had built up, and scattered the nation he had welded together. To this day the remnant of that nation, reverting to the sentimental practice of David, spoils its children, with the result that in dealing with them our grown-up public schoolboys are as clay in the hands of the potter.

As to Solomon himself, unrestrained authority, and the practice of flogging other people, had such an effect on him that, on reaching the age of an admiral, he turned to the worship of Ashtaroth, and never could be reclaimed. A more impressive warning against governing empires on Solomonic principles, and navies on the principles of Captain Kidd's boatswain, is not to be found in the Scriptures.

I quite appreciate the implication that the reverend head of a public school either could, or, if he could, dare, administer such birchings and canings as are given on board ship by able-bodied seamen to boys who have neither social influence nor legal remedy to protect them. Perhaps the admiral will be good enough to pass it on to that amphibious branch of His Majesty's forces at sea which is reputed to be specially susceptible to representations of this character.

Finally, may I point to a recent article in The Boston Transcript, arising out of this correspondence, and shewing how our retention of flogging in the navy, and especially of that degrading and obscene form of flogging officially called birching, convinces other nations that our navy is recruited from the lowest and most worthless classes among us?

From The Morning Leader, 28 January 1907

I write to warn The Leader not to allow itself to be checked in its honorable crusade against flogging in the navy by the letter signed "Reformer," which claims for the present Government the merit of having abolished this practice. I am sorry to say that the assurance with which the Government disarmed the Humanitarian League has proved as delusive in substance as it was equivocal in form. The flogging of two boys last autumn for the hideous offence of having omitted to salute an officer whom they met bicycling in civilian clothes, and whom, they pleaded, they failed to recognize, was as bad as any of the cases exposed in Parliament by Mr Swift MacNeill before the late general election. No Unionist Minister has ever defended coercion by the lash more whole-heartedly than Sir Edward Grey defended the atrocious Denshawai executions, at which seven men got fifty lashes each (not to mention four hanged, two sent to penal servitude for life, one to fifteen years, six to seven years, and three to one year plus flogging) because they mobbed a party of English officers under circumstances of the most outrageous provocation.

Do not for a moment suppose that Liberal Governments need education and shaming—especially shaming—on this subject any less than Conservative ones. As long as the traditions of our county families and public schools make them nurseries of vice and barbarism, and as long as men educated in these nurseries predominate in our Governments, nothing but the most vigilant and implacable campaigning by the Democratic Press will keep the lash in check. Please keep pegging away, now that your friends are in office, just as hard as you did when they were in opposition; for when it comes to flogging there is not a straw to choose between them.

FLOGGING IN OUR INDUSTRIAL SCHOOLS

From the Daily Chronicle, 24 February 1895

THE London School Board will have before it this afternoon a proposal so atrocious that I venture to ask you to allow me to draw public attention to it.

There has of late, it appears, been a considerable change of feeling among our boy population with regard to our truant schools. Formerly they did their best to keep out of them after their first experience of them; now they return cheerfully. The secretary of such a school in Wales goes so far as to declare that as many boys now return in a month as formerly returned in a year.

This extremely desirable result does not please the teachers: it gives them more trouble. They want to return to the old system.

What was the old system? It was very simple. Whenever a boy was brought to a truant school he was flogged, as part of the ceremony of admission, before all the other boys. Naturally he loathed and dreaded the place after this experience, and tried to avoid readmission. The same result might have been achieved more thoroughly by frying him in boiling oil; but apparently the flogging went far enough in the way of cruelty to make things easy for the teachers.

In 1895 somebody realized the infamy of the practice, and it was prohibited. The recent spread of that familiar old neurosis, the flagellation mania, has emboldened certain school authorities to invite the London School Board to join in a deputation to the Home Secretary to procure a return to the flogging system.

It did not occur to anyone at first that the present Board, with its sweeping Progressive majority, could give any quarter to this disgraceful proposal. But it appears that Flagellomania has been victorious by seven votes to five on the Industrial Schools Committee. The matter will come before the Board this afternoon. The decision will help to clear up the growing doubt as to whether our boasted majority is really a Progressive majority or only a teachers' majority.

FLAGELLOMANIA

From Humanity, May 1899

IT is waste of time to deal argumentatively with the petition of the Edinburgh Society of Scotswomen for the flogging of men who commit sexual assaults. These ladies are neither fools nor illiterates: they must know all the arguments against passionate retaliatory punishments as well as every drunkard knows all the arguments against alcohol. They have caught a well-known hysterical disease, of which there have been several European epidemics. It seems to have come to England some years ago with the influenza. Since its arrival, the Press has been inundated with frantic appeals for the revival of flogging. Some of these are so obviously the outcome of a special disorder of the imagination that it is astonishing to find reputable newspapers printing them. In others we find the Edinburgh pretence of a desire to repress crime, invariably accompanied by the statement that the lash has put down garrotting. As there is probably not a single English newspaper in which this mistake has not been exposed, or a Parliamentary debate on the subject in either House in which it has not been authoritatively contradicted, it need no longer be treated as a mistake: it is simply the excuse of the flagellomaniac for the gratification of his (or her) passion. What is wanted is not the refutation of a sham argument but the resolute diagnosis of a real and very mischievous disease. Let this be once well understood by the public, and ladies will as soon think of passing resolutions in support of nymphomania as of flagellomania, which is a cruel variant of the same disorder.

I may remind them that the male flagellomaniac—who is sometimes, unfortunately, a judge—craves intensely for the flogging of women. He generally alleges that the woman who brings a false accusation of criminal assault or incest against a man is much more to be dreaded than a highway robber, and that the lash alone, etc.—you can supply the rest of the excuse.

If you still feel bound to argue with a disease which defies argument, simply ask why the flagellomaniac, with a great variety of exquisitely painful punishments to choose from, invariably insists on the only one that is notoriously sensual? Not long ago a flagellomaniac, excited by the assassination of the Empress of Austria, wrote to the Pall Mall Gazette proposing that Anarchists should be imprisoned for life and flogged *every day*. But why flogged? Why not suspended by the thumbs, or tormented by electricity? And why was this proposed when a romantic and handsome woman was stabbed, and not when President Carnot met the same fate and suffered much more? The same answer fits both questions. The pretended anti-Anarchist was simply a victim of the disease of the debauchees from whom poor girls earn a few pounds by submitting to a flogging. And that is the vulgar secret of the whole agitation. It will die away as former epidemics of it have died away. In the meantime we must see that it does not leave permanent traces on our statute book to deepen the infamy which we already enjoy as the upholders of prisons which are compared unfavorably in point of useless cruelty with the prisons of Morocco by travellers who have seen both.

The subject is so disagreeable that it is necessary to justify the publication of even a warning against it by a practical example of its danger. Early this year the London School Board, in spite of the efforts of some humane members, authorized public floggings at Truant Schools. A boy at one of the schools, having made an accusation against one of the officers and then withdrawn it, was thereupon publicly flogged, receiving the maximum punishment of twelve lashes. Some weeks later, the accused officer was found committing an offence with the flogged boy. The police applied for a warrant; the officer absconded: the boy was transferred to another school; and the flogging majority of the Board stood convicted of having been the dupes of a satyromaniac, and of having propagated his disease by a public exhibition of flogging. Comment is unnecessary.

CHILD-BEATING: A BISHOP'S PASTORAL

From The Irish Times, 25 February 1928

THE Meath correspondent of The Irish Times quotes the Most Reverend Dr Gaughran, Bishop of Meath, as having expressed himself in his Lenten Pastoral as follows:

"In childhood the least sign of anger, untruthfulness, or disobedience must not go unpunished. The rod must be used whenever the child refuses to obey father or mother. Young children especially have no respect for anything else. Let the child feel the rod; it is the best food he could have.

"The surest and most necessary means to bring up children in a Christian manner was to shew them a good example. Instruction was no use without example."

Surely this cannot be an authentic piece of news. We are asked to believe that an eminent Churchman declares that his Church classes children with their tops, which respond only to whipping, and denies that they have any consciences; yet, in the very same breath, enjoins that, if a child does not attain a higher level of conduct than is claimed for God Himself in the Bible, it must be beaten. How could such monstrous propositions be put forward officially by a responsible Irish ecclesiastic? What would be said of me if I urged that Dr Gaughran should be soundly flogged whenever he shews "the least sign of anger," or when his natural kindness of heart impels him to spare his friends the truth, the whole truth, and nothing but the truth?

The final proof that the report is only a bad joke is its last paragraph, in which the parents, who have just been exhorted to behave in this outrageous manner, are told that it will be no use unless they set their children "a good example."

I should not trouble you about a matter which appears to speak for itself were it not that so many people in Meath are incapable of criticizing advice purporting to come from their spiritual directors that Ireland will be deafened by the screams of the unfortunate children of that county, none of whom are either divinely truthful nor heroically able to control their angry impulses, unless their parents are warned that the alleged Lenten Pastoral cannot be accepted as *ex cathedra*.

THE LOGIC OF THE HUNGER STRIKE
10 *September* 1920

WHENEVER an irresistible Government passes a sentence of punishment, however trivial, on an individual, it also passes a sentence of death on him in the event of his determining to die rather than submit to the punishment.

If this consideration did not exist, Governments could impose their wills on their subjects by simple reckless persecution up to the point at which they would provoke a spontaneous general revolution of an overwhelming majority of their subjects; and they could persecute a physically powerless minority without limit.

The Hunger Strike is the practical form of the determination to die rather than submit to a decreed punishment. A prudent Government will therefore be very careful how it decrees any punishment, because in the event of its victim hunger striking, it will be forced either to reduce itself and the law generally to absurdity by an unconditional surrender, or else go through with it and become responsible to the public conscience for the victim's death.

If the victim is a criminal who has incurred the punishment by some act which has excited general abhorrence or even strong reprobation, the Government may safely go through with it. But this case does not arise in practice. Scoundrels do not hunger strike, nor do ruffians, though the latter may in rare cases resist capture by violence to the death. When this happens the general verdict is "a good riddance"; and this would also follow a hunger strike to the death by an ordinary criminal. Ordinary criminals know this very well, and therefore, having to choose between a period of imprisonment and certain and unpitied death, accept the lesser of the two evils. That is why the repeated surrenders of Governments to hunger strikers have conferred no impunity on ordinary crime, and why thieves, homicides, forgers, incendiaries, and even bigamists go on serving their sentences hopelessly when they have seen the prisoner in the next cell released at the cost of a fortnight's fast.

With the hunger striker, therefore, it is always a case of conscience. He (or she) is willing to die, not for himself, but for a principle, or cause, or religion, which he identifies with the public good. He gives his life that these things may live, and dies *ad majorem gloriam Dei.* It is a serious matter for a Government to kill such a man. Even when his conscience seems silly and selfish, his principle fallacious, his cause subversive, and his religion heretical, still the fact that he is one of the few men who can rise above himself to the pitch of dying for them gives him a sanctity that makes it impossible for the public to contemplate his death without great uneasiness, or to feel satisfied with a Government that has provoked a fatal contest between the law and his conscience. This may be unreasonable; but it has to be faced by politicians, for Cabinets cannot escape from the facts under cover of syllogisms. *A fortiori*, if his principle is one of such wide acceptance that the Government itself has done it loud lip service, and has even alleged it as the pretext for a colossal war, and his cause widely popular in the Government's dominions, his death is very likely to prove the doom of the Government, and to be obstinately, but by no means undeservedly, counted against them as an act of wilful murder in the form of morally compelled suicide.

This is clearly the case of the Lord Mayor of Cork. Whether he is alive or dead I have no means of ascertaining as I write these lines: all I know is that the Government has already gone further than it should have gone if it is not prepared to go on to the end. It is, however, such an extraordinarily unintellectual and ignorant Government that it is unlikely that it knows clearly what it is doing; therefore the case may as well be stated clearly for it by some fairly intelligent person.

I may add, in order that my personal bias may be duly allowed for, that I am against all strikes that recoil on the striker instead of felling the adversary, and that I wish I could persuade the Lord Mayor of Cork to eat a hearty dinner and leave the silly Government to the anarchy from which his improvised Court, which is well spoken of and appealed to by the best people in Cork, rescued it. But if Mr Lloyd George really means to make a martyr of the Lord Mayor, I would not be in Mr Lloyd George's shoes for a good deal. The Lord Mayor is the sort of martyr who burns with a very bright and very fierce flame.

P.S. [1931]. The Government nevertheless went through with it this time; and the saintly Lord Mayor died of starvation in the midst of plenty. His Church apparently regarded his action as a justifiable suicide: at all events he was not commanded to eat on pain of dying without absolution. The Government was logically in order and was able to claim that its consistency put an end to hunger striking in Irish prisons for the moment.

SHAM EDUCATION

SHAM EDUCATION

SCHOOLS AND SCHOOLMASTERS

From the Education Year Book of 1918

SOME years ago, in an essay entitled Parents and Children, published, according to my custom, as a preface to a play, I gave a fairly exhaustive account of my view of the process commonly called education. Returning to the subject in 1918 by way of a careful perusal of the Education Year Book of The Workers' Educational Association, to which I had been invited to contribute a preface, I found in that very remarkable volume all the relevant essays by other hands which make up this book. I can assure that the facts are fit for publication, all the hopes, all the failures, all the finance, set forth at worst readably, and at best with rare knowledge, penetration, and literary skill. There was nothing left for me to say except the very simple things that stand as mountains in the path of the writer on education, yet that he must usually ignore if he is to get to his subject at all. And I have said most of them before.

First, there is the fact that education is mostly a pretext under cover of which parents get rid of their duties and escape from the noise, the dirt, the unconscious chaperonage, the perpetual questioning of children. By conniving at this evasion our Churchmen and sectarians are enabled to proselytize the rising generations, our plutocrats to segregate and corrupt them, and our schoolmasters to make money. The tense silence in which my exposure of this radical imposture has been received, in contrast with the garrulous discussions of minor points, shews how deeply guilty our society is on this score. Yet the guilt, as I have insisted, does not lie in the parents' quite natural and socially wholesome desire to escape from the intolerable inroads made by the continual presence of children on their privacy, their quiet, their pursuits, and their pleasures, but in our callous indifference to the methods by which the schoolmaster relieves us for so much a year cash.

SHAM EDUCATION

What does the schoolmaster do with the child when the parent delivers it over with a sigh of relief, having nothing more to dread until the holidays come round? He imprisons it, and hires a body of minor masters to act as warders and turnkeys. An admirable essay by Mr Edmond Holmes in the Year Book deals with the essential slavery of school life, and concludes that we must "defeudalize" education. But strong and deeply felt as Mr Holmes's condemnation is, he flatters our school system in comparing its child victims to feudal serfs. Serfs had rights and a status. School children have neither one nor the other: they are treated as outlaws pure and simple. And their condition is not improving in this respect. One of the contributors to this book, a man not yet past middle age, tells me that during his last two years at Eton he did what he liked. Recent biographies of Etonians (for example, Gosse's Life of Swinburne) shew that the public schoolboy was once left to himself sufficiently to enable him to cultivate tastes of his own and approach and commune with Nature in his own way. Compare this picture of Eton life with the recent ones written by young men, especially those who are so proud of having been at a public school that they delight in describing how they were thrashed because they tried to botanize, or naturalize, or take country walks, or read instead of drudging at compulsory games. In our socially pretentious preparatory schools the boys who are too young to play games are actually forced to stand and watch their seniors playing. Is anyone imposed on by the pretence of liking this and believing that it was good for them with which our eager climbers of the social ladder present their credentials as "public school men"? Yet this modern invasion and enslavement of every moment of a child's waking life is represented as a development of education. The most impressive documentary novel of recent years is Mr Alec Waugh's Loom of Youth, which is almost a diary of life at Sherborne. Compared with the medieval public school curriculum, in which the wretched scholar rose at six and learned Latin for nearly twelve hours without any play at all, it exhibits the complete capture of the school by the athletic schoolboy and the athletic schoolmaster, the medieval system being restored with the substitution of football and cricket for Latin and Greek. Soon a schoolboy caught reading or looking at pictures or listening to music will be thrashed as he once was when caught playing games.

Meanwhile the schoolmaster must not confess himself a mere boy farmer: he has to make his prisoners learn certain things, whether games or murdered languages. Now there are, unfortunately, two ways of doing this. One way is teaching: a process which requires some natural vocation, a good deal of skill and experience, and an honorable character. The other way is open to any fool or blackguard. You do not teach: you set the pupil a task, and beat him, bully him, ridicule him, or torture him in any other way that may be convenient to you unless he is able to perform it. To naturally cruel men, the Creakles and Murdstones and Squeerses, this makes schoolkeeping a delightful occupation. The old cries of "See, Udal, see," and "The schoolmaster's delight is to flog" are still stifled in the breasts of many inarticulate victims of much worse men than Creakle or Squeers; for Dickens never told the worst of the orgiast-pseudo-pedagogue, though he need have gone no further than the boasted records of Bell and Lancaster for evidence of them.

This fact has to be faced if the profession of teaching is to be lifted from the abyss of popular dislike and contempt into which it has fallen. Of all men the most naturally reverenced are teachers. Of all men the most naturally despised are executioners. And as long as the schoolmaster is paid, not for teaching, but for saying to the growing child "Learn this, you little devil, or I will cane you until you will not be able to sleep for terror of me," the schoolmaster will be classed with the executioner in popular esteem. That, and that alone, is the secret of the shameful poverty and low social status of the schoolmaster.

If this were merely an abuse in practice such as must arise in all professions when the practitioner is a scoundrel, there would be no disgrace in it. Most unfortunately, it is the accepted and legalized theory of schoolmastering; and, although the practice is seldom as vile as the theory, it is by the theory that the status of the practitioner is determined. The reader of this book may ask me how I can maintain such a proposition in spite of the spirit informing the essays of Mr C. H. C. Osborne on The George Junior Republic and The Little Commonwealth, of Miss M. L. V. Hughes with her admirable Two Decalogues, of Mr Edmond Holmes already quoted, and of Lord Haldane with his claim that even the technical formula for calculating the strain on a girder should not be taught without relating it, not to the fear of a caning, but to the Cartesian mathematic which is part of a philosophy. I shall be asked if I have ever read Goethe's Wilhelm Meister; heard of Dr Montessori; or met a pupil from President Pearse's Sgoil Eanna.

I will, therefore, mention something that I have read quite recently and that everyone who takes in a newspaper has read. A schoolboy, with an unusually manly mind, summoned his schoolmaster for assaulting him. The schoolmaster's defence was that he was "teaching" the boy geography. The process, as de-scribed by himself, was asking the boy questions in geography and hitting him with a cane when the boy was unable to answer them. The magistrate at once accepted this as the normal and proper business of a schoolmaster; reproved the boy for being (of all things) unmanly; and dismissed the summons. There was no protest either in editorial or correspondence columns. The Press agreed with the magistrate. The parental public agreed with him. That is what education means at present, both in law and public opinion, in spite of the few genuine teachers, who are regarded simply as cranks.

I recommend this case to Dr F. B. Jevons and the other writers who are very justly concerned about the inferior status and wretched pay of schoolmasters as a class. I am a professional man, paid, when I am in luck, two hundred times as much for my work as the poorest schoolmaster is for his, and perhaps thirty times as much as many an envied headmaster. I am invited to feel indignation because this police-court hero, with his cane and his geography lesson, is not placed on my level as to social esteem and income. I admit the claim as to income because I am a Socialist, and because I am perfectly well aware that my income has no reference whatever to my merit. But as to social esteem I must really ask whether I, who am, for good or evil, a genuine teacher by a highly skilled method, am to admit as my equal a person whose "profession" it is to hit a boy half his size hard enough to make him wince with pain. The schoolmaster's gardener, who could probably hit harder than the schoolmaster, and can at least plead that he produces vegetables without assaulting people, makes no such claim. My feeling is that 30s. a week, and the status of a trainer of performing dogs, is as much as a schoolmaster can reasonably expect until he learns to teach. He would probably think this quite good enough for me if my success as a playwright were obtained by imprisoning my audiences in the theatre and caning them when they omitted to applaud, or whispered, or coughed, or shuffled their feet.

I am not for the moment dealing with the question whether it is possible to make all our children learn in any other way, having regard to the multitudes of them and the dearth of teachers of genuine vocation. And I am certainly not proposing that children, any more than adults, should be artificially exempted from physical coercion, or even from summary natural personal vengeance, to the extent of making them imagine that they are living in a moral vacuum and can do as they like without regard to the feelings and convenience of others. I am simply insisting that the forcing children to learn by beating them is unskilled labor of an unedifying and repulsive character. I call it unskilled advisedly. I am aware that it would break down in practice if the curriculum were not planned with some skilled knowledge of the cane's possibilities, and that you cannot teach the infinitesimal calculus to a child of three by any amount of flogging. But the ordinary schoolmaster does not devise the curriculum: he simply carries out a prearranged routine like the school charwoman; and if some practical joker were to slip the calculus into the junior time-table most of the masters would try to whack it into their youngest pupils as solemnly as they used to try to whack the very difficult subject of grammar. While this state of things lasts they will rebel in vain against the tendency of public common sense to class them with menagerie keepers rather than with men of learning.

The remedy is not to give professional pay and status to unskilled men who cannot even pronounce the alphabet presentably, but to exact genuine professional qualifications from the schoolmaster and pay him their market value. His status will then take care of itself. I have not noticed that genuine teachers who now undertake the care of children are at any disadvantage pecuniarily or socially in ordinary professional society. They have, comparatively, a good time of it; for, I repeat, the true teacher can leave the doctor, the lawyer, and even the parson nowhere in the rapidity with which he can gain respect and liking both in his school and out of it, and that, too, without being by any means an angel in point of temper. Most real teachers have occasionally to pretend to be rather shorter tempered than they really are lest they should mollycoddle their charges. But they do not appear in police-courts to explain that in their schools the pupils have to learn without being taught on pain of being beaten, the schoolmaster's department being confined to the beating. They try to make the teaching half of the transaction interesting enough to induce the pupil to do the learning half either for its own sake or for theirs.

The modern tendency is to relieve the caning system for the masters in two ways. One is to confine the use of the cane to the headmaster. That is to say, the head, who ought to be the moral centre of the school, is made a sort of Lord High Executioner, and spends his time between doing the dirty work of his assistants and the making out of the school bills. The other plan, started by Arnold, is to get the boys to do their own caning by the prefect system. This was a natural move enough; for whereas under the old system the masters, if they did not teach, at least had to cane, under the prefect system they neither teach nor cane; and it becomes possible for a comparatively easygoing, lazy, unauthoritative, donnish sort of person to hang on to a mastership. Also the boy who is caned can look forward to the time when he will cane other boys, and can form a taste in that direction, just as he forms a habit of treating servants as fags. But these alleviations of the schoolmaster's lot do not entitle him to call himself a teacher, nor to claim the respect and emolument considered proper to a professional man. He still has to depend for any credit he enjoys on such incidentals as holy orders or a University degree. The common schoolmaster who has neither of these qualifications is still in the most embarrassing of all social positions. The gentry inexorably refuse to accept him as a gentleman; and the common people refuse to accept him as a fellow-creature. And they will both be entirely justified in their attitude as long as his profession of teaching is only a cloak for the practice of a turnkey and an executioner carrying out a law which is purely lynch law.

Under such circumstances it is not surprising to find that when an educationist is also a statesman, he will not support the schoolmaster's claim to be organized and recognized as the medical profession is organized and recognized: that is, as a monstrous tyranny with legal powers of coercion over the rest of the community, and with unlimited power to dictate its own qualifications; to prevent anyone practising as a teacher without its authority; and to set all lay power at defiance. The schoolmasters are not even aware of the fact that the inevitable operation of these powers has brought the medical profession into such disrepute and open conflict with the public interest that nothing but the gross ignorance and superstition of Parliament in regard to political and hygienic science stands between the General Medical Council and the deprivation of its worst privileges, accompanied by a resolute exercise of the powers already possessed by the Government and the Universities to secure a majority of laymen on it. One of the very first things a true teacher should teach is that such bodies as the General Medical Council, and the ideal at which the National Union of Teachers brazenly aims, should be resisted as Star Chambers and Bastilles should be resisted. To Sir Robert Morant's refusal to allow the teachers themselves to be the judges of their own success and the prescribers of their own qualifications, so that they can ruin any teacher who dares to criticize their methods, the Registration Council opposes a simple assumption that a body of men whose notion of teaching is to beat the children for not learning, is omniscient, infallible, and infinitely virtuous, and should, therefore, at once be entrusted with powers which this country made two revolutions sooner than entrust to the Throne and the Church. Those who advance such a demand are not only incapable of teaching, but incapable of learning. By all means let us have a register of teachers; but let the learners keep the key of it.

It must never be forgotten that education is such a dangerous thing that it is very doubtful whether the invention of printing would have been tolerated if more than a very few people had been able to read. The Roman Catholic Church has not to this day consented to place the Scriptures in the hands of the laity. We must either go through with education or let it alone. A state of things like the present, in which everybody knows how to read and nobody knows what to read, and in which the crudest, darkest, poorest minds are allowed to propagate their crudity, darkness, and poverty through the Press for a pittance which leaves them no chance of culture, is disastrous: the war is only one of its disasters, and not the worst of them. For it must be added that the richer classes which have gone through the entire routine of schooling, as established at our public schools and Universities, are, except as experts in athletics, sport, and drawing-room accomplishments, as crude and ignorant as the journalists from the elementary school, who have become journalists because they are so incorrigibly inaccurate that they could not keep situations as clerks for a fortnight. The newspapers which cater specially for public schoolmen and University graduates, for the country-house and the rectory: that is, for the classes which represent our education untempered by the teaching which men of business or professional men get from their daily pursuits, are frankly organs of savagery and snobbery. The war has revealed an astounding ignorance in the classes that actually govern us: one wonders sometimes how any human beings with so much interest in their own ambitions and amusements could possibly be so void of intellectual interests and curiosities as not to have learnt something by merely walking about with their eyes open, nor have reasoned enough about what they see to become capable of a few simple syllogisms.

Take a topical wartime specimen of their powers of reasoning upon what is one of the main interests of their lives: pheasant shooting. They want pheasants to shoot; therefore nobody must be allowed to kill pheasants except gentlemen with guns. Nevertheless, as we shall lose the war by starvation unless we economize food, we must not feed the pheasants. And there the matter was left. The pheasants were strictly preserved; and their food was cut off. The country-houses of England apparently did not contain a single representative person with intelligence enough to infer the result that followed, which was, that the pheasants, not being fed as usual by the gamekeeper, ate the farmer's crops; and the farmer, being forbidden to shoot them, quarrelled fiercely with his landlord, their proprietor. In the same way, when the war imposed a need for economy, we had, instead of the educated man's conception of economy as a facilitation of production, the miser's conception of it as mere abstinence. The first thing we were to abstain from was education, which was sacrificed not merely with indifference to its economic value, but positive malice against its superiorities. The next thing was locomotion, the very circulation of the productive organism. Even communication was restricted to such a degree that the penny post is now a thing of the past. A gentleman who was appointed to control the Air Service because his brother was a rich newspaper proprietor, began by making a speech, in which he described his own official business as murder, like any poor woman in a slum who has seen her child killed by a bomb, and following this up by demanding that the British Museum be cleared out to make room for him and his staff. He did not ask for Westminster Abbey to store petrol in; but it can hardly have been any cultural consideration that hindered him. And the working classes can hardly reproach him after handing over Ruskin College for war purposes with an alacrity which suggested that they were glad of an excuse to get rid of it.

All this means not only that the people we send to school at great expense are ignorant, but that their minds are of very limited use to themselves, and worse than no use to the nation: nay, positively injurious to it. The stupendous blunders made by the Germans, most fortunately for us, shew that their school methods are no better than ours; but they respect education, having an intellectual conception of it, whereas we, having no such conception, dislike and despise it. We actually prefer the ignorant and insolent young barbarians who keep up the reputation of certain Oxford and Cambridge Colleges for rowdiness to those whose civilized instincts and naturally refined tastes lead them to behave like grown-up people with some sense of their duty to their neighbors.

I might say a good deal more about this fundamental vice and error of imposing as education a system of imprisonment and "breaking in" which has no reference to education at all, and is intended only to secure a livelihood for schoolmasters by saving parents trouble and making children quiet and submissive: that is, unfit to be free citizens in a democracy. Suffice it to say here, that the curse of a prison is that by its very nature it reverses every law and aspiration of Christian conduct, being violent, revengeful, coercive, and deliberately planned to destroy happiness. In these pages the essays of Mr Osborne, of Miss McMillan, of Mr J. L. Paton, of Miss M. L. V. Hughes, of Dr Keatinge, and of Mr Holmes are penetrated with a sense of struggle against the prison morality of our schools; but they do not seem to me to grasp the fact that what they are in revolt against is not fundamentally a bad method of education, but a selfish and mischievous purpose of which neither the parents nor the masters are in the least ashamed. That is why I have felt bound to harp on it.

I need hardly add that the fact that at this moment the majority of schoolmasters are schoolmistresses does not affect my argument. They are quite as handy with the cane as the men. What is more important is that as it is possible to make a case for the statement that "corporal punishment is disappearing," we should bear jealously in mind that corporal punishment is only one of many available methods of intimidation and coercion, and by no means the most cruel and injurious. There are worse tortures, both physical and moral, in actual use (I shall not propagate them by giving particulars) in schools where "corporal punishment is not permitted."

I pass on to the controversy as to technical and liberal education which occupies the contributions of Mr S. G. Hobson and Lord Haldane. I do not think that liberal education, which is really recreation, can ever be attained through compulsory schooling. Until English literature was made a school subject the Shakespear nausea which is now common among the secondarily educated did not exist, though already schoolgirls had learned from their music lessons to loathe Beethoven. Now no adult loathes that indispensable subject of compulsory technical education, the multiplication table; nor indeed would any have loathed it in childhood had it been made clear then that a child who knows it can enjoy money and liberty to an extent impossible to one who cannot change a sixpence to buy a tram ticket or visit a picture palace. Technical education is a qualification for living in society. Being necessary to life, it justifies itself by its results even to those who acquire it with difficulty and repugnance, and exercise its accomplishments without pleasure for ulterior objects. But a liberal education cannot be acquired without interest and pleasure. Compulsory Shakespear only provides a public for books written to prove that Shakespear was Bacon by people who lack the literary and dramatic sense to know that the fact that Shakespear was not Bacon is not a matter of evidence or argument, but of the direct evidence of the literary and dramatic sense, just as the fact that Bacon's statue at St Albans does not represent the same man as the Stratford bust is a simple matter of eyesight, and the fact that Wagner was not Brahms is a simple matter of listening to their music. It does not provide audiences for Shakespear's plays: on the contrary, it keeps them away. A liberal education, in short, cannot be imposed: all that can be usefully given is access: water should be provided for the horse; but it must not be forced down with a stomach pump submitted to under threat of the whip.

The distinction between technical and liberal education seems obvious when we contrast a knowledge of the multiplication and pence table with a taste for Shakespear. The obviousness vanishes when democracy forces us to recognize that citizenship is a technical subject and the universal profession of democrat a highly skilled one. Calvin, I take it, though he would perhaps have admitted that the children of Geneva could not be taught to appreciate and enjoy the music of Orlandus Lassus and Josquin Deprès and Van Sweelinck as they could be taught to navigate a ship or build a house, would have maintained that his Institutes should be taught in order to qualify the children technically to become citizens of "the perfect city of God." And I think he would have been right. To live in Geneva in Calvin's time, or in Scotland in the sixteenth and seventeenth centuries, as in Ulster today, without intolerable social friction, a knowledge of the Calvanistic scheme of salvation and damnation was as necessary to the man who abhorred it as to the man who accepted it. Dante's scheme of Catholicism was equally a technical subject for the diplomatists of the Holy Roman Empire and their opponents. What is the matter with civilization at present is that Calvin's Institutes and the divine rights of the Holy Roman Empire having become incredible, and the Church Catechism and the Thirty-Nine Articles in great part unthinkable, chiefly through the discovery of Evolution, there is a void left in our technical education. As Nature abhors a vacuum, this void is being filled by demoralizing pseudo-scientific stupidities like Weismannism and Mechanism on one side, and a mess of crude pseudo-political sentimentalities on the other; whilst the creed of Creative Evolution, obviously the coming religion, has not been formulated and popularized. But it will have to be.

SHAM EDUCATION

The symphonies of Beethoven will never be possible as text-books; but the treatises of Bergson certainly will if we are to have a society as genuinely organized as the Protestant and Catholic societies of pre-evolutionary times. There must be a common technical theory of the goal of Evolution to replace the old common technical theory of the will of God. Not only those who accept it but those who challenge it will at least know where society stands, which no man knows at present.

Science, admittedly a technical subject, must include political science, not only in its elementary branch of police regulation, but in its modern constitutional developments as industrial democracy and Socialism, which subjects, in a modern democratic State, should be as compulsory, up to the limit of the scholar's capacity for them, as the multiplication table. At least a conception of them should be inculcated: such a conception, for instance, as I have of mathematics, though I cannot do the simplest sum in algebra. Even the uneducated should know what education means. Such an epithet as "half educated" should vanish from the language; for nobody who knows what he is talking about imagines that any individual can confidently claim to be even one per cent educated, much less fifty per cent. The old formula "Know something of everything and everything of something" belongs to an age when so little was known that "one small head could carry all we knew." Three hundred years ago Newton, who came as near to universal knowledge as any merely human animal is ever likely to, could not find a figure infinitesimal enough to express how little he knew, and compared himself to a child on the seashore picking up a few grains of sand. Still, Newton knew what knowledge means and what ignorance means; and though we cannot make every boy and girl a Sidney and Beatrice Webb we can at least save them from the democratic delusion that political capacity is not a scientific acquirement but an intuition which descends on every freeborn Briton at the age of twenty-one. It needs no abnormal acumen to see how odd it is that though we will not allow a barrister to practise, or a doctor to call himself a doctor and sign death certificates, or a clergyman to hold a living, unless they undergo a test of technical qualification, anybody may practise political science as voter, or even as Cabinet Minister, without knowing how to read and write. What is worse, anyone may practise abortion and poisoning on the nation's mind and spirit as a journalist or newspaper proprietor with complete impunity and even huge profit, though if he did the same with a mechanical instrument on an unborn baby he would go unpitied to penal servitude. It is even proposed that legislation shall be initiated and imposed, or defeated and cancelled, without discussion or information, by the man in the street acting through a referendum: indeed, this can already be done in some States. The consequences under modern democratic conditions are so appalling that we are in imminent danger of that revulsion against democracy which, instead of saving ancient Athens, hastened its ruin. The people will either throw over democracy altogether in disgust at its disastrous ignorance, and fall back on the hopeless expedient of thrusting dictatorial powers on the nearest adventurer whom they may romantically imagine, at his own suggestion, to be an Earthly Providence, or else they will demand some sort of scientific evidence of political capacity as a qualification for election or office. Already the public services are protected from absolute imbecility and illiteracy by examinations; and sooner or later we shall see the absurdity of demanding educational qualifications from the clerk and none from the Secretary of State, with the result that we have Secretaries of State for Foreign Affairs who cannot speak French at the head of an office in which a knowledge of French is obligatory on everyone else.

The difficulty is that the examination test is useless and even mischievous except for routine workers. Though a knowledge of French and drawing-room dancing may qualify a man to be an attaché, it does not qualify him to be a Foreign Minister. The late President Kruger, who would not have been accepted by the Foreign Office as a hall porter, outwitted all the diplomatists of Britain and Germany until he was in his dotage. People who have a positive genius for passing examinations, and who learn languages with extraordinary facility, are often quite impossible as chiefs of staff, to say nothing of Ministers; and for this reason it has never been possible to apply the examination system throughout the whole public service, the necessary exceptions becoming excuses for a good deal of jobbery. Also, examinations can be manipulated so as to favor or exclude classes; and the shameless resort of our own ruling classes to this device has cooled the enthusiasm with which the examination system was formerly hailed as a democratic reform.

In short, we still lack a trustworthy anthropometric method for high purposes of State. Poets, like other observant people, notice "the straitened forehead of a fool," often in the highest offices or in feudal command of a county; but we have not yet invented the callipers, ascertained the measurements, or discovered the reagents which should test the Prime Minister and the Commander-in-Chief as the tape round the chest and the height measurer test the rank and file of the police and the Army. I remember once being much flattered by a speaker in a discussion following a political harangue of mine, who said, "I did not understand the lecturer's arguments, because, as you will see if you observe the shape of my head, I have not the requisite faculty; but as a professional phrenologist I can assure you that you may trust to his judgment." I followed up this clue far enough to convince myself that the analysis of human faculty made by the phrenologists had not yet carried them beyond classifications so crude and ambiguous as to verge on positive illiteracy here and there, the results being far too imprecise to be of any practical value for political purposes. Nevertheless, the need for some method of measuring personal capacity which shall be as completely beyond the control of the operator or the subject as the measurement of a yard of cloth is beyond the control of the cloth or of the yardstick, is becoming more conscious. I have myself been tested with contrivances designed to ascertain how quickly I can respond to a sensory stimulus, or how long I can distinguish between two colors when they are being substituted for one another with increasing rapidity. The inferences from these tests vary from the simplest statement of the result to a certificate classing you with a Fuegian or with Plato or Shakespear: that is to say, from cautious fact to extravagant romance; but if these contrivances be taken with the various tests used in the Army and other public services, they will appear as part of a growing body of anthropometric devices ranging from the shoemaker's rule to attempts at psychometric machines. These things should not be passed over lightly because some of them are obviously cranky and none have superseded the experienced college tutor who tells an undergraduate what honors it is worth his while to read for in view of his natural capacity. But tutorial measurement is founded on a degree of intimacy and familiarity which is not practicable for general public purposes. We seem far from the day when persons classed by natural capacity (as distinguished from acquirements) will be disqualified or conscribed for public work according to their degree; when Class A1 will be compelled on incorruptible evidence to elect representative peers from their own register to undertake the highest duties of the State, and Class Z17, however self-assertive and noisily popular, will be absolutely debarred from voting at elections, contesting Parliamentary or municipal seats, running newspapers, or possibly even procreating their species.

In making this rough suggestion I am not forgetting that one of the uses of democracy is to save people from being intolerably well governed, and, in fact, discouraged out of existence as savages are by civilized men. I would give Class A1 rights of counsel and criticism, but no vote. The mass of men coming between J and K should neither be dragged in the mud by Z nor dragged up to the clouds by A to share the fate of Phaeton; and my old proposal that Parliament should contain fifty aldermen elected by proportional representation under the original Hare scheme, the whole nation voting as one constituency, should be safeguarded by the proviso that their rights of speech in the Assembly should not include access to the voting lobbies. But even with such safeguards, which would not exclude the popular actor of the day and the popular general, however incapable they might be politically, a wise electorate would still ask for some incorruptible scientific test of capacity, taking capacity in its widest sense to include intellectual integrity and social instinct, and giving no more than its due value to that power of working for sixteen hours a day every day for thirty years which at present enables the stupidest routineers to oust from important posts men of much higher faculty, whose real work cannot be sustained except in emergencies for more than two or three hours, and even at that imposes extensive periods of total recreation.

Now secondary education, as we have it today, wholly fails to supply such a test.

Mr J. L. Paton points out how very little secondary education we actually give. People who have attended a secondary school are in an absurd minority. These two propositions are not, however, the same. There is, fortunately, a great deal of secondary self-education: indeed civilization would not hold together if its culture depended on its schools instead of on its bookshops and lectures and summer schools and general currency of intellectual intercourse. Many of our most cultivated people owe absolutely nothing to their schooling; and some of them, especially among the women, have never been to school at all. Though Ruskin took an Oxford degree, he was never a schoolboy; and he differed from his Etonian and Harrovian fellow-graduates only in being, not worse educated (conspicuously the contrary, in fact), but much less of a blackguard. I can lay my hand on my heart and say that nothing that I know was taught me at school except a collection of foul jests on the very subjects that ought to be kept cleanest in a boy's mind; and even these were not in the curriculum. The place where I was imprisoned for half the day, and which was called a school, kept me from the books, the great public picture gallery, the music, and the intercourse with Nature which really educated me; and admirable as the spirit and insight of Mr Paton's plea for more secondary education seem to me, I am not sure that the extension of what is now called secondary education to the age of eighteen or twenty for all classes would not abolish the little culture we have, and produce a generation of young Goths and Vandals which would reduce all Europe to the intellectual level of an officers' mess. The experiment has actually been tried through Eton and Harrow, Oxford and Cambridge; and the result is that the young gentlemen trained in this way are conspicuously absent from the learned societies, political societies, artistic societies, and other cultural organizations, whilst the hunts, shoots, dances, and dinners which enable men to endure the crushing dullness of the drawing room and the tedium of church on Sunday are recognized as their special provinces.

Even in the enlightened pages of the Education Year Book it is remarkable (though I doubt whether anyone will remark it) that with the single exception of a passing reference by Mr Sidney Webb to "subjects requiring exceptional provision," and a paper on Eurhythmics by Miss Beryl de Zoete which is too special to save the situation, there is not a word about music, painting, sculpture, literature, or to any other department of that education of the senses and refinement of the imagination without which the inevitable division of a life's activity into work and play, or business and pleasure, means nothing but its division between compulsory necessary money-making and voluntary intemperance in eating, drinking, and sexual sensuality. The appalling fact that nobody in this country seems to know that intellect is a passion for solving problems, and that its exercise produces happiness, satisfaction, and a desirable quality of life, shews that we do not yet know even our crude bodily appetites in their higher aspects as passions: a passion being, I take it, an overwhelming impulse towards a more abundant life. We all have to admit that the greatest poets and dramatists, though great because of their philosophic power and biologic instinct, have been artists. But we talk of professional philosophers as if they were only half men, having brains without eyes or ears or souls. Yet the philosophers who have most deeply moved the world, whether for good or evil, are those who have been artist-philosophers.

SHAM EDUCATION

I have already insisted on the fact that the fine arts cannot be taught by school methods: the attempts at it end only in trying to make a boy appreciate Venetian painting by asking him the date of Tintoretto's birth, and hitting him if he cannot give the correct answer. What is needed is plenty of books, plenty of picture postcards of masterpieces of design, plenty of good performances of the best plays and the best music obtainable (not necessarily always in the heaviest *genres*, remember), and plenty of rambles in the country. But of what use will these be if the growing boy or girl is always reading that unreadable imposture, a school book, or imprisoned in a school or in a cricket or football field when the music is going on, or the galleries are open, or the view from the mountain is at its best. Ask any schoolmaster to provide for this method of culture; and he will first demand that the manifestations of fine art shall be changed into school lessons; and when they are thus turned into a deadly seed of hatred of all art, and even of Nature, he will sulk furiously over having to find a place for them in his time-table, first declaring it to be utterly impossible, and then grudgingly squeezing them into half an hour a week, perhaps by sacrificing that *bête noire* of his, the drawing lesson. The moment we come down from pompous phrases about education and fine art to the actual facts of the school and the schoolmaster, we are in danger of being driven beyond all patience into a simple declaration that the first step must be the utter annihilation of both, as of Sodom and Gomorrah.

We have, however, admitted that civic education is a technical subject and one of such infinite scope that it overflows the old boundary between technical and liberal education and confines the latter to knowledge as distinguished from practice. Now no real civic education is possible without discussion and controversy. The dogmatic schoolmaster, with his authoritative textbook and his "sanction" of the cane, or the imposition, or the keeping in, will not do here. Mr J. M. Mactavish speaks in these pages of the difficulty of asking for grants of public money for instruction in controversial subjects. But no difficulty is ever made provided only one side is taken in the controversy: provided, that is, that the controversial subject is falsely taught as a closed subject. It is quite true that there is a certain difficulty in obtaining grants of public money to teach that baptism and the Supper of Our Lord are necessary to salvation; but you can get any amount of public money to teach that vaccination is necessary to escape a horrible death from smallpox. No human being could believe these statements if he had all the arguments for and against presented to him fairly: that is, by hearing them, not from one humbug pretending to be an omniscient and impartial judge, but from two well-informed but strongly partial advocates. Both methods have been amply tried; and over and over again the dogmatically schooled professions, on the very questions which concern their own work, have been proved wrong where the laity, especially the unschooled laity, has been proved right. The doctors, the lawyers, the clergy, have had to yield again and again, after the most uppish resistance, to movements conducted by self-educated men. At last a superstition has arisen that popular ignorance has some mystic sanction which makes it more trustworthy than science and knowledge. This is pestilent nonsense: the truth is that the popular movements are educated by open discussion and vehement controversy, and know all the facts and have balanced all the considerations more thoroughly than the professionals. It is not ignorance shaming education: it is controversial education shaming dogmatic cramming. In every street you may find a doctor who is ignorant of a wide range of fact and discovery concerning his own art that is familiar to every member of the debating class in the nearest Young Men's Christian Association, just as any frequenter of Secularist meetings can knock an average curate into a cocked hat in a religious discussion, though he may drop next day to the gun of a Jesuit who has had to defend his intellectual position against continual challenge in Protestant England.

This point is the more vital because we have developed our civilization, and with it the conditions of social intercourse, without revising our philosophic basis, with the result that, though our social structure has reached a degree of communistic complexity at which it is far more important that every adult should be a good citizen than a confirmed member of the Church of England or a successful trader, we are still teaching a code of personal righteousness and riches, and denouncing Socialism and loyalty to the Common Good, which are now primary necessities of civilized life, as Marxist atrocities. And when any man takes us at our word and, on the authority of his personal righteousness, denies all obligations to accept any State decision of which his individual conscience does not approve, we first admit this anarchic right in the Act of Parliament which imposes the State decision on him, and then, in defiance of that Act, persecute him with murderous ferocity for exercising it. At this moment (1918 war time) the most opprobrious epithet that can be levelled at an Englishman is "conscientious." The controversy is really the old one between the Holy Roman Empire of Dante and Calvin's Perfect City of God, of which our modern Nonconformity and Anglicanism are only muddled, corrupt, and very Laodicean versions. Now both these formulas of the whole duty of man have, I repeat, been made as incredible and unthinkable by the discovery of Evolution as they have been made impracticable by the industrial revolution. Yet the moment anyone proposes to teach children anything else in public schools he is told that public money cannot be spent on controversial subjects. This ends in the children not being seriously taught anything at all on the plane of philosophy, religion, and political science: they are taught scraps of Dante and Calvin with the tongue in the cheek, and learn from their parents that such doctrines are "rot." In consequence we have such a generation of atheists and anarchists as never existed before. In the eighteenth century Frederick the Great, Catherine the Great, and a handful of financiers and philosophers were atheists, with Voltaire defending God and Rousseau defending Jesus Christ against them on modern Free Church Deistic lines; but the common people were Catholic or Lutheran, and men could be and were broken on the wheel for not kneeling down when the Host was carried past them in the street. But today Fred Smith and Kitty Jones are too utterly godless to be even conscious that they are atheists; and the Voltaireans and Rousseauites are classed as ultra-pious chapel folk. Ignorant parsons who used to excite the indignation of Carlyle by absurdly describing Voltaire and Rousseau as atheists are succeeded by the far more dangerously ignorant laymen who imagine that Charles Darwin discovered Evolution and that Natural Selection is an explanation of the universe.

Consider the dilemma we are thus landed in. Nobody who knows what contemporary Governments are would dream for a moment of trusting even the best of them to impose a creed on the children of the nation through the schools. Yet nobody who understands how vitally necessary a common faith is to a common civilization dares persist in the attempt to muddle through as we are. Well, suppose a Minister of Education proposed to adopt Natural Selection or "neo-Darwinism" as the creed of the Empire, with Weismann for its prophet! Instantly he would provoke a raging opposition that would bring any Government to the ground. Calvinist and Catholic alike would declare that they would fight to the last drop of their blood to save their children from the lake of fire and brimstone. The Creative Evolutionists, with Butler and Bergson for their prophets, would offer to swallow the Bible ten times over sooner than the doctrine with which Darwin "banished mind from the universe" and hope from the soul of man. In vain would the Minister of Education exclaim "My good people: what are you making all this fuss about? Dont you know that the scientific sides of our schools and Universities have been teaching nothing else but Natural Selection and purely mechanistic physics for the last half century, and that it would be harder for a teacher who taught anything else to hold a professorship than for Mr Edward Clodd to hold the pulpit of the City Temple or the Deanery of Westminster?" The reply would be that the people had not known it and would not have stood it if they had, and that all the professors on the scientific side must immediately sign either the Thirty-Nine Articles or the Westminster Confession, or else be thrown out of their chairs.

The Australian way out of this difficulty is secular education, meaning total exclusion of religious and philosophic teaching. But it does not mean the exclusion of scientific teaching. Now to teach science without any reference to philosophy and religion is to present the world to the child as an automatic machine worked by soulless mechanical forces and energies without purpose or scruple: the organism called Man going through a course of action as an avalanche does when it rolls down a hill or a hydrogen balloon when it rises through the air. The children may not be interested enough or intelligent enough to question this view spontaneously; but as there will be plenty of theologians at hand to prompt them the teacher will soon be asked whether Will and Conscience are not powers as real as gravitation or magnetism, and where they come in under his scheme of things. He must reply, "Oh, that is the science of psychology: we shall come to that presently." But the moment he comes to it he must overleap his non-controversial limit and plunge into metaphysics; for he cannot enter the domain of Aristotle without poaching on St Thomas Aquinas, nor combine the science of mind and motive with Weismann's dismissal of a butterfly's flight from the sweep of the entomologist's net (and presumably also the movement by which I dodge a motor-bus in the Strand) as mere reflex action responding to a purely sensory stimulus of the retina, without presently having to discuss the pre-Weismannic version of Predestination put forward by Calvin, which at least had the mind of God behind it. Once the question of free will is thus raised you are in the controversy about Determinism, to which there is no answer but Bergson's answer. When purpose is once admitted in the course of a psychology lesson the question whether the existence of evil does not prove an evil purpose behind evolution cannot be staved off; and there is no answer to that except, if I may say so, *my* answer.

Now if secular education thus leads inevitably to the discussion of St Thomas Aquinas, Calvin, Darwin, Bergson, and Shaw, what is the use of pretending that it is non-controversial or that it can steer clear of religion? You can no more draw a line and put a barrier between the temporal and spiritual in education than you can in the soul of man. You may forbid a teacher to mention the Bible or the Koran, or to refer to the Pope or the Archbishop of Canterbury as an authority. But what sense is there in that when you are thrusting on the scholar little textbooks reeking with the crudest theories of creation, destination, and predestination, and claiming an authority for the inoculatory rites of Jenner and Pasteur that St John the Baptist himself would have regarded as blasphemous?

The only solution of the difficulty is controversial education. That is what all the real education we have at present is. The student must be warned that religion, science, and philosophy are all fiercely controversial subjects, and that if he feels interested he must hear champions of the opposed views fighting it out in debate and be permitted to question them afterwards.

The result in many cases will be to leave the student in the very common case of a jury unable to agree on its verdict. But juries learn more from such cases than from the plain sailing ones. Controversy is educational in itself: a controversially educated person with an open mind is better educated than a dogmatically educated one with a closed mind. The student should hear the case, but should never be asked for a verdict. It may take him forty years to arrive at one.

At the same time it must be carefully explained to the young that there is a vast field of human action in which something must be done immediately and they must all agree to do the same thing without stopping to argue about it; for a confident expectation of how other people will behave, though irritating to reformers and improvers and victims of the Tolstoyan *Weltverbesserungswahn* generally, is, nevertheless, a first condition of civilization. The child must be taught, in direct contradiction to the current cult of salvation by personal righteousness, that in all public respects men in society must reform society before they can reform themselves. The individual may see a better line for the main road; but he should be educated to understand that his business is to persuade the authorities to make the new road and plough up the old, and not immediately to trample and trespass along his pet line as if the business concerned himself alone.

Yet who will dare to say that this first lesson in civic education is also the last? "Do as everybody else does; and never disappoint expectation" is as necessary a rule in business and general conduct as at a dinner party or when driving a motor-car down a crowded street; but it is none the less a law of stagnation and not of evolution. There are departments of the greatest importance in which, far from setting up a rule of perfect expectedness, we must be trained to expect and tolerate and even demand the unexpected. Not only are individuality, originality, initiative, moral courage, and a bold preference of the inner light to the neighboring example vital in society, but mere novelty, change for the sake of change, is needed to make human activity endurable. The schoolmaster or parent who teaches a child the occasionally very necessary lesson that it must not do what it likes, presently finds that a child who is not engaged largely in doing what it likes is the worst sort of spoilt child. All kinds of conflicting rules arise. "Act according to your conscience" is a rule no sooner applied than we find that its validity depends altogether on what sort of conscience you have. Do what you like except when there are good reasons to the contrary is a rule which only leads to the discovery that none of the "natural rights" on the recognition of which all stable society must be built are reasonable; and, if they were, nine people out of ten would be unable to state the reasons for them. President Pearse, of the imaginary Irish Republic of Easter 1916, founded a school of romantic heroism, teaching boys to throw away their lives for their ideals, and sealed his teaching with his blood by throwing away his own life. But is it not clear that these boys of Pearse's, stuffed as they were with legends of the Fianna and of Cuchullain, should have heard the other side from Professors Falstaff, Sganarelle, and Sancho Panza, and been encouraged to perform The Wild Duck and A Phenomenon In A Smock Frock as well as The Coming of Fionn and the like? Is a man who does not know the uses of unreason, of perversity, of paradox, of derision, an educated man? Can nothing be done to relieve our unfortunate pioneers from the unwholesome strain of being heroes at the excessive risk of becoming martyrs?

Toleration, Liberty of Conscience, Freedom of Speech and of the Press are all dogmas; consequently no person ignorant of history will accept them; for they are against all reason. It is for want of historical knowledge that they are not accepted at present. No doubt we all profess the deepest regard for liberty; but no sooner does anyone claim to exercise it than we declare with horror that we are in favor of liberty but not of licence, and demand indignantly whether true freedom can ever mean freedom to do wrong, to preach sedition and immorality, to utter blasphemy. Yet this is exactly what liberty does mean. He who remarks that it is a fine morning is not taking a liberty. Galileo took a seventeenth century liberty when he said that snipe shot would fall as fast as cannon balls, and that the earth moves round the sun; but the most abject slave may say both in the twentieth century. It is from history alone that we learn that the obvious and immediate evils of allowing individuals and newspapers to utter and publish revolting propositions and to deny sacred beliefs are not so dangerous as the stagnation and retrogression which follow the enforcement of conformity, and that even in the crises of a war the consequences of deceiving the enemy, involving as they do the consequences of deceiving the nation, may easily be more disastrous than fighting strictly on the facts and discarding bluff. Now there is no sign that this lesson has been effectively taught to our educated classes, or even taught at all. It is the received opinion and practice among us that heresy should be persecuted and "bad taste" punished. There is, it is true, a benefit of clergy and of class and of income allowed in time of peace; and party invective and vulgar abuse are always privileged; but this is not Toleration: we do not tolerate suttee in India, nor did the United States tolerate the cult of nakedness introduced by the Doukhobors.

These two examples bring home to us at once that Toleration is no golden rule: in fact, all laws act in restraint of toleration,

even when they are laws to enforce toleration. In decently conducted churches a Quaker is allowed to walk to a pew before
taking off his hat; but if he were to put his heels up on the back of
the pew in front of him, and light a cigar, he would assuredly be
thrown out and charged with brawling; and no plea of an im-
perative inner light would secure his acquittal. Toleration is a
matter of degree: we all draw the line somewhere; and nothing
will shift that line except education. In a rude village a stranger
may be stoned for wearing his hair two inches longer than usual,
though on the great bridge across the Golden Horn men and
women of every race, class, color, fashion, costume or no costume, on earth pass one another without even looking round, the
reason being that the Turks have been educated by experience to
believe that a long-haired man may be as honest a neighbor as a
short-haired one, improbable as that may seem to a British
islander. Yet in matters which depend on historical education, the
Turk is as intolerant as any other equally ignorant person. One of
the main objects of education is to prevent people from defeating
their own civilization by refusing to tolerate novelties and
heresies which history proves that they had better tolerate. Therefore it is of extraordinary importance that all citizens should be
educated in liberty, toleration, and the theory of natural rights.
At present they are taught nothing but an idiotic demonstration
that natural rights are a fiction of the vulgar imagination, because,
forsooth, natural rights *are* natural, and not derived or acquired:
in short, not logical.

When we turn from the toleration of acts to the toleration of
doctrine, we have to admit that we are not prepared to allow any
doctrine which we believe pernicious to be taught to young
persons dogmatically. For example, I am not prepared to allow
Calvinism to be taught to any infant under any circumstances,
nor to older children otherwise than controversially. I have never
suffered from the fear of ghosts, because when I was a child, and
the servants tried to frighten me with ghost stories, my father
assured me that there are no such things as ghosts, and I believed
him; but I know people who to this day are afraid to be alone in

the dark because their parents were not as careful as my father. Now the dread of ghosts is a trifle compared to the dread of hell; and though there are stages of civilization, like that of the Arabs in Mahomet's time, in which men can be kept under moral restraint only by threatening them with a horribly tortured immortality, yet Mahomet never defeated his own expedient by complicating it and indeed demoralizing it by a doctrine of election and predestination as the Calvinists do. I have enjoyed the friendship and conversation of a gentleman who holds that the two greatest scoundrels who ever lived were Calvin and Robespierre; and though I am not prepared without further consideration to subscribe to this refreshingly vigorous estimate, I should insist that no Calvinist be allowed to proselytize in a school except through controversies with other zealots of the complexion of my friend, and with a sound Nazarene Christian or two as well. This involves, of course, my conceding to the Calvinist in the nominally Christian countries that he should have his say in the schools against Creative Evolution. Calvinism and Paulinism cannot be ignored. The Atonement religions are all much older than Christianity, and have captured it to such a degree that no one can possibly understand human nature or history, even to the very limited extent to which they can be understood at all, without a knowledge of these religions, especially the modern forms of them established by the Reformation.

We are driven to conclude then that civic education must be as compulsory as technical elementary education, but that the former must be controversial, whilst liberal education must be voluntary, though the community must provide the material and conditions for it. But compulsion can only take the form of political or social disability involved by failure to qualify for benefit of clergy. If people have no civic interest or capacity, and therefore cannot be civically educated, it is as absurd to give them political power or admit them to responsible public offices as it would be to give money to a child incapable of counting it. However we may be tempted to say that the only qualification the voter needs is the power of suffering from misgovernment, a moment's reflection will convince us that a baby might claim a vote on this ground. The one thing that is certainly worse than the suffering of a political imbecile is his notion of a remedy for it. Yet if our political imbeciles are disfranchised they will be exploited by their rulers; and the rulers will be corrupted by that power to exploit them. The democratic safeguard against this danger is to give them a choice of rulers. Only, it must be a guided and limited choice. Left to themselves with the whole human race to choose from they will prefer Titus Oates to John Stuart Mill. Elect a world president by universal suffrage, and who would have a chance against Mr. Charles Chaplin? The choice must be limited to persons who have passed certain tests and perhaps taken certain vows. Such a limited choice may seem sufficient. Even if it be limited to Cæsar or Pompey (it may be argued) that will keep both of them in order. It will, provided they are both ambitious of rulership. But suppose they are both very reluctant to shoulder the heavy burden of governing! In that case the competition becomes a donkey race in which the candidates vie with one another in unpopularity and the loser wins. It is conceivable that when we at last learn how to limit the choice of our electorates to qualified persons we may have to compel those persons to accept the mandate as a public duty just as we now compel jurymen to serve. In any case our rulers must be held to good behavior by forfeiture of rulership if they oppress; and as only new brooms sweep clean, old brooms should not be eligible for re-election too often, however popular they may be.

I am fully aware of the difficulties which my suggestions raise, and how impossible it is to carry them out save as part of a social synthesis which involves the reconstruction of many other institutions besides our schools. Reforming our educational system may end like what is called "restoring" a medieval cathedral: we talk of numbering each stone, and replacing carefully and reverently those which are not too far gone to be saved; but in practice the edifice crumbles to pieces at the first touch of the pick and leaves us contemplating a heap of fragments which have miraculously lost all the shape they had a moment before, and now have neither head nor tail, top nor bottom. The school-master as we know him may, like the cathedral stones, be numbered and registered ever so carefully; but when child slavery is abolished, and a new constitutional edifice of children's rights is set up, he will not fit into it. Genuine born teachers will hold their own, and indeed come to their own; but there will not be enough of them to go round; and the teachers who are not born but made by training will have to be a new generation. Still, the change has to come, for democracy without democrats: that is, without civically educated voters and representatives and officials, means, as we now see, red ruin. And civic education does not mean education in blind obedience to authority, but education in controversy and in liberty, in manners and in courage, in scepticism, in discontent and betterment, tempered by the fear, not of artificially manufactured punishments, but of genuine natural consequences, to be faced or funked, as the case may be, in the light of kindness, humor, and common sense.

The human result will probably be much more like the so-called self-educated man of today than the public school man and the university graduate whose cloistered ignorance and inculcated error have made such a mess of things as they are. Yet what self-educated man, if he can afford to send his son to the public school and university, dares let him run wild? He knows too well that even in the matter of schooling it is a questionable kindness to take a child too far out of the common groove. If, like Romulus or Mowgli, it has to live the life of a wolf, it had better be brought up as a wolf. The good school is now, unfortunately, the crank school: the problem is to make the common school a good school. And good schools are not easily tolerated by bad civilizations. The parent may wish in his soul that his son could be taught that honesty is the best policy; but he has to consider that if he is led to take that precept seriously as a practical rule of life in competitive commerce he may starve for it. All our conventional schools at present teach false ethics, false science, false history, and even false hygiene. And if there were sufficient vested interests in false geography and false arithmetic they would teach these too. Truth is a guilty secret, heavily punishable on discovery; and the parent who allows his child to be taught truth without also leaving him an independent income must be prepared to hear his child curse him. This, I think, is the real reason why we dare not embark on controversial education. It would tear away the camouflage from commercial civilization.

For the rest, I can only repeat that if the advance of education is to mean nothing more than the widening of the net of the child prison and boy farm until not one of us can escape it we had better abolish it altogether. Our main disqualifications for citizenship now are ignorance, unsociability, and terror. And the government of the world by people who have been longest at school has been so far an organization of ignorance, unsociability, and terror, exploding from time to time in such monstrous smashes as the so-called Great War, which the belligerents could bear only by persuading themselves that it was a crusade, though it had really no more ethical character than a railway collision. The root of the evil is that though our national life, which is always assumed to be adult life, is and must always remain at least one-third child life, we have never given children a political constitution with appropriate laws, rights, and safeguards. But this I must reserve for another utterance.

WHAT IS WRONG WITH OUR SYSTEM OF EDUCATION?

From The Sunday Pictorial, 16 June 1918

THIS question unconsciously begs another question, which is, whether our school system is really a system of education at all.

I have alleged, and do still allege, that it is not a system of education but a cloak for something else. And that something else is the sequestration and imprisonment of children so as to prevent them being a continual nuisance to their parents.

That children and adults cannot live together comfortably is a simple fact of nature which must be faced before any discussion of their treatment can advance beyond the present stage of sentimental twaddle.

The blood relationship does not matter: if I have to do my work amid noise and disorder, and break it off repeatedly to console the yelling victim of a broken shin or to act as judge, jury, and executioner in a case of assault with violence; if I have to be at call continually as a dictionary and encyclopædia for an insatiably curious little questioner to whom everything in the visible universe requires an immediate explanation; if I cannot discuss the Billing case with an adult friend because there is always a small chaperone within earshot; if I have to talk down to the level of a child's intelligence, and incidentally to humbug it in the interest of my own peace and quietness, for hours every day; if I have to choose between spending my time either answering the question "May we do this?" or shrieking "Dont dare do that"; if I have to be medical officer of health, wardrobe mistress, sanitary inspector, surgeon for minor operations, fountain of justice and general earthly providence for a houseful of children, the effect on my career is the same whether the children are the issue of my own body or of my neighbor's: that is, I shall be so interrupted and molested and hindered and hampered in any business, profession, or adult interest, artistic, philosophic, or intellectual, which I may be naturally qualified to pursue, that I shall have to choose between being a mere domestic convenience and getting rid of my children somehow.

Under these circumstances a modern humane parent who can afford it always does get rid of the children by handing them over in their infancy to servants and later on to schoolmasters. The humane parents who cannot afford it let their children run wild. I insist on the word humane because there is a third alternative open to inhuman people.

By simple cruelty they can tame their children to sit still and ask no questions, to make no noise, not to tear their clothes, not to speak until they are spoken to, to be instantly obedient, and to take extraordinary pains to keep their misdeeds concealed (mostly by lying) from their elders.

SHAM EDUCATION

Many people are so constituted that an occasional exercise in breaking a child's will, punishing it, and seeing it flinch and scream under the rod or go pale with terror, is pleasurable to them. But this is bad for the child.

Any dog trainer will testify that a spaniel can be spoiled for life by a single act of terrorization; and many human beings have been spoiled in this way. It is no doubt desirable that little boys and girls should have sufficient self-control to sit quietly throughout a suitably short religious service once a week, or to hold their breath whilst swimming under water across a bath; but for most of their time they should be as noisy as nightingales, as restless as squirrels, as curious as monkeys, and quite indifferent to the tidiness of their hair, the integrity of their clothes, or the scrupulous cleanliness of their persons.

The humane parent knows this and puts up with it when the children are about; but that is precisely why humane parents are the first to get rid of their children under pretence of "sending them to be educated."

The schoolmaster is the person who takes the children off the parents' hands for a consideration. That is to say, he establishes a child prison, engages a number of employee schoolmasters as turnkeys, and covers up the essential cruelty and unnaturalness of the situation by torturing the children if they do not learn, and calling this process, which is within the capacity of any fool or blackguard, by the sacred name of Teaching.

That is what is wrong with our so-called educational system. Every genuine teacher knows it. Every person who understands children and sympathizes with them, like Dr Montessori, knows it. Everyone who, like the wife of the Master Builder in Ibsen's play, has a genius for fostering the souls of little children, knows it. But I am the only person who ever mentions it; and not one of those who have pretended to discuss my views has ever dared to allude to it.

When I tell the story of my friend who, in a hasty fit of sympathy with a beaten child, punched the head of an elementary schoolmaster, and was fined two pounds and informed that he would have been fined six if he had hit a gentleman, elementary schoolmasters, against whose scandalous underpayment I have always protested, rage at me for disparaging their gentility (as if the valuation had been made by me); but they have never squarely faced the fact that the wages and social standing of the skilled and earnest teacher of genuine vocation is kept down by the competition of the fellow who, because he can lock a school gate and hurt a child with a cane, can therefore do all that the children's parents pay for. Such an unskilled ruffian can always depend on the parents supporting him in any further pretensions he may make; for do they not owe to him the quietude and freedom of their lives?

The result is that when war emergencies subject the so-called education of our governing classes to a stringent practical test, we discover that their ignorance costs millions of money and thousands of lives, and is quite staggering to the two classes who have to save the situation: namely, the self-educated and the truants.

By the self-educated I mean those who have taken advantage of the voluntary associations, the Summer Schools, the professional societies, the propagandist organizations which continually keep up a supply of lectures and controversial discussions under free conditions, and also of the access to literature and art and music provided by our libraries, galleries, concerts, theatres, and the like.

If every secondary school and university in the kingdom were wiped out by an air raid tomorrow, and their staffs buried amid the ill-concealed exultation of their unfortunate pupils, thereby throwing our young people on the agencies I have just named, there would be an immediate and enormous increase in the number of really educated persons in England, and a quite blessed disappearance of a mass of corruptly inculcated error and obsolescence, and of that intense hatred of intellectual and artistic culture which exists today among our public schools and university graduates because it is known to them only as an excuse for loathsome prison tasks.

When young people are as free to walk out of a classroom where they are bored by a dull teacher as grown-up people are to walk out of a theatre where they are bored by a dull playwright, the schools will be far more crowded than the theatres, and the teachers far more popular than the actors. Until then we shall remain the barbarians we are at present.

Formerly, when games were forbidden in schools, and children were expected to study Latin for twelve hours a day, the children were keen on games and fighting.

Now that games have been made compulsory school subjects, boys will soon hate athletics and fighting as they now hate "English literature," and their country will be gathered like a daisy by the first vigorous nation that ventures to cultivate its wits and its muscles in freedom.

For my part, I thank my stars every day that as the German "system of education" differs from ours only in being more thoroughly carried out, and much more sincerely believed in, we may win the war by virtue of being less "educated" than our chief antagonist.

BENEFIT OF CLERGY NO LONGER BENEFICIAL
From The Guildsman, June 1921

THE distinction implied in the slogan "workers by hand and brain" may help the Labor Party to effect a political combination of the office with the factory, the clerks and secretaries with "the hands"; but it had better not be allowed to delude the men whose work can be carried on without soiling their collars into believing that their economic position is any stronger, or, indeed, half as strong, as that of the miner, the navvy, or the steel smelter. Under the capitalist system the value of the employee is determined by supply and demand; and even the most complete trade or professional organization can do little more than secure him the top of his market. Anything beyond this can be attained only by making breaches in the system, and filling them up with more or less communistic institutions. Therefore it is important that the *soi-disant* brain-worker should know where he is: for instance, whilst his pay depends on supply and demand, he should be able to answer the question "Supply and demand of what?"

Industry, under the capitalist or any other system, involves a prodigious quantity of routine work, and relatively very little original work. A century ago any routine work that involved reading, writing, and arithmetic, had a scarcity value, because the mass of the population was illiterate. In a still remoter time this scarcity was so much felt that a man who could read and write could "plead his clergy" if he was condemned to death, virtually telling the State that it could not afford to hang a man with so valuable an accomplishment. Many a gentleman-duellist saved his neck by benefit of clergy; for the institution survived as a class privilege long after it had been carefully ruled out of all legislation likely to affect common people only. Still, it existed as an economic privilege until the Compulsory Education Act of 1870 made the three R's so common a possession that by 1880 the salary of a London clerk was fifteen shillings a week, on which he kept a house, a family, a hymn book, and a tall hat. And yet Robert Lowe, afterwards Lord Sherbrooke, had accepted the Act reluctantly and bitterly, on the ground that "we must educate our future masters." If he had understood the capitalist system he would have embraced the Act joyfully, exclaiming, "Let us cheapen our future slaves."

The lesson of this experience should be taken to heart by all routine workers whose tools and materials are pens and ink. To begin with, let every clerk ask himself whether there is any sense in assuming that the man who writes down "six candlesticks, nine shillings" on an invoice, even if he copies it into three or four books afterwards, needs any more brain than the man who makes the candlesticks. He need not even write a legible hand now: the modern typewriter will not only do that for him, but will actually add up the figures for him; and the books can be balanced by a real professional specialist called an accountant. A woman with a calculating machine now does the work of four

Tim Linkinwaters. All routine work is sooner or later conquered by a machine; and the worst of it from the point of view of the black-coated proletariat is that whereas the machine in the factory often demands as much strength and skill and intelligence from its operator as the old handwork did, the office machine is fool-proof, and requires no more muscle and hardened habit of physical work than any ordinary healthy young woman can supply.

But it is not only the clerk, the copyist, the totter-up of long additions, that is touched. Let us take the opposite extreme: the persons who are employed in observatories and laboratories as mathematicians. It is a mistake to suppose that these are all Einsteins or Newtons or Kelvins. Kelvin would have starved as a clerk or a journalist, because he could neither write readably nor add up his washing bill correctly. But he *comprehended* what the people who could write and add up washing bills were doing. When it came to doing a sum in algebra, he may have been unable to work it without so much irksome trouble and risk of mistake that he handed all such work over to hired mathematicians who could do it on their heads without the slightest comprehension of its need and purpose. Generations of dull schoolboys and duller schoolmasters have learned the routine of algebra and Latin verse making without ever getting as near to the minds of Descartes and Virgil as an engine driver gets to the mind of George Stephenson. But let not our astronomical staffs, our actuarial staffs, our engineering and architectural office staffs deceive themselves: they are proletarians like the rest; and every advance in general education, every office machine, from the one with which Kelvin calculated the routine of the tides (an opera-tion so inconceivably complicated that if it could not defy machinery nothing can) to the duplicator and envelope addresser, still cheapens them relatively to the roughest manual laborers in direct proportion to the roughness. A sum in long division was once a job almost impossible to Archimedes or Euclid: today the office boy does it for less money than a stevedore gets. The value of muscle has fallen far less than the value of mind.

Even the man who feels secure because he makes decisions, which is the accepted rough-and-ready test of the real business brainworker, is not so safe as he thinks. Just as when chess is played long enough, all the gambits become known and are named and catalogued, so the decisions in business become more and more a matter of "seeing what was done the last time"; for even the most exceptional emergencies repeat themselves and get reduced to rule in time; and the time shortens as the volume of transactions increases. Business problems that formerly arose in Manchester once in fifty years (if at all) now arise ten times a day, and have stereotyped solutions. There was a time when the manager of a cotton mill was a maker of decisions who took rank with managing directors. At present he is a mere official, and not even a highly paid one. If he presumed to make decisions now in the directorial sense, he would get the sack. There are thousands of men today making decisions and being highly paid accordingly, whose decisions will presently be classed as routine, and whose posterity will have to accept the wages and share the fate of the routine workers.

Therefore put not your trust in your clergy, nor in your secondary education and professional status, nor even in your decisions; but flee from the wrath to come.

THE ETONIAN IN THE STREET AS OTHERS SEE HIM

From The Eton Review, No. 1, March 1918

IN pre-war days when petrol was plentiful I found myself from time to time driving my car through the royal borough of Windsor. I would cross the river and make for Watford, my way home lying that way. And I was always startled, very much as I might have been at a flock of penguins, by meeting an irresistibly funny figure, or perhaps two funny figures together, followed by others equally ridiculous. They never got nearer to any sort of sociability than walking in couples here and there. Most of them would struggle along singly, all over the road, with an air of strongly reciprocated dislike and mistrust, which resolved itself on closer observation into the burden of a common misery and a common boredom.

They were unlike anything else to be seen on earth, as far as my experience goes; and I have travelled in many lands. The nucleus of each figure was apparently a human boy; but I never could feel quite sure; for the costume was the costume of a stage boy, who is of course often a grown man and the father of a large family. The first absurdity in the costume was a tall hat. To me, who am old enough to remember when every adult of my sex wore a tall hat, and have actually worn one myself, a tall hat can never be quite as extravagantly ridiculous as it is now to people under thirty; but even in my day it was a stock joke to put a tall hat on a boy, because boys did not wear them. A tall hat was then an assertion of gentility and maturity: I remember that when I bought my first, I had to buy a new suit to keep it in countenance. But nowadays all that is changed. About a year ago I met an earl of my acquaintance in a most resplendent tall hat. "In heaven's name," I exclaimed, never having seen him in such a thing before, "what are you wearing that for?" He explained that he had to, as he was going to the House of Lords, where, it seems, they are still worn. Undertakers and their mutes also wear them. In short, they survive only as part of the grotesque pageantry of some ancient ceremonial; and the consequence is that when you put them on a string of melancholy looking boys, the impression that they are going to bury one another, and are not even pretending to grieve about it, produces an effect so uproariously comic that if I could reproduce it on the stage I should make more money than the author of The Bing Boys.

Next to the hat comes a collar of the sort I was compelled to wear when I was a child, and would not wear again if you paid me £100 a year for the sacrifice. It was not like a man's collar, therefore it was humiliating and ridiculous. It would not sit properly; it always got crumpled (in which condition its appearance was unbearably untidy); and its capacity for getting dirty was extraordinary. Every one of these Penguin boys under the adult stature of five foot four sported such a collar. To complete their disgrace, they wore, not jackets, but dress coats with the tails cut off. No human being could wear such a thing with dignity. It is said that in America before the Civil War of 1861, tarred and feathered men, riding on a rail in the hands of the anti-Abolitionist mobs, bore themselves heroically even at that disadvantage. In dress coats with the tails cut off, the noblest cause in the world could not have redeemed them: the very slaves they were trying to liberate must have shouted with laughter at them.

And yet the effect of leaving the tails on is worse, because nobody but a waiter wears such tails before dinner, nor even then under the age of fifty, now that the modern dinner jacket enables us to sit down to that meal without ridiculously tucking ourselves up behind first. The experiment was tried before my eyes; for here and there appeared an enormously conceited Penguin who for some inscrutable reason was not only tailed, but carried a rolled-up umbrella; turned the collar of his overcoat down; wore a jampot shirt-collar; had braid on his coat; and challenged special attention by a flower in his buttonhole. These strange liberties, and the air of inflation with which they were taken, led me at first to suspect that the Penguin was drunk, and had broken into reckless revolution. But as he was neither apprehended by the authorities nor molested by his fellow-victims, who seemed rather to court his patronage, I concluded that he was an officially sanctioned example of the horrors of any attempt at depenguinization. And he certainly proved that those who make half revolutions dig their own graves. Antarctic explorers have told me that you can become accustomed to normal penguins; and I have long since become accustomed to normal human beings. But no man can become accustomed to a moulting penguin; and that is just what these young cranks looked like.

Anyhow, moulting or normal, if any Penguin boy has ever succeeded in outfacing his costume, I have never met him. The Penguin boy gets a peculiar high-shouldered slouch, and hides his hands instinctively in his pockets as if there were handcuffs on them. He knows that his appearance is hopeless. And it is worse at this time than it has ever been before or will be again. Compare, for example, the Bluecoat boy. His get-up of blue gown, yellow stockings, knee-breeches, and hatless head, is not a travesty: it is a genuine sixteenth-century costume. There is nothing ridiculous about it. Early in the seventeenth century it must have been old-fashioned, just as the Tower beefeaters must have been old-fashioned for a while before they, too, became historical. Still, the costume was always genuine, because in the sixteenth century all boys did dress like that. But the Penguin costume, which makes a drive through Windsor so mirthful and yet so pitiful (for nobody who remembers his own boyhood likes to see a boy made ridiculous), was never worn by boys at any time. It was deliberately invented to make the boy himself feel small with his coat tails shorn off and his child's collar, and yet to give notice to the common youth of England, known generally as "the cads," that here came the son of a person with money: one whom vulgar boys must not accost and attempt to play with, though on occasion they might, in mere envy, throw stones at him or assail him with derisive epithets, when the circumstances made such subversive conduct safe.

How can the Penguins bear it? Why do they stand it?

Mind: I do not say that there is not great convenience in a uniform. One of the enormous advantages of being a man instead of a woman is that when you are going out in the evening you never have to think of what you will wear. You have no choice: it is the regulation evening dress or nothing: if you have pawned it you must just stay at home. This saves a lot of thinking and choosing. But the same thing may be said for the dress of a convict. The same thing may be said for the life of a slave. He, too, never has to think or choose: he just does what he is told; and there is an end of it. If a slave is not too hard worked, and has enough to eat, and clothes enough to keep himself warm, he has what many people consider a very easy life. He escapes what the poet Cowper called "the intolerable fatigue of thought." There is nothing so lazy and popular as a comfortable slavery: that is why Shelley, who had a mania for liberty, and was an incorrigible thinker, was not popular at Eton.

But any fool can be a slave: in fact, every fool *is* a slave, though he may be too great a fool to know it. The great aim in life is not to find out how little you *need* do, but how much you *can* do. Liberty is the right to think and choose for oneself. What liberty costs is the trouble of thinking and choosing for oneself. He who thinks liberty worth the trouble, and actually likes the trouble, is the only really free Englishman. Now suppose the Penguin boys began thinking about their ridiculous clothes! What would come of it in the minds of the intelligent ones?

Well, it would be something like this, I imagine. (1) I dont want to be made a guy, as I am at present, and be laughed at by that beastly bounder in his motor-car. (2) But I'd rather be a guy than have the bother of designing my own clothes and choosing the materials, and perhaps being laughed at by the other fellows for my pains. (3) Also, I am rather proud of being a Penguin boy; and I want to be recognized as one in the street. (4) I want to be dressed like the other fellows; so that if there is any laugh it will be on them as much as on me. (5) I dont want to look like a snob advertizing my social position; and I dont want to be made look like a child by silly coats and collars that men dont wear. (6) I dont want to go against the School: I want to stand in with the School if only the School will have some sense and recognize that the boys make the School and not old Henry VI or even the Head. (7) I think a thousand boys in the foremost files of time should count for something in the choice of their own clothes; for unless they have better taste than their elders there is no such thing as progress.

How are all these aspirations to be reconciled in practice? Clearly the boys should form a Sumptuary Committee to regulate the School dress. The Committee should be elected by universal suffrage within the limits of the College; and no master should be disfranchised, not even the Head; for the Sumptuary Committee would eventually regulate the dress of the masters (some of whom dress shockingly) as well as of the boys. A tax should be levied on every voter to supply the Committee with stationery and necessary funds; and the Committee should apply for an annual grant from the funds of the College as well. The Committee should tolerate no amateur nonsense in the way of fancy designs from artstruck boys. The designing of costumes is a profession like any other profession. The fashions of the day, the uniforms, the liveries, the dresses of the actors in *revues*, all have to be designed before they can be made or worn. It would be the business of the Committee to find out the best designers for their purpose, and pay them for working drawings of a School uniform, or of several uniforms, if it was desired to have variety and distinction between different sections or even different houses. It should criticize, modify, improve, change at intervals for the sake of novelty, taking care not to put parents to unnecessary expense in changes or to unreasonable cost in the first instance. It should regulate caps, badges, liveries, servants' dresses; so that everyone connected with the School should be visibly distinguished as such to the eye of the admiring tourist and respectful townsman. And it should be careful to allow certain individual modifications to adapt the regulations to the taste and complexion of the wearers of the costumes. Cæsar's soldiers were uniformly equipped and clad; but they were free to titivate themselves in various ways; and many of them, being dandies by nature, sported all sorts of gold chains and plumes and colored cloaks and so forth. It is not likely that the Penguin boy would under any circumstances make himself a Flamingo boy; but within certain limits variation ought to be encouraged: for instance, if a blond boy and a brunette boy wear collars and ties of the same color, one or other of them is pretty sure to be badly dressed. The tradition that it is unmanly to bother about colors or notice the color of your own eyes and hair should be sternly discountenanced: it is indifference to such points that is boyish in the silly sense. An eye for color is womanly; and all wise men take trouble to acquire the strong points of women, just as wise women take lessons from men. Besides, there may be women to be consulted. The Sumptuary Committee of the future will regulate not only the dress of the housemaids, but of the ladies of the master's household, who can hardly be allowed to be dowdy, or to hide their honorable connection with the School in mufti.

But individual liberty must not be abused. Black and white, being a confession of color-blindness and artistic impotence, should be forbidden. The present costume should not be used even as a punishment: no boy should be degraded in that manner. Let him rather be shot, if nothing else will meet his case. Mourning should be indicated, if at all, by a violet ribbon; and boys who wish to express their rejoicing at the death of a much disliked relative, or at the birth of a brother or sister, or at the news of a successful revolution or restoration, as their sympathies might dictate, could substitute orange for violet ribbons, The undemonstrative boy could wear no ribbon at all, and explain that he was wearing infra-red or ultra-violet, both of which are invisible.

I could suggest many other reforms; but this one will suffice for the present year. When it is accomplished the Editor can call on me again. Meanwhile the moment is propitious; for khaki has broken many traditions, and the ugly Penguin costume may as well share their fate.

THE EDUCATED WORKING MAN
From New Standards, October 1923

THE educated working man resembles the educated gentleman on one point. He knows nothing that he has been taught; and what he has been taught prevents him from learning anything. Search the mind of an uneducated man, and you came across odd scraps of knowledge. He may even have arranged them into something like a body of knowledge from which he gains individuality and culture. But in the mind of the educated man you can discover only a mass of unassimilated stuffing, which is of no use to him, and not only makes his head impenetrable to the lessons of life, but makes intellectual exertion hateful to him instead of healthy and natural. There is one exception to this; and that is the case of the teacher or stuffer. To him education is useful as a stock-in-trade, because he can make a living by imparting it.

The effect of this on the subjects taught is remarkable. Take for example Latin, or music. Latin begins as a living language. It dies a natural death, but walks ghostlike as a medieval Esperanto, and is used as such by the Catholic Church and the learned professions. In due time, the learned professions take to the vernacular, and Latin dies a second death. But it has in the meantime become a subject of technical education as the key to all written learning; and as a result a body of teachers has come into existence who teach scholastic Latin, and know nothing else; and schools have come into existence as places where boys are taught Latin and nothing else.

When Latin dies its second death these schools go on just as before. They are useful to parents as prisons in which their children are kept from worrying them; and Latin is a good enough excuse for this, as it is traditionally indispensable to clergy in its old sense of literateness. But whereas in the Middle Ages, Latin, being really in use, had to be effectively taught, like riding or dentistry, so that the students could read it and write it, however crudely (they even made rhymes in it), when it went out of use the school Latin had no contact with life to keep it straight. It became "a teaching subject" pure and simple: that is, a subject taught by each generation of teachers to the next generation so that the teaching profession might continue to make a living by teaching it, the pupils who did not become teachers (but who paid fees all the same) learning it for no purpose whatever except to pass examinations in it. Those who did not go in for examinations had no use for it at all. Neither the teachers nor the pupils knew Latin in the sense in which Julius Cæsar knew it; and most of them, outside the routine of their text-books, and a convention as to the English equivalents of certain passages from Virgil and Cicero, did not know it in any sense. The result was a spurious

Latin, taught because teaching it paid, and never learnt by the vast majority of boys, even when they had been kept at it for ten years: enough to learn all the languages of Europe.

Music begins as the spontaneous product of individual musical genius. Musical geniuses do not teach music: they compose it. Persons who are not musical geniuses think they would like to "learn music." Parents think it would be a desirable accomplishment. Teachers are asked to impart it. As the request is accompanied by offers of payment, the teachers comply eagerly. Thus music becomes a teaching subject. Boys and girls are beaten or set impositions if they cannot name the date of Palestrina's birth, or if parallel octaves or consecutive fifths appear in their exercises in eight-part harmony, neither students nor teachers having the faintest notion of what these exercises would sound like if anyone was mad enough to perform them. Thus arises an academic music like the academic Latin, which has nothing on earth to do with real music, which has made many a naturally musical student loathe the sight of musical notation, and which is utterly useless as an instrument of culture.

Finally, we get a whole body of teaching subjects masquerading as real subjects, and not only useless for culture, but actively and disastrously mischievous because of the unexplained but patent fact that when uninteresting studies are forced on the human brain they produce imbecility. That is why our educated classes are morally and intellectually imbecile, and are thrusting civilization to ruin by commercial, foreign, and financial policies precisely analogous to the conduct of an idiot who persists in trying to fill a cistern with the tap turned on.

Now the intelligent and conscientious young working man does not understand commercial, foreign, and financial policy well enough to criticize the governing class; but what he does understand as a matter of common sense and immediate experience is that his father was handicapped to hopeless social and political disablement by simple ignorance. He feels that men can do nothing without knowledge and culture. In search of them he goes to the teachers, the schools, the university extension classes, the new working-class colleges at the universities. And in due time he becomes an imbecile more helpless than ever his ignorant father was. That is the tragedy of the educated working man.

Our established system of teaching consists in elementary schools in which children are imprisoned for nine years learning to read, write, and speak their own language decently, at the end of which period they read, write, and speak so badly that they are properly classed as uneducated, illiterate, and unpresentable. We have also secondary and "public" schools and universities from which our graduates emerge very fully accomplished as sportsmen (sport not being a teaching subject), but so ignorant and sheeplike intellectually, that they are the dupes of every charlatan and adventurer who has saved his brains by truancy, or by belonging to the class which lives in a house valued a little above £40 a year, and thus escaping the compulsion of the school attendance officer without incurring the social pressure which makes secondary education compulsory among the well-to-do.

It is not possible for me to go into the remedies for this horror —for it is nothing less than a horror—in a necessarily brief article. I have dealt with the matter elsewhere; but I must leave it to others to deal with it exhaustively. Civilization is dying of what it calls education; and when it wakes up to that fact, it will burn all the examination textbooks, hang all the teachers, and demolish all the schools and universities, only to find that their incidental discipline, communism, and alternatives to petty home life are indispensable in a highly developed society.

The radical remedy is an organization of child life as such on a basis of children's constitutional rights as definite and original as men's or women's rights. If children were really free as adults are free, it would be found that intellectual capacity creates intellectual appetite, and that children grab eagerly at all the learning they can use. And that is all they can take in without injuring themselves. The public school notion that every boy should be forced to do the work of Horace, Plato, and Einstein, is much less sensible than the notion—as yet unpromulgated—that they should all do the work of Carpentier, Dempsey, and Sandow;

and the results are not serried ranks of Horaces, Platos, and Einsteins, but of Tootses and Sparklers. There is far more sense and hope in the Boy Scout and Girl Guide movement (if only it can be kept out of the hands of school teachers) than in all the educational endowments that were ever stolen from the poor by the rich.

Meanwhile, let the conscientious and intelligent young working man learn from the doers and not from the teachers, who are mostly in a conspiracy to calumniate the new doers and misrepresent the old ones. But I must add a practical warning. He may find it necessary to pass an examination to procure entry to some service or profession. In that case he must go to a coach to be prepared with the obsolete and erroneous answers which the elderly gentlemen who will examine him believe to be the latest thing in science and practice. Otherwise he will be ruthlessly and even angrily plucked. And he will probably find bits of this false knowledge sticking in his mind and tripping it up to the end of his days. That is the price one pays for being a successful examinee.

DOES MODERN EDUCATION ENNOBLE?

From Great Thoughts, 7 October 1905

Obviously, no.

If the question were, Is Education a cruel, degrading, and foolish process, carried out by cruel, degraded, and foolish people, we should pay more attention to it, because we should be getting closer to life. Neither form of the question is conducive to good-tempered, clear-headed discussion; but in these democratic days, when relatively uneducated men sit in Parliament and on all public authorities with men of finished education, it is an open fact that the line which divides stupid, ignorant, and prejudiced people from sagacious, well-informed, and open-minded people does not coincide at any point with the line which divides the educated from the uneducated.

SHAM EDUCATION

Dr Johnson and Gladstone were classically educated men of great natural force. John Bunyan and Charles Dickens were virtually uneducated men of great natural force. Dr Johnson and Gladstone were conspicuous among the most ignorant, the most absurdly prejudiced, the most society blind, the most broken-minded and yet undisciplined men who have ever risen to commanding eminence. Bunyan and Dickens were equally conspicuous for great knowledge of men and things, great penetration in exposing social prejudices and making moral valuations, and cheerful co-operation combined with vigorous freedom and initiative in social activity. Such contrasts are the rule, not the exception. Could anything but the education of a gentleman have produced the endless volumes of unashamed tittle-tattle on which Thackeray wasted his genius?

"Modern" education differs from Dr Johnson's education only in substituting Jenner and Pasteur for Plato and Euripides as academic idols, and replacing the recognition of a purpose in the world, and the investigation of that purpose, by a conception of the universe as the accidental result of a senseless raging of mechanical forces, and by a boundless credulity, not outdone in dirt, cruelty, and stupidity, by any known savage tribe, as to the possibility of circumventing these forces by nostrums and conjurations.

The truth is that Education (a question-begging term, by the way) is a gigantic hypocrisy. If all the objects which it professes to produce by imprisoning children for fifteen years could be achieved in ten minutes our school system would go on just as before.

The real object of that system is to relieve parents from the insufferable company and anxious care of their children. If this object, which is a quite right and necessary one, were frankly acknowledged, then it would be possible to frame a constitution conferring rights and liberties on children. At present a child may be beaten, underfed, overfed, overworked with school lessons or otherwise, petted, shewn off, neglected, played with, made the subject of religious and moral experiments, and denied all freedom of thought and action, without remedy. That children should be herded together for hours every day, and beaten or otherwise punished if they fidget, talk, or are inattentive to an uninteresting teacher whom no adult audience would tolerate for five minutes, is taken as a matter of course, and called instruction. It is, of course, nothing of the sort. It is grotesque, unnatural cruelty, both to the teacher and the children, who hate each other as no human beings possibly could hate each other in natural and humane relations. The teacher, being the more conscious victim, suffers the more: highly-strung teachers inevitably have fits of fiendishness, induced by chronic irritation; so that childish, mild, insensible teachers are far safer. But all these evils are outfaced because the school system relieves the parents of the unbearable nuisance of being continually with their children. And until it is frankly recognized that children are nuisances to adults except at playful moments, and that the first social need that arises from the necessary existence of children in a community is that there should be some adequate defence of the comparative quiet and order of adult life against the comparative noise, racket, untidi- ness, inquisitiveness, restlessness, fitfulness, shiftlessness, dirt, destruction, and mischief, which are healthy and natural for children, and which are no reason for denying them the personal respect without which their characters cannot grow and set properly, we shall have the present pretence of inexhaustible parental tenderness, moulding of character, inculcation of prin- ciples, and so forth, to cloak the imprisoning, drilling, punishing, tormenting, brigading, boy and girl farming, which saves those who can afford it from having to scream ten times every hour, "Stop that noise, Tommy, or I'll clout your head for you." When the school system has reached such a point that games are made compulsory, avowedly in order to ensure children going to bed so completely tired out physically that they have no energy left for the worst abuses of monastic and barrack life, even the stupidest people ought to begin to have some misgivings about it.

Certain very simple knowledges must be acquired by children before they can enjoy full freedom of movement. They should know a few simple arithmetical calculations and tables, so as to enable them to deal with money. They should know how to read, not with a view to the masterpieces of literature, but so that they may be dealt with by direction boards and other forms of public notice. But children would learn reading and simple arithmetic for their own use if they led promptly to more freedom and more pence, and if the learners could see the end of their labor close enough to be stimulated to race for the goal. At present they drudge hopelessly at them, knowing that the achievement of a simple task will lead, not to freedom and use of the new accomplishment, but to the imposition of more and more difficult and distasteful ones for years and years to come. They should be taught how to use and enjoy the country without destroying trees or crops, and how to be as sanitary in their rambles as a cat. Instead of being forbidden to do as they like, they should be compelled to dispense with adult guidance, and depend on themselves to the full limit of their resourcefulness; so as to accustom them to that tyranny of Nature and circumstance from which they are only too willing to be shielded. They should be let loose in the country, and not too obtrusively policed. A considerable compliment should be made of teaching them anything beyond what is necessary to enable them to use pennies and shillings, and to take journeys and get meals in a town. The present obligation of the schoolmaster to retain by force an unwilling and consequently unruly child, merely for the sake of its school bill, should be unknown. Under such conditions, real live learning would soon flourish on the boundless basis of human curiosity and ambition. At present it can hardly be said to exist. The grown-up man turns with loathing from all the associations of the penal servitude of his youth. The grown-up woman revenges on the governess to whom she is forced to hand over her own children (because she can see no practicable alternative) the miseries of her own childhood in the schoolroom. The hobbies of both men and women are something they were never forced to drudge at, just as their religion, when they have any, is Positivism, Darwinism, Theosophy, Secularism, Socialism, anything rather than the religion of Bibles and Catechisms, and compulsory pew sittings on fine Sundays.

We pay a frightful and inevitable penalty for our inhuman treatment of children, because of the fact, which we invariably forget, that the world is peopled, not by two distinct races called children and adults, but by human beings of various ages, from a second to a century. The ruthless repression which we practise on our fellow-creatures whilst they are too small to defend themselves, ends in their reaching their full bodily growth in a hopelessly lamed and intimidated condition, unable to conceive of any forces in the world except physically coercive and socially conventional ones.

Exactly in proportion as Parliament consists of thoroughly schooled men, do we find it given to shuffling and prevarication, and convinced that the world can only be held together by flogging, punishing, coercing, and retaliating. And the exponents of this philosophy of cowardice are personally docile, abject to superior rank and royalty, horribly afraid to say, do, or think anything unless they see everybody else setting them the example, incapable of conceiving liberty and equality: in short, schoolboyish. That is, they are exactly what they have been educated to be from their weakest childhood; and they are everywhere beaten in character and energy by the men who, through the poverty, carelessness, or enlightenment of their parents, have more or less escaped education. Great communities are built by men who sign with a mark: they are wrecked by men who write Latin verses.

Under these circumstances it is only to be expected that Modern Education should be very highly spoken of and thought of; for one word of truth or sense would be fatal to its credit. And when we have thoroughly found out the school, the turn of the home will come. The one place in which we never look for social evils is in our own house; and yet if there were no evil there, there would be hardly any in the world. The reason that the Education Acts are supported by people whose opinions are much the same as mine, is that the school is obviously a better place for the child than the home, and a safer place than the streets. Even among the rich, where the home is not a poverty-stricken tenement, and a well-kept park takes the place of the street as a playground, it is recognized that there is something fatally lacking in the character and manners of a man brought up in a private house, between the kitchen and the drawing room, in a narrow private atmosphere, without any society except that of a few people of incongruous ages. Eton and Oxford, Harrow and Cambridge, with all their depravities and impostures, produce something more attractive. This something is neither a trained mind nor a knowledge of classic poetry, but simply the social habit and easy manners which distinguish all men, whether sailors or senior wranglers, bagmen or billionaires, who have lived in common and on equal terms with large bodies of men of their own age and standing. Therefore, it must not for a moment be supposed that the remedy for the evil called Education is to keep children at home. The right course is to respect children; to secure their rights and liberties exactly as those of adults are secured (when they *are* secured); to protect adults against annoyance by them; to stop telling them lies and posing before them as gods; to keep constantly in mind that every child is an experiment which must be carried through on its own lines and not aborted so as to produce a monster of moral perfection and erudition (which is the universal pretence of education); to give children variety of experience and company, the world to live in, homes to sleep in, communal halls to eat and associate in, safe cities to roam through and learn from the crowds and sights, and opportunity to hear every statement that can be made to them controversially criticized so that their conclusions shall be verdicts arrived at after hearing the evidence and arguments pro and con, instead of, as at present, *ex parte* statements (all false) which they will be punished if they do not repeat. Any person professing or attempting to pass off his opinions on children as absolute truths should be classed with the quacks who sell panaceas and "nerve-restorers," and deprived of his teaching licence.

In concluding—or, rather hastily breaking off—this hurried

summary of the impression made on me by Education, let me save some useless trouble to the people who would otherwise pour forth reassuring statements that I know nothing of "modern methods." I flatly deny that there are any modern methods. It is true that I have walked through modern schools, and seen in them cards and cases filled with various objects unknown in my schooldays, and intended to teach children various object lessons in weight, measure, form, and so forth. I have also wondered why the pretence that these things are ever used is not made a little more plausible by dusting them occasionally. The object that *is* used—the cane—has no modernity whatever about it. And when I had occasion some years ago to lecture at Oxford on Education, I took care to obtain from the London School Board time-tables of the half-dozen most up-to-date of their schools. One glance at them was sufficient. They proved that a school today, as far as the curriculum is concerned, is exactly what a school was when I was a schoolboy. And so they will remain until we get rid of schoolboys and schoolmasters altogether and fall back upon human beings.

HAS THE INTELLIGENT SCHOOLBOY ANY RIGHT TO LIVE?

On the Suicide of a Bullied Bluecoat Boy

From the Sunday Chronicle, 28 January 1923

As one who was once an intelligent schoolboy, to whom cricket, save in its humorous, brief, and only tolerable form of tip and run, was a grosser bore than anything else except professional football and the amateur imitation that apes its worst feature by making a business drudgery of play, I should like to know definitely whether boys such as I was are to be finally and frankly outlawed, every bigger boy being free to kick them until their lives are unbearable to them, and their bodies when they commit suicide to be buried in unconsecrated ground to mark the sense of the community that their end was in bad taste, and was caused by carrying a despicable attempt at self-advertisement too far.

If this is to be so, we had better know it, in order that parents whose boys are of this unmanly intellectual type may send them to institutions for the mentally defective, where games are not compulsory, and where persons who kick them are not listened to with reverence when they explain that they kicked without any intention of hurting, and are even asked why, in that case, they kicked at all.

In Christ's Hospital kicking, it appears, has some specially Christian point and purpose which makes it so agreeable to the kickee that a boy who stabs himself after being twice kicked for inattention to the sacred rites of football must be an ungrateful, perverse, conceited, and malicious creature, concerning whom British public opinion must feel that his death (probably half-simulated, if the truth were known) is a good riddance; that the boys who kicked him are fine manly lads; and that the battles of the next war will be won (unless, unfortunately, they be lost) on the Bluecoat playing fields.

We unhappy people whose children prefer mechanical inventions and constructive activities to Soccer and Rugger do not venture to defend our degenerate offspring (we should perhaps be kicked ourselves if we did): we only want to know where we are.

Thank heaven, my school-days are over! It was bad enough to have masters who were down on you with impositions and detentions and canings when you were inattentive for a moment to their uninspired lessons, or made sulky by their infamously bad manners; but to have, in addition, all the bigger boys actually obliged to kick you for inattention to silly games which you do not want to play, thereby changing playtime to tasktime, and making Jack not only a dull boy but a suicidally unhappy boy, is a piling of horror on horror's head that makes wise men want to emigrate to some country where schools are unknown, and become naturalized there before it conquers us.

I notice that the father of the dead boy is a clergyman. I quite expect to see a deputation to his bishop to call attention to his unfitness to have charge of the Church school, and a subscription started to give a testimonial to the boys who upheld the national sport vigorously enough to rid us for ever of a football slacker who wanted to study mechanics and invent things, like a German.

At the same time I cannot help feeling that these despised intelligentsia of the schools may be more numerous than is supposed; for, after all, we cannot be a nation of numskulls. Sanderson, the great Oundle schoolmaster, who entirely agreed with my opinion that Eton, Harrow, Winchester (he said a good word for Rugby), and their cheaper and more pernicious imitators should be razed to the ground and their foundations sown with salt, said to me, when I asked him were there compulsory games at Oundle, that without at least some pretence of them he could never get the boys out of his workshops and libraries, but that there was no moral prestige for muddied oafs and flannelled fools at Oundle.

Nothing will persuade me that any boy, even an English boy hypnotized by inculcated superstition, really likes being kicked and ashplanted into doing the drudgery of a professional footballer or cricketer, without any intention of ever becoming one. Yet by the time, not far distant, when compulsory smoking and drinking are added to the manly curriculum, we shall be able to boast that in England everything foolish and fashionable is compulsory, everything individual and original is kicked, and nothing is optional except honest work, at which point we shall remain a flock of sheep shepherded by a handful of energetic and ignorant blackguards from the happily uneducated backwoods and outskirts of the Empire until we are annexed by some civilized Power and put into reservations, like the North American Indians whose ideals our public schools cherish so devotedly.

That we are well on the way to this consummation is, I think, shewn by the fact that everyone seems to be agreed that the boy who preferred suicide to being kicked into football playing behaved disgracefully.

SHAM EDUCATION

The head of the school, invited to express his opinion, remarks calmly that there is no harm in a mild kick occasionally, which must be deeply consoling to the dead boy's parents. All the schoolmasters assure us that there is no bullying, which, of course, is true now that the kicking is official and authorized. They naturally stand by the ingenious prefect system by which Arnold contrived to make the big boys do all the unpleasant work that the masters are paid to do.

And of course all the novelists who have no other means of making the world believe that they are splendid, breezy, brave public schoolboys and gentlemen, and not cads from the elementary schools and polytechnics, will seize the opportunity of describing how they were kicked and ashplanted, and how they liked it, and how it made men of them.

The sane moral would seem to be to send your son anywhere rather than to school pending such an organization of child life as will enable a boy to learn what he needs to know without serving a sentence of sixteen years' penal servitude.

Otherwise we shall presently have a boy sharp enough to see that if you have made up your mind to commit suicide you may as well emphasize your disapproval of school life by committing a few murders first.

I do not like to conclude without saying that I do not blame the boys who did the kicking. They are evidently just as much the victims of the system as the boy they kicked, and have no doubt often been duly kicked in their turn. They could not have foreseen or imagined that an English boy would die rather than submit to kicked slavery. But what a reflection on the average English boy!

"TAKING IT LIKE A MAN"

From The Daily News, 29 May 1914

Do you seriously expect your readers to believe the report in your issue of Thursday to the effect that the Alderman at the

SHAM EDUCATION

Willesden Police Court refused to grant a summons to a school-boy who had refused to hold out his hand in order that a school-master might strike it with a cane, on the ground that "if the boy had taken his punishment like a man he would not have been caned on the back"?

The boy did exactly what a man would have done. No magistrate could possibly have been so foolish as to make such a comment on a case the whole point of which was that a boy claimed an adult's right of freedom from assault and demanded the legal remedy of an adult. What the Alderman must have said was "if the applicant had taken his punishment like a child he would not, etc." Really your reporter ought to be more careful!

A MODEL EXAMINATION RESULT
From the Women's Dreadnought, 26 February 1916

THE ESSAY WHICH WON THE FIRST PRIZE

On Saturday, January 22nd, the E.L.F.S. gave a party at the Town Hall to the children of the East End. As we filed in, a bag was given to us which contained cakes and fruit, and while we were taking our seats the violinists played. This being finished, a pretty dance was given by two girls which was well applauded. After the dance, a girl played a tune on the violin. Following this was a very pretty dance given by a little girl. It was done very gracefully, and she was applauded as she left the platform. Again we had a dance, but this time it was a tall girl who did graceful actions with a piece of pink muslin.

While this performance was proceeding, we had our tea, which consisted of the contents of our bags, and cups of tea. Our violin entertainers again played to us and when they had finished they prepared to leave. It was then announced that we were going to see something to make us laugh.

A clown was then introduced. He played the "fairy bells" in imitation of church bells. He also played other tunes. After this was accomplished he told us that he would play "The Blue Bell of Scotland" with the violin in various positions.

This he did in the ordinary position, then with the violin in his mouth, and ended by putting the bow between his knees and playing in that position.

He called six boys up on the platform, and shewed what they should do on entering school.

He then retired, and the next to appear was the marionettes. First of all they put up a kind of shop like a punch and judy show. The lights were then put out, and the show commenced by two marionettes appearing who sang some of the latest songs. Then they left the show to change their dress. They next appeared as two Scotchmen and while they sang a Scotch song they danced very prettily. Again one of them disappeared, and then came out dressed as an Irish girl, and while she was dancing the other performer went and changed into an Irishman. On appearing again they sang "When Irish eyes are smiling," and we joined in the chorus. After this they both left the show and appeared again as a sailor and a captain on a ship which rocked up and down as if it was on the sea. While in this attire they sang a few songs about sailors. The show then came to a close after which we gave three cheers for all the workers.

Father Christmas then appeared while we cheered him. He then apologized for coming after Christmas and told us how he came from the sky and had sent the toys before him. The toys were then distributed and we all went home feeling very happy.

ELLEN CRUTCHFIELD.

128 Kerbey Street, Poplar, E.

THE AWARD

I have to award the prize of 5s. to Miss Crutchfield, as she has not made a single mistake; and the rules must be kept. Her essay is so correct that I think she must have got the clergyman to write it for her. If so, she ought to go halves with him.

G. BERNARD SHAW.

THE ONE-AND-SEVENPENNY CONSOLATION PRIZES

2   Miss Ruby Drake
49 Crediton Rd., Tidal Basin, E.

In account with G. Bernard Shaw

Correcting one mistake in grammar	$\frac{1}{2}$d.
Altering "there" to "their" three times	$\frac{1}{2}$d.
Correcting wrong use of the word "ridicules"	1d.
	2d.

I award Miss Drake a special prize of 1d. for businesslike and exact information as to who gave the party and what actually took place. So she has only 1d. to pay.

Feb. 13th, 1916.   G. Bernard Shaw.

3   Miss Mumford,
36 Northumberland St., Poplar.

In account with G. Bernard Shaw.

Correcting four mistakes in grammar	2d.
,, two ,, in spelling	1d.
	3d.

I award Miss Mumford a special prize of 2d. for her careful and regular writing. So she has only 1d. to pay.

Feb. 13th, 1916.   G. Bernard Shaw.

4   Mr J. Hornibrook,
42 Rook St., Poplar, E.

In account with G. Bernard Shaw.

Correcting two mistakes in spelling Miss Pankhurst's name	2d.
,, two ordinary mistakes in spelling	1d.
,, three mistakes in grammar	$1\frac{1}{2}$d.
Supplying one word omitted	$\frac{1}{2}$d.
	5d.

I award Mr Hornibrook a special prize of 4d. for putting all the go he had into the songs. So he has only 1d. to pay.

Feb. 13th, 1916.   G. BERNARD SHAW.

5   Mr J. DRAKE, 49 Crediton Rd.

In account with G. BERNARD SHAW.

Correcting four mistakes in grammar	2d.
,, three ,, in spelling	$1\frac{1}{2}$d.
Altering "their" to "there"	$\frac{1}{2}$d.
Soap to clean up after reading Mr Drake's essay, as it was so untidy	1d.
	5d.

I award Mr Drake a special prize of 4d. for family feeling, as he did not forget his little sister, and Aunt Emily, and Ruby, and Francis and Dad. He has, therefore, only 1d. to pay.

Feb. 13th, 1916.   G. BERNARD SHAW.

6   Miss MOLLY BEER
9 Brabazon St., Upper North St., Poplar.

In account with G. BERNARD SHAW.

Correcting two mistakes in grammar	1d.
Striking out two apostrophes put before "s" when there was nothing belonging	$\frac{1}{4}$d.
Completing the word "affectionately" as it was written "affec."	1d.
Counting 22 kisses for Miss Pankhurst	$1\frac{3}{4}$d.
	4d.

I award Miss Beer a special prize of 3d. for laziness. She was in such a hurry to get into bed that she wrote the shortest essay, and signed herself "Yours affec." to save the trouble of writing "tionately." So she has only 1d. to pay.

Feb. 13th, 1916.   G. BERNARD SHAW.

7 Mr ALBERT MABBOTT,

In account with G. BERNARD SHAW.

Correcting one mistake in grammar	$\frac{1}{2}$d.
Striking out four words repeated	$1\frac{1}{2}$d.
	2d.

I have given so many special prizes that I cannot afford any more; but as Mr Mabbott's handwriting is so easy to read, and so square and regular, and his description of the party is excellent, I will let him off half of my bill; so he will have only 1d. to pay.

Feb. 13th, 1916. G. BERNARD SHAW.

(The point of these accounts is that though each child had its attention called to its mistakes in a manner which suggested that they had cost it something, yet they all got the same sum (eighteenpence) and therefore were not provoked to envy and hate one another as they certainly would have done if their prizes had varied in amount.)

A NEGLECTED SUBJECT OF EDUCATION

A Private Letter quoted in The Weekly Times and Echo, 12 July 1908. It was addressed to Mr Arnold Crossley, author of The Compleat Baby Book.

I AM much obliged to you for the book you have sent me. Some years ago my attention was called to the subject by something that happened in a Great Western express. A woman was travelling in the express, and the only people in the carriage with her were some students. She was the only woman there. In the course of the journey she gave birth to a child. Fortunately it was not her first child; she was able to tell the unfortunate students what to do, and as far as one could gather from the newspapers, neither the mother nor the child were any the worse.

It struck me at the time as a very noteworthy fact that though these students could have found innumerable popular handbooks instructing them in all sorts of exercises and processes, from driving a motor-car to giving first aid to a man with a broken leg, the only popular guides to the conduct of a childbirth are shilling handbooks for married women which no man dreams of as having any bearing on his own education or accomplishments. Now the probability of a man finding himself cast on a desert island with a pregnant woman may not be very serious: the railway instance was certainly improbable and exceptional; but still there are a dozen ways, by no means so improbable and exceptional, in which a man might find himself in the same predicament as the students on the Great Western.

And this, remember, is only the man's point of view. It is a thousand times more important for a woman to be instructed on the subject. I imagine a good many of the cases of infanticide after concealment of birth are really due to the mother, in her helplessness and ignorance, losing her head in mere despair and terror, whereas if she had read your book she might come through quite successfully.

I am not sure that if I were in your place I should not take the bold step of approaching the Board of Education and governing bodies of some of our big school companies, and propose that the book should be made a school book for all adolescent students.

AN EDUCATIONAL CONFESSION

From The Schoolmistress, 17 November 1927

1. WHAT was your favorite subject at school? Has this or some other subject influenced you most in your after-school life?

   I had no favorite school subject. No subject was made interesting to me. My interests, which were keen, lay outside that dreary prison.

2. What was your favorite game?

   I had no choice. We played rough, *unorganized* games, like

Police and Robbers; and I enjoyed roaring and rushing about and struggling.

3. What book most impressed you as a child?

An impossible question. I read everything I could lay my hands on that was readable, which of course excluded school books. The earliest literary sensations I can recall are The Pilgrim's Progress and Arabian Nights.

4. Did you "rag" your teachers?

No. I left school before the ragging age. Boys under fifteen dont rag, as far as I know them.

5. Would you like to have your school-days over again?

Good God, NO! would anybody like to serve a sentence of penal servitude twice over? But then my home was not a prison. The boys who liked school dreaded their parents more than their teachers.

6. Did you find examinations a source of anxiety?

Not in the least. I never prepared for them, and could not understand the boys who did. I instinctively saved my brains from destruction by resolute idleness, which, however, made school tedious and meaningless to me.

7. Is the modern freedom better for the child than the old-time discipline?

I dont know. In the schools I attended there was neither freedom nor discipline. They told you to learn lessons and sit quiet, and hit you or kept you in if you didnt do it. They did not even hit you hard enough to matter. Clearly that was not real discipline.

8. Could you draw a tolerable map of England without access to an atlas? Is this worth being able to do?

1. No. 2. Not under ordinary circumstances except for self-satisfaction. It does not happen to appeal to me.

9. Where does the education of today fail in your opinion?

In that it is only a disguise for relieving parents of the worry of children by caging them and taming them like wild animals, mostly by cruel methods, and because it ends in Latin verse, which is only a vested interest in torture.

10. Do you accept the principle of secondary education for all?

It depends on what you call secondary. A minimum of technical education (the three R's, for example) is necessary to qualify for citizenship in a modern city. Beyond that people will seek all the knowledge they are capable of without compulsion; and it is most important that they should have the fullest opportunities as easily and cheaply as possible.

11. To what extent, if any, should the education of the modern girl differ from that of the modern boy?

Not at all in the compulsory stages (all boys should be taught to mend their clothes and cook); but in the voluntary stages the sexes would find their own differentiation.

12. What can the nation reasonably expect to get for its expenditure on education?

At present, the moral and intellectual imbecility, the illiteracy of pen and speech, that it actually does get. With a reasonable, sincere, and really available system of education, the nation might reasonably expect to become educated after a generation or two.

PUBLIC LETTERS ON SECTARIAN AND UNSECTARIAN EDUCATION

From The Daily News, 25 August 1902

MANY of us who, though under no suspicion of fashionable Toryism, are anxious to see the Education Bill passed, have too much respect for Dr. Clifford to differ from him without offering any explanation.

SHAM EDUCATION

In his letter in your issue of the 20th Dr Clifford puts before us the following case: "St Mary Magdalene's is a notorious Anglican Church. It has large schools, teaches the Confessional, takes children to Mass, and has lately introduced that sign of extreme Romanism, 'the worship of the Sacred Heart.' A recent issue of the Parish Magazine said: 'Many a little Dissenter, so called, has been taught the Catholic faith in these walls, as, though the Conscience Clause is there, it has only once been used to withdraw the child from religious instruction.' " Please observe that this is not an abuse which the Bill will create if passed. It is the *status quo*. Now, the *status quo* is what Dr Clifford is advocating as against the Bill. He is, in fact, urging us to cling to the system under which St Mary Magdalene gets subscriptions by undertaking to "turn little Dissenters into Romanists."

To this Dr Clifford has two replies. First, that he is certainly in favor of the *status quo*, infamous as it is, as against the *status quo* plus the rating of the whole community to pay for it. Second, that to choose the least of two evils is not to be "in favor of" the lesser evil chosen, and that what he is really in favor of is the substitution of the Board School for the Church School.

On the first point I flatly disagree with Dr Clifford. It is precisely because the Free Churchmen do not pay in full for the education of these children in St Mary Magdalene's that the authorities of that school are able to snap their fingers at so powerful a neighbor as Dr Clifford. They actually must so snap their fingers, since they are dependent on Anglican voluntary subscriptions (the Free Churchman's contribution is involuntary; so they need not consult his feelings). To get those subscriptions they have to promise the Anglicans results in the shape of proselytes. This is merely one of the shifts of beggary. Those who voluntarily pay the piper call the tune; and the secret of the energetic support given to the Bill by ultra-Radicals like the Fabians, and by some of the younger clergy of the Free Churches, is the conviction that the elimination of the Voluntary subscriber, and the frank acceptance by the State of the entire cost of education, is an indispensable preliminary to the transfer of the effective control of education from the Established Church to the whole community.

Dr Clifford offers, as an alternative way of doing this, the replacement of the Voluntary school by the Board school. But here we must call upon Dr Clifford to do what he has so eloquently called on us to do: that is, to face facts. The people of England have been offered the Board school; and they have taken as much of it as they are likely to take. And that much is more than is good for them. There is no use in multiplying village School Boards which substitute for the squire's and parson's divided allegiance to education and the Established Church, a perfectly single-minded determination to do away with education and with school rates as far as the central authority will let them. What the big School Boards have become since the death or retirement of the first generation of enthusiasts may be gathered from a comparison of the dominant personalities of the London School Board and those of the Technical Education Board of the County Council. Mr Diggle was for years the Czar of the London School Board. On the Technical Education Board at the same period he was a cipher; and it was the series of object lessons, of which this was a leading example, that induced even Mr Diggle's own political party to recognize what has been apparent to many of us for the last twenty years: namely, that the one thing to be done with School Boards is to abolish them root and branch.

However, this is not the fact I ask Dr Clifford to face. Even if the *ad hoc* School Boards were as conspicuously superior to the Technical Education Board as they seem to me to be conspicuously the reverse, and if, in addition, the rural Board schools were better than the squire-and-parson schools, or the Urban Church schools worse than their relative poverty and beggary might lead one to expect, still the fact remains that a vast proportion of the children of this country are sent to these schools, and cannot for many generations of school children be sent elsewhere, even if their parents disapproved of Church schools, as some, but by no means all, of them do. Once face that fact, and the whole question becomes simply: Is the education of these children to be paid for by the State as liberally as that of Board school children or is it not? I am aware that there are many members of the Free Churches who will reply "Certainly not." In that case the proselytizing power of the parson will be maintained, as at present, at its highest possible point, whilst the education of the children will be sacrificed. Therefore, I find it hard to believe that Dr Clifford would give so impolitic an answer; and yet I cannot infer any other from his speeches and letters on the Education Bill. For my part, I say that so long as there is a school in England to which children practically must go, either because their parents choose to send them there or for want of a better one in the neighborhood, that school should be placed under the Education Department, and fully financed by the State, whether it be Established Church, Nonconformist, Roman Catholic, Positivist, or Parsee.

As to the religious teaching in schools, there can be no general agreement among parents, the great majority of whom are either too indifferent to know accurately the very various tenets they themselves profess, or else violently irreligious persons who believe that members of all the other sects and most of their own are awaiting an eternity of Hell fire. A year ago I should not have dared to say this; but, after the recent dealings with heresy by the Council of the Methodist Church, I think it is as well to take the opportunity of reminding Dr Clifford that a great deal of that Nonconformist sectarianism to which, in his enthusiasm, he attributes a high Cromwellian spirit, is really of so base a quality that he himself, were such a choice forced on him, would place his children under the spiritual direction of Lord Hugh Cecil himself rather than under that of its exponents. The truth is that neither in religious matters nor in those departments of religious matters which we call secular can the truth be told to children at present in any English school whatsoever. Our duty to our children is clear enough. Just as we teach them that the various races and classes and colors of men have such and such customs and laws and habits differing from our own, so we should teach them that there exist in the world divers creeds and observances, theories of morals, and views as to the origin and destiny of life and the moral sanctions of conduct. And we should add that these differences do not connote differences of what children call goodness and badness, and that quite as good men and women, and even (which they will, perhaps, find it harder to believe) just as bad men and women are to be found among "heathens" as among their own fathers and mothers. That is all we have any right to teach children about creeds nowadays. In Cromwell's time it was as true as it is now; but its truth was not then apparent; consequently a moral enthusiasm of revolutionary intensity was available for the protest against Anglicanism. To the Puritans Laud stood for the sum of religious error, and Cromwell for the sum of religious truth. To us there is no absurdity in Laud's belief that cannot be paralleled by an equally obvious absurdity in Cromwell's belief. And in our attitude towards our own contemporaries there is no feeling that Lord Hugh Cecil stands for the sum of religious error, and Dr Clifford for the sum of religious truth. Our deepest convictions are on a plane where sectarian distinctions have no importance, and where matters on which no influential sect has yet dared to utter a sincere opinion are of very great importance indeed. And that, I venture to think, is why Dr Clifford's stirring call to arms has awakened no echo that can be spiritually distinguished from the sportsmanlike electioneering excitement which always follows such dramatic political reverses as the Leeds election.

From The Daily News, 30 August 1902

I am told that unsectarian education would avoid the difficulty. But there is no such thing possible in England as unsectarian education; and if there were the Free Churches would be the first to repudiate it. They all insist on the Bible, and the Bible teaches Judaism and Christianity, peculiar to two sects of the British Empire, besides the Shakespearean pessimism of Ecclesiastes, which is still as much the creed of our reflective University men as it was of Thackeray. I leave out of account the sectarian doctrines which are apparent to Biblical scholars only, and the doctrine of Job, which is beyond the capacity of school children. Consequently, whatever Bible teaching may be, it is not unsectarian even within the limits of Christianity alone. Were the Indian authorities to propose to make education in India unsectarian by simply having an hour of "Koran teaching," the whole Empire would recognize the violently sectarian nature of such a proceeding. If, on the other hand, we banish the Bible, the Koran, and the other sacred books of the Empire from the schools, we get what used to be called "secular education"; that is to say, instead of teaching that every child should be baptized, we teach that every child should be vaccinated; we replace creation in the garden of Eden by evolution from the amœba; and we keep the field clear for the purely physical logic that finds its most striking political application in dynamite (or lyddite, if the logician wears a uniform), and its pet scientific method in vivisection. Religion is a subject that cannot simply be dropped. Nature specially abhors that vacuum. Unless schooling is to include manners and morals—that is, applied religion—the teacher, in imparting the methods of the three R's, must either allow complete anarchy in the classroom or else impose orderly conduct by mute brute force. As neither plan is humanly possible, children cannot be educated without metaphysical assumptions; and once you admit metaphysics it is vain to urge that they shall at least be unsectarian, that is, formless. Forms they must have if children are to apprehend and adults teach them; and when this is admitted everything is admitted; for all forms are sectarian. My plays are just as sectarian as Dr Clifford's sermons; Mr Herbert Spencer is as dogmatic as Calvin; the Hegelians already number many sects; and if all the Bibles were burnt and forgotten, and Voltaire and Rousseau, Schopenhauer and Nietzsche substituted for the Hebrew prophets, their sects would rage as furiously as ever.

Consequently, to me unsectarian education or secular education means, for popular school practice, a counsel, not of perfection, but of impossibility; and though Dr Clifford is fundamentally right in his consciousness that the religious spirit is one though the sects be many, yet the moral of that is not that the forms of the Church of England matter so much that they should be resisted to the death, but that they do not matter at all. And certainly a Church that gets out of its most bitter controversy with Rome by an article of faith which affirms transubstantiation to please the Anglicans, and in the same breath denies it to please the Protestants, cannot be said to be either bigoted or morally impressive.

The truth is, the mischief wrought by the parson in the schools is not done by the Church doctrine he imparts (if he really does impart any), but by the anti-republican social idolatry which he really believes and drives into the children. As a matter of fact, the children in a Voluntary school do not learn the 39 Articles: what they learn is that it is more respectable to go to church than to chapel; that the baronet belongs to a higher order of creation than the blacksmith; and that they must stand up reverently whenever God is bawled and blared at to scatter the enemies of the King. But this sort of teaching is not peculiar to clergymen of the Established Church. All our school teachers aim at being gentlemen and ladies, and recognize that religious instruction, Bible reading, and moral training, whether Anglican, Unitarian, "Secularist," or what not, are conditioned by the laws of good taste and the duty of patriotism. Under which two heads as much moral cowardice and selfish violence, as much sectarian snobbery and intolerance can be taught in a Board school as in a Voluntary one. The difference between the moral influence of lay principals and clerical ones, of Anglican managers and Free Church managers, of Board school teachers and Voluntary school teachers, is the difference between Tweedledum and Tweedledee. In point of sectarian impartiality, there is practically no difference at all; and as to tolerance, the Established Church, though not more latitudinarian than the Congregationalists, is certainly not less so. There is not at present in England a denomination numerous enough to count politically in whose ministry the views of Matthew Arnold and Ernest Renan are not represented as boldly as they are in any other fairly comparable social circle. The notion that liberty of conscience can be increased in schools by shuffling the general pack of managers or teachers out of their seats, lay or ecclesiastical, seems to me an illusion founded on the common practice of comparing the *status quo*, not with the socially practicable alternatives to it, but with an individual's ideal. But the efficiency and independence of the teaching is a very different matter. Here everything depends on money, and on the freedom of that money from the private control of individuals and sects. Let a Voluntary school cost £10,000 a year; if the State gives £9999 15s., and the odd five shillings has to be got from me as a voluntary contribution, then I am the master of that school; and the managers and the principal and the teachers may offend me if they dare! They are in the position of a postman, who depends on his Christmas boxes to make up his budget: the Christmas box may be but a trifle compared to the wages paid by the Postmaster-General, but, as the two ends will not meet without it, the postman is more anxious to please the man who gives him five shillings a year than the Postmaster, who gives him five pounds a month. In short, the sectarian character of the school makes no difference, and is unavoidable anyhow; whereas the voluntary character of the school makes an enormous difference, and is avoidable. In a fully State-financed Church school the parson can be as independent of the local Church zealots as he pleases. He cannot be driven by them to regulate to their taste the conduct, dress, habits, and devotions of the teacher, whereas in a Voluntary school the parson is the slave of the subscriber, and has to see that the teacher is as abject a slave as himself. Surely, then, the reasonable course is to take care that as long as Church schools are indispensable, they should be independent.

I am confident that I represent by these views not only a majority of the Fabians, but a whole movement within the Liberal party. Mr S. G. Hobson is right in saying that all my opinions are not, as far as either of us knows, Fabian opinions. But I am not here abusing the courtesy of The Daily News by making this correspondence a pretext for ventilating ideas which have no political importance. It is clear that I speak in this matter for others as well as myself. The Fabians have always tried to stem the torrent of thoughtlessly traditional Radical opposition to State support of Church schools. The present Bill is perhaps as near an approach to The Way Out prescribed by the Fabian Society in its well-known tract, entitled The Education Muddle and the Way Out, as a Government like the present would be permitted by its supporters to introduce. That the Fabians do not like its concessions to the Church is natural enough. Neither do I. But in a determination that the education of the hosts of children in the Church schools shall no longer be starved by sectarian bigotry or postponed until Dr Clifford's generous ideal of unsectarian education is realized by the votes of sectaries who are, to say the least, very far from being Dr Cliffords, I am thoroughly representative of the great majority of Fabians; and this majority is representative of an important and growing body of opinion on the Progressive side in politics. So far, the result of ignoring that body of opinion has been twenty years of humiliation for the Liberal party. It is because the party has failed to learn this lesson that the suspicion has arisen that it is too old to learn anything.

As to the Free Church Councillor from Waltham, his letter is a frank repudiation of citizenship. It is a pity that with principles which would qualify him to act Robin Hood's chaplain, and all the courage and eloquence of those opinions, he should, with Epping Forest so near at hand, be wasted on the humdrum respectability of Waltham, where no man can do what he likes with his own (at least if he does, the police should be informed), and no man's rates and taxes are spent on his own exclusive personal use and gratification. I leave the gentleman's darkened soul to Dr Clifford, who will know how to deal with it better than I.— Yours, etc.

Coast of Norfolk, August 28, 1902.

A PRIVATE LETTER ON SECULAR EDUCATION

My views on what is called Secular Education are to be found in the preface on Parents and Children in the volume of my plays entitled Misalliance, The Dark Lady of the Sonnets, and Fanny's First Play. In the preface to the Education Year Book published last year by the Workers' Educational Association I have returned to the subject. I cannot add anything to these very carefully considered utterances. There is so much in my criticism of schools generally that is uncomplimentary to them and to their masters as they exist at present, that my special references to the question of secular education have passed comparatively unnoticed. And they do not recommend themselves to the ordinary advocates of religious education because these are mostly proselytizers pure and simple, desiring to impose their own beliefs on the children in the manner hitherto customary.

The propositions I have sought to demonstrate are, shortly, as follows.

1. There is no such thing as secular education. The nearest thing to it is what may be called secular discipline, in which conduct is governed wholly by the fear of punishment and the desire to escape it, without any reference to the merits of the conduct so prescribed. In dealing with ferocious animals, and with moral imbeciles, such "secular" discipline may be necessary; and there is a great deal too much of it in the army and in some schools and private families. But even in the army and in such schools and families, good conduct has to be inculcated as a point of honor, and on the understanding that it is right, and bad conduct wrong. External coercion is always reinforced by appeals to the sense of shame and disgrace: in short, to conscience. And the moment any such considerations are introduced, the system becomes a religious system. This cannot be evaded by mere utilitarianism. It is always possible for an individual to sacrifice the good of the community to his own convenience without having to pay any penalty in his own person; and in such cases there is no utilitarian reason why he should abstain from such unsocial conduct: in fact individual utilitarianism points the other way. Finally, good conduct has to be recommended because it is a fulfilment of the will of God, or because it tends towards the goal of Creative Evolution; and though the one is the phrase of the Plymouth Brother

and the other of the most advanced scientific thought of the day. When this is grasped it becomes apparent at once that the conflict which is spoken of as a conflict between secular and religious education is really a conflict between different forms of religious doctrine based on different histories of the human race.

2. The rights of the children in the matter are plain enough. They have a right of access to all knowledge of which they are capable, and should be made acquainted with all the forms of religion just as they are made acquainted with geography and ethnography. It is not humanly possible that this instruction should be given impartially by teachers whose personal beliefs are involved. If a learner is to be instructed about Christianity and about Islam, the instruction had better be imparted either by a teacher who believes in neither, or by Christian and Mahometan teachers successively, the pupils finally hearing them in controversy with one another.

3. The special question of the Bible would be easily solved if the parties were honest about it. On the face of it the exclusion of the Bible from school is as monstrous as the exclusion of the Koran, or the works of Shakespear or Milton, or Shelley or Blake or Swedenborg or Bergson or Charles Dickens or Darwin or Nietzsche or Goethe, or any other of the vehicles of inspiration and revelation. It has been excluded solely because its advocates wanted to introduce it as an infallible record of perfect truth and the supreme authority on conduct. The admission of any literature on such terms is out of the question. The difficulty is not evaded by the silly proposal to have the Bible read "without comment." If the book of Genesis is to be read without comment whilst the statement that the world stands on an elephant which stands on a tortoise is to be read with any comment the teacher or the pupils choose to make on it, then the Bible is clearly claiming superstitious privileges. No literature can be an instrument of education unless it is discussed with perfect freedom. If both teacher and pupil may not say that the story of Noah's Ark is manifestly a child's fairy tale as freely as they may say that the explanation of the universe as the result of Natural Selection is

damnable nonsense, then Noah's Ark must simply not be mentioned at all; and the children will be brought up in barbarous ignorance of literature and history. For without a knowledge of what the Bible contains, and the part it has played in history, and an equal knowledge of the literature of the theory of Evolution, no one can claim to be educated.

4. Religious education is a necessary part of technical education, because it is a necessary part of the education of the citizen. It is admitted that doctors and ship captains, for example, should be carefully instructed in the science of their professions before they are allowed to practise them. It is much more important that a citizen should be instructed in social and political science and in the final sanctions of conduct before he is allowed to practise his profession by casting a vote or taking a seat on a public authority. He must therefore be taught as much about religion as he is capable of taking in. He must not be taught that it is right to burn widows on the funeral pyres of their dead husbands, even if his own mother has been so burned; and he must not be taught that the conquest of Canaan by the Jews was less open to criticism than the conquest of Belgium by the Germans in 1914. He must, if he is to be told of these things at all, be told simply that as a matter of historic fact men have done these things and claimed divine sanction for them. If the facts are presented controversially he must hear them both denounced and defended. And he must not be left to suppose that society will allow him to choose freely between the views he will act on. After everything that can be taught him as to the danger of intolerance and the vital importance of liberty of conscience, he must still face the fact that if he attempts therefore to burn his mother for being a widow or stone her for being an adulteress he will be treated as a criminal in spite of all the Bible and the Indian gospels. There must be a code; and at the back of that code there must be a view of human nature and destiny: that is, a philosophy of life which will still be called a religion. Young children must be taught this dogmatically. They must be told that lying, theft, and cruelty are wrong; and persons who teach that they are right will be excluded from the

schools. And as, in the current religious and scientific doctrine of today there is a good deal of glorification of lying, theft, and cruelty, there will be a steady reluctance to allow their exponents opportunities of corrupting the souls of children in schools. But as the alternative seems to be that dangerous ignorance of the world which is falsely called innocence, I think we shall at last have to face the duty of making up our minds as to what we really do believe and disbelieve, and teach it with due warning that it is only the best we can do, and that future generations may find it as incredible and indeed as mischievous as we now find any of the forms in which religion and history are presented to the tribes of Africa and Asia.

5. I therefore expect that we shall teach the theory of Creative Evolution as the soundest and most inspiring religion we can formulate; that we shall explain the extraordinary impression made by Christ as due to the fact that His economic and biological teaching was at bottom scientifically right as well as prophetically inspired; that we shall reject Pauline Salvationism as an atavistic corruption which has produced all the mischief ascribed to Christianity; and that we shall warn our pupils against Natural Selection on precisely similar grounds, it being clearly a corruption of the theory of evolution by extracting all the divinity from it, so that through it evolution gained the whole world and lost its own soul. It will be no more possible to tolerate the deliberate inculcation of Calvinism or Darwinism in public schools than Voodooism.

I have treated this distinction between Salvationism and Christianity very fully in my preface to Androcles and the Lion.

I am afraid you will now conclude that I am far too thoroughgoing an opponent of Secular Education to be a safe ally; for to me Salvationism trading under the name of Religion and Secularism trading under the name of Science are equally fraudulent; and if Salvationism can claim any superiority in results it is because it has now much less power of imposing itself on modern children, and incidentally gives them access to the Bible. Genuine Religion and Genuine Science, which are fundamentally inseparable, will still have to fight for their lives against persecution from both sides.

22 January 1919.

EDUCATION AND ELECTIONEERING
From The Daily Mail, 27 February 1904

ONE redeeming feature of the present County Council election is that it provides London with a joke—an enormous, outrageous joke. And that joke is the opposition to the London Education Act of 1903.

The Act is the greatest educational advance ever made by the British House of Commons. It is such a magnificent piece of educational socialism that, knowing what I do of Governments and legislatures, I half think it must have been a huge inadvertence, a blunder into virtue.

However that may be, there is no getting away from the fact that since the Act that created the County Council in 1888, no measure at all comparable to this one has been passed. It is a triumph for the Government; it is a triumph for the County Council, which evolved in its Technical Education Board the model for the new authority that has superseded that poor old School Board (which ought to have been abolished ten years ago); and it is, as usual, a triumph for the Fabian Society, which formulated all the unsectarian demands with which the Act has complied.

But, you will say, where is the joke? Well, the joke is that every good Liberal is bound to abhor an Act passed by a Conservative Government, without the smallest reference to its merits. And the County Council Progressives think that they depend for their majority on the Liberal vote, raised to the necessary strength by a makeweight of intelligent Conservatives who see that Moderatism is a species of municipal pro-Boerism, a repudiation of civic patriotism, and are determined that the Conservative Party shall not be tarred with it.

SHAM EDUCATION

The Problem and the Solution

Thus the momentous question arises: How are the Liberals to be conciliated and the Progressive Conservative Churchmen retained at the same time? The solution is amusing. Though all the Progressives have accepted the Act; though they all know that the opposition to it, so far as London is concerned, will be stone dead in six months' time; though they no more dare hint at repealing its splendid conquest of secondary and university education, its replacement of the present little scholarship ladder to a clerkship by a broad flight of marble steps to the professions for all the clever children, its prospects of unlimited unsectarian training colleges for the Free Churchmen, and its huge increase in the public expenditure on and public control over education, than they dare repudiate Magna Charta—yet they feel bound to accept the Act as men submit to some terrible calamity: no doubt the ordained chastisement of an impious nation which has not given the Liberals a turn for nearly ten years.

The general attitude of the Progressives towards it is that of the eighteenth century towards the earthquake at Lisbon; and because I—who am one of the original patentees and inventors of Progressivism—openly rejoice in the London Act as one of the greatest achievements of the Progressive spirit, I am assured by my Liberal constituents that I am deliberately throwing away my chances of success at the poll. They look at me with volumes of reproach in their earnest, passive-resistful eyes, and then turn away—to canvass for me. That is genuine political heroism. Certainly, to a man with any sense of the pathos that underlies the highest comedy, this is an election in a thousand.

The Rates! The Rates!! The Rates!!!

But the serious side of the election, now as always, is the grim contrast between our magniloquent Progressive projects and programs and the struggle with money worries that never ceases in the homes of nineteen out of twenty of the people who have to find the capital for these glorious schemes, and whose landlords will reap the whole harvest. How long, I wonder, is London going to stand it?

Here am I, expected to canvass a great segment of a circle of houses, with the centre at King's Cross Metropolitan Station. Until you get to the south-west end of the segment, beyond Tottenham Court Road, there is no sensational poverty, no submerged tenth, nothing but street after street of respectable houses for people of modest means. In nearly every window is the same card—Apartments, Apartments, Apartments. The ratepayer cannot afford a whole house to himself, though he is rated on the assumption that he can. The sacrifices that are made in these houses to bring up children respectably and start them fairly in life are appalling.

When I pay my canvassing visit, I know perfectly well that what is wanted in that house above everything else is simply another hundred a year to be spent on its own immediate concerns. And I am expected to talk as if what was wanted was another penny on the rates to spend on colossal Strand and Holborn improvements, and create values which will finally be exported to relieve the ratepayers of Monte Carlo from all rates and taxes whatever, besides providing them with daily processions of motor-cars, thousand-guinea sets of sables, and loose livers, amateur and professional.

The Board of Public Prosperity

As I raise my hand to the knocker, a horrible temptation to expatiate on the merits of the lethal chamber as an instrument of social reform seizes me. My old proposal to bring everybody before a Board of Public Prosperity every seven years, and request him to justify his or her existence on pain of being politely shewn into the other world, returns upon me as the only really sane way of dealing with the hideous waste of life that comes from our idiotic distribution of wealth.

But then comes the thought, Will the ratepayer within think

this quite respectable? Was not my opponent better served when the Liberal Unionist Association invited his supporters to a smoking concert at Frascati's, there to forget the worries which I am foolishly proposing to remind them of.

It ends in my doing as others do. I go in and talk about taxation on ground values, which I do with all the eloquence of a man whose income comes mostly from bank and railway shares. True, I also am a landlord; but as my property is an Irish one, I am guiltless of drawing any income from it.

THE GREAT REVOLT

It is all frightfully unsatisfactory; and for the time we must only rub on as best we can. Some day the revolt of the ratepayers will come; for no human power can stop the growth of public expenditure, nor convince the professional man or the man of business, much less the artisan and laborer, that he should pay both in meal and in malt, in rent and in rates, for improving private property and multiplying the number and intensifying the extravagance of the parasites on it. In short, though I am, as I have said, one of the fathers of County Council Progressivism, I have no illusions as to the possibility of carrying it to its highest developments with capital extorted from people whose most pressing need is more income. Unless we readjust the burden, there will be trouble.

For the rest, the election rubs on in the usual way. Nothing that can make it a nuisance to the householder is neglected. Canvassers call with devastating bundles of "literature," and retire leaving the house strewn with papers like Hampstead Heath after a Bank Holiday, and the householder vindictively swearing to vote for nobody.

In South St Pancras, which I am wooing, there are three thousand people who dont vote; and I shall be beaten unless they make an exception this time and vote for me. I am told that the reason they dont vote is that they have not been thoroughly canvassed. My own conviction is just the contrary. Abstention from the poll is the only revenge open to the canvassed man; and he naturally takes it. I have implored my supporters not to canvass; but they will do it. I now implore the canvassed of South St Pancras not to blame me for it.

The sequel can be gathered from the following letter from The Times of 11 March 1904:

The Church of England will never be a successful electioneering body until it can answer for the political action of its own officials. In the late election the Bishop of Stepney asked me and my colleague, Sir William Geary, for a certain pledge in return for the neutrality of the Church. We gave it. The Bishop very faithfully remained neutral. But the vicar of St John's, who represents the Church in one of the wards of the division we contested, signed an appeal to the electors to vote against us, which they accordingly did. In other constituencies the pledge was refused, and the Bishop denounced the Progressive candidates; but the Radical and Christian Socialist clergymen worked for them none the less. I do not complain of this. It is, no doubt, quite Protestant and independent, and proper; but, regarded as electioneering, it is not cricket. If the Bishop of Stepney were able to say to every candidate, "Unless you give me such and such a pledge, every clergyman in London will work against you," he would be a formidable political power in the county. At present all he can say is, "I should like to receive such and such a pledge from every candidate; but whether it be given or not the action of the clergy will not be affected; the Conservative parsons will back the Moderate candidates, and the Radical and Christian Socialist parsons the Progressives, without the smallest regard to any recommendation I may make." Is it surprising that the Progressives paid no serious attention to the Bishop? It was the prospect of the Government grants that induced the Progressives to pledge themselves to administer the Act, not any hope that the clergy would subordinate their private political opinions to their Church during the election. And what a pledge it was! Virtually the Progressives said, "We pledge ourselves to administer this Act because we believe it to be an infamous one." I was in the unfortunate position of having to say, "I pledge myself to administer the Act because I believe it to be one of the best ever placed on the Statute book." Whereupon the Westminster Gazette accuses me of having thrown away the seat for the sake of a paradox, and the Daily News politely accuses me of "tomfoolery." But the fact remains that, with the exception of Mr Sidney Webb, whose seat was not contested, I and Sir William Geary were the only candidates whose pledge was convincing, with the result that the Church combined with the Catholics to defeat us, and succeeded triumphantly, to the undisguised delight of the opponents of the Act.

In short, the Bishop most effectually deprived us of the support of the Free Churchmen without screening us from political excommunication by the vicar of one of the most important parishes in the constituency.

Naturally the impression made on me is that the Free Church minister, though utterly wrong about the Act, is a man to be reckoned with because he is loyal to his denomination, even to letting his political champion be defeated for its sake, whereas the clergyman of the Establishment is as likely as not to be simply a private gentleman in a peculiar waistcoat and collar, who has no more sense of solidarity with his Church than a stockbroker. Under such circumstances, and notwithstanding my sense of the scrupulousness with which the vicar of St Pancras and the vicar of St Jude's made good their Bishop's guarantee by a neutrality so generously emphasized that it probably won some votes for me, I must say that I regard my case as a conspicuous example of the fact that the Church comes upon the electoral exchange with empty hands, the power to bind and loose being a private matter with the local parson. Again I say I do not complain of this fact; I simply point it out, leaving the Free Churchmen to congratulate themselves on it, and the Establishment to draw what moral it thinks best.

THE END